Zephaniah Kingsley Jr.

UNIVERSITY PRESS OF FLORIDA

Florida A&M University, Tallahassee
Florida Atlantic University, Boca Raton
Florida Gulf Coast University, Ft. Myers
Florida International University, Miami
Florida State University, Tallahassee
New College of Florida, Sarasota
University of Central Florida, Orlando
University of Florida, Gainesville
University of North Florida, Jacksonville
University of South Florida, Tampa
University of West Florida, Pensacola

Zephaniah Kingsley Jr. and the Atlantic World

Slave Trader, Plantation Owner, Emancipator

Daniel L. Schafer

University Press of Florida

Gainesville

Tallahassee

Tampa

Boca Raton

Pensacola

Orlando

Miami

Jacksonville

Ft. Myers

Sarasota

A Florida Quincentennial Book

Frontispiece: "A View of Charles-Town, the Capital of South Carolina," by Thomas Leitch, circa 1770. Image courtesy of the Library of Congress, Prints and Photographs Division, Washington, D.C.

First cloth printing, 2013
First paperback printing, 2024

29 28 27 26 25 24   6 5 4 3 2 1

Library of Congress Cataloging-in-Publication Data
Schafer, Daniel L.
Zephaniah Kingsley Jr. and the Atlantic world : slave trader, plantation owner, emancipator / Daniel L. Schafer.
p. cm.
Includes bibliographical references and index.
ISBN 978-0-8130-4462-0 (cloth) | ISBN 978-0-8130-8078-9 (pbk.)
1. Kingsley, Z. (Zephaniah), 1765–1843. 2. Slavery—Florida. 3. Slave trade—United States—History. 4. Kingsley family. I. Title.
E445.F6S33 2013
975.9'04092—dc23
[B]
2013020093

University Press of Florida
2046 NE Waldo Road
Suite 2100
Gainesville, FL 32609
http://upress.ufl.edu

Contents

Illustrations

Preface and Acknowledgments

Zephaniah Kingsley Jr., 1765–1843, was born in England, reared in colonial South Carolina, and became British Canadian, American, Danish, Spanish, and again American. He was a ship captain, maritime merchant, Caribbean coffee trader, Atlantic trader in enslaved Africans, slave plantation owner in Florida, and patriarch of a large mixed-race extended family that functioned in a polygamous fashion. Nearing the end of life and alarmed by the increasingly discriminatory race policies that threatened his free black family, Kingsley established a massive agricultural colony in Haiti as a refuge for them and for more than fifty slaves he emancipated and carried to Haiti under indenture contracts.

During a long and eventful life, Kingsley witnessed the violence of the American Revolution in Charleston, South Carolina, and exile in New Brunswick, Canada. As a ship captain, he traveled frequently to countries throughout the Atlantic world, witnessed the rebellion that ended slavery in French Saint-Domingue, and sailed to and from ports in North and South America, the Caribbean, and Africa while the violent overseas campaigns of the French Revolution and the Napoleonic Wars were under way. Ships that Kingsley commanded were confiscated by French privateers and ships of the British Royal Navy; he was incarcerated in Martinique and in Florida, and his life was endangered on numerous occasions. During the War of 1812, when British troops captured Washington, D.C., and burned the White House and the U.S. Capitol, Seminole warriors allied with the governor of Spanish East Florida attacked and destroyed Kingsley's St. Johns River plantation. Renegade bandits from Georgia later attempted to assassinate him. During the decades that historians label the Age of Revolution, Kingsley moved throughout the Atlantic world and accumulated a considerable fortune through the sale of enslaved Africans and the labor of slaves at his Florida plantations.

My interest in Zephaniah Kingsley Jr. began in 1975. A friend drove me to Fort George Island in Jacksonville, Florida, for a guided tour of Kingsley

Plantation, then a property of the Florida Park Service (today a National Park Service site). After hearing a brief version of Kingsley's life story, it came as a surprise to learn that no one had done a scholarly study. I began serious, although intermittent, research a few years later, intending to publish an article in a historical journal. The work went slowly. Credible evidence was hard to find, and when found it was located in distant archives. As I learned more about Kingsley's involvement in the Atlantic slave trade, his life as a planter and slave owner in Florida, his theories on slavery and race policies, and his controversial interracial family life, I realized that instead of a journal article the product of the research merited a book-length biographical study. Consequently, I began to follow Kingsley's historical footprints with a sometimes obsessive intensity.

I visited archives and historical societies along the Atlantic coast from Florida to New Brunswick in Canada, as well as in England and Denmark in Europe, Senegal and Guinea in West Africa, and St. Thomas and the Dominican Republic in the Caribbean. Fitting expensive lengthy research travel into a schedule dominated by teaching obligations and the need to publish on less demanding topics to meet tenure and promotion requirements meant that Kingsley's tracks grew cold at times. When time was available and my budget permitted, tracking resumed. This biographical portrait is the result.

Three goals have guided the research and writing: comprehensiveness, accuracy, and objectivity. I have searched for pertinent manuscripts and official documents regardless of where they were located, with the goal of writing a complete biographical portrait of Kingsley even though it meant delaying publication for several years. I also consulted a wide array of secondary sources to fulfill my second goal of accurately interpreting Kingsley in the context of the dramatic events of the revolutionary era in which he lived. That goal is perhaps less important for historians specializing in the era, but for a general readership more extensive interpretation and explanation is necessary. My intent throughout has been to write a manuscript for general readers and scholars alike. The third goal was to write an objective narrative about a controversial man whose main motivation was to amass a fortune to protect himself and his family against the uncertainties of life in the Age of Revolution. This has not been easy. Kingsley amassed a fortune, but it came from participation in the Atlantic slave trade and at the expense of the lives and freedom of Africans enslaved on his plantations. That he treated his slaves humanely and permitted them to live in family units without fear of separation by sale, and to practice their own religions and cultures and self-purchase freedom, mitigates but does not excuse the enslavement and forced labor.

Kingsley chose enslaved girls as young as thirteen for his sex partners. Over time, he moved from one young woman to another, fathering numerous children at his plantations. That he emancipated the young women and their children, educated them and provided financial security and protection, and continued to live with the mothers and children in an unusual extended family unit mitigates but does not excuse the abuse, and the limitation of their independent life choices.

While writing, I tried to keep in mind that Kingsley lived in an era when American presidents, governors, senators, mayors, bankers, carpenters, and even preachers were slave owners. The Atlantic slave trade, although morally repugnant, was legal while Kingsley was a slave trader, and chattel slavery was legal in Florida for many years after Kingsley's life ended in September 1843. Some readers will find it offensive that the tone of the narrative is objective and lacking expressions of moral outrage. Writing history, however, requires objective inquiry. Readers can judge Kingsley from the safe shores of the mores of the present era.

During the nearly four decades I researched and wrote this book, friends and colleagues generously contributed suggestions, source material, advice, peer support, and critical readings of articles and chapters. Jane Landers's scholarship has served as a model for what I have tried to accomplish. She sent copies of documents from archives in the United States and Spain and served as an important mentor. Svend E. Holsoe gave generous help in Copenhagen in November 1994, translated Danish records, and contributed careful and critical readings of drafts. It is this author, not Dr. Holsoe, who bears responsibility for errors of spelling of Danish words and names in the narrative and bibliography. Peter Sørensen also provided special assistance at the Danish National Archives.

I wore out an automobile driving between Jacksonville and the P. K. Yonge Library of Florida History at the University of Florida at Gainesville, and the St. Augustine Historical Society Research Library. While at the P. K. Yonge Library, I received generous assistance and guidance from

James G. Cusick and Bruce Chappell. Dr. Cusick's gift of copies of his M.A. thesis and the bound volumes of his research into Spanish East Florida loyalty oaths was especially helpful. So, too, was Bruce Chappell's help with the East Florida Papers. My work was greatly assisted by Page Edwards and Taryn Rodríguez-Boette, former directors of the St. Augustine Historical Society, and by archivist Charles Tingley. My special friend, Jean Parker Waterbury, the editor of the Society's publications, read drafts and gave kind encouragement. I regret that Mr. Edwards and Ms. Waterbury are no longer with us.

At the University of North Florida, I wish to express my gratitude to Barbara Tuck and Eileen Brady of the Thomas G. Carpenter Library staff. I also thank Dr. Shirley Hallblade, dean of the library, for permitting me to continue using interlibrary loan and other library services. Marianne Roberts, longtime executive assistant at the Department of History, untangled many of my computer messes and assisted with manuscripts. Kevin Hooper, James Vearil, Barbara Parrish, and Ruth Cook helped with research, sent copies of photographs and manuscripts, and transcribed documents. The University of North Florida also granted a one-semester sabbatical leave and professional travel funds that helped with expenses for one of my research trips to Senegal.

Frank Marotti Jr. sent copies of documents from the National Archives and a copy of his doctoral dissertation. I used that dissertation as a guide to documents during several research trips to the National Archives. Ann Burt and Cleve Powell of the Old Arlington Historical Society in Jacksonville have been my guides to the history of the area where Anna Kingsley and her daughters, Martha Baxter and Mary Sammis, lived for many years. It has been encouraging to receive their supportive correspondence. Professor Philip M. Smith, a Jacksonville native whose fascination for Florida history survived exile in New England and Texas, has sent advice and encouragement. For many years, Mr. Everette McNeill Kivette of Burnsville, North Carolina, has generously sent copies of documents and journal articles, even a rare book, related to the family of Kingsley's sister, Martha Kingsley McNeill, the wife of Dr. Daniel McNeill.

I have been fortunate to have had the support of several National Park Service employees who for more than two decades directed operations at Kingsley Plantation of the Timucuan Ecological and Historical Preserve with integrity, common sense, and a professional respect for scholarship. Superintendent Brian Peters arranged a grant from the Eastern National Parks and Monuments Association that assisted with expenses for my 1994 research trip to Senegal. Superintendents Kathy Tilford and Roger Clark gave advice and access to documents at the site. The current director, Susie Sernaker, shares their cooperative spirit. Carol Clark, a former University of North Florida graduate student, now a National Park Service official and an accomplished author, assisted with research on numerous occasions. Roger and Carol are now in New Mexico, but their cooperation continues.

At the White Oak Plantation and White Oak Conservation Center, general director John Lukas has permitted me to explore the ruins of the rice field, pounding mill, and other agricultural structures remaining at the site of Kingsley's most profitable plantation. I would also like to thank Stephanie Rutan and former director Wallace Prince for their assistance.

In Senegal, essential advice was provided by Professors Mbaye Gueye, Mamadou Diouf, Penda Mbow, and Boubakar Barry of Cheikh Anta Diop University. Andre Zaiman and Katy Diop of the Gorée Institute arranged housing, meetings, and transportation. I was also assisted by the Honorable Abdou Diouf, former president of Senegal, and by Dr. Sidi Camara and Andre Sanko of the Ministry of Education.

During two visits to the Dominican Republic, Tony and Sandra Lebrón provided transportation, arranged introductions and interviews, and treated me with familial kindness. Their son, Manuel, like his mother a descendant of Anna Jai and Zephaniah Kingsley Jr., joined in the travels and interviews and has contributed to the research for many years. Ms. Peggy Fried, a New Jersey resident who descends from Sarah Murphy and Zephaniah Kingsley Jr., shared several important documents from her research in archives at the Dominican Republic. At Puerto Plata, Neit Finke and Pablo Juan Brugal contributed their knowledge of Dominican law and history and copies of rare documents.

It is profoundly disappointing that no images of Zephaniah Kingsley Jr. or of his parents are known to exist. No images of Anna Jai, Munsilna McGundo, Flora Hanahan, and Sarah Murphy have been found. With the exception of an 1834 portrait of Martha Kingsley McNeill, Zephaniah's sister, no images of his siblings have been found. The portrait of Martha, by Samuel Waldo and William Jewett, is at the Wadsworth Atheneum, Hartford,

Connecticut. Because of this woefully sparse visual documentation of the Kingsley story, I am especially grateful to Tony Lebrón for restoring an image of Osceola Kingsley, a son of Zephaniah and Flora Hanahan Kingsley (see figure 10). It is the only known portrait of a child of Kingsley. I also wish to thank David P. Stair for contributing a copy of a miniature portrait of Emma Vera Baxter, the wife of Joseph Mocs and the daughter of Martha Kingsley Baxter (the eldest daughter of Zephaniah and Anna Madgigine Jai Kingsley). The portrait of Emma is the only known image of a grandchild of Zephaniah Kingsley. It is my hope that the publication of this book will lead to the discovery of additional portraits and letters of the Kingsley family.

Much of the narrative of this book was written at the summer place in Corea, Maine, that Joan and I have owned for thirty years. The volunteer staff at the Dorcas Library Association at nearby Prospect Harbor ordered dozens of books for me through inter-library loan. Thank you all very much.

I am grateful that what I thought was the final draft of this book became the "nearly final" draft as the result of the careful peer reviews done for the University Press of Florida by the historians Jane Landers, Paul E. Lovejoy, and Larry Rivers. Their suggestions were heeded.

This is my fourth book with the University Press of Florida, all produced under the genial guidance of the director, Meredith Morris-Baab. I thank Meredith and her colleagues at UPF, Sian Hunter, Marthe Walters, and Shannon McCarthy, for their continuing assistance. *Zephaniah Kingsley Jr. and the Atlantic World*, like the two that preceded it, benefited from the excellent skills of copy editor Jonathan Lawrence. Thank you, Jonathan, for improving the text and for untangling the messy threads in the endnotes and bibliography.

Finally, I dedicate this book to Joan Elizabeth Moore, my wife for more than thirty years. Joan has worked beside me at archives and made many stylistic suggestions during repeated readings of chapter drafts. She always found a way to fit yet another research trip into our budget, and with gentle resolution she insisted that I not turn the story of Kingsley's life into a novel or a movie script. I have tried to follow her advice, although with occasional grumpiness. Joan is the essential inspiration for my research and writing.

Introduction

Zephaniah Kingsley Jr., 1765–1843, was born in England, was reared in Charleston, South Carolina, and resided in New Brunswick in Canada after his father's exile at the end of the American Revolution. He became a West Indies merchant, African slave trader, ship captain, plantation owner, slave master, polygamist, father of mixed-race children, and, late in life, the founder of a vast agricultural settlement in Haiti as a refuge for his free colored children and wives. A controversial figure for his views on manumission and his unorthodox marital arrangements, Kingsley is known today for his 1820s publication, *A Treatise on the Patriarchal System of Society*, and for his plantation at Fort George Island in Duval County, Florida. The plantation site is now a featured attraction of the Timucuan Ecological and Historical Preserve, a National Park Service site that is visited by thousands of tourists each year.

Anta Majigeen Ndiaye, the African woman Kingsley acknowledged as his wife but never legally married, is also remembered in Florida. Anta was of Wolof ethnicity born in 1793 in Jolof, in today's Senegal. Her father was a member of the ruling lineage of Jolof, which explains the persistent legend that Anta was an "African Princess." Her privileged status ended in her thirteenth year, when slave raiders attacked her village and marched her in shackles to the coast of Senegal. Sent to a holding pen on the Island of Gorée, Anta was sold to a slave trader and carried in the hold of a slave ship across the Atlantic Ocean to Havana, Cuba. In September 1806, Zephaniah Kingsley Jr. purchased Anta there and transported her to his plantation in Spanish East Florida. In Florida, Anta was generally known as Anna

Kingsley, but also as Anna Madgigine or Anna Jai, commemorating the African name of her mother, Majigeen, and the family name of her father, Ndiaye. In March 1811, Anna was emancipated, along with three children fathered by Kingsley. She was eighteen years old at the time. Anna Kingsley became a planter and a slave owner in her own right.

Zephaniah Kingsley Jr. was born in Bristol, England, in December 1765. His mother, Isabella Johnstone, was a native of Scotland. His father, Zephaniah Kingsley Sr., was a native of Lincolnshire, England, and a third-generation Quaker. Kingsley Sr. moved his family to Charleston, South Carolina, in 1770 and became a successful merchant. As a child, Zephaniah Jr. witnessed the excitement of revolutionary ferment that was transformed into a war for independence. When the war ended, Kingsley Sr. was banished for loyal support of King George III. The Kingsley home and rural properties were confiscated, the mercantile business and accumulated savings lost. The family relocated to the British province of New Brunswick, Canada, where Kingsley Sr. again became a successful merchant. He also became the owner of ships engaged in the Atlantic and Caribbean trade that provided the training and opportunity for his eldest son to launch a career as a ship captain and maritime merchant.

By 1793, Kingsley Jr. was trading for sugar and coffee at Jamaica, Saint-Domingue, and other Caribbean islands to St. John, New Brunswick, as well as at Savannah and Charleston in the United States. His ship, the *Argo*, was seized by a privateer that year and sold at an admiralty court auction held at Charleston. With France and Britain at war, privateers licensed by each nation captured and confiscated commercial vessels owned by citizens of their enemy. Kingsley swore to an oath of loyalty and became a citizen of the United States in 1793, thus minimizing his danger at sea by sailing under the flag of a neutral nation. Ships flying flags of neutral nations were not immune from danger in the Caribbean while the international warfare stemming from the French Revolution was under way. In 1794, British Royal Navy vessels seized another ship under Kingsley's command at Martinique.

Kingsley also became involved in the international trade in enslaved Africans. Looking back on his early life, he said in 1826 that he had "travelled in the early years of his life to Africa, and even been concerned in the hideous traffic of slaves." He resided in "all the West India colonies," including several years in "Cuba and Saint Domingo, as well as the mainland of South America." Between 1793 and 1797, when the southern region of Saint-Domingue was occupied by Britain while a massive slave rebellion was under way, Kingsley lived at Jeremie, in Grand Anse, from where he rode out on horseback through "the south and west of St. Domingo . . . through woods and over mountains, with my saddle bags loaded with specie to buy coffee."[1]

In 1798, at the Caribbean island of St. Thomas, Kingsley took an oath of loyalty to another neutral nation, Denmark, and was employed as a ship captain. In March 1802 he purchased a ship, the *Superior*, and two months later sailed it to Havana with 250 slaves from the coast of Africa. The following year, prompted by Denmark's abolition of the African slave trade, and also by the availability of fertile plantation lands in East Florida, Kingsley sailed to St. Augustine and took an oath of loyalty to Spain. In Spanish colonies the African trade continued for decades, and Kingsley continued to traffic in that trade, even participating in an expedition to the east coast of Africa in pursuit of a human cargo.

In northeast Florida, Kingsley purchased Laurel Grove Plantation and put one hundred enslaved Africans to work in cotton, citrus, and provisions fields. The plantation was operated almost entirely by enslaved laborers. The managers were enslaved men who delegated authority to enslaved drivers and then supervised to ensure that the daily tasks assigned were completed properly. The laborers came from distant locations on the African continent, spoke a variety of languages, and practiced different cultural patterns. Laurel Grove became a transplanted African village where diverse people adjusted to enslavement and the demands of their European owner, and still created a creole culture of their own.

Laurel Grove Plantation was destroyed during the conflict that the scholar James Cusick has labeled the Other War of 1812. Seminole Indian warriors torched the buildings and abducted or killed nearly half of the Africans living on the property. Most of the plantations and small farms in the province were destroyed before this conflict ended in 1814, and for months afterward bandits pillaged at will.

Kingsley refined his unique theories on slavery and race relations at Fort George Island from 1814 to 1838. He believed that the coerced labor of Africans was necessary if planters expected to prosper from agriculture in the semitropical climate of Florida. Only Africans were able to work and flourish amid the heat and diseases of Florida; their pale European counterparts sickened and died under these conditions. Kingsley wrote: "Nature has not fitted a white complexion for hard work in the sun, as it is evident that the darkness of complexion here is a measure of capacity for endurance of labor."[2]

Enslaving and coercing Africans to labor, however, carried the risk of rebellion, which led the pragmatic Kingsley to advocate a humane and patriarchal system of labor. His slaves lived in family units, practiced African customs, owned small properties, and were encouraged to work for themselves when the labor tasks assigned by their overseers were completed. He employed the "task system" of labor rather than the "gang system" practiced in Alabama and Mississippi. Kingsley encouraged other white slave owners to create a caste of free black allies. If the white patriarchs were to survive and prosper, liberal manumission laws and policies were needed to convince "the free colored population to be attached to good order and have a friendly feeling towards the white population." Kingsley believed that "color ought not be the badge of degradation. The only distinction should be between slave and free, not between white and colored." Closing off a path to manumission would turn free blacks into "enemies by degrading them to the rank of our slaves."[3]

Kingsley's marital relations were highly controversial. He lived openly with Anna Madgigine Jai and acknowledged her as his wife. He praised her intelligence and character and authorized her to act as manager of his property during his many absences, but he also fathered children by other enslaved women, whom he emancipated along with their children, and incorporated them all into an extended kinship group. His familial relations with the various segments of his "family" continued until his death. The children were all legally emancipated, educated, and cared for. His unabashed defiance of prevailing customs jarred the sensitivities of his Christian and monogamous neighbors, even some of his siblings, but he made no attempt to veil his amorous predilections.

While Spain controlled Florida, Kingsley's views and practices were in accord with the flexible three-caste system of race relations that recognized the legal rights of enslaved men and women and encouraged emancipation. After the United States acquired East and West Florida in 1821, however,

Spanish racial policies were replaced by a rigid set of laws based on the assumption that all blacks—whether slave or free—were uncivilized and inferior to whites and could not exist peacefully outside the rigorous restraints of slavery. As a member of the Territorial Council, Kingsley resisted the passage of these laws and despaired as the rights of free persons of color, including his own extended family of African women and their mixed-race children, were curtailed.

Kingsley did well financially under American governance, acquiring several thousand acres of land in six northeast Florida counties and several hundred slaves. During the 1830s, however, his contempt for the increasingly discriminatory American race and slavery policies prompted him to sell most of his Florida property and rent a huge tract of land (later purchased in his son George's name) located on the northeast coast of the free black Republic of Haiti, where he established a refuge for his extended family. That land is now part of the Dominican Republic. One of the tracts, Mayorasgo de Koka, flourished under the management of his sons, George and John Maxwell Kingsley. Anna Kingsley and Zephaniah's other "wives" and children lived at settlements east of Puerto Plata in today's Dominican Republic. Kingsley emancipated more than fifty enslaved men and women in Florida and transported them to Haiti as indentured laborers. Promised annual shares of the proceeds of the estates and tracts of land in their own names, the laborers were relieved of all indenture obligations after three to nine years. Kingsley encouraged all of his children, unsuccessfully for two of his daughters who were married to wealthy white men in Florida, to also migrate to Haiti or "to some land of liberty and equal rights, where the conditions of society are governed by some law less absurd than that of color."[4]

During the latter years of his life Kingsley traveled frequently between his home in northeast Florida and the dwellings of his extended family members in Haiti. His plantation affairs in Florida were placed in the hands of a nephew and a son-in-law, while Kingsley dealt with frustrating efforts to claim compensation from the United States Treasury for losses suffered in 1812 during the "Patriot War." He continued to encourage his slaves to "self-purchase" their freedom, although Florida laws were making that increasingly difficult to accomplish. Kingsley still owned more than eighty slaves in Florida when he died in September 1843.

The year before he died, Kingsley justified his failure to emancipate all of his human property in a conversation with the abolitionist Lydia Maria Child. "The best we can do in this world is to balance evils judiciously. If I have no negroes to cultivate my Florida lands, they will run to waste; and then I can raise no money from them for the benefit of Haiti." Child was appalled. She denigrated his "bewildered moral sense" as running the risk of consigning his remaining slaves to perpetual bondage, and called his idea of "balancing evils" a "theory obviously absurd, as well as slippery in its application." She dismissed Kingsley as "one altogether unaccountable."[5]

Given that more than six in ten of Kingsley's remaining slave families suffered some degree of family separation as a result of the lawsuits and auctions that followed his death, Child's condemnation was prescient. But she erred in dismissing him as "unaccountable" and for assuming that he shared her support for abolition. It is true that Kingsley treated oaths of loyalty and other official testimonials cavalierly, and that he treated nationality and flags of several nations he flew on his masthead as a way to profit from his business activities. In general, however, Kingsley was open and honest about other matters and scornful of negative public opinion. Even Child commented on his "heroic candor." Kingsley advocated humane treatment of slaves and liberal emancipation policies, but he was never an abolitionist. Slaves were a necessity for agricultural labor in Florida, Kingsley reasoned, and without slaves he could not make the money he needed to protect himself and his family from the dangers that existed in the Atlantic world during the Age of Revolution. Kingsley was a pragmatic businessman, and he was proslavery to the end of his life. When rejecting Child's urgent call for emancipation, Kingsley said, "To do good in this world we *must* have money." It was a sincere expression of conviction, and the imperative motivation of his adult years.

1 | The Kingsley Family, Charleston, and the American Revolution

After eight weeks crossing the Atlantic from England, Zephaniah and Isabella Johnston Kingsley arrived at a wharf on the Cooper River in Charleston Harbor in late December 1770. Standing at the ship's rail with them were their children: Mary, age six, Zephaniah Jr., five, George, two, and Catherine, four months. Charleston would be home to the Kingsley children for the next fourteen years.[1]

Isabella's brother Charles Johnston was undoubtedly waiting at the wharf to lead the Kingsleys over the sand streets of Charleston to their residence on Bedon's Alley, south of Broad Street between Elliott and Tradd Streets. The rented structure was to be both family residence and retail store, with the living quarters situated above the ground-floor commercial space, a common practice for merchants in Charleston other than the very wealthy. Charles Johnston had migrated from Scotland to Charleston in 1763 and became a partner in a dry goods retail store with another Scot, John Simpson, a future attorney general of South Carolina. John Graham, Savannah's leading merchant and a future lieutenant governor of Georgia, also became a partner of Johnston and Simpson. It is likely that Johnston encouraged Isabella and her husband to move to Charleston and extended a line of credit to a London merchant that enabled Kingsley to acquire the cloth and other dry goods he needed to start a new business.[2]

Like many Britons who migrated to the North American colonies in the decades prior to the American Revolution, Zephaniah and Isabella Kingsley arrived in Charleston after failing to achieve success in England. After marrying in London in 1763, they moved to Bristol, England, and settled

Figure 1. "A View of Charles-Town, the capital of South Carolina in North America," original painting by T. Melish, engraved by C. Canot, London, 1768. Courtesy of the Library of Congress, Prints and Photographs Division, Washington, D.C.

on Wine Street.[3] Zephaniah was reared in the wool-growing region of Lincolnshire, where cloth merchants had prospered for centuries from exports to Europe. He moved to London after the wool and cloth trades shifted to that city and to ports on England's west coast. A cloth merchant in London, Kingsley followed the same occupation in Bristol, and he achieved brief success at a store on Wine Street.[4]

Bristol, one hundred miles west of London, was England's third-largest city in the 1760s and a thriving center for exports to the British colonies in North America and the West Indies. Large supplies of cotton cloth and woolen goods from the surrounding region were brought to wharves on the Avon River at Bristol, where merchants bundled them with products manufactured locally and dispatched them to American markets. Wholesale linen drapers were prominent among Bristol's smaller exporters. A 1768 city directory for Bristol lists five linen drapers as well as cloth dyers (known then as "colour men"), cotton dealers, haberdashers, silk dyers, and several other mercantile establishments located near the Kingsley residence and business on Wine Street.[5]

During the eighteenth century, Bristol merchants and ship captains were also deeply involved in the Atlantic trade in enslaved Africans. From the late seventeenth century to 1807, more than two thousand ships were fitted out for the African slave trade at Bristol's wharves. The vessels returned with sugar, rum, tobacco, rice, cotton, and other produce from American plantations.[6]

Four children were born to Isabella and Zephaniah during the five years they lived in Bristol: Mary on August 24, 1764; Zephaniah Jr. on December 4, 1765; Johnston on May 5, 1767; and George on October 11, 1768. The births are recorded in the register of the Society of Friends, which is surprising since the parents were married by a curate of the Church of England. Contemporary records of meetings of Friends at Bristol indicate that "marriage by a priest" was considered a serious transgression of Quaker practice. Members transferring from other meetings were expected to bring records and letters of introduction from their previous meeting houses, and both men and women were subjected to "careful inquiry" at the Bristol meeting regarding "clearness of marriage." Records of the Bristol Meeting are mute on the specific case of Zephaniah and Isabella Kingsley, indicating that Isabella converted to the faith of her husband and the newlyweds were accepted at Bristol without punishment. Isabella, a native of Scotland and an Anglican before marriage, worshipped as a Quaker for the rest of her life.[7]

In early 1769, Zephaniah Sr. moved his family back to London. His business had failed in 1768, and he was forced to file for bankruptcy. The cause of his financial distress emanated from the troubled relations between Britain and its North American colonies following the end of the Seven Years' War in 1763. Britain's victory led to the acquisition of vast territory, including French Canada and Spanish East and West Florida, but the gains came with a staggering burden of debt that Parliament tried to pay off by imposing customs duties on products imported in the American colonies.[8]

Conflict between Britain and its American colonies began soon after the Peace of Paris. The Sugar Act of 1764 imposed duties on imported textiles, coffee, wine, and other items and increased customs duties on non-British imports. The Currency Act of 1764 prohibited colonial legislatures from issuing paper money as legal tender, resulting in shortages of specie and hindering trade and commerce and the repayment of debts. The Stamp Act of 1765 imposed direct taxes on the North American colonies and prompted protests and riots. Further fury was provoked by passage of the Revenue Act of 1767, which imposed duties on tea, glass, paint, lead, and paper and authorized customs officials to use generalized "writs of assistance" to search ships and homes for smuggled products.

Leaders in America called for boycotts of British goods in an effort to convince Parliament to repeal the revenue measures. Colonial merchants who had previously sided with Parliament became alarmed by the arrogant acts of royal appointees and British judges in the colonies, especially judges of the vice-admiralty courts, and threw their support behind the boycotts. British-American trade declined dramatically, causing financial hardship on both sides of the Atlantic. Smaller merchants in Bristol and other English ports saw their profits plummet and their businesses fail. Kingsley's bankruptcy coincided with this transatlantic turmoil.[9]

Following his return to London, Kingsley again found employment as a cloth merchant and rejoined a meeting house of the Society of Friends. His family resided at Bread Street in the Parish of St. Mildred, only a few blocks from the dwelling he and Isabella occupied in 1763. Then, a personal family tragedy occurred. On June 19, 1769, two-year-old Johnston Kingsley died from unknown causes and was buried at "The Park," the Worcester Street burial ground at Southwark, south of the Thames River.[10]

Early in 1770, Zephaniah and Isabella decided to migrate to Charleston, South Carolina. The desire to start life anew in the North American and West Indies colonies was not uncommon among Englishmen in the second half of the eighteenth century. Between 1750 and 1775 an estimated six thousand Englishmen migrated across the Atlantic seeking careers in British North American cities. For merchants in the cloth trade, New World markets were especially attractive. The historian Robert S. DuPlessis has demonstrated that textile imports represented the "largest single category of consumer items" sent to the colonies, and R. C. Nash has shown that 40 percent of all British exports went to the American colonies in the early 1770s. Charleston merchants were important participants in that transatlantic trading network.[11]

Charleston was the most important shipping port in the southern colonies. In 1770 approximately 450 ships anchored in the harbor formed by the merger of the Ashley and Cooper Rivers. With approximately twelve thousand residents, Charleston was the fourth-largest city in North America, behind only Philadelphia, New York, and Boston. The value of its exports, generated primarily from sales of rice and indigo, exceeded the exports of these northern colonial cities.[12]

Kingsley's move to Charleston coincided with the early stages of a commercial resurgence. On December 13, 1770, after Parliament repealed the Townshend Act (with the exception of the duty on tea), a general meeting of the citizens of Charleston voted to end the local boycott of British goods, sparking a surge in imports of textiles and other British products. Kingsley's business flourished in the 1770s from retail sales of imported linens, linen drapery, cotton cloth, silk fabrics, checked handkerchiefs, calicoes, shoes, stockings, and general grocery and household items. During his first ten years in South Carolina, Kingsley entered into at least three partnerships and purchased several valuable properties. His brother-in-law, Charles Johnston, was a partner in at least one venture.[13]

For Isabella Kingsley, business success did not lessen her fear of losing another child to disease. The Kingsleys arrived in Charleston when a whooping-cough epidemic was menacing families in the town. In June 1770 a Charleston socialite, Mrs. Ann Manigault, wrote in her journal that "a good many children die of whooping-cough." In early December Mrs. Manigault wrote: "the sore throat still very bad in town." Her December 28 notation read: "a good many people died of the sore-throat," and on February 1, 1771, she wrote that the health scare from "sore-throat deaths" was still a serious public health threat.[14]

High death rates from alternating waves of smallpox, diphtheria, scarlet fever, measles, mumps, dysentery, and malarial fever also threatened Charleston families in the 1760s and 1770s. People of means traveled to Newport, Rhode Island, during the summer months. Other residents of Charleston sought medical treatment in Great Britain. Ann Manigault complained in her journal that "these annual migrations drain this province of a great deal of money."[15]

After becoming pregnant in the summer of 1771, Isabella returned to England to ensure safe delivery of her child. Her third daughter, Elizabeth Kingsley, was born April 29, 1772, at Rochester in Kent County, twenty-five miles southwest of London. She and the infant Elizabeth were back in Charleston by December 1772.[16]

William Dillwyn, a Philadelphia businessman vacationing in South

Carolina, recorded in his diary that he attended a Quaker meeting in Charleston on December 6, 1772, and was introduced to Z. Kingsley and his wife. Dillwyn met the Kingsleys at another Quaker meeting on the twentieth. Apparently, Zephaniah and Isabella joined a meeting house of the Society of Friends soon after becoming residents of Charleston.[17]

Zephaniah Jr. and his siblings were too young in the early 1770s to be involved in the business concerns of their father; their days were occupied with parental tutoring in Quaker values and attending private schools in the neighborhood. Living as close as they did to the leading public places in Charleston, they could not have avoided gaining an education in colonial politics by witnessing the dynamic activities that occurred daily in the streets and gathering places of Charleston. The massive protests and mob disorders of the 1760s had dissipated by 1770, when it appeared that Britain would continue to govern the North American colonies without major challenges to its imperial authority. Beneath the appearance of calm, however, the spirit of dissent simmered. Streetcorner orators and speakers at public meetings warned that arbitrary acts of Parliament could limit their rights as Englishmen by abolishing their ability to elect representatives to colonial assemblies and by imposing direct taxes. Mary and Zephaniah Jr. were old enough to personally witness the early events of the Age of Revolution as they were enacted in their neighborhood.

The flash point for massive protests in the colonies came in May 1773 when Parliament passed a Tea Act that eliminated duties on cargoes brought to Britain by the East India Company for re-export to the colonies. This provided a subsidy to the firm by enabling it to lower the price it charged in the colonies and thereby eliminate competition from Dutch merchants whose contraband sales had come to dominate the trade. The availability of less-expensive tea came at a significant sacrifice of principle, however, since buyers still had to pay the three-pence duty imposed in 1767 by the hated Townshend Acts.

Political agitators were joined by influential merchants, the Sons of Liberty, and Committees of Correspondence throughout the North American colonies. In December 1773 the Boston Committee assigned three men to board an East India Company ship anchored in the harbor and toss three hundred chests of tea overboard. Outraged Members of Parliament passed the Coercive Acts in the spring of 1774 and closed Boston Harbor until the East India Company was compensated for the tea it lost.[18]

Similar protests occurred at Charleston on December 2, 1773, when a ship arrived at the harbor carrying 257 chests of tea consigned to Zephaniah Kingsley and two other retailers. Led by merchant Christopher Gadsden, the Liberty Boys warned residents of the city that by purchasing the tea they would be accepting the principle that Parliament had the power to pass direct taxes. Handbills were circulated urging local citizens to prevent the tea from being landed. At an emotionally charged mass meeting at the Exchange Building on December 3, business leaders, artisans, and laborers joined in a pledge to refuse to buy or drink tea, forcing merchants who ordered the tea to announce they would not accept it. The ship remained in the harbor until the end of December, when British officials stored the tea in the basement of the Exchange Building.[19]

The most important outcome of the public meeting was establishment of the South Carolina General Committee, whose initial charge was to enforce the non-importation agreements. When another ship carrying tea arrived at the harbor in June 1774, an unruly mob boarded the ship, forcing the captain to seek safety aboard a nearby British naval vessel. Another ship carrying tea arrived several months later, galvanizing the General Committee to order the merchant consignees to empty the chests into the Cooper River. Zephaniah Kingsley Sr., one of three consignees, tossed chests of tea in the harbor while members of the General Committee looked on. Whether or not eight-year-old Zephaniah Jr. witnessed the traumatic scene of his father's humiliation and its potential for violence, the formative influence must have been long-lasting.[20]

Prompted by Britain's closing of Boston Harbor, the South Carolina General Committee called for delegates from throughout the colony to gather at Charleston on July 6, 1774. At that meeting, five representatives were elected to attend the meeting of the First Continental Congress at Philadelphia. Six months later the South Carolina General Committee voted to transform itself into the First Provincial Congress, which became the governing body of Charleston and the new state of South Carolina.[21]

In spite of the furor over the tea chests and the revolutionary sentiment that pervaded the streets of Charleston, Kingsley prospered during these tumultuous years. Zephaniah Jr. and his siblings were able to attend private schools rather than the Provincial Free School for orphans and children of poor families sponsored by St. Philip's Church. Young Zephaniah may have attended a private school that met only a few doors from the Kingsley residence, "in a large convenient room at Mrs. Knox's in Bedon's Alley," where schoolmaster David Gillespie taught English, Latin, and Greek languages, arithmetic, and writing. Decades later, knowledgeable professional men commented on Kingsley's intelligence and the quality of his classical education.[22]

An important part of the education of the Kingsley children came from observing the action on the streets of Charleston, where events of worldwide significance were occurring. Revolutionary orators like the merchant Christopher Gadsden could be heard leading rallies and speaking to crowds of the city's white artisans and laborers. Meetings of the First Provisional Congress were held at the State House at the corner of Broad and Meeting Streets, only a few blocks from the Kingsley residence. On March 28, 1776, the proclamation that South Carolina would join other states in a Declaration of Independence was announced from the front steps of the Exchange Building, also close by the Kingsley residence. When delegates met in July to elect representatives to the First Continental Congress, they gathered at the Great Hall of the Exchange.

According to the historian Walter Fraser, Charleston was a city of extremes of wealth and income. Half of the city's population was enslaved, and one of every four white residents was considered poor or vagrant. Fewer than 9 percent of the whites "owned approximately 75 percent of the wealth." Influential and wealthy men like the planter and merchant Henry Laurens, whose slave import business was the largest in North America, made up the city's elite class. Laurens was the president of the Continental Congress from November 1, 1777, to December 9, 1778. One of Charleston's wealthiest merchants, Laurens was at first alarmed by the growing radicalism among the white artisans and laborers, but he attended the public meetings and eventually became a leader in the Patriot cause.[23]

Zephaniah Jr. observed the slums and tenements as he walked the city's unpaved streets from where the laboring poor lived to the luxurious waterfront dwellings south of the Exchange Building. When his mother sent him for groceries, he walked to one of three markets in the city: the fish market at the foot of Queen's Street at the Cooper River, the beef market at the corner of Broad and Meeting Streets, or the vegetable market at the west end of Broad Street where provisions were ferried to vendors' stalls from across the Ashley River. The fish market must have fascinated as well as frightened the young shoppers: in addition to the stalls for vendors, city officials installed public stocks to punish drunkards and others convicted of petty crimes.[24]

Throughout the city, Zephaniah Jr. could observe enslaved men and women performing manual labor tasks and working as artisans, coopers, carpenters, draymen, stevedores, coachmen, caulkers at shipyards, boatmen, domestic servants, cooks, seamstresses, and other occupations. Slavery was an integral and essential feature of life in colonial Charleston and vital to its prospering economy. During the years the Kingsley family lived in the city, slaves constituted one-half of the population. More enslaved Africans were brought to Charleston than to any other port in North America prior to the American Revolution, in excess of fifty-eight thousand between 1750 and 1775, and imports of Africans "reached unprecedented proportions between 1771 and 1774." Residents of the city claimed some of the Africans, but planters at rice and indigo estates located between the Cape Fear region of North Carolina and the St. Johns River in Florida claimed the majority.[25]

Given the fact that Zephaniah Kingsley Jr. became a ship captain involved in the African slave trade in his adult years, it is significant that his introduction to the sale of human beings occurred in Charleston. He would have learned then that slave ships arriving from Africa were required to unload their human cargoes at Sullivan's Island north of the Cooper River before proceeding to the wharves at Charleston. Local officials imposed a mandatory quarantine of ten days for newly arrived Africans to inspect for smallpox and other diseases. If symptoms were detected, longer confinement at one of the "pest houses" on the island was required. Any ship passenger sailing near the island experienced the revolting smell of urine, feces, and vomit after the decks and holds of the slave ships were washed with pails of hot water and vinegar. Dr. Alexander Garden inspected the health of Africans arriving on the slave ships; he commented that the "filth, putrid air, putrid dysenter[y]" was so offensive it was "a wonder any escape with life."[26]

Approximately 40 percent of all Africans imported into North America prior to the American Revolution passed through Sullivan's Island before being transferred to the wharves along the Cooper and Ashley Rivers. The general practice was for merchants to advertise in local newspapers immediately following the arrival of a slave ship, announcing the number and ethnicity or place of origin of the Africans and the anticipated day of sale. On April 2, 1771, the *South Carolina Gazette and Country Journal* announced "Eighty remarkable likely New Negroes" for sale; on the ninth, an advertisement read "one hundred and five as likely and healthy New Negroes as ever were brought into this Province, being chiefly of the Coromantee and Fantee Country."

During 1772 and 1773 more than 10,000 enslaved Africans arrived aboard sixty-five ships, and in May 1773 alone 1,900 Africans were introduced aboard twelve ships. On May 31 a single page of the *South Carolina Gazette* contained ads for 1,335 Africans destined for sale on June 7 and 8 aboard eight ships tied to wharves on the Cooper River. Between 1735 and 1775 more than four hundred merchants paid duties for importing Africans. The elaborate mansion at 27 King Street for the city's leading importer of slaves, Miles Brewton, still stands as a monument to fortunes gained from the sale of human flesh.[27]

When auctions were conducted at the wharf, potential buyers clambered aboard the ships to inspect the Africans and shout out bids. Sales were also held at local taverns, merchant's stores, and trade marts. During the "high season" for sales, generally from March to October, it was not unusual to encounter frenzied scenes when the demand for enslaved Africans was intense. Savannah merchant John Graham "attend[ed] a sale of Windward and Grain Coast Negroes" at Charleston with seven assistants "yet could only get in all fifty three [Africans]," prompting him to complain about "the fiery edge" of the aggressive Carolina planters who had been "pulling, hawling and pushing one another down as if they [the Africans] had been to gott for nothing."[28]

Curious youngsters were attracted to the excitement at the wharves when Africans were sold shipboard. In 1775, Charleston residents witnessed numerous sales of black men and women with the distinctive facial markings of their respective African ethnicities visible to bystanders. Zephaniah Kingsley Jr. had his tenth birthday in December 1775. He had likely been a spectator at several slave auctions by then, a witness to the fear and bewilderment etched on faces while raucous crowds of white men milled about shouting bids. Although only a boy, he would have recognized the merchants in charge of the auctions as business acquaintances of his father.

In the decades ahead, Zephaniah Jr. would captain several ships engaged in the Atlantic slave trade and sell his human cargoes at markets in North and South America and the Caribbean. He would become as familiar with credit purchases, interest rates, commission fees, letters of credit, and other financial arrangements associated with the African trade as were the Charleston merchants who sold captive Africans in the 1770s. In May 1806, Kingsley would watch as a crowd of white men inspected 230 African men, women, and children who had survived a lengthy journey from the coast of East Africa in the fetid hold of an African slave ship. The sale was conducted on the deck of the *Gustavia*, a British-built "African Guineaman" anchored off Gadsden's Wharf. Kingsley was aboard that ship during its journey from Charleston to East Africa and back, functioning as the supercargo. Record book in hand, Kingsley identified the buyers, linked them to the Africans they purchased, and listed the sale prices. Lessons learned in childhood would follow Kingsley through life.[29]

Throughout 1775, Zephaniah Kingsley Sr. lived in a state of anxiety as conflict escalated between the city's wealthy and conservative merchants and the increasingly radical laborers and artisans led by Christopher Gadsden and William Henry Drayton. The Council of Safety closely monitored the activities of merchants for possible violations of the trade ban passed by the Provincial Congress in January 1775. Loyal supporters of Britain became targets for mobs of ruffians who pressured them to leave Charleston. Violent incidents occurred in 1775, when angry mobs tarred and feathered outspoken critics of the Patriot cause. In August, a victim of such violence was tossed in a cart and pushed through the streets by a mob of four hundred men. The mob stopped at the residence of every suspected Loyalist to shout warnings that a similar fate awaited the occupants if they did not leave Charleston. Many Loyalists packed their belongings and boarded ships bound for England. On September 15 the last royal governor of the colony, Sir William Campbell, furtively boarded a British warship in the harbor, an action that symbolized the dissolution of South Carolina's ties of empire with Great Britain.[30]

Isabella Kingsley was not in Charleston when the violence escalated that August. During the final months of what turned out to be her last pregnancy, she and the children had traveled to New Jersey, where her daughter Martha was born on August 14, 1775. Zephaniah Sr. traveled to the north in the autumn of 1775 to gather his family and return with them to Charleston. A brief news item in the October 16, 1775, issue of the *South Carolina and American General Gazette* stated: "On Tuesday last arrived here from Philadelphia, in the Sloop Bentham, William Moore, Master, Mr. Zephaniah Kingsley and Family." There were then six children in the Kingsley family: Mary, age eleven; Zephaniah Jr., who would be ten in December; George, eight; Catherine, five; Isabella, three; and the infant, Martha.[31]

Tension was still high in Charleston when the Kingsleys returned from New Jersey, and the intensity escalated in early 1776 when a British fleet under command of Admiral Sir Peter Parker anchored off the bar. Aboard the vessels were three thousand British troops led by General Sir Henry Clinton, who intended to seize Sullivan's Island and control the entrance to the Charleston harbor. Patriot troops from South Carolina and a small force of American Continentals led by Major General Charles Lee were rushed to the defense of the city. Streets were barricaded, exterior defenses strengthened, and reinforcements deployed to a palmetto log fortification being constructed at the southern tip of Sullivan's Island, a strategic point overlooking the entrance to the harbor.[32]

Charleston's Loyalists waited with trepidation on June 28 after gunners aboard Admiral Parker's ships opened fire on the unfinished fort (now Fort Moultrie), while General Clinton ordered an amphibious attack from his base at Long Island (now Isle of Palms) across the narrow inlet north of Sullivan's Island. Both efforts failed. The opening shots of the American Revolution in South Carolina had been fired, and the unthinkable had happened: the Patriots scored a stunning victory. The British army withdrew, although Admiral Parker's fleet remained at anchor off the bar. Loyal supporters of Great Britain pondered their fate: Had they been abandoned by the Crown to fend for themselves in a time of increasing peril?

Additional problems occurred when the hundreds of soldiers encamped in the city crowded the streets and engaged in fights and riots. Tensions were lessened, however, by an economic revival resulting from the need to import provisions to feed the Patriot soldiers and the general populace.

Merchants who went about their business quietly and without gaining notoriety or the hatred of the mob for outspoken support of Britain were not attacked, and some even prospered. But no one in Charleston, Patriot or Loyalist, was safe from the curse of the periodic fires that destroyed hundreds of homes and businesses in these turbulent years.

One of the worst fires happened on January 15, 1778. It started at the corner of Queen and Union Streets, and before the flames were extinguished more than 250 homes had been destroyed along Broad, Church, Elliott, and Tradd Streets and Bedon's Alley. Included in the destruction were the Kingsleys' two-story brick dwelling, retail store, and outbuildings located at 16 Broad Street. Within one year of the fire, Kingsley had rebuilt the structures.

Between 1775 and 1780, while Charleston was occupied by American troops, Kingsley purchased several lots and buildings in Charleston and at Beaufort, along with a 554-acre plantation at Port Royal Island, an 1,800-acre plantation at Black Swamp in St. Peters Parish in Greenville, a store and outbuildings on 20 acres of land seventy miles from Charleston "at Indian Land," and a house and lot on a 40-acre tract at Frederica, Georgia. He later explained that his debts had all been paid by then and that he had cash on hand that was losing value because of currency fluctuation during the rebellion. With the exception of the family dwelling and retail store at Broad Street, the properties were all purchased on speculation at prices far below their pre-rebellion values. The sellers were Loyalists who were anxious to leave South Carolina—one was imprisoned when the transaction occurred—because of the rebellion then under way. Confident that Britain would subdue the rebels, Kingsley chose to play the game of chance. It was a choice he would come to regret.

Pressures on Loyalists increased in March 1778 when the legislature required every male over the age of sixteen to pledge loyalty to the revolutionary government or leave South Carolina. A large group of Loyalists refused, prompting a sympathetic Governor John Rutledge to extend the deadline for compliance. Mobs of laborers rioted, however, incensed by what they judged to be favoritism for people of means.

Zephaniah Kingsley was one of the men who refused to sign the "test oath," although he had been threatened with banishment and confiscation of his property. He instead followed the advice of his neighbor, a justice of the peace, who "out of friendship took his [Kingsley's] signature as an equivalent, and gave him a certificate of his having made an affirmation to the affect of the oath, [although Kingsley] . . . considered himself as being under no obligation therefrom, and that he would sooner have quitted the country than have made the affirmation."[33]

Between 1775 and 1779 Kingsley was imprisoned three times for refusing to bear arms against the British. His refusal was based partly on his Quaker faith, but he stressed that his main motivation was loyalty to Great Britain. He did provide service to the Patriot cause in 1780, when he "was obliged by the Americans to act as an overseer of their Negroes."[34]

In 1780, with the British army poised to regain control of Charleston, Kingsley was confident that his speculative investments would reap a major return. Early in the war the British army had focused its efforts to subdue the rebellion on the northern colonies. Beginning in June 1778, however, Sir Henry Clinton initiated a campaign to reclaim the southern colonies. In December an army of three thousand men under Lieutenant Colonel Archibald Campbell captured Savannah, Georgia. Between November 1778 and May 1779, another British army under General Augustine Prévost advanced from St. Augustine, East Florida, all the way to the walls of Charleston before a larger American force under command of General Benjamin Lincoln arrived to strengthen the city's defenses. British troops then pulled back to Savannah.

Reinforced at Charleston by fourteen hundred Continentals dispatched by General George Washington, General Lincoln ordered a massive fortification project. At the narrow neck of land north of the city between the Ashley and Cooper Rivers, Lincoln's men constructed redoubts, earthworks, lines of trenches, and a wide ditch flooded with water. The entire army of more than five thousand men moved inside the confines of the town's defenses, leaving them vulnerable if the British surrounded the city with a combined naval and land force.[35]

Beginning in February 1780, Clinton sent a force of ten thousand men against South Carolina. By mid-April, heavily armed British ships were in commanding positions on both the Ashley and Cooper Rivers and a land force had constructed a siege line north of the city. Aided by the cover of naval bombardments, the British soldiers advanced the siege lines incrementally, moving closer and closer to the city each day until the American army was trapped behind its defense lines without a means of escape or access to food supplies. Soldiers and residents alike despaired as provisions were consumed and hunger stalked the streets. Repeated bombardments aimed at targets within the town walls destroyed buildings, sparked fires, and spread terror among the town's residents. Finally, General Lincoln capitulated. On May 12, 1780, the entire 5,500-man American army was surrendered and the British reclaimed Charleston.[36]

For the Kingsley family and other Loyalists, General Clinton's triumph was liberating. The Kingsley children could again walk the streets without hearing taunts and threats of violence. Merchants loyal to Britain who had suffered harassment and economic hardship under the Americans now hoped to recoup their losses through revival of the export/import trade. American military authorities had confiscated hogsheads of tobacco, three hundred barrels of rice, dry goods, and other articles worth more than £2,000 sterling from Kingsley, and paid him with devalued paper currency and unredeemed promises. By late August, however, Kingsley and his partner at the time, Edward Oats, had received a shipment from British suppliers containing cloth goods, clothing, table china, glass, tinware, kegs of butter, and chests of tea.[37]

Kingsley joined more than one hundred residents on June 3, 1780, as sponsors of a petition that congratulated General Clinton on his victory and assured him of their loyalty. With British soldiers once more walking the streets of Charleston, the petitioners expected to again live "in ease and affluence." Kingsley was appointed to commissions operating under the Board of Police, including a committee advising military authorities on ways to moderate the rampant inflation that represented a bonanza to debtors but was undercutting the wealth of creditor classes. Another committee was authorized "to examine into and distinguish between the loyal and disaffected inhabitants," an activity unlikely to have endeared him to residents who favored the Patriot cause. Kingsley also provoked lasting enmity by, as he testified, exerting "every influence he had in endeavoring to reconcile the minds of the disaffected in those parts to yield submission to the government of their lawful king."[38]

In June, General Clinton returned to New York and left Lieutenant General Charles Cornwallis in charge of the southern campaign. British arms achieved great success in the early stages of the South Carolina campaign.

However, the decision by Cornwallis to force Carolinians to swear loyalty to Britain and to confiscate estates and plunder property so enraged Carolinians that they joined the Patriots in successful guerrilla forays against British outposts. Inspirational leaders like Thomas Sumter and Francis Marion succeeded in capturing several rural garrisons and inflicting more than a thousand British casualties at the great American victory at King's Mountain.

After victories by a new Continental army under General Nathanael Greene in December 1780, the British army divided its forces. General Cornwallis led his troops north to Virginia's Yorktown Peninsula for reinforcement. Before that could happen, however, an army of American and French soldiers led by General George Washington trapped Cornwallis's army on the peninsula while a French fleet sailed up Chesapeake Bay to block escape by water. On October 19, 1781, Cornwallis surrendered his army, forcing the British to seek terms of peace.[39]

British forces still occupied Charleston, but the countryside was under control of the Patriots. South Carolina's Fourth General Assembly met at Jacksonborough in January 1782. The main business during the six-week session was to identify individuals who had collaborated with the British and were therefore to be banished from South Carolina and their estates confiscated. Historian Walter Fraser describes a "spirit of vindictiveness" that prevailed throughout the session, with some legislators using the confiscation procedure to acquire valuable properties at bargain prices.[40]

Kingsley realized that his reluctance to take an oath of loyalty or take up arms for the Americans had "increased the resentment of the Americans toward him to such a degree that a sentence of banishment accompanied with the confiscation of the whole of his property was passed against him." On August 5, 1782, the Commissioners of Forfeited Estates sold sixteen hundred acres of his confiscated properties.[41]

While British soldiers under command of General Alexander Leslie remained in the city maintaining order and protecting private property, General Greene's American troops were in camps across the Ashley River, patiently waiting for the British occupation to end. Charleston's Loyalists hurried to conclude their business affairs and prepare their families for exile. Merchants sentenced to banishment were given permission to remain in Charleston for six months while they closed their businesses and collected debts owed to them.

Kingsley discovered that residents of the town were unwilling to meet their obligations. Debtors ignored him or refused his entreaties outright. Kingsley had previously formed a partnership with his attorney, Bennett Taylor, a Loyalist, who had managed to avoid publicity or confrontations with Patriot radicals and was permitted to remain in South Carolina. On April 30, 1782, Taylor ran an advertisement for "just imported linen drapery, etc., sold for cash or Government Bills and on no other terms, under the firm of Bennett Taylor and Company . . . Zephaniah Kingsley having declined trade and shortly going to England."[42]

Taylor also became the agent for Kingsley's home and store on Broad Street and the protector of his wife and children when he was forced into exile. Kingsley gave Isabella title to the lot and the "good brick house" he built on Broad Street and to all his remaining properties, and shipped several slaves he owned to Jamaica. An unspecified number of slaves were retained in Charleston under supervision of Taylor, who agreed "to keep the Negroes under an idea that they belong to [Kingsley's] children and indeed he did make a deed of gift of them to his children before he came away."[43]

In August 1782 the residents of Charleston watched as a large British fleet anchored in the harbor. The 4,200 Loyalists awaiting evacuation had requested permission to carry away 7,200 enslaved men and women. In all, three hundred ships transported British soldiers, the Loyalists, and their property away from Charleston. Kingsley went into exile on December 14, 1782, aboard one of the last evacuation ships to depart from the wharves at Charleston. His destination was Bristol, England, the city he had left in 1768 after suffering bankruptcy. Isabella Kingsley and her children remained in Charleston surrounded by Patriots hostile to British Loyalists, unsure of what their fates would be.[44]

2 || New Brunswick Years

Becoming an Atlantic Trader

The British naval vessel that carried Zephaniah Kingsley Sr. into exile departed Charleston on December 14, 1782, and joined a flotilla of British vessels anchored offshore. Stymied by inclement weather, the fleet stayed at anchor until December 19, when it broke into convoys of fifty ships headed for New York, fifty for Jamaica, and twenty for England. Elias Vanderhorst, a former Charleston merchant residing in Bristol, wrote to Henry Laurens on February 1, 1783, with news that Kingsley and several other Loyalist merchants had recently arrived at the port.[1]

Loyalists had been migrating to Bristol since the rebellion began, prompting a former colonial from Massachusetts to comment that "of all the Americans on this side of the water the greatest number are in Bristol." In fact, it was London that drew the largest number of Loyalists from North America. The Loyalist community in Bristol was significant, however, and the city's merchants had for decades carried on a lively commerce with their Charleston colleagues. Kingsley had operated a retail store in Bristol between 1764 and 1769, and after migrating to Charleston he purchased merchandise from suppliers in Bristol. He had departed South Carolina with a burden of debt to English creditors, some of which likely appeared on the books of Bristol merchants. Kingsley's American properties were worth more than £20,000 sterling, but he owed £22,000 sterling to creditors in America and Britain. Residents of South Carolina were indebted to Kingsley for £6,500 sterling, but he had little chance of collecting that money, and he was liable for debts on his American properties even though the legislature confiscated them.[2]

Kingsley intended only a temporary residence at Bristol. Isabella Kingsley remained in Charleston, expecting him to return. Her immediate responsibilities were to care for the children and hold onto as many family properties as the new state of South Carolina would allow. Meanwhile, Zephaniah renegotiated lines of credit in England and sought a pardon from the South Carolina government.

On January 28, 1783, Isabella submitted the first Kingsley family petition to the South Carolina House of Representatives. She requested that her husband be pardoned and permitted to return to Charleston with his confiscated properties restored. As the mother of "six children and being deprived of her Husband's estate . . . [and having] nothing to maintain them with," she pleaded with the legislature to practice clemency rather than "subject . . . her helpless, innocent family to misery and want." The plea was ignored, and the Commissioners of Forfeited Estates sold the Kingsley family home on Broad Street at public auction on June 16. The commissioners also auctioned a Kingsley-owned lot and house on South Bay with an adjoining low water lot. Because the home on Broad Street was purchased by Zephaniah's former partner, attorney Bennet Taylor, Isabella was able to remain in residence while she prepared to join her husband in exile.[3]

News of the rejected petition and the property sales convinced Kingsley to resettle in Britain's North American colony of Nova Scotia, Canada. During July 1784 he arranged a line of credit for a cargo of merchandise to be shipped in his name to the care of William Abbott, a Loyalist merchant at Halifax. By September 3, 1784, Kingsley had relocated to Parr Town (later St. John), at the mouth of the St. John River in what later became the province of New Brunswick. He wrote to Gideon White, a Loyalist merchant located at Shelburne, Nova Scotia, requesting that merchandise from Maltby and Sons of London be forwarded to him at Parr Town, where he had secured a location for a retail business. When the merchandise had not arrived by October 4, Kingsley became impatient and asked White to "inquire of every vessel from England for his goods."[4]

With the same resilience and perseverance he had shown after his business failed at Bristol, Kingsley restarted his life and career at New Brunswick. He had not, however, become reconciled to permanent exile from Charleston. From Parr Town on November 6, 1784, he petitioned the House of Representatives of the South Carolina General Assembly for permission to return to that state, asserting that because of his "very indigent situation, burthened with a numerous and helpless family of a wife and six children three of them natives of [South Carolina] & . . . the infirmities of old age . . . he is rendered incapable of providing for them." Kingsley promised "future deportment . . . [to] atone for his past conduct" if the legislature would "forget his injudicious conduct" and grant "mercy to a distressed family that thereby they may be rescued from want and beggery."[5]

On January 28, 1785, a Charleston resident who had supported the Patriot cause addressed the committee on behalf of Kingsley. "Mr. Brenian" testified that he had known Kingsley for many years and that while imprisoned by the British military in a ship anchored in Charleston harbor Kingsley "supplied him with necessarys the whole time he was a prisoner, even on board the prison ship and that when [a prisoner exchange] took place he [Kingsley] pressed him to take some goods . . . out of his store & he might pay when he pleased." Brenian testified that Kingsley had provided supplies for other imprisoned American officers and frequently heard him "reprobate the conduct of the British officers in the garrison."[6]

The committee that considered Kingsley's petition voted to approve his request. That recommendation did not convince Kingsley's detractors. On March 17, 1785, the House of Representatives voted to deny the petition. Kingsley thereafter focused on a new life and business in British Canada. Isabella remained in Charleston while plans were finalized for the family to reunite.[7]

It is likely that Zephaniah Kingsley Jr. was with his father when he first arrived in Canada, or joined him soon after. He was seventeen years old when his father departed Charleston, old enough to accompany his father into exile, and a port-of-entry record provides evidence that he returned to Charleston from London on August 27, 1783. The *South Carolina Gazette* announced that day the arrival of the *Roman Emperor*, under command of Captain Thomas Davison, inbound from London "with passengers, among whom are listed a son and nephew of Mr. Zephaniah Kingsley."[8]

In *The Loyalists of New Brunswick*, Esther Clark Wright lists both Zephaniah Kingsley Sr. and Jr. as recipients of land grants in the province. Zephaniah Sr. is described as a merchant who received a government grant for a building lot in the new town of Fredericton and a rural tract on Hammond River. Zephaniah Jr. is also listed as a recipient of a land grant on Hammond

River. Zephaniah Jr. was the first in the family to join his father in New Brunswick. Father and son worked together to establish a store at St. John for trade with the thousands of Loyalists who were arriving from the former British colonies in North America.[9]

The first of the Loyalists arrived in Canada late in 1782, searching for eligible harbors, fertile land in the river valleys, and forest land with exploitable timber stands. From the experiences of earlier generations of explorers and settlers, they knew of the vast timber resources and the seemingly endless supplies of fish found in the St. John, St. Croix, Petitcodiac, and Kennebecacis Rivers and the adjoining Bay of Fundy. Edward Winslow, a Harvard graduate and Loyalist from Massachusetts, came to Halifax in 1783 as an advance agent for the New York Loyalists. After exploring the St. John River valley, Winslow wrote that its fishing industry was matchless in North America, the "fund of timber literally inexhaustible . . . and beef and pork are produced in great abundance."[10]

Loyalist refugees began arriving at Halifax in May 1783 and continued into the autumn months. They were provided military supplies left over from the war, including provisions, clothing, axes, agricultural tools, cooking implements, and blankets. Approximately 35,000 refugees arrived in Nova Scotia in 1783, and more followed. Historian Christopher Moore estimates that 70,000 Loyalists left the thirteen British colonies that became the United States of America. Of that number, 46,000 settled in the Canadian Maritime Provinces. Wilderness settlements and small communities of Loyalists began to appear on the coast and along the river valleys.[11]

In August 1784, Loyalist merchant Gideon White wrote to a Jamaican merchant from Shelburne, a frontier settlement west of Halifax, to order a shipment of rum, sugar, and coffee. White added: the "situation we are in . . . is dam'd hard 'tho in the Course of a few years it will be a very eligible Situation." White marveled at the building boom under way, "2700 Houses—above 2000 are framed," and expressed his expectation that "business will soon be sprightly." The resources of codfish seemed endless, White wrote, "next Year I expect to see great exertions—but at present every Man seems intent on a House, Wharfe, Stores &c."[12]

Merchants like White prospered as the population of Nova Scotia more than doubled, prompting the government to carve off a huge unsettled area north of the Bay of Fundy for the new province of New Brunswick. In June

1784, Thomas Carleton, the younger brother of the commander in chief of British forces in North America in 1782 and 1783, was appointed governor. At the place where the St. John River joins the Bay of Fundy, a village called St. John (formerly Parr Town) contained forty families and a small garrison of soldiers living in houses built around the commodious harbor. In June 1784, the government announced that St. John had been selected the first capital of New Brunswick, initiating a building frenzy. Approximately fifteen hundred houses were constructed in 1783 and 1784. Merchants, including Zephaniah Kingsley Sr., competed for space for wharves, warehouses, and commercial houses. A London newspaper reported in September 1784 that the new "settlement of the American Loyalists, at Saint John in New Brunswick" was flourishing because of the "fertility of the soil, the great plenty of fish, and wild fowl, American deer, wild hogs, and other cattle."[13]

At the end of August 1784, Kingsley Sr. purchased merchandise on credit from English firms to sell to the pioneer farmers settling along the rivers north of the Bay of Fundy. Unlike his previous experiences at Charleston, Kingsley's mercantile transactions at St. John would often involve bartering for products the pioneers extracted from the forests and fields. Kingsley and his eldest son toured the frontier settlements searching for land to purchase and observing men at work clearing the forests, building cabins and utility buildings, and processing deer, bear, moose, and other wild game they killed. Later the Kingsleys would purchase skins, furs, and timber products to sell to merchants in England and the Caribbean. After the Kingsley store was established at St. John, ships unloaded imported English merchandise at the wharf and local fishing boats brought cod and other fish. Kingsley would load many tons of dried and salted fish and stockpiles of timber aboard ships engaged in the Caribbean trade.

One of Kingsley's mercantile colleagues at St. John was General Benedict Arnold, the former Patriot hero and major general in the Continental army who defected to the British after his plot to turn West Point over to the British was discovered. In 1786 Arnold purchased the *Lord Sheffield*, a 300-ton ship built at New Brunswick that he sailed between St. John and Jamaica. He acquired numerous city and rural properties before returning to England in 1791, from where he continued to engage in Caribbean trade.[14]

In July 1785 Kingsley advertised in a New Brunswick newspaper "sundry

European goods" from London for which he would accept payment in "cash or bills, or in exchange for moose skins or winter furs of any kind." His April 1786 solicitation read: "Wanted immediately, by Zephaniah Kingsley, to be delivered at St. John at a market price, 200,000 boards." In May of that same year he offered for sale "linen and woolen drapery, [and] shoes" imported from London on the *New Hope*. He also pledged to pay "the highest price given for Beaver, Otter, Muskquash, Moose-skins, and peltry in general, likewise for boards and staves, and any kind of lumber fit for the West Indies." Two weeks later he urged fishermen to bring their catches of herring and salmon to "the old Commissary Store, on Portland Point."[15]

Kingsley placed similar advertisements in subsequent years. On December 18, 1787, he solicited "one hundred and fifty thousand good red oak and beech barrel staves" and offered "skins and furs of all sorts—likewise Castoreum and Musqush Stones." On July 16, 1789, he had merchandise from England for sale "cheap for cash, or in exchange . . . [for] dryed fish, oil, skins, and furs of all sorts, moose hides, otter, bear, etc."[16]

The viability of the St. John merchant community was threatened in 1785 when the provincial capital was moved seventy miles upriver to Fredericton (formerly St. Ann) to encourage settlement of the interior of the province. Surveyors had begun laying out blocks and lots for the new town in July 1784. Kingsley acquired a town lot to establish a second outlet for his merchandise. On December 18, 1785, he joined several prominent businessmen in a petition to Governor Thomas Carleton requesting the establishment of "an academy or school of liberal arts and sciences at Fredericton," an action that eventually led to the creation of the University of New Brunswick.[17]

Insight into Kingsley's business activities are found in the Ward Chipman Papers at the New Brunswick Museum. Chipman, a graduate of Harvard and a successful attorney at Marblehead, Massachusetts, came to St. John with the Loyalists in 1784 as the new province's solicitor general. Chipman served as Kingsley's attorney and used his extensive contacts to facilitate Kingsley's business affairs. In June 1785 Chipman arranged power of attorney for the firm of Cathcart and Mowatt of Kingston, Jamaica, authorizing them to collect money from Loyalist refugees from Charleston who were still indebted to Kingsley and to "sell and dispose of . . . as they shall think fit, all or any Negroes and other things whatsoever belonging to

[Kingsley]." The power of attorney specifically mentioned "a Negro man named Kelsey and a Negro woman named Lucy or, however otherwise named or called in the said Island of Jamaica."[18]

In addition to his mercantile career in New Brunswick, Kingsley Sr. acquired titles to tracts of rural land and town lots and houses in St. John and Fredericton. In February and March 1785 he petitioned Governor Carleton for a land grant, citing his record as a loyal supporter of the Crown and a merchant from South Carolina with six children to support. In August and September 1786 he purchased two tracts on the Little Kennebecasis River, also known as the Hammond River. Signing as a witness for one of these tracts was his son George Kingsley, approximately eighteen years old at the time. On January 13, 1787, Kingsley Sr. and his wife, Isabella, received a Crown grant of nearly nine hundred acres in Sussex Parish of Kings County, located on the west side of the Little Kennebecasis River. Two months later, Kingsley transferred title of this tract to his son Zephaniah Jr., who later deeded the tract to his sisters Catherine, Isabella, and Martha. The stream that flows through the acreage is still known locally as Kingsley Brook. Kingsley Sr. also purchased two half-acre lots with dwellings at Fredericton in 1789.[19]

The property transactions provide evidence that Isabella Kingsley and her children moved to St. John in 1785. Only Mary, Isabella's eldest child, is not mentioned in the New Brunswick records. She may have married by this time and moved to England. According to family legend, Mary was wed to an English naval officer named Charlton and was widowed early in the marriage when his ship was lost at sea. Isabella's presence in New Brunswick is further documented by an April 11, 1786, newspaper reference to "Zephaniah Kingsley and his wife Isabella . . . a prominent merchant at the City of Saint John" and one of three commissioners who supervised construction of the "Westmoreland Road from Saint John to the Bend of Petitcodiac River."[20]

Business success led to social prominence for Kingsley Sr. Drawing on a letter of recommendation for Kingsley, historian Carole W. Troxler described him as "a man of great property and credit," the owner of several houses, and one of the most active of New Brunswick's Loyalist merchants.[21] A London newspaper reported in August 1787 that a St. George's Day celebration had been held at St. John, attended by "a number of respected gentlemen [who] dined together at McPherson's Tavern. . . . An elegant entertainment was prepared, and the evening concluded with every demonstration of loyalty, and with the most perfect harmony and good humor." Kingsley was listed as vice president of the organization that sponsored the event.

Quakers in London who organized a relief effort for their New Brunswick brethren looked to Kingsley for assistance. In September 1788 the London Meeting for Suffering sent £500 sterling and agricultural tools to St. John. The aid package was shipped from London aboard the *True Briton*, a brigantine owned by Kingsley, and he was designated as one of the local merchants responsible for its distribution. The yearly meeting of Philadelphia Quakers sent £384 sterling in cash and relief supplies to Quaker settlers at Beaver Harbor and St. John. The supplies included agricultural tools, sixty barrels of cornmeal, and other provisions.[22]

During his early years in New Brunswick, Kingsley imported goods on credit from English merchants to sell in his retail stores, acquired urban and rural properties, and purchased the produce of New Brunswick's farms, forests, and waters for shipment to markets in England and the West Indies. He also became a shipowner while at St. John. By April 1786, Kingsley had purchased a ship and was using it to transport cargoes from England to New Brunswick. Mather Byles of St. John informed Edward Winslow on April 11, 1786, that Kingsley's ship carrying Irish linen and other goods from England "will be round here from Halifax in a few days," at which time he expected to pick out a piece of fine linen for his mother. On September 4, 1787, an advertisement in a St. John newspaper offered passenger and cargo accommodations for a voyage to Lisbon and London aboard Kingsley's brigantine, the *True Briton*, which sailed twice each year between St. John and London. Cargo space and passenger tickets could be arranged by contacting either Kingsley or the captain of the *True Briton*, Christopher Collins.[23]

Kingsley, or possibly his son Zephaniah Jr., purchased another ship for the lucrative West Indies trade. For decades, ships owned by New Brunswick and Nova Scotia merchants carried grain, timber, barrel staves, and dried and salted fish to ports on the Caribbean islands and returned with sugar, coffee, and rum. In 1790 at the port city of Yarmouth, Nova Scotia, Zephaniah Kingsley (the name was recorded without a suffix) was listed as a real estate owner, a grand juror, and the owner of the *Argo*, a 64-ton brigantine. It is doubtful that Zephaniah Sr. was that person. In 1790, Kingsley Sr. was still an established merchant and residential property owner in New Brunswick. Only a few months before he had purchased two houses and their corresponding lots in Fredericton, New Brunswick, making it unlikely he could have simultaneously satisfied the residency requirements needed to qualify as a grand juror at a city in the neighboring province of Nova Scotia. Zephaniah Jr., however, could have satisfied the requirements. He was twenty-five years old at the time and had apparently served an apprenticeship in Atlantic maritime commerce under his father's direction. Only three years later, in October 1793, when the British ship *Argo* arrived at the Charleston harbor, Zephaniah Jr. was its captain. Yarmouth, with an excellent harbor on the Gulf of Maine and a reputation as a major shipbuilding center, offered advantages to a ship captain trading in the West Indies, which is the occupation that Zephaniah Jr. followed for the next quarter-century.[24]

In the early months of 1791, Zephaniah Kingsley Sr. left New Brunswick and moved with his family to the United States. Barred from returning to South Carolina, Kingsley chose an alternate Atlantic port city, Wilmington, North Carolina, located on the Cape Fear River 150 miles north of Charleston. His reasons for departing New Brunswick are not known. Judging by the comments of his business acquaintances and the properties he had accumulated, his accomplishments in fewer than seven years in New Brunswick had been significant. He had, however, started his days in Canada with a heavy burden of debt. After South Carolina banished him and confiscated his properties, Kingsley had returned to England owing £22,000 sterling to creditors. In the limited body of relevant correspondence found in Canadian archives are references to unsuccessful attempts to collect money owed to Kingsley by Loyalists in Jamaica and Canada.[25]

New Brunswick experienced an economic downturn at the end of the 1780s, and this might explain why Kingsley moved to North Carolina. The British government had by then eliminated relief support for Loyalists and reduced military expenditures, and the seemingly inexhaustible forests had begun to show signs of decline. The proliferation of settlements along the navigable waterways had depleted the readily accessible stands of timber, forcing lumberjacks to move further inland before roads existed. New

Brunswick sawmills that had worked at full capacity for years had reduced production or were sitting idle in 1790, and timber was being imported from forests in Maine. The New Brunswick fishing industry was still productive, but competition from New England fishermen and merchants resulted in diminished profits.

These problems were accentuated after 1789 by the shock waves emanating from France. After King Louis XVI was executed by revolutionaries in January 1793, England and Spain declared war on France. Within weeks, French privateers began capturing ships flying the flags of enemies of France. The British responded in kind; ships of the Royal Navy and privateers sought out and captured vessels with French registration. For the next two decades, all ships engaged in the Caribbean trade sailed at the risk of capture and condemnation. Although not immune, ships flying the flags of neutral nations—at first the United States, Denmark, and the Netherlands—were less liable to seizure. American merchants thus gained an advantage in the West Indies trade, and the prescient and cautious among the Canadian maritime merchants—perhaps including Kingsley Sr.—moved their ships to safe harbors along the east coast of the United States.[26]

The evidence for Kingsley Sr.'s move to Wilmington is found in the correspondence of Ward Chipman, the Loyalist from Massachusetts who became a prominent lawyer and judge in New Brunswick. In July 1791 Chipman received a letter from William Wylly, a Loyalist from Georgia who was the King's Counsel and registrar of the vice-admiralty court in New Brunswick before moving in 1787 to New Providence Island. At his new home, Wylly became solicitor general and chief justice of the Bahama Islands. Wylly had employed Chipman to secure payment of a debt owed to him by Kingsley. His July 18 letter informed Chipman that "Mr. Kingsley has taken his last leave of you and is now here in our neighborhood. . . . I am informed that Kingsley is settled at Wilmington in North Carolina." Although he "feared the money is lost to me and my heirs," Wylly asked Chipman to continue efforts to collect on the debt.[27]

Wylly's 1791 letter to Chipman represents the end of the trail of evidence concerning Zephaniah Kingsley Sr. No further record of his life has been found, although several documents support the conclusion that he died soon after moving to Wilmington. Isabella Kingsley and her two youngest daughters, Elizabeth, age nineteen, and Martha, age sixteen, also moved to

Wilmington. Both Elizabeth and Martha married natives of North Carolina during their years at Wilmington: Elizabeth in 1798 to Wilmington merchant George Gibbs III; Martha in 1800 to Dr. Daniel McNeill, who had studied medicine at Edinburgh, Scotland.[28]

Zephaniah Kingsley Jr. did not move to Wilmington with his family, although he visited the city to care for his widowed mother. There are indications that he utilized Wilmington as an unofficial home, but until he swore an oath of loyalty to the United States of America at Charleston, South Carolina, in December 1793, Kingsley continued to be identified legally as an English citizen residing in British Canada. He was in his mid-twenties by then, with an official residence at Yarmouth, Nova Scotia, the owner and captain of the brigantine *Argo*. Port-of-entry records for Charleston list the arrival of the *Argo* on March 29 and October 3, 1793, both times with Zephaniah Kingsley in command. Kingsley learned the mercantile trade under the tutelage of his father during the years the family resided at St. John, New Brunswick. He served his apprenticeship as a ship captain under masters hired to operate his father's ships in Atlantic commerce.[29]

This early training as a maritime merchant served Kingsley well. For the next thirty years he would command ships engaged in commerce at ports throughout the Atlantic world, exchanging products of North American farms and forests for Caribbean coffee, sugar, rum, and other items produced by enslaved Africans. For nearly two decades, Kingsley's ships also transported human cargoes, enslaved men and women from East and West Africa, across the Atlantic to Cuba, East Florida, and other Caribbean colonies. After becoming an American citizen in 1793, Kingsley pledged loyalty to the king of Denmark in 1798 and to the king of Spain in 1803, and he changed the flags he flew above his ships as often as he changed nationality. He became the owner of several Florida plantations and hundreds of enslaved African men and women. For thirty years, the perilous winds of Atlantic commerce during the era of the French Revolution and the storm clouds of warfare would propel Zephaniah Kingsley Jr. from home to home and from nation to nation.[30]

3 | "My Saddle Bags Loaded with Specie"

Caribbean Commerce in the Age of Revolution

On October 3, 1793, Zephaniah Kingsley secured the *Argo*, a British-registered brigantine, to a wharf jutting into the Cooper River at Charleston. It was a homecoming of sorts for the twenty-eight-year-old ship captain, but it was not to be a happy occasion. Charleston had been his home between 1770 and 1783, but that ended when his father was banished for supporting Great Britain during the American Revolution. The family home for the next decade had been St. John, New Brunswick, although Kingsley Jr. had returned to Charleston occasionally while learning the maritime trade on his father's ships. In the late 1780s he became a ship captain in his own right, and by February 1791 he was master of the *Dolphin*, a sloop employed in the Caribbean trade. On February 23, 1792, he registered as the captain and owner of the *Argo* when clearing customs at Savannah with a cargo from Kingston, Jamaica.[1]

When Kingsley arrived at Charleston on October 3, 1793, he was a seasoned mariner familiar with ports in the Caribbean and the Atlantic coast of North America. The October 1793 voyage, however, was his last aboard the *Argo*. In late September, Kingsley departed Jamaica bound for Wilmington, North Carolina, but his ship was seized as a prize of war by a French privateer, Captain Jean Bouteille and the fifty-man crew of the *Sans Pareille*. Bouteille, out of Saint-Domingue, was operating under license of a "letter of marque and reprisal" issued by an official of the French Republic, which authorized him to confiscate property of the enemies of France. Seizure of a merchant ship on the open seas would normally have been condemned as an act of piracy, but England and France were at war in 1793. The continental war between Britain and the revolutionary government of the French Republic, begun in February 1793, had quickly become a worldwide maritime conflict.[2]

Boteille and his heavily armed crew escorted Kingsley and the *Argo* to Charleston, the nearest neutral port that permitted French privateers to bring their prizes before a court of admiralty. A few days later, the ship and its cargo were condemned as a prize of war and sold for £288 British sterling to a Danish citizen, who immediately sailed for Barcelona, Spain, with a new captain and crew. It was a devastating blow to Kingsley. He lost his most valuable possession and was stranded in Charleston scrambling to find employment. A more cautious person might have considered a less hazardous occupation, but Kingsley was motivated by the lure of fortune from the immense volume of Caribbean trade.

The French colony of Saint-Domingue alone produced roughly 40 percent of the sugar and 60 percent of the coffee consumed in Europe. Nearly all of the sugar, coffee, indigo, and cotton exported from Saint-Domingue was produced by the forced labor of enslaved Africans brought to the colony in astonishing numbers. Nearly 700,000 Africans arrived in chains from 1700 to 1791, more than half that number between 1776 and 1791.[3]

The numbers of ships and sailors involved in the Caribbean trade is equally astonishing. The historian Julius S. Scott has estimated that "roughly 21,000 British mariners traveled to the West Indian colonies each year" in the late 1780s. Jamaica, a British colony, "employed close to 500 ships and well over 9,000 seamen" in 1788, and in the following year nearly 19,000 French sailors were aboard the 710 ships that arrived at ports in Saint-Domingue. Guadeloupe, Martinique, Cuba, and the other West Indian colonies of France, Britain, Denmark, Spain, and the Netherlands all offered shippers the possibility of great profits.[4]

The loss of the *Argo* dramatized for Kingsley that profit from Caribbean trade was tempered by the great peril faced by mariners during a time of international warfare. French and British naval vessels patrolled the waters, yet privateers licensed by both nations lay in wait, eager to seize commercial vessels. Danger was also posed by the violence emanating from the slave rebellion in Saint-Domingue and the civil wars under way in other French colonies.

Fulwar Skipwith witnessed the violence firsthand. A Martinique-based commercial agent employed by the United States Department of State, Skipwith announced in 1793 that he had seen too many violent incidents and informed the secretary of state that he would soon bid "his final adieu to this unhappy island." One of Skipwith's fellow agents, David M. Clarkson, was alarmed when he heard that British privateers were stopping all vessels suspected of having French property onboard and that American ship captains were discharging all French products to avoid having their cargoes confiscated.[5]

Zephaniah Kingsley was not intimidated. He immediately began searching for a commission as captain of another ship engaged in Caribbean trade. He traveled briefly to Savannah, returning to Charleston on November 7 at the helm of the brig *Argus*. He then booked passage to New York City and returned on November 23 in the company of George Gibbs, the future husband of his sister Elizabeth. The wealthy Charleston merchant Charles Johnston, brother of Kingsley's mother, still lived in Charleston and was available for advice and introductions. Johnston, a Loyalist, had been banished in 1782 but was pardoned and retained his position among the influential Scot and English merchants in the city.[6]

Kingsley also utilized a network of Loyalists who settled in Canada and the Caribbean islands after the American Revolution. His deceased father had established commercial relationships that Zephaniah Jr. later revived. This was especially true for Kingston, where merchant associates arranged the sale of slaves owned by Kingsley Sr. after he was banished from Charleston. Kingsley Jr. called on these merchants during his trading ventures in the late 1780s and the 1790s.

Kingsley also associated with another diaspora network of planters and merchants, the French émigrés who fled from Saint-Domingue following the massive slave rebellion that swept across the northern province of that island in August 1791. Thousands of refugees fled and were resettled at Kingston, Charleston, and other cities in the West Indies and the United States. The historian David Geggus found in a study of Kingston that refugees from Saint-Domingue began arriving in that city in September 1791 and that by April of the following year "there were as many French in the capital as British." The influx of refugees, combined with a surprisingly high number of imports of enslaved Africans (23,000 from June 1792 through June 1793), created a booming market for foodstuffs. The French refugee community at Kingston proved highly influential in encouraging an invasion of Saint-Domingue that became, for the British, a five-year occupation with horrendous consequences. It was at Kingston that six hundred British troops boarded ships and departed for Jeremie in the southern province of Saint-Domingue on September 9, 1793.[7]

Kingsley was in Kingston when preparations for that invasion were under way. Only a few weeks later in Charleston, he encountered a similar community of several hundred exiles who were engaging in lively debates and stirring the pot of political ferment while waiting to reclaim their abandoned properties as soon as the rebellion was contained. The citizens of Charleston were grateful to France for the revered General Lafayette and for military aid during the war for independence. More than one hundred Charleston citizens joined the Republican Society to pledge solidarity with the new government of the French Republic and its ideals of liberty, equality, and fraternity and to speak out against the efforts by Great Britain and Spain to drive the French out of Saint-Domingue.[8]

The French Patriotic Society stood in direct opposition to the political goals of the Republican Society. Members of the Patriotic Society came mainly from the ranks of the colonial aristocrats, whose goal was to end their exile and return to their plantations and businesses in Saint-Domingue. A few among them longed for restoration of the monarchy, but most sought either autonomous control of the island's economy within the French Empire or complete independence. The primary goal was to regain their elite race and class privileges and to reimpose slavery, even if it meant conquest of the island by the British.[9]

The American Revolution Society was founded in Charleston in 1792 by men the historian Robert J. Alderson Jr. described as "the more Conservative and British-oriented" individuals in the community, who were horrified by the increasing radicalism of the French Revolution. Members of this society were primarily affluent British merchants who missed few opportunities to denounce the French privateers that preyed on British shipping. At meetings at William's Coffee House in Charleston they loudly proclaimed support for the Royal Navy and clamored for a British invasion of Saint-Domingue.[10]

The leader of the pro-British conservatives in Charleston was the merchant and shipowner Edward Penman, a Scot migrant from Edinburgh who had lost a ship to a French corsair and then armed one of his own vessels as a British privateer. His brother, James Penman, had been one of the leading planters and merchants in British East Florida prior to the American Revolution. Merchant firms like James and Edward Penman and Company, North and Vesey, and Jennings and Woddrop owned numerous commercial ships and routinely searched for dependable ship captains. These firms had established contacts with traders at ports in the southern province of Saint-Domingue, the area that Kingsley would frequent in the years ahead.[11]

In 1794, Zephaniah and his brother George were both employed as ship captains by Edward Penman and Company, and both were sailing between Charleston and ports in the Caribbean. The Penman and Company Daybook for 1794 lists salaries paid to "Zeph Kingsley" and to "George Kingsley." Several entries in the daybook provide details of George Kingsley's voyages to ports in Saint-Domingue as the captain of the schooner *Mary* and of his return to Charleston with cargoes of coffee and sugar.[12]

Early in 1794, Zephaniah Kingsley maneuvered a Penman and Company vessel, the schooner *Rosina*, through the Charleston harbor and charted a course for the Caribbean island of Martinique. Before departing, however, he strengthened his claim to neutral status by changing his nationality from British to American. On December 20, 1793, at the Court of Wardens in Charleston, twenty-eight-year-old Zephaniah Kingsley affirmed an oath of loyalty to the United States of America. He had learned through bitter personal experience that sailing a British ship in Caribbean waters while Britain and France were at war represented a major financial risk. In the future he would sail under the flags of neutral nations, although he soon learned that a neutral flag was not a guarantee of safe passage in Caribbean waters during the era of the French Revolution.[13]

Kingsley was warned before leaving Charleston that British naval vessels and privateers were stopping American ships suspected of trading at French ports. Early in the war the powerful British navy had swept French vessels from Caribbean waters, placing the residents of French colonies in danger of starvation. The French Republic responded by encouraging Americans to bring cargoes of provisions to the French West Indian colonies, and hundreds of merchants dispatched ships as quickly as they could load them with foodstuffs.

The British Foreign Office declared that ships of neutral nations delivering provisions to French ports were providing direct aid to an enemy during wartime in violation of the rights of neutrality. The ships involved, along with their cargoes, were subject to confiscation. With this interpretation, Britain was adhering to policies first proclaimed in 1756 at the beginning of the Seven Years' War, barring ships of neutral nations from trading in ports of their enemies if those ports had been closed to neutrals before the war. The U.S. government insisted on the principle of "free ships make free goods" and protested vehemently, but the British Foreign Office paid little attention.[14]

Hundreds of U.S. vessels were stopped and escorted into British ports for inspection during 1793. Coffee and other products loaded at French colonial ports were condemned as contraband of war and confiscated, a process that resulted in expensive delays and losses of cargo, but the ships were returned to their owners. When the Baltimore schooner *Peggy* was seized by a British vessel in August 1793, it was escorted to Jamaica and relieved of its cargo of coffee purchased at Saint-Domingue. After a six-week delay, the ship was returned to its owner, John Smith and Company of Baltimore. That same firm's brigantine *John* was captured twice in 1793 but released each time.[15]

David Clarkson, the American commercial agent at St. Eustatius in 1793, reported to the State Department that U.S. vessels were being seized. In 1794 his frustration turned to anger after the British navy implemented the Orders in Council decreed by the Foreign Office on November 6, 1793. The orders had been kept secret for two months to facilitate a planned naval campaign, which resulted in large numbers of American merchant ships trapped in French West Indian ports when the British fleet arrived. In contrast to previous practices, British officials hastily condemned and sold both ships and cargoes. Clarkson witnessed as dozens of American ships were condemned and sold at Montserrat and St. Kitts. Two months later at St. Eustatius, agent Fulwar Skipwith learned that 250 U.S. vessels had been seized by British warships and carried into ports at the Windward Islands. All the ships taken into Dominique, Antigua, Montserrat, and St. Kitts were condemned and sold, the captains and crew stranded and in desperate need of passage home.[16]

Zephaniah Kingsley was the captain of one of forty American ships that entered the harbor of St. Pierre, Martinique, in January 1794, unaware that Britain was about to implement its controversial policy. When a British fleet under command of Admiral John Jervis arrived on February 3, 1794, to begin a siege of the island, egress from the harbor was blocked. Fourteen days later, British troops took possession of the town and seized all vessels in the harbor. In a joint statement written three months later, the still-confined American ship captains charged that British officers boarded their vessels and tore down the flags, forcibly removed the captains and crewmen without permitting them to take along a change of clothing or to secure their personal possessions before being "carried on board a Ship of War, and after undergoing a contemptuous examination . . . [forced] on board a Prison Ship crowded together to the number of two hundred and fifty Persons in a small ship." After three days without food, the captains requested permission to go ashore to procure provisions, but the British officer in charge condemned them as "a set of damned Rascals [who] might starve and be damned." Eventually, the confined sailors were provided provisions and the captains were permitted to live ashore at their own expense. The captains later discovered their ship "Cabbins had been shamefully and wantonly plundered . . . Trunks and Chests broke open and robbed of everything of value" and personal papers destroyed in acts "of malicious revenge or the frenzy of intoxication." Some imprisoned American sailors were forced to serve on British warships, while others "died daily on board the prison ship."[17]

John Shallcross, another U.S. commercial agent, traveled from the Island of St. Vincent to St. Pierre in early April 1794 and discovered the captured American ships anchored carelessly in the harbor, some moored so closely they slammed together when the tides changed. Four were damaged and sank in the harbor, and two others pulled loose from their moorings and drifted out of the harbor and were lost at sea. Shallcross verified that captains and crew members had been treated brutally and that sailors were still confined in the decrepit prison ship moored in the harbor. British army commander Lieutenant General Charles Grey appointed an unauthorized judge and then pressured him to condemn and immediately sell the American ships at St. Pierre and ten others anchored at Fort Royal.[18]

Shallcross assembled a list of the captured ships, the ports where their owners resided, and the names of their captains. Five of the ships were registered at Charleston, including the schooner *Rosina*, whose captain was identified as "Zephinia Kingsley." Like the other captains, Kingsley had been confined aboard the prison ship and was later released to live ashore at his own expense. Forced to give testimony at the liable proceedings and to observe deliberations as the ships and cargoes were condemned and sold, Kingsley and the other captains accused the judge of denying them "the benefit of an argument through our attorney, and condemning us all . . . as Bad men, supplying the wants of Bad Men in a Bad Cause, and were and ought to be considered as Enemies to Great Britain."[19]

Sales of the captured ships began on April 10, 1794. In late May, Shallcross wrote: "All the vessels at Martinique were condemned in one breath by the judge. All . . . [privateers] have been called in since there are no more American vessels bound to the French Islands." The British fleet had moved from Martinique by then and conquered the Island of St. Lucia. Shallcross advised owners of American vessels to instruct their captains to avoid the French islands, as every British ship in the West Indies carried orders to capture all craft of neutral nations bound for French ports.[20]

For the residents of the islands, the British conquest and implementation of the Order in Council had serious consequences. Shallcross observed that stores of provisions had dipped "extremely low" in May 1794, prompting officials to warn of possible starvation if American ships were not permitted to return with cargoes of flour, corn, and other provisions. After traveling from island to island to observe conditions and assist American sailors, he concluded that "the residents of these islands cannot live without our vessels bringing provisions."[21]

By the end of June 1794, the British campaign had succeeded in capturing most of the French islands in the West Indies. Naval commanders were instructed to stop seizing American ships carrying provisions. In August, Shallcross wrote: "We are allowed to trade with all the islands held by Britain in these seas, and we can take into all the islands, including the French, flour, corn, bread, peas, horses, mules, all livestock and lumber, and we can carry out rum and molasses."[22]

News that the British navy had stopped seizing American ships had not reached managers at John Smith and Company of Baltimore on September 1, 1794, when they warned a ship captain that "The British privateers and ships of war are capable of anything." A Smith and Company ship had delivered a cargo of flour to a Saint-Domingue port where the residents "were starving." The port was occupied by British forces at the time, yet a British privateer captured the ship "almost within the port."[23]

The fury provoked in Washington prompted Congress to pass an order of embargo in March 1794 that required all ships in U.S. ports, whether American or European, to remain at anchor for thirty days. The order was extended for another thirty days. American ships that normally supplied desperately needed provisions to West Indian residents remained at their moorings and suffered significant financial losses. President George Washington sent Chief Justice John Jay to London in an effort to mitigate the ship seizures and negotiate an end to the infuriating British practice of "impressment"—seizing sailors aboard American ships and forcing them to crew on British naval vessels—and to resolve other vexatious disputes between the two countries. The controversial "Jay's Treaty" was agreed to in November 1794 and, after extensive and rancorous partisan debate, was ratified by the U.S. Senate in June 1795. Although highly controversial in America, the treaty resolved many of the issues in dispute and averted a war between the two countries, and the British Foreign Office revoked the Order in Council.[24]

In France the treaty provoked outrage. French officials expected gratitude from Americans for assistance rendered during the war for independence. They now felt betrayed by terms that appeared to grant favorable trading status to Britain. As a consequence, France once again authorized the seizure of American ships. It was Victor Hugues, the commissioner sent to Guadeloupe by the French Republic, who most effectively implemented the new policy. Hugues had arrived off Point-au-Petre in June 1794 with a French army of only fifteen hundred men, yet he quickly purged the French colonials who had welcomed the British invaders after the French National Convention decreed emancipation of slaves in the French West Indian colonies in 1793. Hugues recruited the former slaves of Guadeloupe to augment his army, urging them to solidify claims to freedom and repay the French Republic for emancipation by fighting in the army or returning to work at their former plantations. The island's free people of color and the local whites who supported the French Revolution joined with the thousands of former slaves recruited by Hugues and drove the British from the Island of Grand-Terre.[25]

Hugues also unleashed a makeshift navy by licensing civilian mariners with "letters of marque" to prey on ships involved in commerce with the British. The historian Laurent Dubois has written that "Hugues turned Guadeloupe into the main hope for French privateers in the eastern Caribbean." During the four years of his administration, "1,800 enemy and merchant vessels suspected of trading with the British were destroyed or captured by corsairs operating out of Guadeloupe." Dubois estimates that more than three thousand formerly enslaved men were among the sailors manning these corsairs and that at least fifteen of the ship captains were former slaves. With the currency, merchandise, and produce the privateers brought back to Guadeloupe, and with crops for export from the plantations where the former slaves were working for wages, Hugues was able to maintain a viable economy to fund his military force and stave off British efforts at conquest. For American ship captains and merchant firms, Hugues's privateer navy meant several years of devastating losses.[26]

Following a difficult four-month ordeal at Martinique, Kingsley returned to Charleston in late June 1794. He had been one of the fortunate captives: forty Americans died at St. Pierre of diseases contracted aboard the floating prison ship. Many of the other survivors were befriended by John Shallcross and Fulwar Skipwith, the consular agents of the State Department who persuaded American ship captains to transport the stranded and impoverished mariners to ports along the east coast of the United States. Kingsley returned to Charleston in a more triumphant manner, as the master of yet another ship. The "Marine List" of the *Charleston City Gazette* announced the June 27 arrival of the schooner *Polly*, under command of Captain Kingsley, terminating a twenty-seven-day voyage from Martinique.[27]

Two schooners named *Polly* were condemned and sold at St. Pierre during the months of Kingsley's confinement. One was likely the ship that Kingsley sailed from Martinique to Charleston in June. Mercantile firms that engaged in the risky Caribbean trade during the era of the French Revolution anticipated incidents of seizure and confiscation by British naval vessels or French privateers, and they often arranged letters of credit that enabled their captains to purchase vessels at the admiralty-court auctions. Hundreds of vessels were sold in this manner each year, generally at prices well below their true value. Penman's "Daybook" entries document the continued use of the *Polly* in Caribbean trade in 1794; in September and again in November the vessel carried cargoes of rum into Charleston.[28]

As challenging and dangerous as the seizure and captivity ordeal at St. Pierre must have been for Kingsley, it did not turn him away from the seafarer's life. Demand for grain and flour was especially acute at Saint-Domingue, and return cargoes of coffee, sugar, and mahogany logs found ready markets in the United States. With the rebellion under way and a continuing threat from privateers, mercantile trade continued to be precarious, but merchant firms countered by maintaining constant communication with their counterparts throughout the region. When John Smith and Company of Baltimore sent Captain Thomas Makool to the Caribbean in March 1795, he was instructed to proceed first to the Danish island of St. Thomas, a neutral port. If he arrived safely, Makool was to consult with local merchants before proceeding to the southern province of Saint-Domingue where the British navy was on patrol. There, he was to exchange his cargo of provisions for coffee or sugar but avoid taking on board incriminating "French letters or passengers." In the event his ship was captured, Makool was instructed "to be particularly careful in protesting and in having all your papers perfectly regular and in case of being carried to a British port and a condemnation taking place, you will enter an appeal to the courts in Great Britain."[29]

In June 1796, Kingsley experienced the third seizure of a ship under his command when a privateer licensed by Victor Hugues stopped him at sea and escorted his vessel to Guadeloupe. He had been at Essequibo (today, part of Guyana) on the Atlantic mainland of South America, a Dutch colony united with Demerara noted for prosperous sugar and coffee plantations. During his stay, a British fleet arrived and accomplished a bloodless occupation of the colony. A British officer administered the oath of loyalty to the Dutch officers governing the colony and left them to continue their administration. Kingsley, apparently caught in the harbor when the fleet arrived, was recognized as a neutral trader and permitted to depart on June 3. Six days later, his ship was seized by a French privateer and escorted to

Guadeloupe. Kingsley's ship was detained for only two days, and by June 24 he was back in Charleston.[30]

Kingsley lived a vagabond existence between 1794 and 1798, when his main commercial activity was purchasing coffee at Saint-Domingue. Like many other ship captains of that era, he lived in the captain's quarters of his ships while at sea and in rooming houses or hotels at port cities when his ships were in port. Although city directories do not record a Charleston residence for him, the 1797 issues of the *Charleston City Gazette* provide evidence of his commercial activities. An advertisement printed January 17 announced that Kingsley would be selling a cargo of coffee at William's Coffee House on March 2. Potential customers were encouraged to contact Kingsley on board his ship, the schooner *Apollo*. William's Coffee House was the establishment favored by Charleston's conservative British merchants. Kingsley departed later that month for the port of Petit-Goâve in Saint-Domingue. He and the *Apollo* returned to Charleston on September 20 after a twenty-seven-day journey from St. Jago, Cuba.[31]

Thirty years later, Kingsley reminisced in print on his mercantile experiences in the West Indies. By then he was an American citizen living in northeast Florida and the owner of several plantations worked by enslaved Africans. He revealed he had previously resided in or visited all of the West Indies colonies and had "spent several years also in Cuba and Saint-Domingue as well as the main land of south america." Between 1794 and 1798 he lived briefly at "the Town of Jeremie," and then resided for "a long time at petitgoave [Petit-Goâve, Haiti, today] where he often had occasion to travel backwards and forwards on horseback sometimes across [and] all over the western and southern part of the island alone with my saddle bags full of specie."[32]

His "residence in Jeremie" was during the years the British occupied the town. Kingsley also mentioned residing "in the south or west of St. Domingo, under the government of Touissant, or Rigaud" for "nearly a year, at one period." While in Saint-Domingue he rode "on horseback, from Leogane to the Cayes, and from Petit-Goave to Jacquemel, through woods and over mountains, with my saddle bags loaded with specie to buy coffee; and though I frequently met large groups of armed negroes in the woods, I neither received insult or hinderance, but was always treated with kindness and civility."[33]

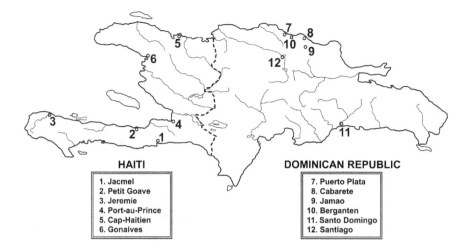

FIGURE 2. The island of Hispaniola, showing Haiti and the Dominican Republic. Towns identified on the map of Haiti locate places visited by Zephaniah
Kingsley while purchasing coffee in the 1790s. Locations identified on the map
of the Dominican Republic, with the exception of Santiago and Santo Domingo, are properties Kingsley acquired in the 1830s as a refuge to protect his
mixed-race family from racial discrimination in the United States. Map drawn
by Jerome Humery of Cranberry Point Computers, Corea, Maine.

Based on Kingsley's own recollections, it is clear that between 1794 and
1798 his principal commercial activity in the West Indies was buying and
selling coffee and that he lived in temporary quarters in Saint-Domingue
when he was not at sea. The trade was undoubtedly lucrative, but it was also
fraught with peril, being conducted while the most explosive slave rebellion ever experienced in the Western world was under way. Between 1791
and 1804, tens of thousands of French colonials and French and British
soldiers died in a decade of incredibly violent warfare. David Geggus has
calculated that 37,000 British troops sent to the Caribbean between 1793
and 1798 died there, primarily of yellow fever and other diseases. The number of black and free colored men and women that died during those years
is not possible to estimate accurately. Torture, mass murder, burning at the
stake, and severed human heads impaled on stakes in city plazas and along
the roadsides were commonplace. Warfare at Saint-Domingue became so
dehumanized that one of the island's French planters could advocate a plan
calling for "an immense slaughter of the Negroes," possibly killing 200,000

or more in order to bring the rest of the enslaved population back "under proper subjection." The planter casually estimated that in the aftermath of the slaughter it would require two or three years and renewed imports of enslaved Africans to restore the island's plantations to prosperity. General Charles Victor Emmanuel Leclerc, sent to Saint-Domingue in 1802 by Emperor Napoléon Bonaparte to reinstitute slavery, called for mass murders of blacks, sparing only children under the age of thirteen, and replacing the lost laborers by importing fresh supplies of Africans.[34]

Given the shocking violence committed by all of the armies during the revolution at Saint-Domingue, it is disconcerting to read Kingsley's reminiscences of traveling alone over the mountains on horseback and being "always treated with kindness and civility" by the armed bands of black men that he met. More than a few readers of Kingsley's *Treatise on the Patriarchal* have wondered if his account was fictional. However, recent monographs focusing on the southern province of Saint-Domingue during the British occupation have clarified that conditions in that section of the island were compatible with the activities Kingsley described.

The preeminent historian of the British occupation of Saint-Domingue, David Geggus, has written that "the isolated, coffee-growing region of la Grand' Anse, at the tip of the southern peninsula, the sole area that had not submitted to the [French] Commissioners," remained stable and operated independent of the colonial administration. The majority of slaves continued to produce coffee for export throughout the British occupation, and hundreds of British, Dutch, and American merchant ships continued to trade at port cities of the region. Privateers were a continuing menace to shipping, but for captains who completed their missions profits were high enough to risk another journey.[35]

It was in the northern province of Saint-Domingue that the slave insurrection exploded in August 1791. The free population of the colony, approximately 30,000 whites and 28,000 free people of color (mixed-race and black), had been distracted by the rebellious activities of white colonials who were themselves enraged by reforms passed by the National Assembly in Paris. Anticipating that the principles inherent in the Declaration of the Rights of Man and Citizen passed in August 1789 would lead to emancipation in Saint-Domingue, radical whites demanded local autonomy. The free people of color were often wealthy and educated land and slave owners who also opposed emancipation, yet the white colonial elites refused to concede the rights of citizenship granted to free people of color by the French National Assembly in May 1791. The result was a brief civil war pitting whites against free people of color in June and July.[36]

In August, slaves in the northern provinces took advantage of the turmoil and launched a massive rebellion. More than fourteen hundred sugar and coffee estates were put to the torch in the first two weeks of the insurrection, hundreds of whites were killed, and several thousand more fled to refugee centers outside the colony. The initial slave rebels became an army of twenty thousand.

Spain, already at war with France in Europe, saw an opportunity to drive the French away and expand the border of Spanish Santo Domingo westward to incorporate the entire island. The Spanish governor negotiated with the rebel leaders, Georges Biassou, Jean-François, and Toussaint Louverture, all free men born on the island, and commissioned them generals in the Spanish army. Slaves who soldiered for the Spanish were promised freedom, but Spanish officials intended to reenslave the black population when the island was under their control.

Great Britain also sensed that Saint-Domingue was vulnerable to conquest. An invasion was launched from Jamaica in September 1793 that succeeded in capturing the coastal towns of the southern peninsula. The towns of Jérémie and Petit-Goâve, where Kingsley resided during the British occupation, were among those captured. British troops expanded their occupation to port cities in the west and north, but the offensive faltered and the troops were generally confined to a narrow coastal zone.

Faced with what seemed like insurmountable opposition, commissioners from Paris played the only trump card they held. In the fall of 1793 they announced the emancipation of the enslaved population of Saint-Domingue and stepped up recruiting of the liberated black men to serve in the army of the French Republic. The emancipation decree convinced General Toussaint Louverture to abandon the Spanish and ally his legions of former slaves with the French Republic.[37]

Spain's leaders negotiated peace with France and relocated Biassou and Jean-François away from Saint-Domingue. By 1796 Touissant's army controlled the north and west of the island in the name of the French Republic. The British occupation in the northern and western provinces was limited to control of military garrisons at port cities, while the hinterland remained, according to David Geggus, "places under siege, cut off from the surrounding countryside and ringed with fortifications. Hemmed in by mountains, crowded, claustrophobic, and tense, they awoke with the morning gun and fell silent at curfew."[38]

Circumstances were different in the four parishes of the southern province, where Kingsley resided and traveled. The British occupation was successful here in its first three years, and local white and free colored planters retained control of their estates and workers. The British invasion had occurred at the urging of local white planters, who remained on their estates between 1791 and 1793 under protection of armed bands of former slaves recruited into military service with offers of freedom. The free colored planters of the southern parishes offered freedom to trusted slaves in exchange for loyal military service. Although the local white and free colored planters faced a divide caused by persistent race discrimination, their mutual desire to hold onto their extensive property in land and slaves helped forge an uneasy alliance.[39]

The result was semi-autonomous local control and continued production of coffee. With British troops in control of several port cities, merchants were able to supply the neutral American, Dutch, and Danish ships, even after emancipation was implemented in October 1793. The plantation owners in the south adapted pragmatically and convinced the freed laborers to continue working for wages. In a careful examination of Acquin Parish, historian John Garrigus has argued that Commissioner Polvérol implemented the policies of a prominent free man of color, Julien Raimond, who called for a ban on capital punishment and a promise to provide workers with garden plots to feed their families. Each worker was to be guaranteed a share of profits and the opportunity to purchase small plots of land. Raimond warned the former slaves they would have to work if they wanted to feed their families, and he advised them that without income from exports of coffee Saint-Domingue would be conquered by foreign enemies and slavery would be reimposed.[40]

In June 1794 governance of the region was passed to General André Rigaud, commander of the army of the French Republic in the southern province. Rigaud, a wealthy free man of color born in the south of Saint-Domingue, directed a campaign that forced the British to withdraw in 1798.

He also ordered his soldiers to use force when needed to keep reluctant freedmen at work. Rigaud's procedures paid dividends: laborers remained at work, the volume of exports remained high, and the southern province was stabilized under armed units of the French Republic.

The revolution as experienced in the southern province differed dramatically from the overwhelmingly violent and unstable conditions elsewhere. As a result of the insightful research of Professors Garrigus, Geggus, and Dubois, it is now possible to judge as factual the claims by Zephaniah Kingsley that he resided at Jeremie and at Petit-Goâve and traveled by horseback "through woods and over mountains" to purchase coffee, and that he encountered "large groups of armed negroes in the woods" without being insulted or hindered. These activities occurred in the south of Saint-Domingue. The port cities where Kingsley resided were under British control for much of the period; the "groups of armed negroes" he encountered were not slaves in rebellion, but freedmen and soldiers armed by local planters or the army of the French Republic under command of General Rigaud. Several American merchants resided at ports in the south of Saint-Domingue at the time, and most of the coffee they exported went to the United States.[41]

By the end of 1798, however, the revolution in Saint-Domingue had reached a dramatic turning point, with major consequences for Kingsley. American ships stopped frequenting the southern ports, and coffee exported from the Aquin ports was routed through the neutral ports of the Dutch at Curaçao and the Danes at St. Thomas. The stability of previous years had disintegrated into chaos and violence. After suffering horrendous manpower losses to disease and warfare, British general Thomas Maitland ordered a complete withdrawal of British forces. Increasing conflict between Generals Louverture and Rigaud sparked a brutal two-year civil war fought relentlessly in the south by more than fifty thousand soldiers. With Louverture's army, under command of Jean-Jacques Dessalines, pursuing Rigaud's army across the peninsula, travel to the interior estates to purchase coffee became impossible. When Rigaud's men began plundering American ships at Petit-Goâve and Jacmel, the coastal towns were no longer safe for Kingsley's vessels.[42]

The president of the United States, John Adams, thought of Louverture as an independent head of state rather than a subordinate of the French

Republic, and supported his initiatives. Adams ordered an American blockade of the ports in the southern peninsula to prevent arms from reaching Rigaud, who maintained a firm alliance with the French government. Adams was influenced by outrage among Americans over the seizure of hundreds of American commercial vessels by French warships and privateers out of Guadeloupe. American merchants were clamoring for increased trade access in Saint-Domingue, and for naval protection against the predatory French privateers infesting Caribbean waters and boldly patrolling the Atlantic coastline near America's port cities. After unsuccessful attempts to negotiate with France, the U.S. Congress authorized President Adams to reconstitute the U.S. Navy, which had been without a warship since 1785. On July 7, 1798, Congress rescinded all treaties with France, and for the next two years the United States and France fought an undeclared war at sea.[43]

For a ship captain like Kingsley, flying an American flag in Caribbean waters had become untenable. For years, British warships had routinely stopped American vessels and forcibly removed sailors to fill manpower shortages on their own ships. In 1796 and 1797, American commercial agent Silas Talbot traveled repeatedly to Jamaica, Martinique, Antigua, St. Christopher, Nevis, and Saint-Domingue, attempting to rescue American seamen impressed by British ship commanders. He seldom succeeded, but his letters to the State Department alarmed American officials. In addition, the threat from the French navy and the privateers operating under Victor Hugues at Guadeloupe posed great danger for American shipping. With the ports in the southern peninsula no longer in British hands, and the bloody civil war being fought between the armies of Rigaud and Louverture disrupting the stability that had previously prevailed, Kingsley was forced to either drop out of Caribbean trade or make major changes in the way he conducted it.[44]

By October 9, 1798, the practical advantages of neutral status as an American citizen had become minimal for Kingsley. On that day, at the port of Charlotte Amalie on the Danish island of St. Thomas, Kingsley pledged an oath of loyalty to the king of Denmark. For the next five years he continued to fly a neutral flag above his ships, but it was the "Dannebrog" of Denmark rather than the "Stars and Stripes" of the United States.[45]

4 ‖ Shifting Loyalties

St. Thomas and the Transit Trade
in African Slaves

On October 9, 1798, Zephaniah Kingsley stood before a magistrate at the
Danish port of Charlotte Amalie on the island of St. Thomas to pledge loyalty to the king of Denmark. This was the second time in five years he had
switched national allegiance. He had been a British citizen who resided
in England and the British colonies of South Carolina and New Brunswick until December 1793, when he swore allegiance to the United States
of America at Charleston, South Carolina. That action was the result of a
calculated decision meant to enhance his success as a West Indies trader.
By flying the flag of a neutral nation, he expected to gain a degree of protection from the hundreds of French and British privateers seizing commercial vessels during the wars spawned by the French Revolution. That the
flag of a neutral nation did not guarantee immunity is a lesson he learned
at Martinique in January 1794 when he lost a schooner to a British warship.
The change to American nationality nevertheless increased his chances of
avoiding additional confiscations. By 1798, however, with the United States
and France engaged in an undeclared naval war and a renewed threat from
French privateers, Kingsley sought protection under the flag of Denmark.[1]

Charlotte Amalie, the only town on St. Thomas, was recognized as a
leading trade entrepôt in the West Indies by the time Kingsley became a
"burgher" (Danish citizen). Acquired in 1672 by the Danish West India
and Guinea Company, a joint-stock company with a royal charter and a
trade monopoly, St. Thomas disappointed officials expecting immediate
profits from sugar and tobacco plantations. The fertility of the arable land
on the small island was quickly depleted by repeated planting of sugar and

tobacco, prompting the West India and Guinea Company to claim more land by annexing a smaller neighboring island, St. John. It was not until a larger island, St. Croix, was purchased in 1733 that sugar production in the West Indies became profitable for the Danes. Raw brown sugar processed at sugar works on the three Danish islands was shipped to Copenhagen for refining and sold at ports on the Baltic Sea.[2]

What St. Thomas lacked in agricultural potential, however, was more than compensated for by the port of Charlotte Amalie, one of the best natural harbors in the West Indies. The location served as a convenient first stop for ships sailing from Europe, as well as a welcome port of call for ships hoisting sails for return voyages. Merchants at Charlotte Amalie routed European products to markets at Caribbean and American colonies and combined cargoes of sugar, tobacco, cotton, and coffee from the West Indies for dispatch to Europe. It was as a transshipment center that St. Thomas prospered.

Denmark revoked the monopoly charter of the Danish West India and Guinea Company in 1754 and made St. Thomas a royal colony and free port. Opening the port to ships of all nations attracted merchants from throughout Europe and the Americas. During the American Revolution and the Anglo-French wars, Charlotte Amalie became a significant commercial center. Managers of large commercial houses based in Europe and the United States established branch offices or hired agents there. The historian Julius S. Scott has written that free ports "became destinations where seafaring folk from across the region could put their heads together free of mercantilist restrictions to make deals, swap stories, plant and harvest rumors, and gather news . . . throughout the greater Caribbean."[3]

Dozens of European and American merchants and ship captains migrated to Charlotte Amalie in the late eighteenth and early nineteenth centuries. Johan Peter Nissen arrived from Denmark in 1792 and marveled that "trade and navigation increased with every year," keeping pace with population growth and construction of new homes and businesses. Nissen tallied "1,569 persons" who took "burgher's briefs" between 1792 and 1801, including "Three hundred and twenty-four persons" who became burghers at Charlotte Amalie in 1799, the year after Kingsley took his oath. In a memoir of the forty-six years he lived at St. Thomas, Nissen recalled the harbor filled with "a great many small and large vessels, and the streets filled with

FIGURE 3. The harbor at Charlotte Amalie, on St. Thomas Island, a West Indies colony of Denmark from 1666 until 1917, when it was purchased by the United States of America. Zephaniah Kingsley moved to Charlotte Amalie in 1798 and pledged loyalty to Denmark in 1798 to facilitate his involvement in the Atlantic slave trade. In 1803, Kingsley pledged loyalty to Spain and moved to a plantation on the St. Johns River in Spanish East Florida. Image courtesy of the Danish Maritime Museum, Copenhagen, Denmark.

people of all colours and nations." Referring to the years 1792 to 1801, Nissen wrote: "it was indeed a very good time, and much opportunity in it for earning money." He noted that profits often were as high as 100 percent on ship cargoes but pointed out that privateers were a major problem for Caribbean traders even when they flew the neutral flag of Denmark on the mast of their ships. Nissen complained of being "captured and plundered seventeen times by these ruffians." In 1798 two of Nissen's ships were sold by admiralty-court judges, one at Tortola, the other at Martinique. The neutral flag of Denmark offered significant protection but not total immunity, especially when Great Britain and Denmark quarreled over shipping access to the Baltic seaports.[4]

While touring the West Indies in the 1850s, the English novelist Anthony Trollope said of St. Thomas: "many men . . . of many nations go thither to make money, and they do make it." It was that very desire, to "go thither to make money," that motivated Zephaniah Kingsley to settle at Charlotte Amalie a half century before Trollope's visit. The driving force of Kingsley's

FIGURE 4. "The Fredensborg II heading for St. Croix with a Cargo of Slaves," circa 1792. Artist unknown. The *Fredensborg II* was a Danish frigate involved in the slave trade. It measured one hundred feet in length and had three upright tubes extending above the deck to ventilate the cramped and unsanitary storage holds below, where slaves were confined during the ocean passage. Image courtesy of the Danish Maritime Museum, Copenhagen, Denmark.

adult years was to accumulate wealth and thereby achieve what he once described as the "wished for object of independence." At the end of 1798 he decided that wealth and independence might be within his grasp if he relocated to St. Thomas, a decision influenced by his younger brother, George Kingsley, who had become a Danish citizen at Christiansted, St. Croix, in June of 1795.[5]

Danish involvement in the Atlantic slave trade began long before Kingsley moved to St. Thomas. The Danish West India and Guinea Company acquired forts on the West African coast in the late 1660s at today's nation of Ghana, between the city of Accra and the Volta River to the east. The company's efforts were never profitable, and control of the trade and the African properties passed back and forth between the Crown and a series of private companies until 1792. In that year, Denmark became the first European nation to call for an end to the importation of enslaved Africans. The Crown decreed that on January 1, 1803, involvement in the Atlantic trade in slaves would terminate for all Danish citizens.[6]

During the intervening decade, importation of enslaved Africans was permitted as a means to increase the population base of slaves on the St. Croix sugar plantations and to establish a sustainable labor force based on procreation rather than importation. A decade-long boom in the sale of slaves on the Danish islands, focused on St. Croix, was fostered by the 1792 decree. Arnold R. Highfield points out that the decision to eliminate restrictions on foreign merchants involved in the slave trade greatly increased the volume of the trade in Denmark's Caribbean colonies. The St. Croix ports of Christiansted and Frederiksted became prime destinations for ships carrying enslaved men and women directly from Africa and from other West Indies islands. The leading scholar of the Danish slave trade, Svend E. Green-Pedersen, estimated that in 1799, 1800, and 1803, years that Kingsley resided at St. Thomas, an average of 2,842 enslaved laborers were brought into St. Croix each year.[7]

The majority of enslaved Africans that arrived at Charlotte Amalie were not purchased by planters in the Danish Virgin Islands. Rather, ship captains coming directly from Africa with large numbers of slaves took advantage of the port's neutral status and sold their cargoes to merchants based at St. Thomas. The slaves were off-loaded to smaller vessels and dispatched to Havana and other markets. Ships with smaller cargoes also found it convenient to sell to merchants engaged in the transit trade in enslaved Africans at St. Thomas.

A proviso in the 1792 decree exempting merchants from paying customs duties on slaves in transit added to the popularity of Charlotte Amalie for international traders. As a further incentive, the transit trade continued after the slave trade to colonies of Denmark ended on January 1, 1803. Danish ships and citizens were prohibited from participating in the transit trade, and enslaved Africans could not be imported to the Danish Virgin Islands, but the transit trade continued until December 1807, when the British captured St. Thomas and occupied it for the next eight years. For four of the years that Kingsley resided at St. Thomas, the transit trade accounted for an annual average of 3,036 enslaved Africans dispatched to other markets.[8]

On October 22, 1799, Kingsley received a Danish West Indian sea pass as captain of the bark *Cornelia*, a ship owned by Peter Vedder. Unlike an Algerian sea pass, which authorized travel to Africa, a West Indian sea pass was valid for six months and authorized travel within the region. Eight months later, on June 27, 1800, Kingsley received another Danish West Indian sea pass that authorized him to bring the schooner *Thomas* from Guadeloupe to St. Thomas.[9] One month later, on July 26, 1800, his third sea pass authorized a return voyage from Guadaloupe as master of the brig *George*. Five months later a sea pass authorized him to bring the brig *Brandywine* from Guadeloupe to St. Thomas. The *Thomas*, *George*, and *Brandywine* were owned by a St. Thomas merchant and burgher, John P. Jennings, an American merchant who traded at Charleston before relocating to Charlotte Amalie.[10]

The timing of these passes suggests that Kingsley traveled to Guadeloupe to assume command of ships purchased for Jennings at admiralty-court auctions of vessels seized by French privateers. Records of these sales indicate that many of the confiscated ships were carrying cargoes of enslaved Africans when they were brought into port. Jennings had the opportunity to take advantage of the bargain prices prevalent at these auctions to purchase ships and human cargoes for the transit trade at Charlotte Amalie.[11]

Evidence that Kingsley transported both produce and enslaved Africans at St. Thomas is found in a series of letters he wrote to a friend and business associate, the Charleston merchant James Hamilton. On May 1, 1801, Kingsley wrote from Port-au-Prince, Saint-Domingue, a city he was surprised to find "peaceful and quiet" despite the bloody revolution ravaging other parts of the colony. Kingsley came to that city seeking a cargo of coffee or sugar. His next destination, necessitated "by business," was Kingston, Jamaica, where he had purchased coffee in the past. After Jamaica, he planned to travel to his mother's home at Wilmington, North Carolina, prompting a request that Hamilton send a message to "inform my Mother that I am on the road home."[12]

The May 1 letter is also noteworthy for Kingsley's bitter complaints about his inability to collect a large amount of money owed to him by a merchant in Saint-Domingue and for a comment that reveals a side of his character seldom seen in his letters. He reported that he had finally caught up with a runaway ship captain he had been pursuing for several months: "I have caught him and strapped him & perhaps may never get any other satisfaction." Kingsley did not return immediately to Charlotte Amalie. British forces occupied the town for eleven months, beginning March 28, 1801, prompting Kingsley to stay at sea and to take up temporary residence away from St. Thomas.[13]

A letter written to Hamilton from Havana on June 13 is the most convincing evidence that Kingsley was involved in the slave trade by 1801. Kingsley had been in Havana only a few days when he booked passage to New York City while his ship "performed quarantine" at the port of Havana. Evidently, Kingsley expected others to supervise the Africans while he traveled to New York to meet with the merchant Richard T. Tucker concerning business "of very considerable importance."[14]

Kingsley had family as well as business matters to attend to in New York. His mother, Isabella Kingsley, and his sister Elizabeth (Isabella) Kingsley Gibbs were moving from Wilmington to New York City, and Kingsley secured a residence at 50 Greenwich Street for them. The move was accomplished by August 1, 1801. George Gibbs, married to Kingsley's sister Isabella, moved into the residence in late September after closing his commission business in Wilmington. Kingsley and Gibbs formed a partnership that functioned until 1820. Kingsley said about Gibbs: "I owe him much for the attention he has paid my Mother in my absence, in short I have determined to support him in the strongest manner in my power."[15]

After completing business at New York and Havana, Kingsley returned to St. Thomas in an attempt to settle affairs there and to "recover [a debt of] five thousand dollars." He "partially succeeded" and was confident he had "no other Risque now to contend with [other] than the commercial solidity of the House with which my concerns existed." This matter had evidently been a major threat to Kingsley's financial security. On July 20, 1801, he informed Hamilton: "I hope very soon to be free and call myself my own master again for I have been led away terribly against my will."[16]

Kingsley conducted illegal business with Hamilton by smuggling enslaved Africans into Georgia. In mid-August 1801, George Gibbs wrote to Hamilton to report his frustrating efforts to persuade a ship captain to deliver "your negroes to St. Simons." The man had arrived at Wilmington only to hear accounts "of the difficulties of a Captain who had some time before taken a few negroes to Savannah for sale." Fearful of being apprehended, he refused to make the delivery, and Gibbs's frantic efforts to recruit a replacement captain failed. The letter does not specifically state that Gibbs was referring to importing enslaved Africans in violation of the 1789 Georgia law banning imports of Africans, but there is little doubt that he meant exactly that. Kingsley's subsequent activities make it clear that slave smuggling was one of the ways he conducted business.[17]

Kingsley was not the only ship captain secreting Africans into South Carolina and Georgia in violation of laws banning the trade. A U.S. consular agent assigned to Cuba, Vincent Gray, informed Secretary of State James Madison in late October 1802 that "the slave trade between this place [Cuba] and Nassau and St. Augustine and the states of South Carolina and Georgia is now carried on to a great extent." Slaves were being purchased at Havana, Jamaica, and St. Thomas and transported to South Carolina and Georgia "in small vessels, generally large pilot boats . . . where they are disposed of generally to great advantage." Gray was particularly interested in "a person from St. Augustine, who states himself to be by birth an American, has been here lately offering to introduce into the State of Georgia a cargo—or any quantity of Negro slaves at a certain price."[18]

The business records of merchant Christopher Fitzsimmons contain revealing evidence of a flourishing commerce in enslaved Africans smuggled into Charleston. Letters from Fitzsimmons to ship captains throughout 1799 and early 1800 instruct them to load coffee, sugar, cocoa, and other West Indian produce for their return voyages to Charleston. Beginning in June 1800, however, the correspondence contains instructions to include small numbers of "New Negroes" in their return cargoes. A June 5, 1800, letter to Thomas Powell, executor for the estate of deceased trader William Skelton, formerly a resident of "Dashea, Africa," demanded that Skelton's debt of £777 sterling be paid off in "merchantable slaves at £20 a head" and loaded aboard a ship Fitzsimmons would send to Skelton's establishment on the Pongo River in today's Republic of Guinea. Two years later, Fitzsimmons directed one of his captains to proceed with the brig *Maria* to the port of Nassau, at New Providence Island in the Bahamas, to "take on Africans from a vessel bound for Havana."[19]

In 1803, when it was still illegal to import enslaved Africans, Fitzsimmons's requests for cargoes of slaves became the dominant topic of his letters to ship captains. In February, Captain William Cory received orders to sail the brig *Maria* to St. Thomas to sell the cargo from Charleston and proceed to Havana to purchase "prime new negroes" and molasses or sugar.

Fitzsimmons sent Cory to Havana again in June for a cargo of molasses supplemented by "ten negro girls about the age of sixteen for about $150 to $180 per head, and ten likely man boys about sixteen or eighteen years at the price of $200 to $220 per head." At the entrance to Charleston harbor, Cory was ordered to remove the Africans from his inbound cargo before it was subjected to a customs inspection and to "put them on board one of the pilot boats to come up to Paul Pritchard's wharf."[20]

In October 1803 Fitzsimmons instructed a ship captain to sail to St. Thomas, or alternately St. Croix or Guadeloupe, to buy "new negroes...none but prime men or man boys...if necessary take as few females as possible." That same month he assured James Eagan, a St. Thomas merchant, that he could "find buyers for Negroes as soon as they are landed. I did every service I could for Mr. McCormick, [even] housed and fed his Negroes and was out the greatest part of one night in landing them."[21] While Fitzsimmons could brazenly order his captains to secrete Africans on the harbor pilot boats for delivery to the readily accessible wharf of a well-known merchant and shipbuilder like Paul Pritchard, he also operated under cover of darkness and directed deliveries to remote beach locations well away from the city.

Kingsley avoided the more risky deliveries at Charleston harbor and limited his slave-smuggling activities to plantations at remote locations on the coastal islands off South Carolina and Georgia. Hamilton Plantation, located near today's city of Brunswick, Georgia, at Gascoigne Bluff on St. Simons Island, was an important destination. A mariner familiar with the intricacies of the maze of waterways in the area could evade patrols by disappearing from the Atlantic at St. Simons Inlet between St. Simons and Jekyll Islands, proceeding through St. Simons Sound to what is today the Frederica River, and then north to Hamilton Plantation.

During one of these deliveries, Kingsley informed Hamilton that he was contemplating major changes in his life. On January 10, 1802, Kingsley sent a reminder: "I mean to try hard for three or four months yet to make a little money if possible before I change the ground, notwithstanding the terrible disappointment of the peace.... Debts here have become like wild geese, the more you run after them the farther they are off." By "change the ground," Kingsley was signaling his plan to leave St. Thomas and change his national identity again, from Danish to Spanish.[22]

Kingsley's mention of the "disappointment of the peace" referred to the preliminary agreement signed by officials of Britain and France on September 30, 1801, that later became the March 1802 Treaty of Amiens. It resulted in a temporary halt to the hostilities that had been ongoing since 1793. Peace reduced the danger of seizure by privateers, but it also increased competition from ships of the combatant nations and diminished profits for neutrals, explaining Kingsley's "terrible disappointment."

This interpretation of the treaty was not shared by Vincent Gray, a consular agent with the U.S. State Department, who noticed in October 1802 that the treaty had boosted American trade at Havana. Gray and his colleague John Norton had for years witnessed Spanish officials at Havana facilitating the seizure and condemnation of American ships by French privateers. Spain and France had been allies in the European wars since 1796, so it did not come as a surprise to Norton when in January 1802 he counted seventy-five American ships, all victims of seizure by French privateers, floating at anchor in the harbor and awaiting condemnation by an admiralty-court judge. Norton accused Spanish officials of delaying auctions until so many ships backed up in the harbor that prices dropped precipitously when the sales were finally held, creating bargains for acquaintances. Havana port officials had also denied entry to American ships engaged in legitimate commerce. By October, however, Gray was pleased to report that American ships were being admitted for trade and that flour, horses, and lumber were in great demand. "Upwards of ten thousand Negroes have been imported into this port since peace . . . [and they have] risen in price from twenty to thirty dollars."[23]

Kingsley may have found the treaty disappointing, but his profits from trade permitted the purchase a 156-ton frigate, the *Superior,* at St. Thomas in January 1802. It was suggested by Danish historian Svend E. Green-Pedersen, in notes he left in a private archive donated to the Royal Archives of Denmark, that Kingsley was aboard the *Superior* in 1801 when it purportedly departed St. Thomas for Africa. This would explain the December 22, 1801, chance encounter in the Atlantic between Kingsley, aboard an unnamed ship, and Captain David Bowers of the *Commerce,* owned by James Hamilton. The *Commerce* had departed Messina, Sicily, bound for Havana when the two ships met. Kingsley gave Bowers a letter to deliver to Hamilton on his return to Charleston, and the two ships went their separate ways, Bowers "bound to Leeward" and Kingsley to St. Croix. Kingsley later explained that the letter contained a request for information "on the subject of New Negroes" and whether South Carolina or Georgia would be "a better market than might be found in Havana if one knew exactly how and where, what quantity could be sold at once and the terms of payment and risks one would have to run, etc." With spring planting about to commence, Kingsley predicted "the good season with you is advancing." Planters tried to avoid adding newly arrived Africans during winter months for fear of losing them to illness and death from pleurisy and pneumonia before they could become acclimated to their new environments. In the early spring months, however, as weather conditions moderated and demands for labor intensified, planters paid higher prices to purchase slaves.[24]

It is not known with certainty if Kingsley had been at the coast of West Africa prior to his meeting with Bowers. Records of his activities and locations between October 4, 1801, when he was at New York, and December 26, 1801, when he was at St. Croix, have not been found. Given optimal conditions, those twelve weeks would have been sufficient to complete a journey to Senegal or Guinea, or another accessible location on the West African coast.

On December 26, 1801, four days after meeting with Bowers at sea, Kingsley arrived at St. Croix and immediately booked passage on a ship bound for St. Thomas. He returned to St. Croix twice more in the next month, and to St. Thomas on January 5 and February 9, 1802. The three journeys he made as a passenger from St. Croix to St. Thomas on December 26, 1801, January 5, and February 9, 1802, suggest that he may have traveled between the two nearby islands to handle the business details of the sale of a cargo of enslaved Africans. This assertion is highly speculative, but it fits with Kingsley's later statements about purchasing slaves on the African coast and with evidence of his employment as supercargo of slaving voyages to Africa.[25]

What can be said with certainty is that Kingsley purchased the *Superior* at Charlotte Amalie on February 27 for the sum of six thousand pesos and that three days later he received a West Indian sea pass as the owner and captain of the same ship. On March 3 he sailed for Havana with a cargo of 250 "New Negroes." The careful research of Dr. Svend E. Holsoe has established that the 250 enslaved Africans that Kingsley transported to Havana in

March 1802 had not been part of a human cargo carried from Africa aboard the *Superior*. Instead, they arrived at St. Thomas on February 25 aboard a Liverpool-based ship known as the *May*. With Captain Patrick Callen in command, the 312-ton ship cleared Liverpool on July 30, 1801, destined for Bonny, a trade center with a population of approximately 25,000, located in a mosquito-infested area of mangrove swamps at the Bight of Biafra, one of the eastern tributaries of the Niger River delta. After the ship arrived at Bonny (date unknown), local merchants traveled in caravans of war canoes carrying European trade goods to inland markets fifty or more miles up the Bonny River to barter for enslaved men, women, and children captured in raids or purchased at markets further inland. The canoes then returned to Bonny carrying armed guards and forty or more captives. Such exercises were generally completed in less than two weeks, permitting ship captains to depart with minimal loss of life to malaria and other diseases. According to the historians Paul E. Lovejoy and David Richardson, it was "the quick turnaround time for ships" that enabled Bonny to "achieve a dominant position in the trade of the Bight of Biafra" and to export more than 250,000 slaves, primarily from Igbo and Ibibio cultural backgrounds, between 1791 and 1810.[26]

On February 22, 1802, seven months after departing Liverpool and still flying the British flag, the *May* arrived at Christiansted, St. Croix, and off-loaded twenty Africans to the account of John Dunlop. Within a day, the *May* sailed for St. Thomas, arriving on February 25 with a cargo of 280 Africans consigned to the merchant John Souffraine, an American who had become a citizen of Charlotte Amalie. In the next few days the officials involved in the transit trade worked at full efficiency. On February 27 Kingsley purchased a ship and registered it with Danish port officials, acquired all but thirty of the Africans who had arrived on the *May*, obtained a sea pass, and sailed for Havana on March 3. All of this was accomplished in less than a week, a remarkably efficient example of a combined commercial and bureaucratic transaction. Hidden between the lines of the official records, however, are the abysmally cruel and often fatal experiences of the Africans who were caught in the maw of the Atlantic slave trade.[27]

The African victims were captured in villages located more than one hundred miles inland from the Gulf of Guinea, then bound and carried down the Bonny River in long war canoes. When they arrived at Bonny, the unfortunate victims were sold to Europeans and thrown into what soon became a vomit- and excrement-filled hold of a slave ship. Before leaving Liverpool, Captain Callen had received a permit that authorized him to carry a maximum of 290 slaves across the Atlantic aboard the *May*, yet more than 300 survivors of the horror and disease of the passage were counted when the *May* arrived at St. Croix. The total number forced aboard at Bonny is not known, but the Atlantic passage generally claimed the lives of 13 percent of the human cargoes.[28]

From St. Croix the *May* sailed to St. Thomas, where the anchor was thrown for the second time in three days. The Africans were brought on deck, bathed in sea water from the harbor, given rough physical inspections, ferried by armed guards from the *May* to the smaller *Superior*, and forced below deck into another dark confinement. Soon, the anchor was raised, the sails were lifted, and the *Superior*, under command of Zephaniah Kingsley, departed for Havana. One can only guess at the reaction of the 168 men (7 were "male youths" and 14 were "boys") and 61 women (23 were female youths and 11 were girls) crowded again below the deck of the ship as it pitched and rolled in the waves during the journey to Havana: fear, rage, despair, horror, despondency. One life after another was lost as the imprisoned watched the death toll of their shipmates mount.[29]

No mention of the suffering below deck is found in the letter Kingsley wrote to Hamilton after the *Superior* arrived at Havana and cleared customs and quarantine. Kingsley's concern was with making as much money as possible, and he was disappointed when the price that buyers at the slave market were willing to pay for "New Negroes" was less than anticipated. Kingsley informed Hamilton by letter on March 14 that he was considering leaving Havana with his cargo and sailing to Georgia, apparently willing to risk violating that state's law banning African slave imports. "It grieves me to be changing one Dollar for another without profit," Kingsley wrote. "If the sale here does not turn out as well as I expect necessity will oblige me to try a part of them at some other market. If I was sure you was on your plantation it would not be long before you would see me. I will perhaps see you as it is for I wish to see whether we cannot do some good business again together."[30]

Kingsley remained at Havana until he "disposed of the Cargo," as he referred to the Africans aboard the *Superior*. He then loaded a return cargo and sailed back to St. Thomas and continued purchasing Africans in the transit trade. His next human cargo was fated for clandestine delivery to estates at the sea islands in Georgia. Kingsley informed Hamilton on March 27: "Without bad weather or some uncommon accident prevents me, I shall call off St. Simons on purpose to have some conversation with you upon business." Evidently, they did more than converse about business. On April 11, George Gibbs wrote to Hamilton: "I am glad to find the Negroes have been shipped to you and I hope you get them safely to land."[31]

Kingsley next traveled to New York to make arrangements with his agent, Richard T. Tucker, regarding the financial disarray caused by the "improvident conduct" of "Mr. Barclay," the North Carolina partner of Kingsley's brother-in-law. As Gibbs described the debacle: the failure of "the House of William & Henry Ross of Liverpool nearly ruined Barclay and Gibbs," thereby wiping out funds Gibbs and Kingsley had committed to a speculative investment in the West Indies. After meeting with Tucker, Kingsley returned to his home base at St. Thomas.[32]

On May 16, 1802, Kingsley informed Hamilton by letter that he had "begun to put in execution what I mentioned to you and expect to sail in ten days. . . . If the ground is as pleasant as your description leads me to hope, it may induce me to [repeat] the visit." Throughout 1802 and 1803, Kingsley was intently focused on making money through the transit trade at St. Thomas. The market for Africans at Havana was booming, and the opportunity to profit from illegal sales at Georgia and South Carolina beckoned.[33]

Kingsley also recognized that it was a time of transition for everyone involved in the transit trade in slaves at St. Thomas. The deadline imposed by the Royal Decree of 1792 was looming: on January 1, 1803, legal importation of African slaves to the Danish West Indies would terminate, and Danish ships and citizens would be banned from further participation. Until December 21, 1807, when a decade-long British occupation of St. Thomas began, enslaved Africans continued to arrive at Charlotte Amalie's harbor as the key component of the transit trade, but Danish ships and citizens were banned from participating. This meant that the December 31 deadline for importation of slaves from Africa was drawing near for Kingsley. He had recently entered into a business partnership in New York with his brother-in-law, and he was still trying to collect several thousand dollars owed to him by a merchant at Port-au-Prince. He was also concerned about the health and financial stability of an elderly business associate with whom he had investments at Charlotte Amalie. Anticipating an end to the lucrative profits from the transit trade at St. Thomas, Kingsley was searching for another safe harbor, and he was willing to pledge loyalty to a new nation if that would permit him to continue profiting from the sale of enslaved Africans.

Finding a safe harbor during the Age of Revolution posed difficult choices. The 1802 Peace of Amiens, which Kingsley derided as a "disappointment," was abrogated fourteen months later when Britain again declared war on France. By remaining at St. Thomas, Kingsley was assured of the protection of a neutral flag, but Denmark's ban of the transatlantic slave trade at the end of 1803 barred him from participating in that trade at St. Thomas. A return to Charleston to sail again under the American flag was a possibility he no doubt considered, but the resumption of war between England and France raised the menace of French privateers. Furthermore, Spain and France were still allies, which posed potential problems for American ships at Havana.

No records have been found for Kingsley's activities for sixteen months after May 1802. This suggests that he continued in the Atlantic slave trade, purchasing men and women on the African coast and transporting them to either Havana or the sea islands of Georgia and South Carolina. His name is not listed as captain of any of the slave ships that entered the Havana harbor during those months, although he may have been employed as a supercargo on voyages between Cuba and Africa (only the names of captains were listed on the Havana port-of-entry records).

On September 24, 1803, Kingsley registered with Spanish customs at the port of St. Augustine, the capital of Spanish East Florida. Four days later he pledged fidelity to Spain and changed his nationality for the third time. He again acted "to change the ground" and settle in a new safe harbor. Two months later, he purchased a large tract of land on the St. Johns River and began importing enslaved men and women from Africa as his labor force. In addition to opening a new chapter in his life as a plantation and slave owner, Kingsley continued to command ships in the transatlantic slave trade. East Florida would pass from Spanish to American sovereignty in 1821, but Kingsley would reside in East Florida for the remaining forty years of his life.[34]

5 | "Fortune Is Neither to Be Won by Prudence nor Industry"

A Slaving Voyage to East Africa

Zephaniah Kingsley's decision to "change the ground" from St. Thomas to East Florida was driven by Denmark's decision to outlaw the slave trade in its overseas colonies. His time as a Danish colonial had been challenging, with Britain and France fighting an overseas war in the Caribbean and privateers seizing ships, but Kingsley reaped financial rewards in the face of these dangers. Residing in Spain's East Florida colony, where importing slaves would continue to be legal for decades, meant Kingsley could continue to profit from the trade. The location of his new home provided convenient access to markets at Havana, Savannah, Charleston, and the Georgia sea islands, as well as the supply base at Charlotte Amalie, while the transit trade in slaves continued. The colony's huge reserves of unpopulated land also represented a portal into the Atlantic world of the future that Kingsley envisioned. The seismic shock of the slave revolution in Saint-Domingue, Denmark's termination of the slave trade in its colonies, and the undercurrents of abolition in other European countries alerted Kingsley that slavery as a legal institution would continue within nations but that importation of slaves from Africa would soon be illegal in the entire Atlantic world. The time was right to transition to legitimate maritime commerce and to the life of a planter and slave owner. For another decade Kingsley would frequent ports in North America, Europe, Africa, the Caribbean, and South America, still engaged in the Atlantic slave trade. At the same time, he was creating a personal empire of plantations in East Florida, worked by enslaved Africans.

On September 24, 1803, when he pledged fidelity to Spain at St. Augustine, Kingsley claimed assets of 67,160 pesos, including the value of one hundred enslaved men and women (equal to approximately $2,350,000 in today's currency). The slave dependents qualified Kingsley for a "head rights" land grant from the government. Under a policy implemented in 1793 to encourage immigration, Spain promised grants of free land to new settlers: 100 acres to the head of household, plus 50 acres for each dependent. Kingsley was eligible for a grant of 5,100 acres.[1]

Kingsley was not the only maritime merchant seeking land and citizenship in East Florida. Between 1790 and 1810, East Florida attracted numerous American and European ship captains and merchants engaged in the Atlantic trade. Spain's decision to eliminate restrictive mercantile policies within its empire, combined with the continuation of legal importation of enslaved Africans and grants of free land to immigrants, attracted hundreds of foreign planters and traders. This was especially true for Florida after Great Britain banned the Atlantic trade in enslaved Africans in 1807 and the United States forbade slave imports in all of its ports in 1808. Ship captains and merchants involved in the slave trade sought out Spanish ports, where importation of slaves was still legal.[2]

Spanish East Florida experienced a massive expansion of commerce in the aftermath of the 1807 decision by President Thomas Jefferson and the U.S. Congress to ban imports from Great Britain and France and to prohibit American ships from leaving U.S. ports. Jefferson hoped to avoid entanglement in European wars, but his embargo policy resulted in huge financial losses for American merchants, grain and cotton planters, and exporters. Commerce at American ports stagnated, and some shipowners became privateers while others moved their vessels to Canadian or Spanish harbors. Amelia Island, located at the northeast corner of East Florida, possessed an excellent deep-water harbor that soon attracted mercantile firms, ship captains, and smugglers. The sleepy settlement with fewer than two dozen families and a small military and customs post experienced a construction frenzy as wharves, storehouses, and dwellings were constructed at the new town of Fernandina. Longtime East Florida resident George J. F. Clarke, the man appointed to survey and lay out the streets and blocks, described the frenzy: "Every man was making money hand over hand as fast as he could, and in consequence of the restrictive measures of the

American government, the trade of the United States with all the world, except Spain, centered in Fernandina."[3]

Between 1790 and 1804 approximately 750 immigrant heads of households pledged loyalty to Spain at East Florida. More than eight in ten claimed birth in a British North American colony (by then part of the United States) or in England, Scotland, or Ireland, and 270 claimed ownership of slaves and more than 800 family members or white laborers. They also testified that they would bring nearly 5,000 enslaved men and women into the province.[4]

In 1803 alone, sixty-three new settlers claimed ownership of 2,270 slaves, an average of 36 for each owner. Kingsley and Charles Ash each claimed 100 slaves, John Kelsall 222, Santiago Main 190, Daniel O'Hara 300, and Daniel McNeill 400. Beginning in 1809, Scotsman John Fraser, who operated a slave-exporting "factory" at Bangalan on the Pongo River in today's Republic of Guinea, settled 370 Africans on two tracts he acquired in East Florida. The largest was Greenfield Plantation, a 2,500-acre property located south of the St. Johns River and west of Pablo Creek, which Fraser dedicated to cultivation of cotton and provisions. Fraser also put Africans to work in rice and corn fields at Roundabout Plantation on the St. Marys River. From across East Florida's northern border, the prominent Georgia planter John H. McIntosh purchased Fort George Island and Ortega Plantation and migrated with 140 enslaved men and women. McIntosh was one of the first entrepreneurs to set up a steam-powered sawmill on the St. Marys River in East Florida.[5]

The combination of the government's promise of free land and the prospect of huge profits to be gained from employing enslaved laborers in plantation agriculture prompted men like McIntosh to move to Spanish East Florida. By 1813, so many Africans had been shipped to East Florida that the enslaved black population of St. Augustine outnumbered the white residents. At Fernandina black slaves outnumbered whites two to one, and at Amelia Island nearly seven in ten residents were black.[6]

When Great Britain abolished the slave trade throughout its empire in 1807, numerous slave traders followed Kingsley to East Florida. John Fraser took an oath of loyalty at Charleston in 1807 while it was still legal to import enslaved Africans. One year later, when the African slave trade was outlawed in every U.S. port, Fraser relocated his ships to Fernandina in Spanish

East Florida. Other slave traders who migrated were Fernando de la Maza Arredondo and his son Juan Arredondo, George Atkinson, William Cook, Francisco Ferreyra, Joseph Hibberson, Daniel Hurlbert, William Lawrence of Panton, Leslie and Company, George Long, John McClure, Daniel Mc-Neill, Bartolomé Mestre, and the brothers Henry and Philip R. Yonge. Numerous slave ships were listed for sale in 1807 and 1808 at Charleston and other ports by Liverpool firms ending their involvement in the trade. In addition, dozens of slave ships captured by British naval patrols and condemned at British vice-admiralty courts in the West Indies and elsewhere were auctioned and sold at bargain prices to slavers like Kingsley who were anxious to acquire more ships and continue the trade.[7]

Soon after pledging allegiance to Spain on September 24, 1803, Kingsley applied for a free tract of land under Spain's land grant program. Governor Enrique White denied the request, based on his personal belief that uncultivated land in the province should be granted to poor settlers, not wealthy foreigners like Kingsley. The governor's decision forced Kingsley to delay his return to Charlotte Amalie while he searched for property to purchase.[8]

Kingsley searched for land along the St. Johns and St. Marys Rivers, where his planting interests would focus for the next four decades. On November 26, 1803, he purchased a 2,600-acre tract located west of the St. Johns River and north of Doctors Lake. Rebecca Pengree, the widow of William Pengree, agreed to sell the tract for 5,300 pesos. The tract had been partially developed during East Florida's two-decade rule by Britain, then abandoned during the American Revolution. The Pengrees acquired the tract in 1787, and with fifty-four slaves they built several houses and barns and cultivated 400 acres of cotton and provisions and an orange grove. The improvements were destroyed in 1794 when an insurgency threatened the province. Following William's death, Rebecca attempted unsuccessfully to restore the estate and so decided to sell. In August 1809, Kingsley purchased the adjacent Fuente del Alamo tract from Ysabel Kane, bringing his purchases to 3,000 acres of prime riverfront property known as Laurel Grove Plantation, portions of which had already been cleared and cultivated.[9]

Laurel Grove Plantation was the first of many valuable plantation tracts Kingsley acquired in East Florida. He would become the owner of several hundred enslaved men and women, but in 1803 he may have exaggerated when he claimed he already owned one hundred. The absence of a Kingsley entry in the tax registers for St. Thomas and St. Croix suggests that although he was living at Charlotte Amalie as a Danish citizen and working as a ship captain in the Atlantic and West Indian trade, he owned neither real nor personal (including human) property in the Virgin Islands. It is likely that Kingsley owned a small number of slaves based elsewhere and that he intended to return to St. Thomas, purchase Africans in the transit trade, and settle them on his St. Johns River tract to fulfill requirements of his land grant application. It was a reasonable plan since he was again eligible—after his change of citizenship from Danish to Spanish—to participate in the transit trade in slaves at the Charlotte Amalie harbor.[10]

Kingsley immediately began assembling a workforce. In late November 1803 he brought ten slave from Charleston. It is possible these slaves were property acquired from his father, who testified that he placed some of his slaves under control of his attorney and partner in Charleston, Bennett Taylor, and that he "made a deed of gift of them to his children" before he was banished in 1782. This may explain how Abraham Hanahan, an enslaved man of mixed-race ancestry who became Kingsley Jr.'s trusted plantation manager, first arrived in Florida. In a certificate of emancipation registered at St. Augustine in March 1811, Kingsley testified that Hanahan was reared in his father's Charleston household. There is further evidence that Hanahan resided at Laurel Grove as early as 1804 and that he was considered by Kingsley's white neighbors to have been a free man when he arrived in the province. Hanahan was not kin to Kingsley.[11]

On April 2, 1804, Kingsley was back in St. Thomas, where he purchased the schooner *Little Jim* for $600. The previous owner of the ship claimed it was registered at Charleston, but a Danish port official ruled the ship was "condemned as unfit to proceed with her lading," suggesting that the ship was in reality owned by a Dane and had arrived in port with a cargo of slaves after Denmark's ban on slave imports became law. In 1800, James Murphy and Company of Charlotte Amalie had employed the *Little Jim* in the Atlantic slave trade. Under command of Captain Laurence Fitzpatrick, the *Little Jim* departed St. Thomas on April 4, 1800, destined for Cape Verde and the coast of Africa. At that time it was legal to introduce enslaved Africans to St. Thomas and St. Croix. After January 1, 1803, however, the same act was illegal. The transit trade in slaves was still legal, but only if conducted in foreign vessels owned by foreign citizens. Port officials judged Captain

Robert W. Leary's claim that the *Little Jim* was registered at Charleston to be fraudulent.[12]

Kingsley renamed his newly purchased ship the *Laurel* and received a Danish West Indian sea pass. Even though he had pledged fidelity to Spain seven months before, Kingsley conducted business at Charlotte Amalie as if he were still a Danish citizen. Apparently, he treated citizenship as a business license and claimed to be Danish, Spanish, or American according to the present circumstance.

Traveling in the newly christened *Laurel*, Kingsley returned to St. Augustine on May 5, 1804, and requested permission to introduce twenty-five "Negro bozales" (newly arrived from the coast of Africa). A Spanish official notified the governor that Kingsley claimed the Africans as "part of his property manifested at the time of swearing the oath of fidelity. It is of major importance . . . [for] his plantation, planting on it suffers due to lack of arms to attend it."[13]

On June 15 Kingsley again anchored off St. Augustine, this time with a cargo embarked at Havana. After a ten-day quarantine, a government official inspected ten enslaved Africans brought by Kingsley from Cuba. Six males, three females, and one boy, "all newly arrived from the coast of Africa," were admitted and transported to Laurel Grove. Ten days later, Kingsley entered St. Augustine harbor with another cargo from Havana: 155 barrels of corn and 4,000 feet of pine boards for his plantation. In seven months he had transported forty-five enslaved laborers to his St. Johns River settlement, at least thirty-five of whom were "new Negroes," but all were in need of provisions and lumber to construct dwellings.[14]

After little more than a two-week-residence, Kingsley sailed down the St. Johns, stopping to register the *Laurel* at the Spanish customs post on July 19, 1804, before entering the Atlantic. It would be more than two years before he returned from an odyssey that included stops at St. Thomas, Charleston, Liverpool, South Africa, Mozambique, and the Zanguebar coast of East Africa in a quest to purchase enslaved Africans. It was an unusually long and dangerous adventure, consisting of a complicated series of individual initiatives strung together by a man intensely driven to accumulate wealth. The plantation experiment at Laurel Grove continued in his absence under the direction of managers and drivers. Before leaving on his odyssey, Kingsley gave command of two of his ships, the *Esther* and the *Laurel*, to captains

Enrique Wright and Juan Friac, along with orders to purchase foodstuffs and miscellaneous items at Savannah, Charleston, Norfolk, and New York to supply his plantation and the new mercantile business he had initiated at Laurel Grove.

Kingsley's first destination was probably Charlotte Amalie, where he purchased another ship, the *Gustavia*. Captain Wright returned to East Florida aboard the *Laurel* while Kingsley piloted the *Gustavia* to Savannah. He then booked passage to Charleston in search of a new owner for the ship he had just purchased. The multinational Kingsley testified on August 14 that he was a resident of the "City and State of New York, at present in the City of Charleston, [and] a native Citizen of the United States of America." In exchange for $10,500, Kingsley sold the 300-ton *Gustavia*, "together with her masts, yard, sails, rigging, anchors, cables, boats, tackle, apparel and appurtenances, as she now lies in Savannah in the State of Georgia," to Spencer John Man, a Charleston merchant and the son of a prominent merchant in St. Augustine when East Florida was a British province. To command the ship, Man chose Captain Theophilus Hill, the son of Greek indentured laborers at the East Florida plantation of Dr. Andrew Turnbull from 1768 to 1777. Kingsley agreed to serve as supercargo during the voyage. Man loaded the ship with cotton for the Liverpool market and instructed Hill and Kingsley to have the ship refitted for a slaving expedition to Africa when the cargo was unloaded.[15]

Captain Hill brought the *Gustavia* up the Mersey River at Liverpool on January 22, 1805. As supercargo, Kingsley represented the owner of the ship and was in charge of selling the cargo and purchasing provisions and trade goods for the voyage to Benguela or Luanda at Angola on the southwest African coast. Liverpool was then the "undisputed capital of the country's slave trade," according to the historians Gail Cameron and Stan Crooke. In one sixteen-month period, Cameron and Crooke claim, "185 slavers cleared from Liverpool and carried nearly 50,000 Africans to slavery in the Americas." Connected by rivers and canals to nearby manufacturing centers, Liverpool benefited from a superior transportation network for supply of textiles, copper and iron bars, cutlery and tools, firearms, powder, flints, and brandy, all standard trade goods Europeans used in barter for enslaved Africans.[16]

Hill and Kingsley expected a quick turnaround, but instead they suffered through a debilitating period of inactivity that lasted for several months. Refitting the ship proceeded as planned. In the eighteenth century, one of every four ships engaged in the Atlantic slave trade was built at Liverpool. The historian Stephen Behrendt has documented that three of every four British slavers were converted from other types of trade. The result was constant demand for refitting services and a large pool of ship's carpenters, caulkers, blacksmiths, masons, sail makers, and coopers available for hire. Carpenters willing to crew aboard slavers were the highest-paid employees, after the ship's officers.

The Liverpool carpenters constructed a barricade on the main deck of the *Gustavia* to separate captain and crew from the slaves when they were brought topside for food and exercise. Below the main deck, sleeping areas for the slaves were fitted out and barricades erected to separate the men from the women. For a ship the size of the *Gustavia* it was customary to install two half-decks, attached to both sides of the hull for the length of the ship, immediately below the main deck. These would be sleeping and confinement quarters for the women and children purchased on the African coast. Approximately four and one-half feet below, a second deck was installed on each side of the ship to accommodate the male slaves purchased.

While the carpenters worked, masons installed brick platforms to contain the fires needed for the large iron and copper cooking pots, and the exterior hull was sheathed with copper to protect against damage from the worms that infested African waters. Ventilation shafts were cut into the topside deck and the sides of the vessels to allow sufficient air to enter the sleeping compartments to keep the Africans alive during the passage. Iron gratings secured the shafts against escape. Similar gratings were placed over widened hatchways that could be opened or closed and locked securely to keep the slaves below. On some ships air scoops that functioned as wind tunnels were cut into the main deck to force fresh air into the hold. Hill bought hundreds of iron chains with wrist and ankle shackles that were later used to secure the slaves to their bunks and to protect against rebellion and escape when they were brought topside.[17]

The problem that kept the *Gustavia* in port so long was a general shortage of provisions in the area. Most overseas vessels arrived at Liverpool between June and October, when supplies of textiles for trade goods and provisions for feeding crew members and human cargo during a transatlantic voyage were generally plentiful. After reaching the wharfs at Liverpool in February, however, Kingsley and Hill discovered that stores of provisions were depleted, and they experienced a frustrating five-week delay. Meanwhile, rumors circulated among mariners that France had sent out two naval squadrons and that a French invasion would soon force Portugal into the ongoing war between France and England. Kingsley finally conceded that it would not be possible to "take on board the necessary provisions" and that he was "obliged reluctantly to set off for Mozambique which could have been done much more advantageously from any port in America. What success I shall have time will show but my expectations are not sanguine."[18]

Kingsley's frustration reflected his understanding that provisions would have been readily available if the *Gustavia* had sailed for Liverpool earlier in the year. He also knew that American ports like Charleston and Baltimore had an abundance of ship carpenters to refit vessels for the slave trade. Had the *Gustavia* not carried cotton to Liverpool, it could have sailed for Africa months sooner. Kingsley's correspondence does not explain why he changed the destination from Angola to Mozambique, but it may have been motivated by news that France was planning to occupy Portugal (an ally of Britain) and convert Portuguese commercial ships to privateers flying French flags. If that happened, slavers trading at the West-Central African ports of Cabinda, Luanda, and Benguela, Portuguese colonies, would have been endangered. David Eltis and David Richardson, using the transatlantic slave trade database compiled at the W. E. B. Du Bois Institute of Harvard University, have concluded that "the dominant regional supplier of slaves in the eighteenth and nineteenth centuries" was "West-Central Africa," from the Zaire River south to the Luanda and Benguela region.[19]

Ships trading at Mozambique, on the southeast coast of Africa, were less likely to be seized by privateers, and prices for enslaved Africans were likely to be lower than at Angola. Slaves from East Africa had been exported for centuries, primarily to locations around the Indian Ocean. French ships carried thousands to the Mascarene Islands, and Portuguese traders operated a thriving export trade in slaves to Brazil until the Napoleonic Wars and the British navy made that route too precarious to continue. Ships from neutral nations continued this trade, and at the end of the Napoleonic Wars it was greatly expanded. The historian Edward E. Alpers has estimated that six to ten thousand slaves a year were exported to Zanzibar between 1811 and 1820, half of them passing through Kilwa. Between 1820 and 1830 "at least 10,000 slaves a year were legally embarked at Mozambique for Brazil alone," while another 5,000 were transported each year to Mauritius and Réunion.[20]

Two ships owned by Charleston merchant James Hamilton, the *Commerce* and the *Isabella*, experienced delays at Liverpool while the *Gustavia* was being outfitted. Captain J. M. Bowers informed Hamilton that instead of sailing the *Commerce* directly to Charleston he had chartered it to a Liverpool firm. The contract obligated him to depart for the Windward Coast to load a slave cargo before returning to Charleston, with the expectation that "we shall be six months on the voyage."[21]

For Kingsley, the delay was troubling. His plantation in East Florida was progressing, but this was a more complicated and expensive undertaking than anticipated. A debt of nearly $6,000 owed to him by a merchant at Petit-Goâve in Saint-Domingue was still outstanding, and two of the principals in the firm had been killed at Port-au-Prince. Kingsley was already six months into the African voyage for Spencer Man, and he now realized that it might take another year to complete.[22]

On December 4, 1804, Kingsley had marked his fortieth birthday aboard the *Gustavia*. The winter wind blowing off the Mersey River must have been bone chilling for a man accustomed to a West Indies climate. After years of continuous involvement in the dangerous and turbulent Caribbean and African trade, Kingsley found himself uncharacteristically immobilized. By the end of February his letters had become introspective and melancholic. He confided to Hamilton that the past year had been so filled with misfortune that he was in "despair of ever accomplishing the wished for object of independence which seemed to be sometimes within my reach and then again totally to disappear. By experience I have learnt that fortune is neither to be won by prudence nor industry and have only to thank god that ambition the attendant of health has not yet deserted me and keeps hurrying me on like a soldier in hopes of victory, yet well aware that if not soon obtained the period must come when nature will relax the springs and leave me distanced in the course." Kingsley regretted that he had been unable to leave Liverpool briefly to "inquire after those companions of my youth and dearest connexions."[23]

It is not clear if the *Gustavia* remained at Liverpool until provisions became available, or if foodstuffs were purchased at a stop along the route to East Africa. European ships generally sailed south to Cape Verde, west of Senegal, then veered further west in the Atlantic and proceeded south parallel to the South American coast. South of Rio de Janeiro ships encountered currents and winds that moved them in a northeasterly direction toward Benguela on the Angola shore and beyond to Luanda and ports further north near the Zaire River.[24]

The *Gustavia* was anchored at the Cape of Good Hope at the end of July 1805. Kingsley wrote to George Gibbs that the *Gustavia* "sailed fast and was light and strong" and the crew was "very healthy." The town at the Cape was "the neatest and most beautiful I ever saw, situated between hills resembling heaps of jagged rocks bounded by barren looking valleys bare of wood and even grass. What trees surround the houses and gardens are all planted and of European seed consisting of White Oaks and short-leafed hummock pine of a slow growth." Kingsley found that wine was "cheap and abundant, brandy in proportion but every kind of bread is at present dear on account of a drought last season. Our pease and beans cost us two dollars per bushel, more than double the common price." The people in the town were "handsome and very hospitable and the climate temperate and the healthiest I believe in the known world." Anxious to resume the journey, Kingsley wrote to Hamilton: "in another week we shall sail for Mozambique about 20 days passage to the N.E., to which no guineamen have passed lately to the region, thus that commodity [captive Africans] must be cheap."[25]

After departing the Cape on August 15, Hill sailed south and east to avoid the seasonal westerly winds and currents, then turned north to pass between Mozambique and Madagascar Island. The continental landfall on the west from north of the Limpopo River to beyond Mombasa was known at the time as the Zanguebar coast. By mid-September they were beyond Inhambane and Quelimane on the Mozambique coast and at Mozambique Island. The coastal region was under Portuguese control, but Arab and Swahili merchants seeking gold, silver, ivory, and enslaved Africans had frequented the port cities for centuries and had extended their trade networks south along the coast as far as the Limpopo River. The historian R. W. Beachey dates the ivory trade back to "the Second Century A.D." and contends that "in the sixteenth century 30,000 pounds of ivory passed through the port of Sofala yearly," much of it delivered by caravans organized by African middlemen to the Portuguese post at Mozambique Island. The historian Pedro Machado has found a 1782 inventory that documents Gujarati merchants from today's India trading as far south as the Zambezi River.[26]

French merchants were responsible for expanding the slave trade in this region in the 1770s, transporting 3,000 slaves a year from Quelimane and Mozambique Island to plantations at Mauritius and Réunion. From further north at Kilwa, even more slaves were shipped each year. Between 1784 and 1794, 4,000 captives from the interior left Mozambique each year for the French West Indies. The Anglo-French wars and the slave rebellion in Saint-Domingue brought the latter trade to a halt between 1794 and 1811, but ships carried East Africans to the Portuguese colony of Brazil, and slavers from the United States and other neutral nations entered the trade and drove up demand along the Zanguebar coast.[27]

The scholarly literature on the East African slave trade is sparse compared to that for the West African trade, and it focuses primarily on Zanzibar and the Indian Ocean trade after the Napoleonic Wars. There are similarities on both sides of the continent in that inter-ethnic wars and organized raids in the coastal hinterlands produced most of the captives. In the seventeenth and eighteenth centuries, the Yao of Mozambique were the middlemen who organized caravans to transport ivory from the interior to Sofala, Inhambane, Quelimane, and Mozambique Island. Further north, the Nyamwezi controlled the caravans from the interior of today's Tanzania.

Prior to 1810, most of the enslaved persons came from the hinterland adjoining the coastal littoral. Malyn Newitt contends that ivory came from deep in the interior, carried on the backs of enslaved porters, whereas coffles of slaves came from the hinterland adjacent to the coastal littoral, supplied primarily by the Makua people located north of the Zambezi River. Abdul Sheriff believes that by the mid-eighteenth century the people residing in the Makonde Plateau of northern Mozambique and southern Tanzania were "constantly at war to make each other prisoners and sell as slaves."

Edward Alpers writes that "most of the slaves in East Africa came from the southern interior and were brought to the coast between Kilwa and Mozambique Island." In the early years of the trade, the war captives came "from the coastal hinterland, people like the Makua, Makonde, Ndonde, and Ngindo; but by the beginning of the nineteenth century, Yao and even some Malawi slaves were becoming increasingly common at Mozambique and Kilwa, as were Nyamwezi to the north."[28]

The *Gustavia* remained on the Zanguebar coast for more than three months, trading at several ports and purchasing Africans captured from diverse homelands and cultures. As supercargo and captain, Kingsley and Hill decided where to conduct trade based on the availability and market prices. The logical first port of call would have been at Quelimane to the south, next at Mozambique Island, and finally at Kilwa on the north. According to Newitt, the Quelimane merchants were receiving large numbers of war captives from the interior in 1805. Kilwa, the likely northernmost port at which the *Gustavia* called, became the leading trade center on the coast in the early nineteenth century.[29]

Only vague clues have been found to the ethnic identities and places of origin of the captive Africans brought aboard the *Gustavia*. For example, a Charleston newspaper noted the ship's arrival from "Zanguebar on the Eastern Coast of Africa" with a cargo of "natives of Gondo, Mocoa, and Swabaytie nations, much distinguished by the Planters of Mauritius." French slavers, of course, had transported captives to Mauritius from all of the East African ports. The mention of "Gondo" may be a clue, since a town of that name exists today in Mozambique, inland between Inhambane and Quelimane. "Gondo" could also be the result of a European slavers' confusing ethnic names for the "Ndonde" and the "Ngindo" people who became embroiled in the wars for captives. "Mocoa" may have been a transliteration of "Makua," meaning people located north of the Zambezi River who supplied captives to coastal buyers, and sometimes became victims.

There may be another clue in Kingsley's *Treatise on the Patriarchal, or Co-operative System of Society*, written in 1828, in which he discussed one of the men purchased at Zanguebar. This man became notorious in the antebellum South as the enslaved ship carpenter Gullah Jack, accused of conspiring with a free black man, Denmark Vesey, to foment a rebellion at Charleston in 1822. Kingsley wrote: "Gullah Jack or Jack the Conjurer was a priest in his own country, M'Choolay Moreema, where a dialect of the Angola tongue is spoken clear across Africa from sea to sea, a distance of perhaps three thousand miles: I purchased him a prisoner of war at Zingue-bar. He had his conjuring implements with him in a bag which he brought onboard the ship and always retained them."[30]

During a May 1806 sale aboard the *Gustavia*, Gullah Jack was sold to Charleston shipbuilder Paul Pritchard. Contrary to several claims, Gullah Jack did not become a slave at a plantation in Florida. Kingsley did select other Africans from the cargo, two of whom became carpenters and were abducted in an 1813 raid by Seminole warriors. Kingsley identified the two as carpenters and as "Zinguibari." The first was Jack, age thirty, with a wife, Tamassa, and four children (Ben, "M Toto," Molly, and Rose). The second was "M Sooma," age twenty-eight, with a wife, Eliza, and one child (March). Kingsley also listed a woman named Jenny, age twenty-eight, with a son (Billy), and identified her as a Zinguebara. In addition, a "Martin, MGuinda" is on the list. Two other carpenters, Bill and Bonafi, both born in Africa, were still enslaved by Kingsley at the time of his death and may also have been purchased in East Africa and carried across the Atlantic aboard the *Gustavia*.[31]

The fact that Gullah Jack, sold at Charleston, and "M Sooma" and Jack, the "Zinguebari" men abducted in 1813, were all employed as carpenters may be a coincidence rather than evidence of a shared ethnic background. It is likely, however, that Jack and Tamassa and their children, along with "M Sooma," and also Jenny (listed by Kingsley as Zinguebara), were of Kamba ethnicity and originated at today's Kenya or Tanzania. Tamassa may equate to Tamasha, a Swahili name for females used in East Africa. Jack and Tamassa's youngest son, "M Toto" (the Swahili word for "boy"), is a further suggestion that the parents were from East Africa. The other Zinguebari carpenter, "M Sooma," has been tentatively identified as a Kamba, possibly from a village located at the headwaters of the Tana River in Kenya.[32]

As Captain Hill moved the *Gustavia* from south to north along the East African coast, he and Kingsley were responsible for acquiring provisions and water to supply the human cargo and crew members during the return voyage to Charleston. Barrels of rice, dried manioc root (cassava), corn, beans, or millet were purchased, along with sun-dried or salted meat or fish, peppers, and palm oil. By the 1780s, slave ships had begun providing lime juice or vinegar as a scurvy preventive. According to Herbert S. Klein, it was the norm after 1770 for slave ships to carry supplies of "provisions and water for double their expected voyage times" and to use "fairly standard foods" and follow "similar methods of hygiene."[33]

Consider the water needs alone: each of the approximately forty crew members consumed about one quart of water a day, plus rations of rum and beer. The general formula followed on slave ships called for one quart of water daily for each slave. As it turned out, approximately 330 slaves were packed aboard the *Gustavia* on this voyage. When spillage, evaporation from the barrels, water needed for cooking, and the needed water for crew, officers, and slaves were factored in, more than one hundred gallons of water would have been expended each day of the journey. If the journey lasted four months, 12,000 gallons of water would have been consumed. At 62 gallons per barrel on average, a bare minimum of 194 barrels of water would have been required, and if doubled for protection against emergency the crew would have packed 388 barrels of water in the hold.[34]

By mid-December, 330 enslaved Africans were secured aboard the *Gustavia* and Captain Hill ordered the sails hoisted for the homeward journey. Beginning on the day the first captive Africans were purchased, the captain, officers, and sailors all became armed guards on a floating prison whose primary responsibility was to protect against escape and rebellion. Crew members continued to do the normal work of sailors, but they also became jailors on full alert to avoid becoming victims like their prisoners. David Richardson has estimated that one in ten of the slave ships experienced insurrections.[35]

Generally, when the enslaved were brought aboard they were assigned a number, stripped naked, their heads were shaved, and on some ships they were branded. Males were shackled and affixed to another man by irons placed on the left wrist and ankle of one man and the right wrist and ankle of another. Secured in chains, they were packed tightly together on the platforms or deck surfaces, and a few large tubs were dispersed in each compartment to collect human waste. For shackled men, maneuvering to access the tubs was difficult, especially when the ship was in motion and sickness was common. The result was a deck that became covered each day with vomit and excrement, and a stench that made it mandatory for crew members to scrub the deck daily and fumigate routinely. After surviving the terror of wars in the interior and a brutal march to the coastal barracoons, the captives next experienced an elevated level of violence and degradation that became central to their shipboard existence.

Armed crew members brought the slaves topside every morning, chained them to the deck, and sloshed them with water while a surgeon searched for individuals who were ill. Women and children were separated from the men by a barricade on the main deck, as they were below, and were not shackled unless they appeared to be rebellious. Food and water were distributed, and the slaves were forced to exercise by dancing vigorously on the deck, "encouraged" by frequent lashing with the "cat-o'-nine-tails." On many ships a drink of rum was dispensed in the afternoon, followed by another meal of soup or gruel and a forced, closely guarded procession to the compartments below. Fourteen or more hours of darkness, painful cramped conditions, and unbearable heat and stench followed before the trek to the main deck was repeated.

At all times when the slaves were on the deck, armed crew members pointed blunderbusses through holes in the barricade, and a gunner with a swivel cannon loaded with small shot trained his weapon on the men. Frequent whippings were the norm throughout the day. The accounts of life on the slave ships left by captains and crew members describe a level of violence that is shocking to modern sensibilities.

An enslaved woman aboard a slave ship endured a special kind of horror: sexual abuse and rape by the crew member that first claimed her as his "favorite." On many ships, although not all, the captains and officers, as well as the crew members, claimed favorites among the enslaved women and used them for sexual purposes for the duration of the voyage. Looking back on his prior experiences as the captain of slavers, the Reverend John Newton remembered African women boarding his ships "naked, trembling, terrified" and "exposed to the wanton rudeness of white savages. . . . In imagination, the prey is divided, upon the spot, and only reserved until opportunity offers." In two carefully researched studies of slave ships and their sailors, Marcus Rediker and Emma Christopher have concluded that, in Christopher's words, "the sexual abuse of women on slave ships was . . . a demanded perquisite of the job of seafaring."[36]

John Newton wrote that involvement in the slave trade "gradually brings a numbness upon the heart" and caused sailors to become "indifferent to the sufferings of their fellow creatures." He may have been remembering the threat of sickness and death that, like violence, was endemic to the Atlantic trade in slaves, or the horror-inducing sight of sharks as they circled and followed slave ships across the ocean waiting to devour the bodies of the men, women, and children who perished and were thrown overboard during the crossing. During the *Gustavia's* Atlantic passage, approximately seventy-four Africans died and were disposed of in the ocean.

The death rate aboard the *Gustavia* was approximately 22 percent, higher than the 19.3 percent death rate calculated by David Eltis and his colleagues for slaves embarked in southeast Africa between 1527 and 1866. The limited records of the voyage contain no references to major storms, pirate attacks, or rebellions, so it is logical to assume that disease, complicated by the lengthy four-and-one-half-month passage, was responsible for most of the casualties. Studies based on journals kept by surgeons aboard slavers have established that the leading causes of death were gastrointestinal disorders like dysentery (known then as the "bloody flux"), malaria, and yellow fever. Suicides, sometimes by slaves who refused to eat despite severe punishment, happened on most slave ships.[37]

After departing Zanguebar in mid-December 1805, Captain Hill steered the *Gustavia* around the Cape of Good Hope and into the South Atlantic on a journey destined to end at Charleston. An unexpected two-week stop at Saint Helena Island occurred along the way. On February 11, 1806, Kingsley dispatched a letter to George Gibbs aboard a ship departing Saint Helena. Gibbs did not receive the letter until April 15, but after months of worry he spoke for Kingsley's family when he wrote: "We are all rejoiced to hear he is so far on his way back, and that he was safe at that time. I hope he will visit us before he goes out on any other expedition."[38]

For the relatives and loved ones of the Africans confined on the *Gustavia* there would be no reassuring communications. Irrevocably torn from family and homeland, thrown together with a mix of relatives, acquaintances, and strangers from other ethnic backgrounds, they would never again see their loved ones or homelands. The Africans had been counted when forced aboard the ship, their numbers listed in an account book, but their names and ethnic identities were unrecorded and lost to history. When the *Gustavia* left the East African coast, it became one of the more than 35,000 ships that carried 12.5 million enslaved Africans away from the continent and into the Atlantic, a traffic in human commerce that David Eltis and David Richardson have called "the largest transoceanic forced migration in human history." Seventy-four men, women, and children, approximately one in every five brought aboard the *Gustavia*, died during the passage. Their bodies, along with the bodies of 1.8 million other nameless victims, were disposed of in the Atlantic. Those who were still alive when the *Gustavia* arrived at Charleston on April 28, 1806, became a tiny part of the nameless mass of 10.7 million enslaved Africans who survived the Middle Passage during the four and one-half centuries of the Atlantic slave trade.[39]

6

Family Ties

Anna Madgigine Jai Kingsley

The *Gustavia* arrived in the United States on April 21, 1806, dropping anchor first at the quarantine station on Tybee Island off Savannah, Georgia. After sixteen months away from Charleston, Kingsley wrote to a merchant there to inquire about the current market for Africans: "We anchored this day for orders with 240 Negroes. . . . We are entire strangers to who is doing well and who ill." While waiting for a reply, sailors scrubbed and fumigated the ship to minimize the stench of human waste and sickness generated by so many people confined in chains for four months. Fresh fruits and vegetables were added to the diet of the Africans, and they were scrubbed and polished with oil in preparation for a shipboard auction.[1]

On April 28 the *Gustavia* cleared customs at Charleston and was secured to Gadsden's Wharf on the Cooper River. The "Marine News" of the *Courier* announced the arrival of the "Gustavia, Captain Hill, 134 days [from] Zanguebar, 230 slaves." Spencer John Man alerted prospective buyers: "Will be opened To-Morrow, The 1st of MAY, on board, off Gadsden's Wharf, the SALE of 230 PRIME SLAVES, imported in the ship Gustavia, Captain Hill, from Zanguebar, on the Eastern Coast of Africa, being natives of Gondo, Mocoa, and Swabaytie nations, much distinguished by the Planters of Mauretius."[2]

When the shipboard sale at Gadsden's Wharf was completed, Kingsley had fulfilled his obligations to Man and collected his wages. He also collected eight men, two women, and eight children from the cargo, a common practice on slave ships, whereby ranking officers claimed "privilege slaves" as partial payment for services. Man then advertised the *Gustavia* for sale, calling it "a very commodious American Guineaman, completely sound in African materials . . . British built, copper fastened and copper sheathed, has undergone a thorough repair twelve months ago in Liverpool . . . may be dispatched immediately for the Coast of Africa."[3]

Kingsley's eighteen Africans were placed aboard Captain Joel Dunn's ship, *El Pele*, and carried to East Florida as part of a cargo that included forty sacks of beans, cotton and linen cloth, twenty-four small iron pots, a corn grinder, and miscellaneous items. Kingsley was not aboard the *El Pele* when it arrived at his plantation in mid-July. He had instead booked passage for New York to visit his elderly mother and arrange employment in Caribbean and African trade.[4]

Kingsley had been away from his Florida plantation for nearly two years. For much of that time he had been immersed in the daily violence and death systemic to the Atlantic slave trade. During the long nightmare of that commerce, many mariners vowed on their first slaving voyage to never repeat the experience. But Kingsley was intent on amassing wealth to achieve his "wished for object of independence," and so he continued in the trade.[5]

For the next five months Kingsley was involved in Caribbean maritime commerce from his old base at Charlotte Amalie, St. Thomas. Employment opportunities abounded for experienced captains and supercargoes capable of managing ships and cargoes in the Atlantic slave trade and trans-shipping slaves from St. Thomas to Cuba and other Caribbean ports. Kingsley's schooner, the *Esther*, captained by Henry Wright, was recorded as shipping out of Charleston, South Carolina, and Natchez, Mississippi, in the summer of 1806, and on September 18 the *Esther* cleared customs at Havana with a cargo of forty-three enslaved Africans, all males. If Kingsley was aboard the *Esther* during these months, his name does not appear on the port records. He was aboard the ship on October 10, 1806, the day he testified at the American Consulate in Havana that he was the owner of the *Esther*, which was "riding at anchor in the harbor of Havana and bound for Charleston." His cargo manifest listed "four hogsheads molasses, twenty-eight half pipes and twelve whole pipes of rum, and tres negras bozales" (three females newly arrived from Africa). It is almost certain that one of the three female slaves was a Wolof girl named Anta Majigeen Ndiaye, who would soon become a prominent part of Kingsley's life.[6]

When Kingsley finally returned to Laurel Grove Plantation at the end of October 1806, after an absence of two years and four months, major changes were under way. His participation in maritime commerce would continue for several years, but he increasingly turned his attention to plantation management and to his role as the owner of enslaved Africans. He was five weeks shy of his forty-first birthday, but he had never married or entered into a familial relationship other than with his parents and siblings. In 1806, however, Kingsley impregnated two enslaved African women, and in the following year he became the father of a daughter and a son.

The mother of the first child was Munsilna McGundo, an East African of unknown ethnicity whom Kingsley apparently chose as a "favorite" from the human cargo aboard the *Gustavia* during its journey from Mozambique and selected as a "privilege" slave when the ship reached Charleston. Munsilna's daughter, Fatimah Kingsley, was born in February 1807 and emancipated by Kingsley in March 1811. Munsilna is only infrequently mentioned in records of the remaining years of Kingsley's life, but she continued to live at his plantations and gave birth to several more children.[7]

The mother of the second child fathered by Kingsley in 1806 was Anta Majigeen Ndiaye, one of "three African females" Kingsley purchased at Havana in late September or early October 1806 and transported to his Florida plantation. She was thirteen years old at the time. In June 1807, Anta gave birth to a son, George Kingsley. In Florida, Anta would be known as Anna Madgigine, Anna Jai, Anna Kingsley, or combinations of those names. In March 1811, at age eighteen, Anta was emancipated by Kingsley, along with her son, George, and two daughters, Martha and Mary. In the years ahead Anta became the most important woman in Kingsley's life, and he publicly acknowledged her as his wife, although they were never legally married. The daughter of a member of the ruling patrilineage of the state of Jolof in Senegal, West Africa, and a survivor of a slave raid and the dreaded Middle Passage, Anta became a free black woman and a plantation and slave owner. Her remarkable life story is an important part of the history of Florida and of the African diaspora in the Americas.[8]

Anta Majigeen Ndiaye's early years were tragically linked to the wars and slave raids that ravaged the Senegambia region of West Africa for centuries. Wars between the Wolof states, the dominant ethnic group in Senegal, and the Fula of Futa Toro and the Trarza emirates to the north raged periodically in the eighteenth century. Wolof states also fought other Wolof states, generally in attacks initiated by Cayor (also Kajoor) that destroyed villages and dispersed or enslaved the residents. Civil wars and dynastic disputes within each state further disrupted normal social and political life.[9]

Raids to capture slaves had been endemic prior to the arrival of Europeans at West African coastal ports in the fifteenth century. Captives of war were incorporated into Wolof villages as laborers or sent north across the Sahara to Arab and Berber outposts to exchange for trade goods, the most prized being the Arabian and Barbary horses of North Africa that permitted cavalry of powerful nations to plunder rivals. The proliferation of Portuguese ships and the unceasing demand for enslaved captives, however, diverted a significant portion of the trans-Sahara trade to the coastal ports and greatly increased the level of violence and disintegration of political stability in the region.[10]

Prior to arrival of the Portuguese, the Empire of Jolof controlled the lands between the Senegal and Gambia Rivers. In the mythic traditions of Jolof, the empire was founded by Njaajaan Ndiaye, a Pulaar-speaking migrant from an Islamic state to the north who settled among fractious Wolof-speakers and brought peace and Islam to the region and unity to the local people. As Buurba Jolof (king of Jolof), Njaajaan Ndiaye established a capital near the Ferlo River in the interior of what is today Senegal. Located astride the important trade routes of that era, Jolof prospered and consolidated three other ethnic Wolof states—Waalo, Cayor, and Baol—and the Serer states of Sine and Saloum into the Empire of Jolof. As European coastal trade increased, the Wolof states with direct access to the Atlantic ports gained wealth and power and became independent states. By the eighteenth century, the Empire of Jolof had disintegrated.[11]

The coastal Wolof states expanded production of grain and other foodstuffs for sale to captains of the slave ships. To acquire agricultural laborers and human cargoes to sell to European buyers, the Wolof states raided Serer, Bambara, and other African nations located to the east and south. Rivalries increased, and wars between the Wolof states were intermittent throughout the eighteenth century. By 1790 Cayor had become the dominant Wolof state, due in part to the military prowess of the feared tyeddo warriors, a caste of slaves owned by and paying allegiance only to the damel (king). The tyeddo were in reality a standing army of professional soldiers, fierce cavalrymen who captured slaves in raids throughout the region. With little regard for Wolof villagers, the tyeddo plundered at will and escalated the level of violence. Writing about the establishment of warrior states, the historian Boubakar Barry observed: "*Ceddo* [also tyeddo] monarchies established violence as the determinant value, not only in relations between Senegambia's states, but also in political and social relations within each state."[12]

The crisis of the Wolof states heightened between 1790 and 1809, when internal religious wars broke out in Cayor. An Englishman who witnessed these events said the villages on the Senegal River were destroyed and the residents "carried into captivity and those who remain are constantly subjected to plunder."[13] Professor Brahim Diop and a team of historical geographers in Senegal have discovered the remains of dozens of rural villages that were deserted as a result of the incessant violence. Anta Majigeen Ndiaye's years in Senegal, from 1793 to 1806, coincided with this intense violence and long tradition of wars and slave raids.[14]

Most Wolof people had converted to Islam before 1790. The leaders of many rural villages were Muslim clerics whose followers were pious farmers, fond of quiet family life and forbidden by their faith to imbibe alcohol or engage in sinful acts. They became resentful of the immorality of the ruling families and of the hard-drinking, flamboyant, and violent tyeddo warriors of Cayor, who in theory raided only non-Wolof people but, when supplies of luxury goods or weapons ran low, also raided distant Wolof villages.[15]

As Cayor's repression worsened, thousands of Muslim Wolof fled south and west to form their own state at the Cape Verde peninsula, enclosing their families in walled villages for protection. The tyeddo warriors crushed the rebellion and sold thousands of prisoners as slaves, but violence spread beyond the borders of Cayor to pit one Wolof state against another and to draw the Fulbe of Futa Toro into the fighting. Warfare was suspended in most of Senegal in 1806, but the tyeddo continued raiding villages in Jolof as punishment for that state's previous support of Futa Toro. In 1806 many Wolof captives from Jolof were marched to the coastal slave markets.[16]

Most slaves from Senegal were exported through a French fortification at St. Louis, an island in the mouth of the Senegal River. In 1806, however, captives were routed to Gorée Island. Major Richard Lloyd, the British commandant at Gorée, reported in 1805 that the French garrison at St. Louis had been depleted by warfare with "some of the Native Princes on the River, with whom there is no probability of being on peaceful terms." French raids of "indiscriminate plunder" had infuriated Africans of the region, who closed the routes to St. Louis. The caravans of captured slaves were therefore routed to Gorée Island, two miles offshore at the tip of Cape Verde, the westernmost point on the African continent. Commander Lloyd reported that one thousand Africans were available for purchase in 1806.[17]

Enslaved Africans passed through the doors of Gorée's holding pens for generations. Men, women, and children, their total number lost through the centuries of slave exporting, were incarcerated in walled courtyard prisons and in basement dungeons beneath the spacious homes of the island merchants. African captives who reached Gorée remained only until the next slave ships arrived, when they were led before the European buyers and prices were agreed upon. Ships rode at anchor offshore while barrels of water, food, and other items were packed into crowded holds beneath the decks. The newly purchased slaves were placed in canoes and carried to the ships anchored offshore. Once aboard, they were forced through an opening on the deck to descend into the darkness and agony below.[18]

That Anta Majigeen Ndiaye was captured during one of the tyeddo raids into Jolof in 1806 is a conclusion based partly on her testimony in Florida that she was a "native of Senegal" and on the fact that she continued to identify herself with her mother's name, Majigeen (generally spelled Madgigine in Florida), and her father's name, Ndiaye (Jai), throughout her life in the Americas. The evidence is persuasive that the slave ship that carried her across the Atlantic stopped at Havana, where she was purchased by Zephaniah Kingsley, and that she arrived in Florida in late October 1806 at the age of thirteen. In Florida there is a persistent legend that Anna Kingsley had been a "royal princess" in Africa prior to her enslavement. This legend corresponds to a legend among Wolof people of Darha, a regional market town located in the interior of Senegal in the district of Linguère, and the nearby village of Yang Yang, a former capital of Jolof. In that legend, Anna Kingsley is identified as the former Anta Majigeen Ndiaye, the daughter of a member of the ruling Ndiaye lineage who was an unsuccessful contender for the position of Buurba Jolof.[19]

Based on her age at the time she was emancipated in Florida, Anta Majigeen Ndiaye was born in 1793, during the reign of Mba Kompas Ndiaye, the Buurba Jolof from 1762 to 1797. Vincent Monteil, the author of respected studies of lines of succession of the rulers of Jolof, lists Mba Kompas as the thirteenth ruler. Mba Kompas's successor, Mba Buri-Nyabu, is believed to have held power for approximately thirty-five years, circa 1798–1833. During his tenure, incessant and violent dynastic disputes as well as wars between the Wolof states devastated the towns in Jolof.[20]

Mr. Abdou Cissè, a respected local historian at Darha, has maintained the oral traditions memorized by his great-grandfather, the griot (official oral historian) attached to the last Buurba Jolof. Mr. Cissè has on three occasions identified Anna Madgigine Jai as Anta Majigeen Ndiaye, the daughter of a man who was a member of the royal lineage of Jolof. It is his opinion that between 1797 and 1806, Anta's father contended for power in a bitter dynastic dispute within the Ndiaye patrilineage. The rebellion failed, and Anta's father was sent into exile carrying only a gun and a sack of possessions on his back. His wives, children, slaves, and other properties were confiscated.[21]

There is further elaboration in a May 2000 interview with Mr. Cissè by Mr. Ababacar Sy, professor of English at the regional school at Dahra. Mr. Cissè again identified Anta Majigeen Ndiaye as a daughter of a contender for the throne and said: "The family of Anta Madjiguéne doesn't want to say that Anta Madjiguéne was a slave. This seems to be a dishonor in the family. For the family, Anta Madjiguéne had traveled in 1806 and hadn't come back. They didn't know more about her." As a representative of the former ruling family, Mr. Cissè chose a polite way to say that Anta was either captured and enslaved or sold into slavery by the family. "The real truth," in the judgment of Mr. Sy, is that Anta, "like many Senegalese or African people," was enslaved and "deported abroad."[22]

A similar account was narrated in March 2000 by the elders of the village of Yang Yang. Anta, they said, was born in their village, the daughter of a direct descendant of Njaajan Ndiaye. She was reared as a privileged daughter in a stratified society of nobles, free farmers, and slaves. That changed, however, when her father led an unsuccessful contest for the kingship.[23]

That challenge may have followed the death of Mba Kompas in 1797, or it may have been one of many unsuccessful uprisings during the rule of Mba

Buri-Nyabu after 1798. Mr. Cissè stated that two of Anta's brothers survived the violence of the dynastic dispute and later returned their branch of the family to power. Judging from the lines of succession collected by Oumar Ndiaye Leyti and Vincent Monteil, which are based on a number of griot renditions collected early in the twentieth century, the brothers may have been the twenty-first and twenty-second Buurba Jolofs, Lat-Kodu Madjiguéne Peya Fal Malik and Birayamb Madjiguéne Peya Fal Malik, rulers from 1848 to 1853. Anta would have been in her late fifties by then, a widow living in Florida unaware that two of her brothers were the current rulers of the strife-ridden homeland from which she had been forcefully separated more than four decades before.[24]

The legends of Anna Jai in Florida as well as in Senegal, when combined with Anna Kingsley's own statements about her origins and the judgments of the leading historians of Senegal, are persuasive that the thirteen-year-old "negra bozal" Kingsley purchased in late September 1806 from a ship captain at Havana was Anta Majigeen Ndiaye. The teenage girl who became Anna Kingsley in Florida was of Wolof ethnicity, born in the interior nation of Jolof. Before she became a captive and a slave, she had been a privileged child living in a royal household. After her father was forced into exile, Anta and other residents of her village were captured in raids by tyeddo from Cayor, sold as slaves to merchants at Gorée Island, resold to European slave traders, and carried in the hold of a slave ship to Havana.

The name of the slave trader who purchased Anta at Gorée and the name of the ship in which she was transported to Havana is a mystery. Spanish officials registered six slave ships at Havana in July 1806, three flying the flag of Denmark, and six more in August and September. These are the months when the ship carrying Anta most likely arrived. The twelve vessels unloaded 1,260 enslaved Africans. The port-of-entry registries list names of ships, captains, nationality, and the gender and approximate ages of the enslaved Africans. Personal names of the slaves were not recorded, however, which makes it impossible to locate the thirteen-year-old Anta on a specific ship, and thereby identify the name of its captain. The *Sally*, a schooner under command of Francis Ghisolfi, a ten-year veteran of the transit trade at Charlotte Amalie, merits consideration. Ghisolfi, an acquaintance of Kingsley, debarked 120 slaves at Havana, 99 of them female, including 22 teenage girls. This happened at a time when the normal gender ratio was two males to one female, and two other slave ships at Havana delivered all-male cargoes.[25]

What is known is that on October 10, 1806, Zephaniah Kingsley testified at the American consulate in Havana that he was the owner of "tres negras bozales," part of the cargo aboard his schooner, the *Esther*, anchored in the harbor waiting to sail to Charleston. A Spanish customs record reveals that the ship sailed instead to St. Augustine, East Florida, arriving October 21. Because the cargo manifest stated that the cargo was consigned to an American merchant at Charleston ("nothing being property of the owner of said vessel"), the *Esther* was sequestered in port until October 25, when import duties were assigned and the cargo, including three "new Negro females," was admitted into the province. Anta Majigeen Ndiaye was almost certainly one of the three.[26]

A vital related document has been found in the Spanish records of slave emancipations in East Florida. On March 4, 1811, four and one-half years after the *Esther* debarked its Havana cargo at Laurel Grove, Kingsley testified before a Spanish magistrate in St. Augustine that he "possessed as a slave a black woman called Anna, around eighteen years of age, bought as a bozal in the port of Havana from a slave cargo, who with the permission of the government was introduced there." He also testified that "the said black woman has given birth to three mulatto children: George, about 3 years 9 months, Martha, 20 months old, and Mary, one month old." Kingsley acknowledged that he was the father of Anna's three children and stated: "I have resolved to set her free . . . and the same to her three children."[27]

The final portion of Anta Majigeen Ndiaye's Middle Passage from Senegal to the Americas is explained in these Spanish documents. The evidence is conclusive that Zephaniah Kingsley purchased Anta as a slave at Havana in late September 1806, fathered children by her, and freed her in 1811. What needs further investigation is whether Kingsley saw Anta Ndiaye in Africa before he purchased her at Havana and whether he was involved in her purchase and transport across the Atlantic.

Kingsley was based at Charlotte Amalie and involved in the transit trade in enslaved Africans during the summer and fall of 1806. The Danish port city had been his place of residence between 1798 and 1803, and he continued to conduct business there until 1809. For decades, large ships with slave cargoes acquired in Africa anchored in the harbor at Charlotte Amalie to off-load their human cargoes to smaller vessels for delivery to markets throughout the Americas. Kingsley participated in that trade, and he also delivered human cargoes off-loaded at Charlotte Amalie to Havana. The cargo of forty-three male slaves that Kingsley's ship registered at Havana on September 18, 1806, was no doubt acquired at Charlotte Amalie.

It is theoretically possible that Kingsley was at Gorée Island in the summer of 1806 at the same time that Anta Majigeen Ndiaye was incarcerated there. That would match with the assertion found in an essay published by the abolitionist Lydia Maria Child, editor between 1841 and 1843 of the *National Anti-Slavery Standard*. Already familiar with Kingsley's monograph, *A Treatise on the Patriarchal*, Child arranged an interview with the author when she learned he was in New York in 1842. According to Child's published account of their conversation, she and the former slave trader fenced back and forth, Kingsley acknowledging his visits to the "coast of Africa" and involvement in "the slave trade [for] several years." He confirmed that he still owned a large number of slaves and advocated amalgamation of the races. In the most relevant exchange, Child asked: "Where did you become acquainted with your wife?" Kingsley responded: "On the coast of Africa, ma'am. She was a new nigger, when I first saw her."[28]

The quotation is troubling and possibly inaccurate. Child's phrasing may have served her didactic purpose and matched her conception of a slave trader, but it seems out of character for Kingsley. A veteran of the slave trade would not have labeled an African who was then in Africa a "new nigger." The term is comparable to "new Negro" in English and "bozal" in Spanish and would only have been applicable to Kingsley's "wife" when she was at Havana or Florida, in which case Kingsley would have said she was "*from* the coast of Africa, ma'am." Changing, or inaccurately hearing, only one word could, in this instance, have had distorting consequences.

However, if the quotation was accurate it means that Kingsley saw Anta Ndiaye at Gorée Island weeks before he purchased her at Havana. This eventuality makes the following section of Kingsley's Last Will and Testament, dated July 1843, highly relevant. Kingsley expressed concern about how American territorial laws would "consider my acknowledged wife, Anna Madgigine Jai, as our connubial relations took place in a foreign land, where our marriage was celebrated and solemnized by her native African customs altho' never celebrated according to the forms of Christian usage." The harbor at Havana was in 1843 a foreign land for a Florida resident, and so was Gorée Island.[29]

Information to resolve this dilemma would be expected to exist in the registries of slave ships arriving at Charlotte Amalie from Africa in 1806, but these records have not been found at the National Archive of Denmark. Were they available, it might be possible to clarify whether or not Kingsley was part of the crew that purchased Anta Ndiaye at Gorée, since the odds are high that she was transported from Senegal on a ship that off-loaded its cargo to smaller ships at Charlotte Amalie, from where the smaller ship carrying her proceeded to Havana.

Rumors and legends of Anna Madgigine Jai Kingsley are abundant, and they continue to be created. The legends concern her origins in Africa, how she came to be enslaved and transported to the Americas, and her relationship with Kingsley. Although she testified that she was from Senegal, and Kingsley described her as "jet black," legend makers have characterized her as from Madagascar, as a woman of "Arabian" descent, and as a person of mixed racial ancestry. The most persistent legend situates Kingsley in Africa—at different locations depending on the legend—bargaining with a king for the purchase of slaves. During negotiations, the king is said to have arranged the marriage of his daughter to Kingsley and provided a dowry of numerous slaves. Even thirty-five years after Kingsley's death, a journalist traveling in northeast Florida heard rumors of "an African princess twelve years of age presented to [Kingsley] by her father. He brought her to America, gave her some little education, and took her to his bed." The actual story of Anna Kingsley's life is more tragic than the romantic fantasy found in the legends; its basic outline is now known, although some pieces of the puzzle will always be missing.[30]

Anna Kingsley's contemporaries in East Florida, those who lived near Laurel Grove, testified years later that she was always treated as a free woman. John M. Bowden, a white planter residing east of the St. Johns River, testified in the 1830s that he had known Anna Kingsley "from the time she first came into the country and she was always called and considered a free person of color." She lived apart from the other slaves, either in Kingsley's residence or in a separate dwelling nearby. In time she was assigned control of domestic matters in Kingsley's household, and according to contemporary witnesses and to Kingsley himself, her authority was gradually enhanced to include temporary management duties.[31]

One year after she was emancipated, Anna Jai and her children moved from Laurel Grove to a five-acre homestead at the "Horse Landing," located across from Laurel Grove on the east bank of the St. Johns River. Kingsley sent enslaved carpenters to construct a two-story home plus additional dwellings for two men, three women, and seven children, all slaves owned by Anna. Less than one year after her own emancipation, Anna had become a slave owner. It may have seemed improbable to neighbors that a nineteen-year-old African woman, only recently released from slavery, would so quickly hold others in bondage, but in Anna Jai's homeland and in the family compounds of her father and uncles, slavery was integral to the social fabric. From her subsequent record as a slave owner, which lasted into the 1860s, there is no evidence that she was anything less than committed to the propriety of the institution of slavery.[32]

Anna Jai was not the only free black woman in Spanish East Florida to own land and human property. Although concentrated at St. Augustine, free black property owners could be found throughout the province. Under Spanish law all persons, whether free or enslaved, male or female, white or black or brown, were believed to be creations of God, who gave each person a soul and a moral personality. The enslaved differed from free persons only in that they were considered the victims of fate or war, and they were all granted rights that were enforced by the provincial courts. Sanctity of marriage, the right to be emancipated for meritorious actions, and the right to purchase one's own freedom were among these rights. Enslaved persons were able to work at extra jobs after their prescribed duties were completed and to use the wages earned to purchase their freedom. Slave status was temporary and changeable, not a status preordained by God or human action. An enslaved person could be freed by self-purchase or by an owner, and as a freed person he or she possessed the right to own property, including human property.[33]

Anna Jai was one of several free black women in Spanish East Florida holding title to land and to enslaved persons. She undoubtedly encountered

racist individuals, but prejudice was not built into the legal, religious, or social fabric of Spanish Florida society as it was in the American states across
the border. As a free black woman, Anna was able to own property, testify
in court, initiate legal action, and operate a business. As a convert to Catholicism, she had access to the sacraments of the church and could form
extended kinship and patron networks by choosing influential godparents
for her children.

After Kingsley returned to Laurel Grove Plantation with his cargo of "tres
negras bozales," he participated briefly in management of his growing agricultural enterprise. There were undoubtedly numerous consultations with
his manager, Abraham Hanahan, the enslaved mixed-race man who had
been reared in Kingsley's father's household in Charleston. It was unusual,
although not unprecedented in Florida, for an enslaved man to exercise authority during the crucial startup years of a major slave plantation. Kingsley
had repeatedly failed in efforts to hire a white manager, and his brother-in-
law George Gibbs had searched for an overseer for Laurel Grove from 1804
through 1806. Gibbs feared that Kingsley's property would become "much
neglected" while he was involved in the Mozambique venture.[34]

Kingsley's participation in management at Laurel Grove lasted only
until February 21, 1807, when he left for St. Thomas. He stopped first at
Savannah to unload a cargo of forty-three bales of cotton harvested at Laurel Grove, then turned command of his ship over to Henry Wright and
booked passage to Baltimore in another effort to collect outstanding debts
from his previous business dealings in Saint-Domingue. He traveled next
to New York City, arriving on May 10 for a three-week visit with his mother
and sisters before departing for St. Thomas as a passenger aboard Captain
Bartlett's ship, the *Libra*. He arrived at Charlotte Amalie on June 26, 1807,
and in the next several months he traveled back and forth from St. Thomas
to St. Croix and Tortola (the largest of the British Virgin Islands). He purchased two more schooners, the *San Juan* (aka the *Welaka*) and the *Industria*, and returned to East Florida on March 24, 1808, at the helm of the *San
Juan*. Captain Giles Mumford returned in command of the *Industria*, carrying "ten bozal Negroes for [Kingsley's] plantation, slaves of both sexes,"
bushels of salt, pipes of Catalan wine, and miscellaneous items.[35]

Kingsley traveled again to St. Thomas in July 1808. A few days after arriving he was cleared for departure aboard the *Industria* by a British naval officer. His previous experiences and business contacts at St. Thomas were of little assistance during this visit: British naval forces had seized the island on December 21, 1807, and begun an eight-year occupation of Denmark's Virgin Island colonies. The transit trade in enslaved Africans previously tolerated in the harbor at Charlotte Amalie had been terminated. Kingsley departed on July 27 for Savannah with his ship in ballast.[36]

He entered the St. Johns River again on August 24, 1808, and registered at the customs post at San Vicente Ferrer (today known as St. Johns Bluff) as owner and captain of the schooner *San Juan*. At some port, probably Savannah, Kingsley and one of his hired captains had exchanged ships. Manuel Romero, the Spanish customs inspector, reported to the governor that the *San Juan* carried only miscellaneous items, and he made a special notation that the crew members were all enslaved black men owned by Kingsley. These same six men, while still enslaved, would comprise Kingsley's sailing crew for the next several years. As the historian W. Jeffrey Bolster points out in his book *Black Jacks*, black seamen were far from a rarity on ships sailing the Atlantic in the early nineteenth century.[37]

Kingsley remained at Laurel Grove for only a few weeks, long enough to procreate a second child with Anna Madgigine, Martha, born in June 1809. Kingsley maintained a hectic pace of maritime travel between East Florida and Havana throughout 1809, stopping only long enough to exchange one cargo for another. He transported rum, coffee, sugar, agricultural tools, and items of clothing, primarily merchant goods suitable for resale. Later, Kingsley built an elaborate retail store at Laurel Grove. Spanish East Florida customs records for 1804 through 1809 document several ships owned by Kingsley, under command of various captains, transporting dozens of cargoes of merchant goods from Savannah, Charleston, Baltimore, Norfolk, and other American coastal cities to East Florida. Henry Wright, Juan Friac, Antonio Sabulache, and Giles Mumford worked for Kingsley as ship captains in charge of the *Esther*, *Laurel*, *San Juan*, *Industria*, and *Isabel*.

Anna Kingsley's five-acre homestead was adapted as a retail establishment for merchandise Kingsley brought into the province. Kingsley's former associate Henry Wright had previously applied for title to the Horse Landing property but failed to complete the process. From his retail store at Laurel Grove, Kingsley dispatched boats to peddle merchandise to farms along the river. From Anna Jai's homestead he expanded his business to farms east of the river.[38]

Kingsley was well aware that flying the flag of Spain was at that time beneficial for trade in the Caribbean, and even in American ports after the U.S. government imposed the embargo on its own commercial vessels. American consuls at Cuban ports had repeatedly warned the secretary of state that French privateers were swarming off the Cuban coast and bringing dozens of American ships to admiralty courts for confiscation. In 1805 an American consul at St. Yago denounced the "scenes of robbery, destruction, evasion, perjury, cruelty and insult" he had witnessed when American ships were brought into Cuban ports. Similar complaints were voiced by U.S. consuls at St. Thomas and at Martinique about the British squadrons blockading Caribbean ports and seizing the American ships that were later condemned before admiralty courts.[39]

Kingsley had anticipated these events, and with American ships idled by the Embargo Act he took full advantage of the enhanced trade opportunities for ships flying Spanish flags. For the time being, his plantation would have to operate under the management of Abraham Hanahan and his assistant manager, a fifty-year-old enslaved African named Peter.

7 | Laurel Grove Plantation, Slavery, and East Florida's Booming Economy

When Kingsley's ship was secured to the wharf at Laurel Grove in March 1808, the total number of slaves he imported for his plantation was seventy-four. Four years later the number of "fully taskable hands" (healthy men and women capable of a full day of labor) had increased to one hundred, in addition to the children. Nearly all the adults were "new Africans" who were immediately thrown into a confusing world of strangers, ordered to clear land, plant and harvest crops, and construct dwellings, barns, and storage buildings.[1]

Information concerning daily life and labor at the plantation is exceedingly sparse until June 1810, when an incident occurred that pitted two of Kingsley's enslaved managers against armed white planters of the St. Johns River militia. On June 4, militiamen conducted raids along the St. Johns River in search of weapons rumored to be hidden in slave dwellings at several plantations. After experiencing "little interruption while the Negroes were at work in the field," the mounted raiders confiscated forty-one guns which they brought back to militia headquarters at the Cowford on the St. Johns River (today Jacksonville's central business district).[2]

When the militiamen rode into the residential quarters at Laurel Grove, Kingsley was not in residence. They were met instead by two enslaved men who claimed to be the managers of the property during Kingsley's absence. The senior manager, Abraham Hanahan, ordered the mounted troopers to leave. Supported in protest by a second black man, named Peter, Hanahan confronted militia members as they searched the plantation's slave quarters and confiscated eleven guns. According to one of the militiamen, Abraham used "improper language [and] conduct" as he demanded that the militiamen return a gun they confiscated from him. When told the militia acted under orders of government and must be obeyed, Abraham said he would "go and see Mr. [William] Craig [the judicial official in charge of the St. Johns River district] and that if he did not give him satisfaction he would go to governor [Henry] White, that he would speak his mind to him and that he might send him to the guard house to the fort or to the Devil that he did not care."[3]

Hanahan went the following day to the home of militia member Andrew Maclean. In front of witnesses, he once again stated that "he was going to the governor and that he did not fear going to the stocks nor anywhere else for he would have his gun." Andrew Atkinson heard Abraham declare that neither "Mr. Craig, the governor or anybody else had any right to interfere with his master's plantation."[4]

The two black managers continued their protest at a June 6 meeting of area planters and militia members held at the Cowford Ferry. They appeared outside the meeting hall, with Peter boldly demanding the return of his personal weapon and becoming irritated when the white men refused. He allegedly declared loudly that "things would take a turn and . . . Negroes would yet have their arms."[5] This was more black protest than the white planters and slave owners would tolerate. After hearing what they claimed were "very improper and disrespectful expressions used in the [presence of white men] by a Mulatto man [Hanahan] . . . and the expressions of disrespect and insubordination uttered by an old Negro man named Peter," Craig had the men manacled and marched to St. Augustine.[6]

Two influential white planters angered by the raids wrote to Governor Henry White demanding compensation for weapons confiscated from slaves at their St. Johns River plantations. George Fleming, a prominent Irish-born planter and militia officer who had been in East Florida since 1790, claimed the armaments seized from his enslaved men were used for "defense and security [against] savage indians, [and] animals eating corn." María del Carmen Hill Sánchez, the widow of wealthy Florida-born planter and merchant Francisco Xavier Sánchez, warned of "dangers now due to lack of firearms" and said her enslaved workers "must have weapons to keep animals away from planted seeds."

Craig had ordered the militia raids in an atmosphere of hysteria prompted by rumors of a pending slave insurrection in Georgia. In early April, rumors had begun circulating of "secret correspondence subsisting betwixt the Negroes and a mulatto man named Morris who had lately come in from Georgia," after reports spread of his "active encourage[ment] of the intended Insurrection there." Even more frightening stories made the rounds: planters heard tales of more than one hundred Florida slaves who owned guns, and reports of behavior "more Insolent and disobedient than usual." Convinced they had stemmed a potential disaster and that further vigilance was needed, militia members brushed aside protests from whites as well as blacks and made plans for further raids on plantations.[7]

Hanahan and Peter were incarcerated in St. Augustine and tried before a judicial tribunal. Hanahan insisted his actions were justified by the authority placed in him by his owner, Zephaniah Kingsley. As first manager, he was responsible for Kingsley's estate and his one hundred enslaved Africans, yet the soldiers had ignored him and instead demanded "keys to all the habitations from a female slave in charge of all the interior interests of our master and as she . . . did not have it in her power . . . they broke the doors of the houses of the Negroes [and destroyed] as much as it was their pleasure to trample."[8] The tribunal instead focused on the charges of insubordination and found the two men guilty. Governor White sentenced the two men to "fifty lashes to each one . . . [and] forced labor for one month in chains or shackles" to "make them understand and observe due submission and respect to the magistrates."[9]

The events surrounding the militia raid of 1810 reveal a troubled and divided white community. Settlers experienced economic hardship and chronic instability in the first years after Spain resumed control of East Florida in 1783. Reforms instituted in the 1790s prompted an influx of migrants and brought improved economic conditions, but in 1794 the gains were interrupted when Governor Juan Nepomuceno de Quesada reacted to an invasion threat with a scorched-earth policy that devastated settlements north and west of St. Augustine and weakened the new settlers' loyalty. Free black militia companies were effective in stemming that threat, and in 1800–1803 also helped defeat William Augustus Bowles and an Anglo-Creek invasion force that attacked Spanish forts and settlements.[10]

To the recent white migrants from Georgia and South Carolina, dependence on a nonwhite militia raised great fears. Bitterness lingered from the Spanish sanctuary policy that allowed slaves who escaped from the British North American colonies and professed their adherence to Catholicism to remain in Florida and join free *pardo* (mixed-race) and *moreno* (black) militia companies. In 1738, Gracia Real de Santa Teresa de Mose, a new town for blacks who were granted sanctuary, had been established two miles north of St. Augustine. The sanctuary policy served as a beacon of freedom for escaped slaves, infuriating British planters and public officials in Georgia and South Carolina. When the Spanish returned to govern Florida again in 1783 after twenty years of British rule, the sanctuary policy was reinstituted and Florida again beckoned to blacks seeking self-liberation. The sanctuary policy was finally terminated in 1790 under an agreement negotiated by Secretary of State Thomas Jefferson and the Spanish government.[11]

Another vexing problem for slave owners was the bloody revolution on the island of Saint-Domingue that eventually drove the French away and ushered in the free black state of Haiti. In East Florida those fears became more acute after General Jorge Biassou arrived in St. Augustine from Saint-Domingue in 1796 and took command of a black militia company. Biassou, a former military leader of an army of former slaves during the rebellion in Saint-Domingue, had allied with Spain and commanded an army of forty thousand men. One of his subordinates was Touissant Louverture. After Spain and France agreed to peace terms in 1795, Biassou, his family, and fellow officers were sent by Spain to the troubled East Florida frontier. The historian Jane G. Landers has described the effective military service Biassou and his black troops provided the government in East Florida, but the presence of a "decorated, militant, independent, and propertied" black man who "fought his way out of slavery in the hemisphere's bloodiest revolution" greatly alarmed Florida slave owners. They feared Biassou and his free black militia fighters would incite unrest among their own slaves.[12]

Spanish governors also relied on Seminole warriors from the nearby Alachua Prairie for military support, which further troubled the province's white planters, especially migrants from Georgia who had experienced troubles with Creek Indians in their former homes. Others feared that slave runaways who found sanctuary in Seminole territory would tempt other slaves to abscond. East Florida in 1810 was a promising frontier area with

huge reserves of undeveloped land. The fact that the Spanish governor depended on black militia and Indian allies for security created an unsettling
prospect for white slave owners recently migrated from the United States.[13]

In the decade preceding the militia raid of June 1810, planters had experienced record prosperity from exports of lumber, cotton, and rice. The slave
population increased dramatically following the 1790 decision by Spanish
officials to open East Florida's borders to foreign and non-Catholic immigrants and to implement a land grant policy. Between 1790 and 1804 approximately 750 immigrant heads of family took loyalty oaths in St. Augustine,
270 of them slave owners claiming nearly five thousand bondsmen. Most
migrants came from the American states along the southeast coast. More
than eight in ten were of British origin. Another 10 percent were of French
ancestry, including refugees from the slave rebellion in Saint-Domingue.[14]

The Georgia planter John H. McIntosh brought more than two hundred
slaves. The Scot-born slave trader John Fraser imported hundreds of workers directly from Africa. After the international trade in enslaved Africans
was banned in the English and Danish colonies and in the United States,
slave traders moved to Florida and other Spanish territories where the
trade was still permitted.

The combination of huge reserves of unclaimed land and a booming
agricultural export market drew slave owners as well as settlers who purchased inexpensive African slaves after pledging loyalty to Spain. The result was black and enslaved population majorities at St. Augustine, Amelia
Island, and along the St. Johns, St. Marys, Nassau, and Mosquitoes Rivers. Planters in need of laborers eagerly purchased the Africans as they arrived at Fernandina and St. Augustine, but always there was fear of slave
rebellion. Fear easily became hysteria at remote frontier estates with black
slave majorities, as the 1810 militia raids on the St. Johns River plantations
illustrate.[15]

Kingsley and other planters who had resided in East Florida for several
years and supported Spanish laws governing slavery and racial policies generally welcomed the protection provided by the black militiamen and the
province's Seminole allies. By 1810, however, Kingsley and his counterparts
were living amid recent migrants from Georgia and other American states
who opposed Spanish race policies. American frontiersmen had been drift-
ing westward into Spain's West Florida and Louisiana territories as well

as south into East Florida. As early as 1787, East Florida governor Vicente Manuel de Zéspedes had warned that an expansionist-oriented American government might act through its former citizens to foment rebellion and call for annexation by the United States. Georgia's population nearly doubled between 1790 and 1800 (from 82,540 to 161,667), and climbed to more than 250,000 by 1810. With land values in Georgia rising in step with population, planters hungry for affordable land viewed the vast unpopulated expanses of land in the Florida territories with envy.[16]

The 1810 militia action was a direct consequence of the disparate attitudes of the established settlers and the recent migrants from the United States. The plantation raids revealed a deeply divided white community, but the immediate impact was negligible for planters, who were experiencing generally prosperous times. That was not the case for Abraham Hanahan and Peter, who each suffered the lashes of a jailer's whip and forced-labor incarceration. Both men returned to Laurel Grove after being released from confinement, but they were no longer in charge of the plantation. In the aftermath of the insurrection hysteria of 1810, Kingsley was pressured to employ a white manager at Laurel Grove.[17]

Kingsley emancipated Hanahan in March 1811 and gave him a plot of land at Laurel Grove. John M. Bowden, a white planter who lived across the St. Johns at today's Mandarin, said that Hanahan "marked off and called his own place" a plot of land where he built a home and outbuildings, grazed cattle, and raised poultry and hogs. Bowden's neighbor, Rebecca E. Read, called Hanahan "a good Spanish citizen" and, like Bowden, thought that he was a free man upon arrival in Florida in 1804. After being emancipated, Hanahan continued to assist with management at Laurel Grove; he also became an independent farmer and traveling merchant employed by Kingsley to peddle supplies from a retail store at Laurel Grove to farms on the St. Johns. His wife, Sophy Chidgigane, and their children, still the enslaved property of Kingsley, lived with him at Laurel Grove.[18]

In 1811 Kingsley acquired two additional tracts of land: Drayton Island and White Oak. Drayton Island was a two-thousand-acre experimental coffee plantation located in Lake George and the St. Johns River. Kingsley at first rented the island from Charles Sibbald, a Fernandina merchant. In 1811 he gained title from Sibbald's widow, Jane Sibbald, for satisfaction of debts. Title to White Oak on the St. Marys River, a vacant thousand-acre tract that had been a rice plantation during East Florida's British years, was a land grant from Governor White as compensation for African laborers Kingsley brought into the province.

Kingsley's operations thrived until invaders from Georgia crossed into Florida in March 1812 to claim the Spanish province as theirs by right of conquest and rename it the Republic of Florida. The invasion force, consisting of American soldiers and sailors and land-hungry adventurers, was joined by East Florida residents who had recently migrated from Georgia and South Carolina. The invasion was characterized by renegade bands of plunderers intent on self-enrichment through violence and theft, although the publicly announced goal was annexation of East Florida to the United States. The so-called Patriot War caused the destruction of most of the family farms and major plantations in the province. Between July 1812 and November 1813, Laurel Grove Plantation was destroyed by Seminole warriors acting in league with the Spanish colonial government to drive the invaders out of Florida.

Kingsley compiled a remarkably detailed inventory of property destroyed and stolen during the violence at Laurel Grove. He lost dwellings, barns and other farm structures, and agricultural fields and citrus groves, all put to the torch by the warriors. Forty-three enslaved laborers were abducted, and two others were murdered. The inventory makes it possible to re-create the basic features of his estate and the Africans who populated it For names, ages, gender, family units, and ethic origins of most of the slaves lost to the raiders see appendix A.[19]

Nine different witnesses gave testimony during the investigation. They established that in July 1812 approximately one hundred "full task hands" worked at Laurel Grove. Neighboring planters judged them to be "prime" workers. The workers and their spouses and children lived in family units in dwellings located at three separate agricultural villages on the three-thousand-acre property, cultivating long-staple cotton, orange groves, and fields of corn, peas, and sweet potatoes. The storage bins held nearly three thousand bushels of corn immediately prior to the attack on the plantation. An abundance of provisions, hogs, poultry, and cattle were raised at each of the three villages. Hay meadows scattered in clearings amid the uncleared reserves of pine and oak forests produced fodder for the draft animals.[20]

The largest of the three agricultural villages, the Laurel Grove Settlement, was an elaborate complex of eighteen hundred acres that extended north and south along the St. Johns River for two miles and west along Doctors Lake for one mile. Two dwelling houses, probably located in the vicinity of the present site of Club Continental off Kingsley Avenue in the city of Orange Park, were destroyed. The first was "a good frame building measuring thirty by thirty-five feet with double piazzas and brick chimneys." Contents of the dwelling included "a large quantity of household and kitchen furniture, beds . . . and one spring shuttle loom." A detached kitchen stood nearby.

In 1812 Kingsley had ordered a second two-story wood-frame building constructed in the same general vicinity. Measuring thirty-six by forty feet, this building with "cedar shingles" and "brick chimneys" functioned as a retail store on the first floor and a residence on the second. The residence held "a quantity of furniture and beds, valuable books, charts, and crockery ware." Kingsley said the retail store "contained a large supply of every article for plantation and family use and was kept for the supply of the surrounding country." An inventory of the store's contents valued the supplies at $2,685 (at least $83,400 today). A nearby wood-frame warehouse, measuring twenty-six by thirty feet, was stocked with 1,500 bushels of salt, 120 gallons of Jamaican rum, sugar from Havana, barrels of gunpowder, and other items for retail sale, and valued at $2,780.[21]

Kingsley must have feared violent attacks on his property at the time the new building was constructed, as he surrounded it with a seven-foot-high vertical log barricade. Inside the enclosure he situated ten muskets with bayonets, two 4-pounder cannons with carriages, and cartridges, iron balls, and grapeshot.

Near the two dwellings stood a framed barn measuring thirty by forty feet that stored bales of cotton harvested from fields at all three settlements on the estate. Sixty bales of ginned cotton from the 1811 harvest (seeds removed), weighing 21,000 pounds, were stored for transportation to Charleston. With long-staple cotton selling for fifty cents a pound at the time, Kingsley expected the bales to bring $10,500. An additional 30,000 pounds of "unginned" cotton (seeds still attached) from the 1810 crop was still on hand, estimated to be worth fifteen cents a pound, or $4,500. Only 200 acres were planted in cotton in 1812, but Kingsley and expert witnesses predicted a yield of 200 to 300 pounds per acre, or 40,000 pounds, worth $20,000 when ginned and baled.

To clean the seeds from the cotton fiber, Kingsley had purchased three double-size cotton gins at a cost of $250 each (nearly $12,000 now) and installed them in a large gin house. A large waterwheel measuring forty feet in diameter provided power for the cotton gins. It is possible that the wheel was powered by tidal waters on the St. Johns River, but more likely the source of power was water diverted from a creek that fed into the St. Johns. The waterwheel and gin house were likely located at the Springfield settlement, where a stream with a larger flow of water existed that could power the mill. The naturalist John Bartram and his son William Bartram visited the Springfield site in February 1765 and described the stream as "half a mile or more broad, and 6 or 7 long; at the head of which is a large creek. . . . On the west side there is a hamock of oak, hiccory, magnolia, and hornbeam, and a fine spring of clear water almost big enough to turn a mill, boiling up from under the main body of the country rocks."[22]

Three additional wood-frame mill houses were installed to accommodate mills to grind flour and meal for weekly rations, as well as a barn measuring twenty-five by forty feet. In July 1812, 800 bushels of corn and 300 bushels of peas were in the barn. The remaining structures included a wood-frame carpenter shop measuring thirty by forty feet where coopers manufactured barrels. It contained saws, drills, axes, hatchets, adzes, planes, and augers. Another workshop, operated by the slave blacksmith Montarro, was equipped with two pair of bellows and two anvils, along with mauls, froes, grindstones, and other expensive tools. Kingsley described Montarro as a "very prime young man" and valued him at $1,000. There was also a fodder house and a cart house with three carts, three plows, and harnesses. Kingsley lamented the loss of twelve "good Negro houses" that were burned, along with clothing, furniture, and work tools.

The secondary commercial crop at the Laurel Grove settlement was citrus. A nine-acre grove with 750 choice mandarin orange trees was located near the dwelling houses, surrounded by a two-thousand-foot "bearing orange hedge," which in turn was enclosed by a twelve-foot-high cypress picket fence. Two men worked for three months installing the picket fence. The same men worked for another four months constructing a rail fence extending thirty miles around all of the fields and buildings.

The second village on Kingsley's property, called interchangeably Ship Yard and Canefield, was located north of Doctors Lake, approximately two miles west of the St. Johns River. The shipyard revolved around a workshop measuring twenty by thirty feet that was equipped with a large steaming stove and kettle. The flats and boats used at the plantation were built and repaired at this shipyard. Kingsley received government permission to import shipbuilders and to construct oceangoing vessels for his commercial trade. A dwelling house, a storehouse, a twenty-by-thirty-foot blacksmith shop, three grindstones and stands, and nine slave houses—all surrounded by live oak trees—completed the structures at Ship Yard settlement. The dual names—Ship Yard and Canefield—suggest that sugarcane was planted on the north shore of Doctors Lake, a practice followed by a subsequent owner of the property, John H. McIntosh.[23]

Springfield was the third agricultural settlement at Laurel Grove. Located west and north of the shipyard at Doctors Lake, Springfield was devoted to the cultivation of cotton, corn, and peas. The manager was the enslaved black man named Peter who joined with Hanahan in protest at the militia raids in 1810; Kingsley described him as a "mechanic and valuable manager." At age fifty-two, Peter was the oldest enslaved person listed on the inventory, yet he was considered so important to operations that he was valued at $1,000.

Buildings at Springfield included a barn that stored 700 bushels of corn and 400 bushels of peas in 1812. The mill house produced rations for the forty working hands living at fifteen "new Negro houses." Kingsley's inventory listed four stacks of fodder, 150 hogs, and fifteen dozen ducks and chickens destroyed during the Seminole raid.

Laurel Grove Plantation was completed in less than a decade and represents a considerable achievement created by the labor of approximately one hundred enslaved Africans. It included four dwelling houses for owners and managers, thirty-six houses for the laborers and their children, wells, waterwheels, tools and farm implements, two well-equipped blacksmith shops, a shipyard, retail store, barns and other storage buildings, stocks of poultry, hogs, cattle, and horses, and a network of roads and fences, citrus trees, provisions, and cotton fields. Laurel Grove was an agricultural factory with three African villages transplanted to the East Florida countryside.

Kingsley's inventory is an invaluable document. It left behind evidence of the dwellings, agricultural fields, farm structures, and industries the workers engaged in, along with valuable information about the enslaved Africans who were brought to East Florida. Without the inventory, Kingsley's Africans would have joined millions of anonymous victims of the Atlantic slave trade who perished without leaving behind a personal identity.

Kingsley's inventory contains the name, age, gender, family affiliation, occupation, and presumed ethnic or regional origin of each enslaved laborer (or child of) abducted or killed during the July 1812 raid on Laurel Grove. The inventory makes it possible to give a personal identification to otherwise anonymous Africans in the North American diaspora and to place them within the families and community they created. It also permits a partial reconstruction of the first slave community owned by Kingsley and to imagine the complex process of cultural adjustment and culture-building at a major colonial plantation.[24]

One striking feature of the men and women on the list is how young they were: the median age was twenty-four; nineteen were children (twelve boys and seven girls) between two and eight years of age. The remaining twenty-two were adults between twenty-four and forty-eight years of age. Seven of the thirteen adult males were between twenty-four and thirty, four were between thirty-two and thirty-six, one was forty, and "Old Paul" was forty-eight. All nine adult females were between twenty-five and thirty. With the exception of the two eldest men, the adults were all rated "prime" or "very prime" workers.

Four other enslaved men were listed on Kingsley's inventory of lost property. "Driver Peter, a mechanic and valuable manager," age fifty-two, and "Montarro, the blacksmith, a very prime young man," age not listed, were both killed at Laurel Grove during the July 1812 attack. Pablo, age forty-five, and Juan, thirty, were abducted from Drayton Island, located upriver from Laurel Grove at Lake George in what is today Putnam County. Pablo and Juan previously lived and worked at Laurel Grove.

If this is a representative sample, Kingsley was the owner of a young and valuable slave community that was rapidly increasing in numbers through the birth of children born in the family compounds. Nine men lived in households with a woman designated as "his wife," of which eight households contained one to four children from two to eight years old. Only one household was childless. Two men were carpenters, one was a driver, and another was a sailor. The women as well as the men were field laborers.[25]

It is important to point out that the adult men and women were all born in Africa. Nearly half of the twenty-two adults retained African names, while all but two of the twenty-nine children were listed with Anglicized names. Eight adult males and their wives were listed as natives of the Niger River delta region in southeastern Nigeria in West Africa: six "Eabo," four "New Calabar," and six "Calabari." Two males, both carpenters, and one female were labeled "Zinguebari," which probably reflects that Kingsley purchased them on the Zanguebar coast of East Africa in 1805. Three males (including Juan from Drayton Island) were from the region of Guinea on the West African coast: two were "Soo Soo" (Susu today), an ethnic group living near the Atlantic and along the coastal rivers; a woman listed as "Rio Pongo" may also have been Susu or from the neighboring Baga, Landuman, or Nalu people. The historian George Brooks has suggested that "Man Cabo Mouse" may have been a head boatman, with the name a combination of the Portuguese word *cabo*, for "chief" or "headman," and the French word *mousse*, for "cabin boy" or "ship boy." Cabo Mouse may have come from Bissau or Cacheu, ports at what is today Guinea-Bissau (formerly Portuguese Guinea).[26]

The inventory supports Kingsley's claim that he encouraged his workers to live in family units. Husband-and-wife combinations, judging from the ages of the nineteen children on the list, must have occurred soon after the Africans arrived at Laurel Grove, or possibly before. Jack and Tamassa, parents of two sons and two daughters, were listed as "Man Jack, Zinguebari, carpenter, very prime, 30," and "Woman Tamassa, his wife, very prime, 28." By listing "Zinguebari," Kingsley identified Jack and Tamassa as natives of East Africa, possibly selected from the cargo of the *Gustavia* at Charleston in April 1806. The age of their eldest son, "Boy Ben . . . 8 to 9," suggests he was born in East Africa prior to the tragic events leading to their enslavement. The name of their youngest son, M'toto, is the word for "boy" in Swahili, the common language of trade along the East African coast for centuries. The name of the second "Zinquebari" carpenter, M'Sooma, has been tentatively identified as a "Kamba" name. The identification was made by a man born in Kenya who now lives in Miami, Florida; he stated that people with the name "M'Sooma" still live at a village located at the headwaters of the Tana River.[27]

Jacob and Camilla made up another of the family units: he was "Eabo," she was from "Rio Pongo," possibly a Susu or Baga. They were parents of Jim, who learned the Igbo language of his Nigerian Delta homeland, and Susu, a Mande language spoken in his mother's home village in Guinea. For each family unit other than Jacob and Camilla, only the male was specifically assigned an African identity, but the listing order—male first, female second—suggests the female shared the male's ethnic and regional background.

Diversity was a key feature of daily life in the slave quarters, with numerous languages spoken each day and great cultural variations in food preparation, hair styles, songs, musical instruments, facial markings, and perhaps clothing when it wasn't supplied by the owner. It is fascinating to imagine children at play or engaged in light tasks under supervision of an older woman, conversing in several African languages, laughing perhaps at the "strange" words Jim used when he mixed his father's Igbo and his mother's Susu words as he spoke. As they played and conversed, however, using words from East and West African languages, with English and Spanish words thrown in, they were unknowingly engaged in the process of constructing a creole language that would be used by Kingsley's enslaved workers over the next decades.

A June 1814 Spanish census of East Florida lists Kingsley with only twenty-one slaves still in his possession, but that is undoubtedly an incomplete count. Kingsley customarily sent groups of enslaved men to work at distant properties he rented or owned, and by 1811 he held title to Drayton Island in today's Putnam County and to White Oak on the St. Marys River in Nassau County. Workers not in residence at the specific site where the census of human property was recorded would not have been counted. The names of Kingsley slaves listed on 1840s inventories— Bonafi, Qualla, Abdalla, Bella, Tamassa, Comba, Coonta, Tamba, Penda, Nassebo, Yamba, and Jenoma—suggest the continuing influence of Africans at Kingsley's estates. In addition, Anna Kingsley was an ethnic Wolof from today's Republic of Senegal, as was Sophy Chidgigane, the wife of Abraham Hanahan.[28]

Kingsley's inventory of Laurel Grove represents an effective challenge to the judgments of historians who have concluded that East Florida in the late eighteenth and early nineteenth centuries was a stagnant economic backwater in a disintegrating Spanish empire. Thomas Jefferson, James Monroe, James Madison, and other U.S. leaders saw Spanish East and West Florida and Louisiana standing in the way of America's destiny to expand the blessings of progress and democracy throughout North America. The historian David J. Weber has best addressed what he calls the "the Black Legend" among Anglo-American historians writing about Spanish North America. Kingsley's single example cannot counterbalance these cumulative negative judgments, but when combined with the recent insightful findings of the scholars Jane Landers, Frank Marotti Jr., and James G. Cusick, the misconceived legend crumbles.[29]

Landers's definitive study, *Black Society in Spanish East Florida*, makes it clear that Kingsley's investments in labor, machinery, work animals, and buildings and the wealth he accrued at Laurel Grove were far from unique among East Florida's planters. Beginning in the 1790s but expanding dramatically from 1800 to 1812, dozens of other proprietors established comparable estates. Francisco Xavier Sánchez, John Fraser, Francis Philip Fatio, John H. McIntosh, Andrew and George Atkinson, James Cashen, Francis Richard, and Farquhar Bethune are only a few of the planters who operated profitable estates.

Marotti's *Cana Sanctuary* and his *Heaven's Soldiers* are compelling examinations of the lives of the free people of African descent in St. Augustine and in antebellum East Florida. His exhaustive research in the underutilized manuscript sources of the Department of the Treasury at the National Archives adds greatly to understanding of the Spanish legacy of Florida's history. James Cusick, in *The Other War of 1812*, discusses the impact of the American soldiers, sailors, marauders, and bandits that joined in the destructive mayhem that characterized the so-called Patriot War of 1812–14. Relying on a huge array of American and Spanish primary sources, Cusick follows the invaders as they torched crops, buildings, machinery, and animals at small rural settlements and major plantations alike. The cumulative effect of the work of these three scholars is convincing support for Zephaniah Kingsley's contemporary remark that the decade preceding 1812 was East Florida's most profitable era.[30]

The following sample of plantations clustered near the juncture of the St. Johns River and the Atlantic Ocean illustrates the larger themes of plantation development and economic progress achieved in East Florida between 1800 and 1812. It also shows the overwhelming reliance of the landowners on enslaved African and African American laborers. Comparable estates existed elsewhere in the province, concentrated in what the historian Paul E. Hoffman has called the Atlantic "tidewater frontier" extending south from the St. Marys River to Mosquito Lagoon.[31]

Had a visitor explored this frontier in 1810, traveling by ship thirty miles up the St. Marys River and by horse from Fernandina to the southern tip of Amelia Island, several dozen small, medium, and large settlements would have been viewed. The traveler would also have seen thriving fields of long-staple cotton, the dikes and canals of rice fields, and plots of corn, peas, and beans. Interspersed along the waterways were timber camps where hundreds of black men worked with axes and saws and floated rafts of logs toward sawmills and the flotilla of ships anchored off Fernandina waiting for cargoes consigned to merchants at Liverpool.

Even more agricultural settlements and timber camps would have been viewed during a journey on the St. Johns River. A traveler on horseback bound for St. Augustine from the south bank of the St. Johns where it joins the Atlantic Ocean would have passed by dozens of settlements and several thousand head of cattle grazing on the prairie grasses. South of St. Augustine, settlements large and small abounded as well.

Travelers were often drawn to John H. McIntosh's East Florida plantations prior to 1812. McIntosh, an established planter in Camden County, Georgia, migrated to East Florida in 1803 accompanied by 180 enslaved men and women. He purchased additional workers after acquiring Fort George Island and Ortega Plantation on the St. Johns River. John McQueen, who owned these properties before McIntosh, had migrated to East Florida in 1791 with 280 slaves. At Fort George Island, McIntosh located 160 of his human properties, primarily women and children. Overseer John G. Rushing worked approximately eighty full-task hands in provisions and 300 acres of Sea Island cotton fields. At Ortega Plantation, McIntosh employed between thirty and forty men and women cultivating the same crops. Two framed cotton storehouses were constructed at Fort George Island, each measuring forty by fifty feet and costing $500. McIntosh was also accumulating a fortune via the labors of more than sixty enslaved black men and twelve white men at timber camps and a steam sawmill on the St. Marys River. His timbering operations brought in clear profits of $36,000 annually from exports to England.[32]

Spicer Christopher, an American-born farmer, arrived in the province in 1790 with a wife, two sons and two daughters, eighteen horses, and ten slaves. He settled at Talbot Island, immediately north of Fort George Island, to cultivate cotton and graze six hundred head of cattle with one hundred full-task slaves. He was wealthy enough to give his son Lewis Christopher a wedding present of a plantation on the St. Johns River complete with a newly constructed honeymoon home and farm buildings. A deathbed inventory of his property reveals that he still owned ninety-seven slaves in 1811.[33]

South of the entrance to the St. Johns River and east of Pablo Creek, John Forbes and John Leslie of John Forbes and Company owned the San Pablo Plantation. The firm specialized in trade with Native Americans but also owned 250 slaves and thousands of acres. An 1815 inventory listed 117 enslaved men, women, and children living in the quarters who cultivated cotton and provisions and herded cattle.

Zephaniah Kingsley was familiar with the estates in this vicinity of East Florida. He commented that the Philip Dewees plantation, located south of the St. Johns and bordering the San Pablo, was "a very productive place for cotton" and cattle and that Dewees was considered wealthy until 1812, when "the American troops and their allies swept the whole country of cattle, hogs, and stock . . . and drove them into camps." Eight of the enslaved men owned by Dewees were abducted and taken to Amelia Island. They attempted to escape and were drowned when their boat capsized.[34]

Further south at San Diego Plantation, Francisco Xavier Sánchez operated the best known of all the East Florida cattle ranches. Sánchez was born in East Florida during the first Spanish colonial administration, and he continued his tenure during East Florida's British years. When the Spanish returned in 1783 he prospered from cattle ranching, planting cotton, and partnering in a merchant firm. Sánchez died in 1807, but five years later his widow, Maria del Carmen Hill Sánchez, still held title to four of his plantations. During the 1812–14 uprising she lost property valued at $35,015

($1,225,525 today). Raiders abducted ninety-two slaves, 4,800 pounds of Sea Island cotton, 1,350 head of cattle, 380 hogs, and 27 horses.[35]

Four miles upriver from the entrance to the St. Johns, on the south bank immediately west of Pablo River, John Fraser established an elaborate 3,000-acre plantation known as Greenfield. Fraser, born in Scotland, was active in the Atlantic slave trade and the proprietor of a "slave factory" at Bangalan on the Pongo River (today north of Conakry in the Republic of Guinea). In 1799 he married an African woman named Phenda at Crawford's Island of the Isles de Los. Fraser purchased African victims of slave raids and wars in the interior of Guinea and transported them from his "factory" across the Atlantic in his own ships or sold them to other slavers who frequented the Pongo and Nunez Rivers.[36]

Fraser pledged loyalty to the United States and established a residence at Charleston in 1807, after Britain outlawed the African slave trade. He moved to East Florida in 1809, one year after the United States banned imports of enslaved Africans, and continued to travel between northeast Florida and West Africa. The reopening of slave imports to South Carolina in 1803 had prompted several Liverpool-based traders to relocate to Charleston during the final years of the American trade. Thomas Powell and William Lawson, Liverpool agents for John Fraser, moved back and forth between Liverpool, Pongo River, and Charleston. British citizen George Irving had an African family and a trading establishment at Pongo River and residences at Charleston and Liverpool. This was a time of flux for slavers as Denmark, England, and the United States moved to abolish the trade between 1803 and 1808. The American ban in 1808 prompted John McClure, a slave trader based at Charleston during the previous decade, to relocate his ships to Fernandina and to purchase the nearby Louisa Plantation.

Among the other men who migrated to the port of Fernandina, where it was still legal under Spanish law to import enslaved Africans, were Joseph Hibberson, Henry and Philip R. Yonge, James Wilson, Daniel O'Hara, James and George Taylor, and James English. When Denmark, Britain, and the United States banned the slave trade, hundreds of slaving ships were idled in American and Caribbean ports. The slaving firms that relocated to East Florida purchased surplus ships at auctions and moved them to Fernandina.[37]

Fraser's schooners continued to bring slaves across the Atlantic after his move to Florida, but his main project was acquiring laborers for his own plantations. On May 2, 1810, Governor White approved Fraser's petition for a grant of 500 acres on the St. Marys River known as the "Roundabout" for the circuitous path the river cut around the 300-acre peninsula its previous owner had turned into a rice field. The following year Fraser purchased a 3,000-acre cotton and provisions estate at St. Johns and Pablo Rivers known as "Taylor's Old Field" and renamed it Greenfield Plantation. His overseer at Greenfield, Francis Richard, said Fraser brought "one hundred thousand dollars in hand, in negroes and other effects" to East Florida.[38]

The 370 laborers at Fraser's plantations were called "prime Africans" and "picked young negroes" by Florida planters who saw them at work. The planters also said it took two years for Africans new to America to "become an equal worker to a country born slave," referring to the period needed to regain health and strength after the rigors of the ocean passage and the time needed to learn a new language and work routine. After subtracting for children and sick or injured workers who could not complete full daily tasks, approximately 270 full-working hands labored at Roundabout and Greenfield. On "first-rate hammock land" at Greenfield the workers tended 750 acres of Sea Island cotton, 400 acres of corn and peas (planted together), and fields of sweet potatoes, as well as personal gardens, in both 1810 and 1811. The average annual yield was 150,000 pounds of cleaned cotton, 7,200 bushels of corn, 3,200 bushels of peas, and 10,000 bushels of sweet potatoes, for a total value of $82,087. At Roundabout, the 15,000 bushels of rice harvested in 1810 and 1811, along with corn and potatoes, were valued at $11,600 each year. The value of the annual harvests at the two estates would exceed $3,000,000 today.[39]

George Gianopoli, a clerk at the nearby San Pablo Plantation who was familiar with Greenfield, searched through the charred ruins after renegade "Patriots" pillaged and torched the buildings and fields. Gianopoli described the two-story dwelling house where Fraser and the white overseers resided as measuring thirty by fifty feet, with five rooms below and two large rooms above. Piazzas surrounded the wood-frame structure that Gianopoli valued at $3,000. He also remembered a second dwelling worth $1,200 and a brick kitchen measuring fourteen by twenty feet.[40]

Living accommodations for some of the enslaved laborers consisted of several African-style "bark and palmetto houses" that Gianopoli estimated to have a total value of less than $500. He was impressed, however, by approximately thirty other residential buildings made of brick. Each building contained two apartments and accommodated one family per apartment. Each of the duplex structures was valued at approximately $500. Work buildings included a gin and cotton house measuring twenty by sixty feet that contained a horse-powered roller gin. Gianopoli saw two very large corn bins, a stable, a small milk house, and thirty poultry houses in which "the Negroes raised all the poultry on the place."

Gianopoli inspected a five-mile-long "fence of the worm form, with stakes and riders, ten rails to a panel." In his estimation, Greenfield was a remarkably valuable property until "War ruined the place." The brick walls were left standing, but the interiors were burned and destroyed. When torches ignited the structures at Greenfield and other plantations clustered near the entrance to the St. Johns River, it must have seemed like all of East Florida was in flames.[41]

In December 1813 Fraser drowned near the entrance to the St. Johns River as he attempted to avoid marauding insurgents. He was considered the "wealthiest and most extensive planter in Florida." His properties in East Florida, South Carolina, Britain, and West Africa were all bequeathed to his African wife and their five children. The story of John Fraser and his Anglo-African heirs reveals the complex multinational and multiracial nature of slavery and the slave trade as it existed on two frontiers of the Atlantic world: Spanish East Florida and the Pongo River region of the Coast of Guinea.[42]

The 1812–14 American invasion of East Florida signaled the end of a promising and prosperous era ushered in by the liberal reforms introduced in Spain's American colonies in the 1790s. Spain's decision to open Florida to immigrants and offer free grants of land, coupled with free trade and legal importation of enslaved Africans, led to a rapid population increase and economic prosperity for free Spanish citizens. As in the Spanish colony of Cuba, which experienced a massive expansion of sugar plantations following the collapse of the sugar industry in Saint-Domingue after the slave rebellion there, prosperity became widespread in East Florida in the decade prior to 1812. Robert L. Paquette's description of the transformation of post-1800 Cuba from "a sluggish, undersettled, largely self-sufficient outpost to a booming plantation society of masters and slaves" applies to East Florida as well.[43] In Cuba, however, economic expansion and prosperity continued for decades, while in East Florida the 1812–14 invasion/insurgency left the province in flames and led to Spain's decision to cede the province to the United States in 1821.

The insurgency that resulted in the destruction of Laurel Grove Plantation in July 1812 brought devouring flames to dozens of small farms and large estates situated along the Atlantic coast from the Georgia border to Mosquito Lagoon. The barns and dwellings that stood on the banks of the St. Marys and St. Johns Rivers were torched and reduced to rubble and ashes. When the brigands calling themselves "Patriots" finally crossed the border back into Georgia, two decades of population and economic expansion in Spanish East Florida had ended.

8

"Left by the Patriots a Perfect Desert"

The Patriot War in East Florida

After a decade of economic growth and prosperity, the so-called Patriot War initiated a calamitous downward spiral for the planters of Spanish East Florida. "Everything was thrown into disorder," Kingsley testified, "the houses all burned, the inhabitants flying or keeping up a feeble warfare against the Indians; fields were ravished; the cattle destroyed or driven away; slaves were left to the mercy of the Indians, or to their own control or discretions." It was Kingsley's opinion that "The country was in a very flourishing state when the revolution commenced. The lumber and cotton trade made it so. It never was so prosperous before or since. It was left by the Patriots a perfect desert."[1]

There was nothing patriotic about the 1812–14 insurgency euphemistically referred to as the Patriot War; it was instead a war of aggression that destroyed a Spanish colony. The insurgency was instigated by the government of the United States of America and participated in by soldiers and sailors of that government. Also involved were dissident Spanish subjects, recent migrants from the United States who plotted to foment rebellion and invite the United States to annex East Florida. Land-hungry Georgians and Carolinians, acting in response to reckless promises of free land grants once East Florida became an American territory, were joined by bands of thugs anxious to loot and plunder properties of Spaniards and sell abducted enslaved men and women north of the Florida border. Banditry, arson, and murder at isolated plantations, a continuing economic depression, a new invasion of West Florida, and the seizure of Fernandina in East Florida convinced the Spanish government it would not be able to stabilize the province and protect its residents. Spain gave in to the inevitable and ceded East Florida to the United States.[2]

In plan, if not in execution, the events of 1812 in East Florida reflected what had previously occurred in West Florida, where American settlers flocked to the rich lands along the Mississippi River and became nominal Spanish citizens. They may have pledged fidelity to Spain, but their loyalties remained with the United States. On September 23, 1810, a band of approximately eighty American migrants captured the fort at Baton Rouge, declared independence, and requested annexation by the United States. President James Madison sent American troops to occupy the territory and incorporate it into Louisiana, justifying his order by proclaiming that the territory was part of the Louisiana Purchase of 1803 and that he was acting to prevent either Britain or France from seizing it. Few were fooled by the ploy.[3]

In 1811, President Madison authorized General George Mathews, a Revolutionary War hero and former governor of Georgia, to negotiate the acquisition of the portion of West Florida that remained under Spanish control. Making no headway with Governor Vicente Folch, Mathews traveled to St. Marys, Georgia, and focused on recruiting dissident Spanish East Florida residents like wealthy planter John H. McIntosh, formerly of Georgia, with promises of political office and lavish awards of land. With a filibuster army assembled in Georgia that supposedly represented the "Republic of East Florida," Mathews and the designated president, McIntosh, led rebels calling themselves "Patriots" into Spanish East Florida on March 14, 1812. Fernandina was quickly captured, and the so-called Patriots continued their southward advance toward St. Augustine.[4]

Zephaniah Kingsley was one of many East Florida residents seized by the invaders and forced to join their army. Some eagerly embraced the goals of the insurgents, while others, like Kingsley, joined involuntarily after being threatened with the loss of property. As Kingsley recalled the incident, twelve men on horseback took him prisoner on March 20 or 21 and "carried him off by force . . . to the Patriot camp near a place called 'Cowford' upon the [St. Johns River]." At the camp, Kingsley recognized General Mathews and his personal secretary, Colonel Ralph Isaacs. He also identified the "two hundred to three hundred" armed men as "Americans from Georgia who had . . . become united with the American troops." Kingsley was more

familiar with McIntosh and with two other migrants from Georgia: Daniel Delany and Lodowick Ashley.[5]

The encounter at the camp was anything but a gathering of old friends. Kingsley said that "General Mathews and the others" relentlessly pressured him to join the Patriots, but despite being promised "great advantages" for joining, he "absolutely rejected all their offers and refused." After hours of badgering, "an act of Independence drawn in writing" was placed before Kingsley at 2 a.m. and he was ordered to "either sign the tract, or be out-lawed and have his property confiscated." Kingsley signed the paper, but in his later years he repeatedly insisted that he did so only because of the "force and compulsion" used against him. After receiving assurances that his property would be protected, Kingsley returned to Laurel Grove.

The Patriots continued upriver and captured Fort Picolata on March 23. Two hundred insurgents moved east to the outskirts of St. Augustine and camped two miles north of the town, outside the range of Spanish artillerists at Castillo de San Marcos. The campsite had formerly been Gracia Real de Santa Teresa de Mose, or Fort Mose, established in 1738 as a free black town and sanctuary for slaves from South Carolina and Georgia.

McIntosh and the Patriots established a siege line and sent a demand for surrender to Governor Juan José de Estrada. The Spanish governor defiantly rejected the demand and issued orders to prepare for an attack. American forces under Colonel Thomas Smith arrived on April 11, but the invaders lacked artillery and the U.S. Navy's gunboats were unable to seal off access to the harbor. The attack bogged down outside St. Augustine.[6]

Kingsley remained at Laurel Grove, hoping to be left alone but expecting a summons to join the Patriots. Judging from his April 1 letter to James Hamilton, he had reluctantly joined the Patriots: "I have been some time past on Indian service on the West side of St. Johns but expect daily to be sent for to assist at the siege and perhaps storming of St. Augustine before which the Revolutionary Army is now lying and only waiting some small reinforcement to proceed against by storm as we are without cannon." Hamilton could assist "by sending some soldiers and military characters who wish to be shot at. We will pay them in hands [slaves] such as might produce sugar etc. and perhaps Coffee. God knows what will be the end of this. We must now either conquer or fall like soldiers, perhaps both."[7]

A few days after writing to Hamilton, Kingsley was ordered to St. Augustine, where the stalemate continued. The poorly disciplined Patriots began foraging for supplies in raids that deteriorated into looting, arson, and violence in an ever expanding cycle of destruction that eventually engulfed plantations throughout the province. Hundreds of slaves were abducted and sold across the border, thousands of cattle were slaughtered for consumption and for spite, and the once-productive countryside was left in ruin.

The momentum of the insurgents was further retarded by the ambivalent support of President Madison. In response to congressional opposition to the military filibuster in Florida, and to protests from Spanish and British diplomats in Washington, Madison revoked the commission previously granted to General Mathews and appointed Georgia governor David Mitchell to negotiate with the Spanish governor. Madison considered a withdrawal of U.S. troops but instead ordered Colonel Smith to hold his position while negotiations proceeded.

On June 18 President Madison signed a congressional declaration of war against Great Britain. The Patriots expected the American president to send additional troops, but two weeks later the U.S. Senate rejected a bill authorizing a formal military occupation. Henceforth, reinforcements would have to come from short-term militia volunteers from Georgia. The stalemate continued.

A new Spanish governor, Sebastián Kindelán, arrived at St. Augustine in mid-June, bringing with him from Cuba much-needed supplies of provisions and arms and three companies of black militia. In an effort to break the stifling enemy lines that encircled the city, Governor Kindelán authorized a series of raids by East Florida's most dependable and experienced soldiers, the free black militia. He also sent emissaries to Alachua to negotiate an alliance with Seminole leaders. In July, Seminole warriors launched a series of raids on the farms and plantations of Spanish citizens who had joined the Patriots. News of the raids propelled an exodus from the already under-manned siege lines: plantation owners rushed home to defend what remained of their properties.[8]

Kingsley was one of the planters who left the siege line and returned to his home. A July 25 attack by Seminole warriors had severely damaged Laurel Grove. Three weeks later, Kingsley wrote to James Hamilton: "While

I was busy about scaling ladders and pikes before St. Augustine, tired of the siege and earnestly wishing for some event that would put an end to our revolutionary troubles, an unexpected irruption of Indians from the west overturned my plantation." Two enslaved men, a driver and mechanic named Peter and a blacksmith known as Montarro, were killed and scalped. A white Frenchman, an interpreter at meetings with the Seminoles, was also killed, and Abraham Hanahan, the mulatto manager of Laurel Grove emancipated in 1811, was wounded. Kingsley said the warriors "killed and drove off 36 of my most valuable negroes and all my horses besides burning and destroying everything but a new unfinished house to which three white men and some Negroes retired and saved themselves by defending it. Since then we have been closely besieged: one white man killed and one wounded and some Indians killed and wounded." Kingsley lamented the loss of the best crop he had "ever made in Florida. . . . The cotton is now beginning to scatter with the wind, my fields are all open, my cattle driven off and I dare not go out even to gather an ear of corn. . . . Many people about have been scalped and murdered but they are now chiefly fled and some have saved their property. . . . The army still holds on before St. Augustine nor have we abandoned the object of being Independent. Large reinforcements are soon expected and we even contemplate driving off both Spaniards and Indians."[9]

The American force was still at St. Augustine, but Kingsley was living a nightmare at Laurel Grove. He had managed to erect a stockade around his main dwelling and to fortify it with two brass cannon. Gathering his overseers and his "remaining Negroes" inside the stockade, Kingsley decided to fight rather than abandon the premises. "If I evacuate I have no means of living," he wrote to Hamilton, "and I have no vessel to carry off a sufficiency of provisions or my remaining moveables so that I have concluded to hold out and go the wholes."

Much had changed during the ordeal, including Kingsley's outlook on life and survival. "Habit modified everything while the savages surrounded the house and watched opportunities of shooting us on every side, at the same time trying to involve us in the general conflagration of the surrounding buildings. I felt a great deal heated and anxious about the flows of wind." After the fires had burned out and the warriors had left, Kingsley observed: "I have already habituated myself to look at a good many bare skulls. I begin to hold scalping in less dread and think I may escape myself by very good luck." He asked a friend to send him a pair of dueling pistols, as "Every instrument of death these days has its value and may be of service."

Kingsley survived and kept his scalp, thanks in part to the arrival of Colonel Daniel Newnan and three hundred men of the Georgia Volunteers at Camp New Hope (today at Goodbys Lake in South Jacksonville) in August 1812. Patriots and American troops also encamped further upriver at Kingsley's Laurel Grove (on the west bank) and Fatio's New Switzerland (on the east bank). Captain Tomlinson Fort and a detachment of 125 Georgians set up camp at Laurel Grove. On September 14, after East Florida's free black militia under command of a self-liberated enslaved man from South Carolina known as Prince Witten (Juan Bautista Witten) defeated a supply convoy guarded by U.S. Marines at Twelve Mile Swamp, Colonel Smith decided to end the siege of St. Augustine and pull American troops back to Camp New Hope. With American soldiers, Patriot troops, and Georgia militia patrols in the vicinity, Kingsley felt more secure at Laurel Grove. He enhanced his safety by making Laurel Grove available for Patriot meetings and by supplying boats, flats, and horses and ferrying provisions for Colonel Newnan's September 1812 invasion of the Alachua region.[10]

On October 11, Newnan wrote to Colonel Smith from Laurel Grove, describing the disastrous seventeen-day campaign in which the Seminoles had inflicted heavy casualties on his men. His troops were "worn down with fatigue and hunger" and suffering from shock and fever, Newnan wrote, and he was "very ill of a fever and hardly able to walk." Two days later, Newnan's health and spirits had revived. He greeted reinforcements of "forty two horsemen" and informed Colonel Smith that another "eighty or one hundred more" were expected in a few days. Newnan and forty of his men agreed to join another campaign "to complete the destruction of the Indians." Kingsley was in residence at Laurel Grove during these months, assisting Newnan by shuttling supplies and munitions between the various Patriot camps.[11]

In February and March 1813 Kingsley again acted as supply agent for U.S. troops under Colonel Smith that joined with militia from Georgia and Tennessee in an invasion of Alachua that captured herds of cattle and horses and confiscated or burned thousands of bushels of corn. Hundreds of Seminole homes and entire villages were destroyed. The Seminoles and their black allies abandoned Alachua and relocated to the Suwannee River and further south near today's Okahumpka, west of Leesburg.[12]

This signaled the end of direct American military involvement in East Florida. Secretary of State James Monroe still wanted to salvage a victory, but Congress refused to acknowledge or sanction the invasion. Monroe informed President Madison of Spain's promise to grant amnesty to the Spanish citizens involved in the rebellion and recommended that the president order American troops to withdraw.

Governor Kindelán had announced the amnesty program in St. Augustine on March 18, 1813. Several Patriots accepted the offer and renewed their pledge of loyalty to Spain, but John H. McIntosh denounced amnesty as "hollow and deceitful" treachery and urged his fellow Patriots to reject the offer. The motivating circumstances are unclear, but even Kingsley signed a petition requesting that American troops continue to occupy East Florida. The petition stated in part: "We the Inhabitants in our feeble situation must fall a sacrifice to the ambition of a Band of Black Troops introduced from foreign Countries, and other merciless Savages, or abandon our homes in a forlorn and beggarly situation."[13]

Many in the Patriot camps agreed, and the insurgency continued. The Americans withdrew, but the Patriot volunteer adventurers recruited allies and dug in their heels at key points along the St. Marys and St. Johns Rivers. Calling themselves endangered victims of Seminole savages and of black revolutionaries from Spain's Caribbean colonies, the rejuvenated Patriots issued bombastic calls for recruits in Georgia through blood-curdling newspaper accounts of their supposed plight. They boldly harassed Spanish outposts and raided farms and plantations of residents suspected of seeking amnesty from Spain. Their main targets were free blacks and slaves at estates north of St. Augustine. For the next two years the province became a lawless and violent "no-man's land."

On April 16, 1813, General Thomas Pinckney issued orders to Major Lawrence Manning of the Eighth U.S. Infantry to abandon Camp New Hope and return to Point Peter, Georgia. The bitter soldiers complied but took revenge at every plantation they passed that was owned by a loyal Spanish resident. Torches were repeatedly applied, and the dwellings of loyal East Florida residents became the flames that lighted the departure route for the vengeful American soldiers.[14]

The American army was finally gone. Kindelán sent troops to reoccupy defense posts between St. Augustine and Fernandina, but the countryside north of St. Augustine remained a dangerous place for anyone loyal to the Spanish colonial government. In Kingsley's vicinity, the closest reclaimed garrison was Fort San Nicolas, located on the south bank of the St. Johns near the ferry crossing known as the Cowford. Further downriver, a post was established at San Vicente Ferrer (St. Johns Bluff). The next secure point to the north was Fernandina, which made travel and mail deliveries via the Inland Passage (today the Intra-Coastal Waterway) precarious. All of the posts were undermanned, and the gunboats patrolling the waterways were few in number and limited in firepower. Patriot bands used hit-and-run tactics to raid and pillage settlements and vanish into the woods when Spanish gunboats or soldiers approached.

The man in charge of Spanish militia based at Fernandina in October 1813, wealthy planter Andrew Atkinson, sent a letter to Governor Kindelán that conveys the tenuous nature of the government's control. Atkinson had received a message from Buckner Harris, self-appointed head of the newest version of the Republic of East Florida, announcing a forthcoming campaign to conquer and occupy Alachua. Harris pledged a willingness to negotiate with Spanish officials but boasted that his troops could defeat any armed force sent against them. Atkinson summed up his predicament: "the Banditti are eighty strong in number in front of this place. . . . I have it much at heart to attack them but disaffected conduct of the militia and the want of discipline in the black troops induces me for the present to continue putting this Island into a state of defence."[15]

Outside Fernandina, Harris and his men were in control, although Spanish gunboats were able to destroy rebel strongholds at Cedar Point on the St. Johns River and at Sawpit Bluff on the Nassau River. The most notorious of the criminal bands operated under the leadership of Colonel Samuel Alexander, who targeted enslaved workers at northeast Florida plantations on both sides of the St. Johns. Alexander's men brazenly captured slaves and sold them to planters in Georgia.[16]

Kingsley led a precarious double life during these traumatic months. He pledged loyalty and received amnesty, and he provided information to Governor Kindelán in the expectation that the government would eventually prevail. At the same time, he cooperated with the successive bands that headquartered at Laurel Grove in the hope of protecting his remaining property. And there were occasions when he was forced to seek protection from Commander Thomas Llorente at San Nicolas.

On November 25, 1813, Kingsley wrote to Governor Kindelán from Fernandina, where relative stability had been maintained for several months under martial law imposed by the U.S. troops and, after their departure, by Spanish soldiers. Kingsley reported a recent attempt on his life, probably by Colonel Alexander and the marauding criminals who were raiding and terrorizing estates on both sides of the St. Johns River. Kingsley praised the commandant at San Nicolas for intervening: "You no doubt heard of my being on my way home as far as Cowford where I believe I should have been massacred but for the exertions & presence of mind of Don Tomas Llorente whose goodness & humanity will be long remembered not only by myself but by all other Inhabitants of St. Johns."[17]

The assassination attempt interrupted Kingsley's effort to return to Laurel Grove to reclaim slaves and other property that remained there. His plantation was occupied at the time by several dozen Patriots under command of a wealthy Florida-born man, Francisco Roman Sánchez, whose family had been in the province for nearly a century. When his own efforts were thwarted, Kingsley informed the governor that he arranged for a man named Morgan to confer with Sánchez to collect the Kingsley slaves at Laurel Grove and bring them overland to Fernandina. "I shall wait their arrival which if no impediment offers I shall expect in about a week."

Kingsley then offered to arrange a meeting to mediate differences between the government and the rebels who remained in control of the territory west of the St. Johns River and the northern reaches of the province. "Once my Negroes are safe I shall have no fear or reserve in trusting my person among them [the Patriots], and I think I could persuade them to accept of any reasonable terms which if Government is so disposed I could sound & make known."[18] Because of his services to the Patriots and long acquaintance with many of their leaders, Kingsley felt confident he could persuade them to entrust their futures to the Spanish. If amnesty was granted and minor concessions were made, it would be possible to attain peace "without compromising the Dignity of Government or Interests of the King's . . . [and to thereby] reconcile these People to Order & industry by only granting them the privileges of Settlers & benefits of subjects on the West side of St. Johns by which . . . Policy one part of them would be made to police the other & would support government for the security of their own property." In Kingsley's estimation, Governor Kindelán's policy of relying on the Spanish moreno and pardo militia companies to restore order was doomed to failure. He discounted the military skills of the militia as "worse than nothing" and recommended instead that "with a little management" an accommodation be offered that would "turn the banditti into useful Subjects."[19]

Governor Kindelán emphatically rejected Kingsley's proposal. Recent events had convinced Kindelán that migrants from the United States and Britain could not be assimilated into a Spanish colony. He refused to compromise and said he would rather see Florida deserted than populated by American rabble.[20]

Although Kingsley was unaware of it on the day he wrote to the governor from Fernandina, his dwelling at Laurel Grove had already been destroyed in a fire. In one of the great surprises of the Patriot insurgency, the fire had been planned and accomplished by Anna Kingsley, who deliberately burned down the dwelling to deny its protective shelter to the rebels. According to historian James Cusick, "The burning of the house at Laurel Grove destroyed the last Patriot refuge on the St. Johns River and made a local heroine out of Anna."[21]

The events surrounding this conflagration are recounted in a series of reports written by gunboat captain José Antonio Moreno and the commander of Fort San Nicolas, Thomas Llorente. Patriots headquartered at Laurel Grove had persistently obstructed Spanish gunboats when they departed San Nicolas and attempted to patrol upriver in the vicinity of Doctors Lake and Mandarin Point and beyond. Throughout November, Llorente had received reports of increased incidents of cattle rustling on the east side of the river, and even more disturbing news of arson, murder, and abduction of free blacks and slaves by the criminal gang led by Colonel Alexander. Spanish soldiers sent against the bandits had little success.

Anna Kingsley's home was located in the center of this zone of violence. After her emancipation in 1811, Anna and her three children moved to the east bank of the St. Johns River, where she became the owner of a five-acre homestead and twelve slaves. For a short time her life was tranquil, until

Samuel Alexander and his band of renegades began pillaging and torching St. Johns River settlements and capturing enslaved and free blacks to sell in Georgia. Beyond skin colors, clothing, and hairstyles, little of substance differentiated the black slave raiders who had seized her in West Africa from Alexander's brutal marauders from Georgia.[22]

In November 1813, Anna became fearful that she and her children were in grave danger. She crossed the river with her dependents and sought shelter under terms of the arrangement Zephaniah had negotiated with Roman Sánchez and the Patriot band then in control of Laurel Grove.

On November 21, 1813, Commander Llorente sent two gunboats upriver from San Nicolas to patrol the St. Johns and to confer with Spanish troops searching for Alexander and his men. Captains José Antonio Moreno and Lorenzo Avila, with the sailors aboard the *Immutable* and the *Habanera*, sailed upriver cautiously, watching for snipers hidden in wooded areas along the shore. Llorente had instructed Moreno to sail to a place known as Kingsley Point, where Kingsley's dwelling house, surrounded by a sturdy seven-foot post-and-clapboard cedar stockade and fortified with two 4-pounder brass cannons pointing out at the river, was being used as a stronghold to harass Spanish vessels. It was evening when they anchored in deep water opposite Kingsley's fortified dwelling.[23]

Early the next morning, Moreno recalled, "Right away with the clear of daylight they opened fire upon us with one of the cannons they have therein, to which we both responded."[24] The rebels were able to direct effective volleys, but eventually the superior firepower from the 24-pounder cannons aboard the gunboats "wrecked the whole front of the house although they stayed firm, protecting themselves therein; we fired upon them with grapeshot, and they no longer were shouting and challenging."

After he thought the rebels had fled to the woods, Moreno moved to the eastern shore to confer with the officer of a Spanish squadron searching for bandits in the vicinity of Anna Kingsley's homestead. While the conference was in progress, the lookout on the masthead of the *Immutable* scanning the west bank of the river saw a canoe push off from the dock at Laurel Grove. When it came within voice range of the *Immutable,* one of the two passengers shouted a password and they were permitted to board. Moreno was surprised to discover "the free black woman Ana Kingsley" was a passenger.

She handed Moreno a letter addressed to Thomas Llorente, commander at San Nicolas, entrusted to her by Sánchez. He had informed her that the Patriot band was in the process of abandoning Laurel Grove.

After receiving assurance from Moreno of protection for her children and enslaved laborers, Anna and the other passenger, one of her male slaves, pushed the canoe away and rowed back to the western shore. "Shortly afterwards she returned with . . . three small children [presumably George, Martha, and Mary Kingsley] . . . two male blacks and three mature female blacks with seven children . . . whom she had hidden in the forest." She also brought back a number of Zephaniah Kingsley's slaves whom "she had saved from the rebels."

Seventy men had been at Laurel Grove when cannon fire from the gunboats prompted them to flee to the woods, Anna told Moreno. Their rifles were left behind during the hasty departure, but when they realized the only casualty had been a horse, they came back to retrieve weapons. The gunboat shells had caused damage to the stockade and the house, but the cannons remained in place and were still functional.

Anna then surprised Moreno by volunteering to lead a party of Spanish soldiers to the abandoned house to confiscate the cannons and bring them to the gunboat. As a token of her fidelity, she left "her children and the slaves as hostages" and joined twenty free black and mulatto soldiers in a journey across the river. As they approached the shore, the lookout on the *Immutable* spotted rebels hiding near the landing and shouted a warning to his commander. Moreno, convinced that his men were being lured into an ambush, signaled his men to return immediately to the gunboats.

Moreno, furious with Anna, accused her of initiating a treacherous plan to lead his men into a death trap. She denied the charges and insisted that it was she who had been deceived. Sánchez, she now realized, had with calculated cunning permitted her to transport her children and slaves to the east side of the river as a ruse to set a trap for the Spaniards.

Later that day, Anna approached the skeptical Moreno and offered to return to the Kingsley house without a military escort to search the nearby woods for enslaved Africans who may have escaped the rebels. She also promised to "set [a] fire so that the house would burn and the rebels would not have this sanctuary." With Moreno's consent, she again departed in a canoe, paddled this time by two of her enslaved black men. The ship's lookout watched as the men tied the craft to Kingsley's wharf and Anna walked toward the dwelling. After a long absence, the canoe returned at seven o'clock in the evening. No smoke could be seen rising from the buildings. Moreno confronted Anna: "You went to set a fire, and you have done nothing?" Her response was: "Wait a moment."

Moreno scanned the shoreline with growing skepticism until he observed a trace of smoke and then "a flare that came out which grew and reduced the house to ashes, the cannons firing off by themselves when [the fire] reached them." Anna had entered the house and "lit a fire in a trunk full of combustibles so that it would give her time to move away, and the enemies, if they were thereabouts, would not come and catch her." The rebels had been completely surprised by the ruse and "unable to do anything to prevent the fire." Moreno reported that the daring young black woman was "greatly pleased to see that the Spaniards' adversaries had nowhere to take refuge and be protected with the artillery." She said "her master would be very content with this as soon as he knew the reasons . . . for carrying it out."

Moreno did not again doubt Anna's honesty or question her courage. When she asked him to cross to the east side of the St. Johns where her homestead was located, he gave the order to hoist anchor. In his report of the incident, Moreno wrote: "Kingsley had recently made [a home] for her on a small plot that the government had conceded to her." Anna's homestead was located directly across from Laurel Grove on the eastern shore of the St. Johns. Once the canoe was secured to the dock, she moved quickly to the dwelling house. "As soon as she was in she brought out a little corn and two rifles and set fire to the house [and] a considerable amount of corn that was inside," Moreno reported. Anna later told Moreno she burned her home "so that the rebels would not avail themselves of it, and that it was more gratifying to lose it than that the enemies should take advantage."

When Anna returned to the gunboat after torching her home and the dwellings of her slaves, it was late in the evening of November 22. Moreno and his crew had been at war since daybreak, yet he gave orders to his crew to sail downriver for the safety of the Spanish fortification at San Nicolas. In his official report Moreno wrote: "[I] cannot help but recommend this woman, who has demonstrated a great enthusiasm concerning the Spaniards and extreme aversion to the rebels, being worthy of being looked after, since she has worked like a heroine, destroying the strong house with the fire she set so that the artillery could not be obtained, and later doing the same with her own property."

Thomas Llorente informed the governor that Anna Kingsley and her household had arrived at San Nicolas and were under his protection. In praise of her courageous actions he wrote: "Anna M. Kingsley deserves any favor the governor can grant her. Rather than afford shelter and provisions to the enemies of His Majesty . . . [she] burned it all up and remained unsheltered from the weather; the royal order provides rewards for such services." She would later receive a 350-acre land grant as compensation for her losses and for her heroic defense of the province.[25]

On December 13, Kingsley sailed a rented sloop from Fort San Nicolas to Laurel Grove in another effort to retrieve whatever remained of his personal property. With the support of Commander Llorente, he sailed this time under protection of Spanish gunboats. When "Kingsley's fleet," as Llorente referred to the sloop and several flats, arrived at Laurel Grove, twenty rebels appeared who were "in no way hostile toward Kingsley, and on the contrary they told him . . . he could come ashore and pick up whatever he wanted . . . and assured him that nothing would be stolen." Captain Moreno was dismayed by the cordial treatment Kingsley received, especially by a gift of venison the rebels presented, and after spontaneously killing and butchering a beef, half of the carcass was sent to the gunboat crew for agreeing to a mutual cease-fire. The Spaniards welcomed the offerings and the lack of violence, but not trusting the rebels, took every precaution to avoid an ambush. Moreno noticed that the entire dwelling and stockade had been consumed by fire; only the chimney was still standing. He was disappointed that Kingsley's two cannons had been removed by the rebels.[26]

In addition to dozens of buildings and two years of agricultural harvests, Kingsley had lost more than forty-five slaves to the Seminole warriors (for their names, ages, gender, family, and ethnic derivation see appendix A). Kingsley repeatedly, although unsuccessfully, tried to retrieve his lost slaves. He did not attempt to re-create the buildings at the three Laurel Grove settlements, although he retained ownership of the site for many years and sent laborers to cultivate its fields and harvest the oranges from the groves that survived the violence. He also rented the land to other planters. He had invested large sums of money in developing Laurel Grove, and it had all gone up in smoke. Already, Kingsley's attention was focused on creating another plantation.

On December 16, 1813, Thomas Llorente noted that "Kingsley's fleet" departed San Nicolas with "the Negro Ana, his son" George Kingsley, age six at the time, along with six other slaves and several white men. Sailing under protection of a gunboat, the flotilla of four flats and several large canoes burdened with slaves, tools, and miscellaneous property traveled downriver on the St. Johns, then turned north on the Inland Passage (today's Intra-Coastal Waterway) west of Fort George, Talbot, and Amelia Islands. During the voyage, passengers could look over the deck rails and view the charred ruins of plantations burned by Patriots, American troops, and criminal bands under Samuel Alexander. The message was obvious: settlements along the shores of the interior waterways of East Florida were still endangered properties. It would be late in September 1814 before Governor Kindelán felt confident enough to proclaim that the province was again tranquil and at peace. Even then, groups of bandits continued to torment settlers north of the St. Johns.[27]

Kingsley's fleet stopped at the north end of Fort George Island to unload tools, supplies, and slaves at the plantation that John H. McIntosh had previously occupied. McIntosh, then in Camden County, Georgia, had ignored Governor Kindelán's offer of clemency out of concern that his leadership role in the insurgency would result in continuing persecution if he returned to Florida. He accepted Kingsley's offer of a lease/purchase contract for Fort George Island.[28]

The two-mile-long island, encompassing roughly twelve hundred acres, had been a successful indigo and long-staple cotton plantation. Of great importance to Kingsley was the island's location. It was situated immediately north of the point where the St. Johns River enters the Atlantic Ocean. From the wharf on Fort George Inlet at the owner's dwelling on the north end of the island, Kingsley could sail east and merge onto the Atlantic. During seasons when storms disrupted travel on the Atlantic, he could reach his wharf at Fernandina by following the inlet west for a half-mile and turning north at the inland waterway to sail behind the protection of Talbot and Amelia Islands. A south turn at the inland waterway put him on Sister's Creek and a passage to the St. Johns River. From there he sailed upriver to

Fort San Nicolas and the Cowford Ferry (later Jacksonville), and beyond to Laurel Grove and Drayton Island. Located far from the violence that continued to torment the planters further upriver, the isolated location was advantageous.

When Kingsley's ship entered Fort George Inlet, the view from the deck encompassed Fort George Island on the right (to the south) and Talbot Island on the left. On each side of the waterway were vast expanses of marsh grass, with small inlets of water interspersed throughout, and tall trees with overhanging limbs of green foliage that reflected outward on the water and were playfully distorted by the wake of the vessels as they proceeded toward the wharf. All thoughts of calm and peacefulness ended rudely when the passengers stepped ashore. Only one building remained standing on the entire island, the large two-story house facing the landing, and it had been badly damaged. Beyond the dwelling, vandals had pillaged and burned the barns, outbuildings, and former living quarters of more than two hundred enslaved workers domiciled on the island prior to the war.[29]

Kingsley had previously inspected the island and was aware the damage scars ran deep but were reversible. Fort George Island was the first hurdle in his quest to restore the fortune lost during the Patriot War. Kingsley was already issuing orders to his overseers and directing the workers to cut saplings and palmetto fronds to fashion temporary African-style houses with thatch roofs. It was already late in December, and the immediate construction of shelters was of the essence. After that was accomplished, fields had to be restored and agricultural buildings and stables constructed. The main dwelling house could not be occupied until it was refurbished.

Kingsley also planned to initiate a shipbuilding enterprise on the island. His shipyard at Doctors Lake had been destroyed in 1812, and he placed a high priority on restarting the enterprise at Fort George. With the United States and Great Britain still at war, and ships of His Majesty's Royal Navy blockading ports on the Atlantic and Gulf of Mexico, Kingsley expected that ships flying the flag of neutral Spain could pass through the blockade and engage in lucrative commerce.

The ship carpenters that traveled with Kingsley during the journey from San Nicolas began work at an improvised shipyard soon after landing on the island. On February 2, 1814, the commander at San Nicolas informed Governor Kindelán that Kingsley was building a ship at Fort George Island.

The governor issued an order to stop construction, but after further investigation he decided to encourage the enterprise. Commander Llorente even borrowed the services of a carpenter and a ship caulker to repair a Spanish gunboat damaged by a hurricane. On October 1, 1814, Spanish gunboat commander Joaquin Navarro reported that Kingsley's carpenters had already launched the first vessel completed at the Fort George shipyard.[30]

A few days after the convoy arrived at Fort George, Kingsley boarded his sloop and sailed to Fernandina with Anna Jai and their children. Fernandina was a town of approximately six hundred residents and a thriving import/export trade. For his financial well-being, Kingsley thought it vital to re-engage in Atlantic trade as quickly as possible. Importing slaves was still legal in Spanish East Florida, and planters who had lost workers during the Patriot War were desperately seeking replacement workers. Kingsley was optimistic he would be able to revive his formerly lucrative business as an Atlantic trader while his managers and overseers directed planting at Fort George Island. He intended to reside at Fernandina and make brief visits to Fort George to check on progress when his ship was in port.

Kingsley's hopes for a quick return to the booming economy that East Florida had experienced in the first decade of the nineteenth century would not be realized. From 1814 to 1821, East Florida would suffer from continued bandit raids in the countryside and invasions across the border. Fernandina would be seized by a gang of revolutionaries who claimed to be liberating Spain's colonies in America but who in reality engaged in piracy and smuggled slave cargoes into Georgia. They were quickly driven out by an American naval force and replaced by a permanent U.S. occupation. Life in East Florida continued to be precarious, and an economic recovery would not occur until after East Florida became a territory of the United States in 1821. Confronted by forces beyond his control, Kingsley would make major life changes. The ship captain, African slave trader, and West Indies maritime trader would become Kingsley the resident planter, directing the labor of slaves at Fort George Island and White Oak Plantation.

9 | "Like a Turtle without a Shell"

Spain's Final Years in East Florida

In August 1814, Governor Sebastián Kindelán informed Juan Ruiz de Apodaca, captain general for Cuba and the Floridas, that the "province is at peace," a pronouncement more hopeful than realistic for East Florida. American troops had withdrawn from the province in May 1813, and most of the Patriot insurgents either petitioned for pardons and returned to their rural properties or sought refuge outside the province. One band of disgruntled Patriots under Buckner Harris returned to Alachua in the winter of 1814 in an attempt to establish the Republic of East Florida in the rich farmlands the Seminoles had been driven from in February 1813. Their goal was recognition by the American government and eventual annexation as a U.S. territory. When a Seminole war party killed Harris in Alachua in May 1814, the Patriot adventurers broke up and returned to their former residences in Georgia and East Florida. East Florida was at peace, but turmoil soon resumed.[1]

The booming economy that East Florida experienced in the first decade of the nineteenth century was a major casualty of the Patriot insurgency. It would not be until after East Florida became a territory of the United States in 1821 that the economy would recover. Zephaniah Kingsley was nevertheless hoping for a quick economic turnaround and anticipating a revival of his career as a ship captain and maritime trader. His base at the end of 1814 was Fernandina, although he traveled often to his new plantation at Fort George Island where his enslaved Africans and overseers were at work. His expectations were high, but like others in East Florida he would suffer through continued bandit raids and violence as well as another series of American invasions. Life under Spanish rule would continue to be precarious.

The first of Kingsley's traumatic experiences in the post-Patriot era occurred at the end of November 1814 in the form of a near fatal shipboard brawl. The incident had its origins in the evening of November 25, when the anchor line of Kingsley's sloop, the *Providencia*, became entangled with the line of another ship tied to a wharf at Fernandina harbor. Kingsley's sloop had only recently been completed at his Fort George Island shipyard, and the rigging and anchor ropes were still being adjusted when it was tied to the wharf that evening, not long before a sudden storm blew in off the Atlantic. Accompanying Kingsley were five enslaved black sailors and John Ashton, a white carpenter from St. Augustine hired to build a house in Fernandina.[2]

Kingsley tied his ship next to the *Dolores*, a Cuban slaving vessel captained by Joaquin Zorrilla. For several days Zorrilla had been waiting impatiently for favorable sailing weather that would permit him to depart for Africa. While waiting, he and his crew members engaged in heavy drinking. A few hours after Kingsley secured his vessel, the wind commenced blowing hard from the east and the *Providencia* banged against the side of the *Dolores*. Zorrilla became enraged and shouted intemperate and drunken accusations at Kingsley, threatening violence if the vessels collided again. Kingsley and his crew rectified the problem, and the evening passed without further problems. The two captains conversed cordially the following morning, and Kingsley sent a gift of Florida oranges to the crew aboard the *Dolores*.

The next evening the storm revived with increased intensity, causing the vessels to again collide. On this occasion, Zorrilla shouted out threats of violence against Kingsley. The two captains exchanged insults while Kingsley disentangled the vessels and promised to find a new anchorage in the daylight. When Kingsley said the dispute could be resolved in the daylight after everyone aboard the *Dolores* had sobered, Zorrilla became enraged and ordered seven of his crew to join him in an armed attack on the *Providencia*.

As the men advanced, Kingsley ordered his black sailors to take shelter in the hold of the ship and to secure the hatch. He and Ashton, who was incapacitated with severe fever at the time, withdrew to the captain's quarters below the deck. Kingsley tucked a dagger in his belt and prepared to defend himself with a rifle and a pistol as the group from the slave ship burst into the quarters. Shots were exchanged, and the pilot of the slave ship, Genaro Garay, received a flesh wound. Kingsley was subdued and nearly killed, as Zorrilla ordered his men to tie Kingsley's arms behind his back and throw him into the hold of the *Dolores*.

Later that evening, port commandant Francisco Ribera arrived. Kingsley mistakenly thought Ribera had come to hear his complaints and mete out justice, but the commandant instead behaved like "a furious person with a naked dagger in hand and insulted me, and said it was 'strange they had not just killed such a scoundrel,' and put my feet in shackles." Naked and covered with blood, Kingsley was brought ashore and imprisoned. He was confined in double shackles for the next twenty-two days. Joseph F. Gault, a Fernandina physician who treated Kingsley's injuries the morning after the violent incident occurred, testified that his patient suffered "a very large wound on the left side of the head, through which the bone could be seen," and additional saber cuts and stab wounds to his nose, lower lip, other parts of his face and neck, the lower part of his abdomen, his knee and right heel, and "other small dagger cuts in various parts of the body." Kingsley's forehead had been "terribly crushed" and his left eye blackened and swelled shut by a pistol blow. Gault said that Kingsley's "shoulders, back, buttocks and thighs were very beaten and of all colors."

It was only after the intercession of Kingsley's colleagues in the Fernandina merchant community that he was able to covertly send a letter to Governor Kindelán and arrange to be moved to St. Augustine. Once there, bail was posted and Kingsley was released to lodge with an innkeeper until his case could be heard by a Spanish tribunal scheduled for January 1815. Zorrilla and Garay were also ordered to stand trial, and the governor ordered Ribera to remove the sails and rudder from the *Dolores* to prevent Zorrilla from escaping. Witnesses at the trial included residents of the town, along with Ribera, Garay, Kingsley, the slave sailors Sam and Tom, carpenter Ashton, and physician Gault. Zorrilla had disappeared.

The tribunal exonerated Kingsley, ruling that his and Garay's injuries were the result of the "imprudent and violent [acts] of Joaquin Zorrilla," and directed the governor to prosecute the captain of the *Dolores*. The governor went even further: after hearing accusations directed against Ribera by more than a dozen of the leading merchants of Fernandina, Kindelán denounced his misconduct and ordered that he be replaced as commandant. Ribera did not respond with humility and regret, but instead refused to surrender his command and rallied supporters among dissident troops of the garrison and disaffected residents of the town. Finally, after a weeklong standoff, Ribera capitulated.[3]

Kingsley, meanwhile, returned to Fernandina, still recovering from the saber wounds. Only days later, he traveled to Cumberland Island in an attempt to retrieve slaves who had escaped to the military camps established there by British rear admiral George Cockburn. He arrived at Cumberland in the third week of January 1815.

Early in the War of 1812, Vice-Admiral Alexander F. I. Cochrane, in charge of British naval forces in North America, had recognized the importance of diverting American attention away from major attacks on Canada. He also deemed it necessary to draw defenders away from New Orleans, a future target for a British offensive. Cochrane assembled five thousand army troops and marines at Bermuda and implemented a blockade of America's Atlantic ports. American ships were seized, and maritime commerce was thoroughly disrupted. Cochrane called on Admiral Cockburn to lead attacks on America's coastal cities and to burn and plunder farms and plantations that could be reached from rivers that emptied into the Atlantic. The capture of Washington, D.C., and the burning of the Capitol Building, Library of Congress, and White House during the summer of 1814 were the major successes of this campaign. Cockburn's relentless raids on settlements located along Chesapeake Bay confiscated hundreds of slaves and provoked additional mass desertions.[4]

After American defenders turned back the British invaders at Baltimore in September 1814, Cochrane and Cockburn targeted the coast of Georgia. Cochrane had issued a proclamation in April 1814 that promised freedom to all slaves of American owners who boarded a British naval vessel. Hundreds of slaves in Virginia and Maryland heeded the call of freedom and found refuge on British ships that carried them to camps at Virginia's Tangier Island on Chesapeake Bay and at Bermuda. Several hundred refugees volunteered to serve in the Royal Marines.

In January 1815 Admiral Cockburn intensified attacks against the mainland of Georgia and the islands off its coast, unaware that American and

British peace negotiators had already agreed to terminate the war. News from the peace conferees meeting in late December at Ghent in today's Belgium would not reach the armies and navies fighting in North America for several more weeks. During the interval, large numbers of enslaved families in Georgia discovered that freedom was as close as the nearest British naval vessel. On January 10, 1815, the British captured the small port town of St. Marys, Georgia, located on the border between Georgia and Spanish East Florida at the entrance to the St. Marys River. They next seized nearby Fort Peter. Cockburn established headquarters at Dungeness Mansion at the southern end of Cumberland Island. British troops, supplemented by newly recruited black companies of Royal Marines, raided plantations at Jekyll Island and St. Simons Island and returned with shiploads of black refugees confiscated from Thomas Spalding, James Hamilton, and other wealthy planters.[5]

News of Cochrane's proclamation and the British raiding parties traveled across the border to Spanish East Florida and inspired slaves living at settlements along the St. Marys and St. Johns Rivers to seek freedom aboard the British vessels. Sixty-six men and women slipped away from the St. Johns River plantation of merchant John Forbes one evening. Using stealth and cunning to evade detection, they made their way along northeast Florida's waterways until they arrived at British headquarters. According to historian Roger Morriss, British officers registered nearly eighteen hundred black refugees before the last of the British vessels departed Cumberland on March 18, 1815.[6]

Several Spanish East Florida planters traveled to Cumberland Island hoping to reclaim human property. Because Britain and Spain were not at war at the time, the Florida planters expected Admiral Cockburn to facilitate the return of their enslaved laborers. The planters were received graciously and permitted to tour the refugee camps, even question black refugees, but their pleas to Cockburn for the forced return of self-liberated refugees were rebuffed. A representative of the governor of East Florida, Captain Benito Pangua, was told by Cockburn that Cumberland Island was a British possession by conquest of war and that slavery was not recognized in his country. Cockburn would not consent to the release of the black refugees unless they voluntarily agreed to return to their former Spanish owners.[7]

Kingsley arrived at Cumberland Island seeking the release of eighty-five Africans from the estate of John Fraser, a native of Scotland who had migrated to East Florida in 1809. At the time of his death, Fraser was considered the "wealthiest and most extensive planter in Florida." In December 1813, during the Patriot insurgency, he drowned when his ship foundered at the entrance to the St. Johns River. As an executor of the Fraser estate, Kingsley represented the legatees, all of whom resided at Bangalan on the Pongo River in today's Republic of Guinea, West Africa. In his will, Fraser listed his widow, Phendah, and their five children, James, Margaret, Mary Anne, Eleanor, and Elizabeth, as heirs and legatees to two major plantations and 370 enslaved Africans in East Florida, as well as properties in South Carolina, Britain, and West Africa.[8]

Prior to his death, Fraser had asked Governor Kindelán for permission to move his enslaved laborers to Cuba until the violence and banditry accompanying the Patriot insurgency subsided. Denied permission, Fraser rented eighty-five of his Africans to a planter at St. Simons Island, considered a safe location until Admiral Cockburn's Royal Marines began raiding the coastal islands in late 1814. Kingsley acknowledged that Fraser's enslaved laborers had been employed by an enemy civilian, but he nevertheless requested their return since their owner had been a citizen of neutral Spain.[9]

Kingsley toured the camps of the black refugees, an experience he remembered vividly two decades later. What impressed him most was how quickly the former slaves were transformed into effective soldiers. Looking back on the event years later, Kingsley wrote: "Whoever was so unlucky as to see, on Cumberland Island . . . the magical transformation of his own negroes . . . into regular soldiers of good discipline," must tremble when considering "the consequences had there been a larger force able to maintain a position on the main[land]. . . . Where would they have stopped," Kingsley asked, and "what could have stopped them?"[10]

After returning to Fernandina, Kingsley asked Governor Kindelán to write a formal letter of protest to Admiral Cockburn. Kindelán wrote the letter on January 31, reminding Cockburn that Spain's neutral status mandated the return of escaped and confiscated slaves. Cockburn responded two weeks later, assuring Kindelán that his concern was a needless worry, as he had "made the necessary enquiries relative thereto and found that very few of these people have in fact appeared here." He pledged that no human property owned by Spanish colonials "shall ever be brought by boats or vessels belonging to His Britannic Majesty or under my control." Preventing desertions from the Spanish territory, however, was not his responsibility.

Cockburn's response blended truculence with diplomacy and must have infuriated the Spanish governor. Cumberland Island, the admiral asserted, was conquered by British forces and would therefore be governed by British laws "which know *not* of slavery." He denied that he had the power to force slaves to return to their former Spanish owners after they had escaped "at the risk of their lives" and placed themselves under "protection of His Britannic Majesty." However, "in consideration of the amity and good understanding so happily existing between" Spain and Great Britain, Cockburn pledged that Spanish citizens would be permitted to come to Cumberland Island and search for their human properties. If they located their former slaves and "persuaded [them] to return to Florida voluntarily, ready permission and every facility for their so doing shall be immediately granted, which will I trust satisfy your Excellency."[11]

Cockburn's response convinced Kingsley that it would be impossible to reclaim Fraser's escaped slaves, but he did not abandon his responsibilities as an executor of the Fraser estate. In fact, he continued to exercise those duties for the next three decades. The immediate problem he faced was the rigidity of Spanish law, which lacked safeguards for legatees who were not citizens of East Florida. Kingsley and co-executor Philip Yonge petitioned the governor to delay testamentary proceedings in order to prevent mandatory confiscation and sale of the estate's properties, with the proceeds assigned to the Spanish Treasury and thereby lost to the legatees. Kingsley reminded the governor of the "dangers and vicissitudes" encountered daily in a province that had fallen into a "total decay of commerce and agriculture and [where] very frequently the slaves desert to the Indians who protect them, and also to other vagabonds of the interior, and in this manner several inhabitants have lost the greater part of their slaves." He predicted that an auction during this time of depressed economy would result in only one in twenty of the Fraser slaves selling for two-thirds of their true value.[12]

When the delay was granted, Kingsley and Yonge offered to purchase the 158 slaves remaining in the estate and to pay the full price of $35,285 assigned by the governor's tribunal. Each man pledged to pay $17,643, plus 5 percent annual interest, in return for 79 slaves. Kingsley provided the court deeds to four plantations with a total value of $52,400 as security for the slaves he acquired. Kingsley and Yonge acted out of self-interest in that they were both in need of laborers after losing slaves during the Patriot insurgency, but there is no doubt the legatees would have suffered significant losses if the proposal had not been agreed to. Over several years, the labors of the African men and women Kingsley acquired from the Fraser estate produced profits for him, yet it is important to note that he redeemed the mortgage and fulfilled his financial obligations: he paid the annual interest and the full purchase price to the legatees.[13]

Kingsley also sought the return of his own slaves lost during the Seminole raid on Laurel Grove Plantation in July 1812. A small number escaped later and reportedly found sanctuary in the black maroon villages located near Seminole settlements in Alachua territory. Bob, Jim, and Buck were captured and returned to him at Fernandina. When Buck escaped again, Kingsley offered an $80 reward for his capture and return to Fernandina in chains. Kingsley was convinced that his other lost slaves had moved with the Alachua Seminoles either to new villages along the Suwannee River or further west to Prospect Bluff on the Apalachicola River. Kingsley therefore took advantage of an unexpected opportunity when Colonel Edward Nicholls arrived at Fernandina harbor aboard a British naval vessel in mid-June 1815.[14]

Nicholls and Captain George Woodbine, as part of the British war against the Americans, were seeking allies among the anti-American faction of the Native Americans residing in the states and territories of the American Southeast, especially among the Red Sticks, a militant faction of Upper Creeks. Slaves were encouraged to desert their masters and join companies of the British Royal Marines. In June 1814 at Apalachicola River on the Gulf Coast, Nicholls distributed several thousand muskets and rifles among the Red Stick and Choctaw fighters who had escaped from Andrew Jackson's avenging army after the March 27, 1814, Battle of Horseshoe Bend in Mississippi Territory (today central Alabama). Large numbers of Seminoles and Black Seminoles, as well as self-liberated blacks from Georgia and Spanish Florida, were also settled along the Apalachicola.[15]

Nicholls ordered construction and armament of a fort at Prospect Bluff, located fifteen miles inland from the Gulf. Captain Woodbine distributed British arms and trained the recruits, whom Nicholls planned to combine with British forces in an attack on New Orleans. When Jackson's army turned that offensive back in January 1815, Nicholls withdrew British troops and four hundred black Royal Marines from Prospect Bluff to new quarters at Tampa Bay and at Manatee River (today's Bradenton), where black and Native American villages had been settled for decades. Left behind at the fortification at Prospect Bluff, which became known as Negro Fort, was an arsenal of weapons and ammunition. With more than a thousand armed warriors and villages of escaped slaves that extended for miles along the river, the area quickly developed a reputation as a sanctuary, attracting hundreds of additional self-liberated slaves from Florida and Georgia.[16]

In June 1815, Fernandina residents were startled to learn that the man made notorious by these Gulf Coast exploits, Colonel Nicholls, had arrived at their harbor aboard a British naval vessel. Kingsley was residing at Fernandina at the time, still recovering from wounds suffered during the violent encounter with the captain and crew of the *Dolores*. "I have been sick," he wrote, "everything looks discouraging & no prospect of security on any side." When he learned of Nicholls's presence, he quickly arranged an interview. According to Kingsley, Nicholls said "he left the [Negro] Fort well furnished with stores, amunition, ordinance & provisions guarded by two hundred blacks & all the Creek nation whom he has declared free and independant and made a treaty offensive & defensive with them in favour of G. Britain with whom alone they are allowed to trade."[17]

Before departing Fernandina, Nicholls left a letter in Kingsley's care addressed to William Hambly, a bookkeeper and trader in the employ of the Panton and Leslie Company, the Indian trading firm that operated stores throughout East and West Florida. The letter contained an order forbidding "Lieut't Hambly & the chiefs . . . to harbour or protect any runaway negroes." Subsequent events indicate that Nicholls had no intention of enforcing a ban on future runaways, but the statement was nevertheless gratifying to Kingsley. He wrote immediately to Joseph Hernandez at St. Augustine that he intended to "forward [the letter] through Bowlegs [the Seminole leader] of whose probable arrival I wish to be informed so as to comply with my promise [to Nicholls]. When I come to town I shall bring the letter and show it to the governor." It must have been disturbing to newly appointed Governor José María Coppinger to learn that British military forces were treating parts of his province as a possession of Great Britain.[18]

The deep concern of the United States about British military involvement with Native Americans, Black Seminoles, and escaped slaves along the Gulf Coast had been exhibited earlier. In November 1814, Andrew Jackson and American forces seized Mobile and forced Nicholls and Woodbine to withdraw, first to Apalachicola and then further south to Tampa Bay. When enslaved blacks continued to escape from Georgia plantations to Negro Fort, Jackson ordered General Edmund Pendleton Gaines to eliminate this sanctuary. On April 27, 1816, Negro Fort was destroyed and more than three hundred of its black defenders were killed or captured. Survivors fled to Seminole villages nearby and to other villages along the Suwannee River. Some of the refugees traveled further south to the Big Hammock area in today's Citrus County and the already established villages at Tampa Bay and Manatee River.

When Kingsley heard the news about the destruction of Negro Fort, he suspected that some of his enslaved Africans were among the captives taken by the Americans, and revived his efforts to reclaim them. Convinced that the ineffectual Spanish government would not be able to muster the strength or diplomatic skill needed to negotiate their return, he wrote to Georgia governor David Brydie Mitchell on September 13, 1816. He told Mitchell of his certainty that "some of mine were amongst" the blacks captured at Negro Fort, "as I have a great many with the Indians, who refuse delivering them up or allowing any one to take them, and as there is no efficient Government in this country to oblige them or protect the inhabitants, we are thus iniquitously deprived of our property by those villains who laugh at us."[19]

Kingsley offered a generous incentive to individuals willing to capture the runaways. He told Governor Mitchell that he owned more than "Forty Negros at Sawanee or about between there and the big Hamack and Tampa and a few about Makasukee. I am willing to give one half to those who will go and seize them and bring them out by force and all the Florida people have agreed to the same and authorise the captors to take them wherever they are to be found. Of that description there must be two hundred Negros or upwards owned about this Neighbourhood." Because pressing "circumstances" in Florida prevented Kingsley from looking "after this business personally," he solicited Mitchell's intervention, trusting the governor would "have my interest in view and should any part of the property appear to be mine, [ensure] that I may be fairly dealt [with]." He offered to meet with the adventurers at either St. Marys or Savannah, Georgia, to pay for their services "on demand: Being a Citizen of the U. States unto which country my Negroes are lawfully imported."[20]

The claim to U.S. citizenship is intriguing. Kingsley did own property at St. Marys, and he posted letters from there frequently. It may be that a residence of convenience at the St. Marys port had been helpful for his commerce as an African slave trader. Of course, citizenship was a flexible commodity to Kingsley, a means to enhance one or another of his ventures. Born in England and reared in two British colonies, South Carolina and New Brunswick, Canada, he had taken pledges of loyalty to the United States at Charleston in 1793, to Denmark at St. Thomas in 1798, and to Spain at St. Augustine in 1803.

Kingsley may have reclaimed some of his missing Africans, specifically "the few about Makasukee" he mentioned in his letter to Mitchell. But if that happened, it came about as the result of an unexpected action by the Indian trader Edmund Doyle, an employee of the Panton and Leslie Company. Doyle had previously reported on black families that fled from American troops after the destruction of Negro Fort, saying that some took shelter in the Miccosukee villages that stretched for miles along the west shore of today's Lake Miccosukee near Tallahassee in Leon County, Florida. According to United States Indian agent Benjamin Hawkins, "Micco Sookee [was] the main town of the Simenolies, they have six towns, and scattered settlements." The general turmoil in the region prompted one group of black refugees to leave the Miccosukee and ask for shelter at the Indian trade store at Prospect Bluff. Doyle wrote on January 23, 1817: "four negroes came here from the Mikasukkys and demanded of me protection which of course was offered; they returned same day to bring the rest of their party." The total number in the party was not mentioned, but Doyle did state that "they belong to a Mr. Kingsley of St. John's River." Since Prospect Bluff and the trading company still operated under the authorization of the Spanish government, it is possible that Kingsley reclaimed the group that Doyle sheltered. A record confirming such a return has not been found, however, nor has evidence been found that Kingsley's September 1816 proposition to Governor Mitchell resulted in a return of slaves to his custody.[21]

Mitchell resigned as governor in 1817 to accept appointment as United States Indian agent. It was in this new position that Mitchell plotted with Andrew Jackson and Lower Creek chief William McIntosh for a controversial invasion of Spanish Florida. It is intriguing to contemplate whether Kingsley's 1816 letter helped inspire the nefarious invasion.

Red Stick Creeks, Black Seminoles, and black refugees from Georgia had been fleeing southward along the Florida Gulf Coast since Negro Fort was destroyed in 1814. The numbers increased dramatically in 1818 after Jackson led three thousand American soldiers and militia on a plundering rampage through much of north and central Florida. This invasion, the First Seminole War, was ordered in 1817 by Secretary of War John C. Calhoun after a series of violent confrontations between American settlers and soldiers and Miccosukee villagers in southwest Georgia. Between March and June, Jackson's army burned hundreds of homes and destroyed agricultural fields and entire settlements near Tallahassee, as well as along the Suwannee and Enconfina Rivers. The American army also captured Fort St. Marks and Pensacola. International protests followed, and Secretary of State John Quincy Adams apologized for the invasion. Spanish officials realized they could not control East and West Florida and agreed to the Adams-Onis Treaty of 1819, which ceded the colonies to the United States.[22]

Jackson, however, had not finished his relentless pursuit of Red Sticks, Black Seminoles, and former slaves from Georgia. Although he was appointed provisional governor in January, the formal transfer of power did not take place until July 17, 1821. During the interim, Jackson wrote to Secretary of State Adams expressing his desire to force the Red Sticks to leave Florida and move to treaty lands set aside in Georgia. Jackson's request was denied, but the man known as Old Hickory was not easily dissuaded.[23]

At his home in Milledgeville, former Georgia governor David B. Mitchell, by then a United States Indian agent, met with Lower Creek chief William McIntosh, a former ally at the Battle of Horseshoe Bend. The historian Toni Carrier writes that Mitchell and McIntosh agreed to send Lower Creek warriors into Spanish Florida to bring "away the blacks among the Red Sticks and return them to slavery." The next step in the plot involved Jackson, who commissioned McIntosh "a Brigadier General in the United

States Army, [and] ordered a Lower Creek war party into Florida. Led by McIntosh's man Colonel Charles Miller and Jackson's Red Stick protégé William Weatherford, the raiders wreaked havoc as they progressed down the peninsula." Focusing their attacks on the black settlements at Manatee River and Tampa Bay, the Lower Creek raiders captured more than three hundred blacks, most of whom mysteriously "disappeared as they were being returned to the United States." The blacks who survived the raids escaped to the Florida Keys and traveled by water to sanctuaries at Andros Island in the Bahamas.[24]

Late in his life, Zephaniah Kingsley told the abolitionist Lydia Maria Child: "I should be the last man on earth to give up a runaway. If my own were to run away, I wouldn't go after 'em." If Ms. Child accurately reported their conversation, it is troubling to contemplate that twenty-five years before making that statement Kingsley had been so desperate to profit from the labor of enslaved Africans that he encouraged the governor of Georgia to deputize ruthless renegades—men not unlike the so-called Patriots who had rampaged through East Florida for more than two years—in order to regain his lost human property. Although the evidence is circumstantial, it is possible that Kingsley's 1816 letter to Mitchell initiated the idea for the plan that became the shockingly cruel Lower Creek raid on the Manatee River and Tampa Bay settlements in 1821. It must have left a bitter aftertaste in Kingsley's mouth when none of the black men and women re-enslaved during the Lower Creek raids were returned to him by the raiders.[25]

Bitterness was common among East Florida residents in the decade before Spain ceded the province to the United States. In addition to the ill-named Patriot War, there were repeated American invasions of north-central Florida and the Gulf Coast from Pensacola to Tampa Bay. The violence, arson, and theft that plagued the rural settlements between the St. Johns and St. Marys Rivers continued well beyond Governor Kindelán's August 1814 pronouncement that the Patriot insurgency had ended and peace had returned to the province.

In 1816, Spanish governor Coppinger authorized George J. F. Clarke, Phillip R. Yonge, and Zephaniah Kingsley to negotiate with residents of the largely lawless area between the rivers in an effort to reestablish order and stability. Settlers in the area had been hostile toward the colonial administration and contemptuous of Spanish officials. As historian Susan Parker has demonstrated, the settlers living north of the St. Johns River differed from St. Augustine residents in terms of national origins and religious affiliation, having originated in one of the American states, Great Britain, or elsewhere in Europe, and professing Protestant rather than Catholic beliefs. Governor Kindelán had initiated a decentralized governmental plan in 1812 by delegating some functions to local magistrates and militia captains. The reform minimized the difficulty and danger of travel to the distant provincial capital and garnered support for the colonial administration. The Crown had previously authorized constitutional reforms that included elective municipal governments for the colonies, but Kindelán, fearful that residents north of St. Augustine were "transients" whose loyalties were to countries other than Spain, decided to appoint the local officials rather than hold elections. His partial reforms proved to be popular, but a few months after they were implemented the "Patriot" and American invasions occurred and turned the northeast portion of the province into an ungovernable region.[26]

By 1816, with violence and turbulence in the region somewhat reduced, Kindelán's successor, José M. Coppinger, decided to revive the initiative. He urged Clarke, Yonge, and Kingsley to travel to the "northern frontier" and meet with disaffected residents. They convinced forty men to meet at Mill's Ferry on the St. Marys River, where a gathering of all residents at nearby Waterman's Bluff was planned for three weeks later. Several hundred settlers attended the second meeting. After vigorous debate, the majority in attendance agreed to participate in a revised governing structure. The vast area between the St. Johns and St. Marys Rivers (essentially today's Clay, Duval, and Nassau Counties) was divided into three separate districts, each with its own magistrate's court and militia, with officers to be elected by the residents of each local district.[27]

The Waterman's Bluff meeting represented a new beginning for the "northern frontier" of the province, but while the program was still in its infancy another foreign invasion negated its promise. Early in 1817 Governor Coppinger began receiving warnings of a possible invasion targeted on Fernandina on the Atlantic coast. East Florida residents heard the same rumors. Soon, the Charleston and Savannah newspapers published detailed accounts of recruiting and fund-raising activities under way in American coastal cities by men calling themselves revolutionaries intent on liberating Spain's American colonies from oppressive monarchal rule.[28]

On June 21, 1817, Kingsley wrote from Fort George Island to his attorney, Joseph Hernandez, that he was delaying his trip to St. Augustine because he feared an invasion was eminent: "I can hear nothing which induces me to believe that any force is expected from without by sea, only that some Chiefs who derive their consequence from Insurgent commissions are endeavouring to raise men and means amongst our well disposed & charitable Neighbours of the US—Land bounties & promises which they never can fulfil would doubtlessly be their principal dependance."[29]

Kingsley predicted that promises of land bounties in exchange for military service would have little appeal to the "Inhabitants who already have property granted to them from Gov't, but a great many residents have no property nor any interest to defend, of these we have most to fear. Government may however depend upon the endeavours of all the principal people who alone are the objects of these plundering expeditions that from motives of loyalty & still more strongly from their own interest they will use every means to maintain peace and good order throughout the province." A prominent member of the planter elite, Kingsley viewed the world through the lens of class conflict.[30]

The rumors of invasion also prompted regret that the recent experiment in local government for the area north of St. Augustine was about to be negated by yet another foreign invasion. "It seems a pity that they will not let us alone 'til another year so that our good governor [Coppinger] might have the pleasure of enjoying the effect of his liberal policy so as to convince the world that the great secret of governing a people lays in making it their interest to defend its government. We are now like a Turtle without a shell, vulnerable on all sides & endeavouring to hide from the vilest animals until we gather strength which time alone can bestow."[31]

A respite from bandit raids and turmoil was needed, a gift of time in which the residents could rebuild their lives. Kingsley told Hernandez that "hardly a family but what is looking forward with anxiety to the ripening of its corn field for subsistence & being the first year few have houses to shelter them from the Rain—nothing less than another season can produce that kind of comfort which alone could render them fit to combine for defending the country ag't invasion—or so as to be formidable to an enemy." Kingsley closed his disheartening letter with a promise to write again if "todays mail will bring us some more certain information."[32]

Mail would not be necessary. Only one week later—June 28, 1817—the invading force arrived at Fernandina harbor with fewer than one hundred men and seized the city. The Spanish garrison was surrendered without firing a shot, and Amelia Island was proclaimed "The Republic of Florida." The local government initiative that Kingsley had praised only one week before died in its infancy.

The leader of this invasion was Gregor MacGregor, a native of Scotland, who claimed to be a revolutionary engaged in a noble republican struggle to liberate the oppressed colonial subjects of monarchal Spain. MacGregor boasted that Amelia Island would serve as a springboard for the conquest of the rest of Florida, after which his liberating heroes would join forces with revolutionaries in the Caribbean, Mexico, and Latin America and drive all vestiges of the Spanish Empire out of the Western Hemisphere. His expedition was financed by a network of revolutionaries in Philadelphia, Baltimore, Charleston, and Savannah, but the funds they provided proved woefully insufficient, prompting him to declare a blockade extending from Amelia Island to the Perdido River on the Gulf Coast. MacGregor established an admiralty court at Fernandina and issued dozens of letters of marque to privateers, authorizing them to prey on Spanish shipping. The occupation soon disintegrated into disorganized exploitation and piracy, and MacGregor departed in early September.[33]

The Republic of Florida continued after MacGregor's departure, led by Commodore Luis Aury and reinforced by additional troops that included Haitian soldiers and sailors. Aury, a French-born sailor who deserted his country's navy to become a Caribbean pirate, later became a revolutionary. Both Aury and MacGregor claimed legitimate pedigrees as veterans of the Latin American revolutionary movement—MacGregor in Bolivia and Venezuela, Aury at Cartagena and Mexico—but during the occupation of Amelia Island they were motivated as much by self-enrichment as by commitment to liberation.

The favorite targets of the privateers commissioned by the Republic of Florida and by Aury's small fleet of ships were Spanish slave ships carrying cargoes of Africans to Havana and other Caribbean ports. The slaves were sold at Fernandina, primarily in clandestine transactions with Georgia planters. Even as prominent a man as former Georgia governor David Brydie Mitchell was caught up in a scandal concerning a slave cargo sold at Fernandina and subsequently smuggled through Georgia to markets in Alabama and Mississippi. Mitchell was forced to resign his post as United States Indian agent when President James Monroe learned of the allegations. According to historian T. Frederick Davis, Aury sold more than a thousand slaves at Fernandina in a two-month span. Some East Florida planters, including Kingsley, were suspected by Governor Coppinger of clandestinely purchasing Africans from cargoes brought to Fernandina by the privateers.[34]

The U.S. Navy stationed up to five naval vessels off Cumberland Sound at the entrance to the St. Marys and Amelia Rivers to monitor Aury's actions. Under command of Captain J. D. Henly, privateers were stopped and boarded to verify the legitimacy of registration and cargoes. Secretary of State John Quincy Adams was keenly aware of events at Amelia Island and was concerned by the volume of slaves being smuggled into Georgia. Politicians outraged by the presence of black soldiers and sailors from Haiti manning Aury's ships and the Fernandina garrison pressured the Monroe administration to bring an immediate end to the occupation. On December 23, 1817, Captain J. D. Henley of the U.S. Navy and Major James Bankhead of the U.S. Army acted on President Monroe's order to seize control of Fernandina and shut down all traffic into and out of the harbor. Aury and his occupying army were ushered out of Florida, thus ending the six-month tenure of the Republic of Florida, one of the most bizarre episodes in the history of Florida.[35]

The American occupation represented more than the ejection of Aury's forces. Rather than invite Governor Coppinger to resume Spanish governance of Amelia Island, American forces remained at Amelia Island until Florida became a United States territory three years later. Secretary of State Adams used the U.S. occupation to dramatize for Spanish minister Luis de Onis the tenuous nature of Spain's control of its Florida colonies. Adams's pressure was a key factor in Spain's decision to cede East and West Florida to the United States in the Adams-Onis Treaty of 1819. It would be two years before the two nations ratified the treaty and the formal transfer would occur, but during the interim the American occupation continued.[36]

Zephaniah Kingsley's activities between June 1817 and January 1821 are only sparsely documented. Popular legends abound of his smuggling Africans to Fort George Island, training them there, and selling them to Georgia planters willing to pay high prices for coveted "Kingsley niggers." No evidence supports these legends. Kingsley certainly had a prodigious knowledge of the waterways of the American Southeast, and based on what is known of his earlier life, he was experienced in smuggling cargoes of enslaved Africans into South Carolina and Georgia. Yet it is hard to imagine him so foolhardy as to risk capture by ships of the U.S. Navy patrolling off Cumberland and Amelia Islands and on the St. Marys River. Kingsley may have purchased Africans for his own plantations from the cargoes brought into Amelia Island by Aury's pirate ships, but it is highly doubtful that he smuggled slaves between 1817 and 1821.[37]

In 1819, treaty terms were agreed upon by Spain and the United States that would result in a transfer of sovereignty. Kingsley supported ratification, but with only tepid enthusiasm. He confided in Joseph Hernandez: "I wish it not from any belief that we shall acquire a better government than our New Constitution (if Established) but that we shall be more fixed and less liable to misfortune." He became more inclined to endorse an American takeover after threats to his property forced him to cancel an important business trip to St. Augustine two months later. "My property has no other protection than my presence," he protested, and "until we are organized according to the New Constitution or have some other government there can be no responsibility nor security for property. Whoever is strongest now makes law & every day growing worse."[38]

10 | "Discreetly Restrained under the Patriarchal System"

Life and Labor at Kingsley's Plantations

In early 1815, Zephaniah Kingsley moved to Fort George Island, his primary residence for the next twenty years. In the previous decade he had been an absentee owner and intermittent resident at Laurel Grove Plantation, observing and directing, but his attention was primarily focused on maritime enterprise. Beginning in 1815, he became involved in the day-to-day operations of Fort George Island and his other properties.

Eventually, Kingsley expanded his property holdings to more than 17,000 acres in five of today's northeast Florida counties: Nassau, Duval, Clay, St. Johns, and Putnam. Other than 2,500 acres at White Oak Plantation on the south bank of the St. Marys River in Nassau County, Kingsley's properties were primarily located along the St. Johns River. They included Fort George Island and neighboring Batten Island, St. Johns Bluff and Sawmill Creek, Reddy's Point and Baxter's Bluff (aka St. Isabel), San Jose (aka Yellow Bluff), Little San Jose (aka Ashley's Old Field), Naranjal de San Jose, Goodbys Creek, and Beauclerc Bluff, all in Duval County; Laurel Grove, in Clay County; Pivot Swamp, Twelve-Mile Swamp, Six-Mile Creek, Chancery, Wanton's Island, Forrester Point, Deep Creek, Buena Vista, and Orange Grove (also known as Buena Vista Point) in St. Johns County; and Drayton Island and a 400-acre tract on the east shore of Lake George in Putnam County.[1]

Kingsley also became the owner of a large number of human properties. The numbers of enslaved men and women he owned varied from 250 to 300 in the 1820s and 1830s to the 84 who lived at his San Jose Plantation when he died in 1843. It was during the years that he personally managed

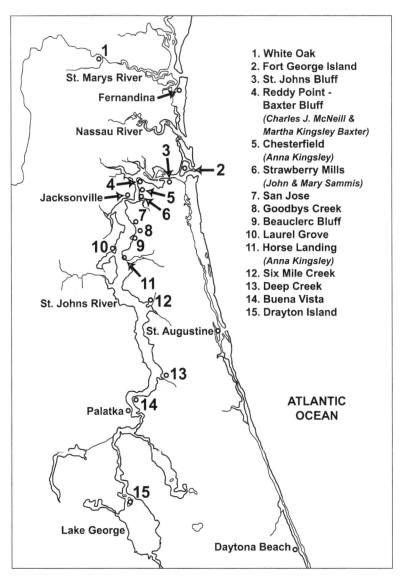

1. White Oak
2. Fort George Island
3. St. Johns Bluff
4. Reddy Point -
   Baxter Bluff
   (Charles J. McNeill &
   Martha Kingsley Baxter)
5. Chesterfield
   (Anna Kingsley)
6. Strawberry Mills
   (John & Mary Sammis)
7. San Jose
8. Goodbys Creek
9. Beauclerc Bluff
10. Laurel Grove
11. Horse Landing
    (Anna Kingsley)
12. Six Mile Creek
13. Deep Creek
14. Buena Vista
15. Drayton Island

FIGURE 5. Northeast Florida properties owned by Zephaniah Kingsley. With the exception of White Oak Plantation on the St. Marys River, Kingsley's East Florida plantations and farms were located along the St. Johns River. Kingsley also owned properties that adjoined or were nearby those identified on this map. Some of his properties were sold by the time of his death in 1843, but titles to most of the tracts were transferred to members of his family. Map drawn by Jerome Humery of Cranberry Point Computers, Corea, Maine.

his Florida plantations that Kingsley developed the views on race and caste, and the managerial practices regarding slave labor that became the basis for his proslavery booklet, *A Treatise on the Patriarchal, or Co-operative System of Society.*[2]

Kingsley would no doubt have chosen his former career as an Atlantic maritime trader over day-to-day supervision of planting operations at his slave plantations. But to have done so in the aftermath of the Patriot insurgency, the British coastal blockade, and the invasions of East Florida between 1812 and 1814 would have required moving to another Spanish colony. Kingsley had learned from repeated personal tragedies how precarious life and fortune could be in the Age of Revolution.

Kingsley was the fourth Anglo-American planter to acquire title to Fort George Island, and the third to occupy the owner's wood-frame dwelling built for John McQueen in 1798. The dwelling's foundation of coquina rock came from a quarry at Anastasia Island, across the Matanzas River from St. Augustine. The building had a full-size basement with cooking facilities and numerous ventilation openings. On the first floor a rectangular "great room" in the center of the house was divided by large folding doors and flanked by six-foot fireplaces on the east and west walls. Doors from the great room opened to attached piazzas on the north and south that were enclosed by wooden blinds. Access to the bedrooms at each of the four corners was gained via the piazzas. The second floor of the dwelling was divided into two large bedrooms above the great room and was accessed by stairs that led upward from the south piazza. The observation deck on the peak of the roof was reached through the attic.[3]

Construction of permanent housing for Kingsley's slaves began as soon as they moved into the temporary dwellings erected on arrival in December 1813. The labor force was tasked with a variety of work assignments: some shouldered axes and machetes and cleared fields of weeds and brush for corn, peas, and beans, while others entered the nearby forest to fell trees and split and saw logs. A small detail of men loaded oyster shells from the huge shellfish refuse mounds found on the island onto mule-drawn wagons to carry back to the residential complex. A portion of the shells was poured into large cast-iron kettles and burned to make lime, which was mixed with sand and water and the remaining oyster shells to make a cement-like mixture that hardened into walls for the permanent dwellings.

FIGURE 6. The Zephaniah Kingsley residence at Fort George Island is the oldest plantation house in Florida, built in 1798 by slaves of John McQueen. The house was designed to maximize the flow of cooling air to the four corner bedrooms on the first floor. The two bedrooms on the second floor were accessed by an external stairway on a porch at the rear of the house. Cooking facilities were located in the full-size basement. The bow windows and the room between the bedrooms on the east side of the building were added circa 1880. Image courtesy of the Library of Congress, Prints and Photographs Division, Washington, D.C.

Carpenters fashioned rafters, trusses, and decking for roofs and cedar shingles. The ground level of each cabin was divided into two rooms, one with a brick-lined fireplace for food preparation, the second for sleeping, with a loft for children above. Thirty-two tabby cabins were constructed, each intended to accommodate a nuclear family.

In addition to the slave cabins, a house was built for Anna Jai and her children. The first floor was constructed of tabby bricks, and the second floor was wood-frame. The rectangular north room of the stable was also constructed of tabby brick, while the walls of the south room were of poured tabby. The main house, the Anna Jai house, the stable, and the walls of most of the slave dwellings still stand.

Tabby construction was familiar to Kingsley from his time in South Carolina and from his travels in Africa and the Caribbean. The prominent and

FIGURE 7. The Anna Jai Kingsley House at Fort George Island, built circa 1820 and located close by Zephaniah Kingsley's residence. A sitting room for Anna, along with a food preparation area and an oversize fireplace and cooking room, were located on the ground floor. Bedrooms were on the second floor. Some of the food preparation for the main house was done here under Anna's supervision. Anna Kingsley lived here until 1839, when she moved to her son George's residential compound at Cabarete in today's Dominican Republic. Image courtesy of the Library of Congress, Prints and Photographs Division, Washington, D.C.

influential Georgia planter Thomas Spalding may have inspired Kingsley to build tabby dwellings. Spalding built an eclectic array of tabby buildings at his numerous properties, including the fifteen thousand acres he owned on Sapelo Island. He wrote on one occasion of assigning "six black men and two boys" the task of constructing a "massy building" and of being astonished that they completed the work in a few months. "They collected their own shells, burnt their own lime, mixed their mortar, consisting of equal parts of oyster shells, lime and sand, removed and filled their boxes—all the art that was necessary was to know the use of the plummet and the level, to keep the walls strait and perpendicular."[4]

The thirty-two cabins at Fort George were placed on a half-circle facing north toward the main dwelling house. Twenty-eight cabins measured twenty-one feet by fourteen feet, each spaced twelve feet from its neighbor. The remaining four cabins were six feet longer and four feet wider, with the additional space intended to provide special rewards to the plantation managers known as "drivers," who were also enslaved men owned by Kingsley. Each driver's cabin was spaced twenty feet from its nearest neighbor.

Visitors traveled from a wharf at Batten Island over a causeway to the southernmost point of Fort George Island and followed a sandy cart road on the west of the island, passing through cultivated fields to the plantation complex at the north end. The road entered the complex between two "driver" cabins located at the center point of the arc of cabins. The end cabins on the east and the west of the arc were also occupied by "drivers." They faced inward directly across from one another at a distance of approximately two hundred yards, providing an unobstructed view of the entire slave village.

The half-circle design for slave dwellings was rarely seen in the American South. Historic preservation expert Wayne W. Wood has speculated that the design was intended to promote "privacy and individuality" for the families living in each cabin. The semicircular configuration of the cabins "seems designed to benefit the quality of living for [the Kingsley] slaves and the development of a residential community."[5]

Kingsley's own writings support this conclusion. He wrote in *Treatise on the Patriarchal* that his African slaves' "strong attachment to their homes, to their women and children, and to domestic life, are likewise great securities for their good behavior; which, with a fair and equitable allowance of clothes and provisions, kind treatment . . . and fair words . . . will, in most cases, insure good behavior, obedience and attachment." In describing the Africans he brought to Laurel Grove Plantation in the previous decade, Kingsley wrote that he "never interfered with their connubial concerns nor domestic affairs, but let them regulate these after their own manner. . . . I encouraged as much as possible dancing, merriment, and dress, for which Saturday afternoon and night, and Sunday morning were dedicated; and after allowance, their time was usually employed in hoeing their corn, and getting a supply of fish for the week." Kingsley was unwilling to permit his slaves to travel away from Laurel Grove on weekends, but he "encouraged the decent neighboring people" to come to his property and "participate in their weekly festivity, for which they always provided an ample

FIGURE 8. "Remains of Slave Quarters at Fort George Island, Florida," circa 1865. The unidentified free black families shown on this image are not Zephaniah Kingsley's former slaves. Kingsley moved his human property from Fort George Island to San Jose Plantation between 1839 and 1842. Image courtesy of the New-York Historical Society, 170 Central Park West, New York, N.Y.

entertainment themselves, as they had an abundance of hogs, fowls, corn, and all kinds of vegetables and fruit." Kingsley's comments indicate that the structural design was intended to enhance a community feeling.[6]

Other observers have concluded that the design was intended to maximize control over the laborers while providing a comfortable distance from them. Kingsley's dwelling was located 350 yards to the north. In the intervening space stood a tabby stable and mule sheds large enough to accommodate up to one hundred of the work animals, in addition to horses and teams of oxen. Beyond the stables were corn and vegetable gardens and small groves of citrus trees, fig trees, and freshwater wells dug between every two cabins. In 1904, Mrs. Hanna Rollins, an owner of the island, recalled that the stable was not complete when she first arrived in 1868. She also remembered a large oak tree beside the sand road running from the cabins to the main house, and "under it a still visable darkey grave yard." The author of an 1878 publication wrote that the slave "grave yard" was "placed there by Captain Kingsley . . . to prevent the slaves, who were excessively superstitious, from leaving their cabins at night to steal corn from the barn." Recent archaeological excavations by Dr. James M. Davidson of the University of Florida discovered a burial site in the space between the cabins, but it is likely the placement had more do with cultural practices of Africans who sought to honor their departed ancestors than a scheme to stop petty theft.[7]

Master and slave lived apart, the historian Daniel Stowell has written, yet not too distant to deny Kingsley "the best opportunity to observe and control his slaves." If desire to control was a motive for the placement of the cabins, it was an insignificant one. Kingsley's dwelling was sufficiently distant from the slave cabins to minimize any potential control he could have exercised by direct observation.[8]

Discussions of the design configuration have not considered the possibility that African conceptions of spatial usage, human community, and aesthetics may have influenced the design. Anna Kingsley lived in a Wolof village in Senegal, West Africa, as a child. Wolof villages at that time contained family housing compounds with multiple dwellings, granaries, and other structures, all with entries facing an open area in the center. Each family compound was surrounded by a circular wall. The adjoining family compounds were similarly configured, and the entire village was surrounded by a circular wall. The historical archaeologist Brahim Diop concluded that the ravages of the slave trade forced the Wolof to reshape their villages to defend against raiders on horseback, but until late in the eighteenth century the predominant design was circular.[9] The building complex at Kingsley's plantation symbolically evokes images of circular Wolof villages.

The design configuration may also have symbolized security. Strangers who entered the compound from the south passed between two roadside dwellings occupied by drivers, people with authority delegated by the master. Theoretically, they could only reach Kingsley after traveling through the entire slave village. This also followed a pattern of deference to male authority among the Wolof, with the focal point of the village community being the dwelling of the master or headman at the north end. According to Wolof paternal protocol, visitors would pass first through the men and women of the slave community before advancing to the residence of the "father," or family head. In March 2001, a delegation from the Ministry of Education of Senegal toured the ruins of the slave quarters at Kingsley's plantation. The design layout reminded the leader of the group, Dr. Sidi Camara, of very old Wolof villages in Senegal, where time-honored patterns of paternal protocol persist to the present.[10]

While the buildings were being constructed at Fort George Island, a larger group of men and women were at work clearing land and planting corn, beans, peas, and potatoes. Turmoil in the province had disrupted Kingsley's planting for years, and it was important that the expense associated with purchasing provisions be minimized. Sea island cotton and other commercial crops would be planted later.[11]

Observers commented on Kingsley's innovative farming methods. He rotated crops and fertilized with animal manure and discarded corn and sugarcane stalks (bagasse). The nutrient-rich muck in the marshes surrounding Fort George was raked and spread over the cultivated ground after rainwater washed out salt residue, and he periodically left the fields idle to regenerate productivity. Seeds and plants were acquired during Kingsley's travels to Caribbean islands and South American countries and planted as experiments: coffee trees at Drayton Island, orange trees at Laurel Grove, and sea island cotton at multiple locations.[12]

Florida planters in the 1820s were enamored by the possibility of becoming rich from cultivating sugarcane. Many sugar planters south of St. Augustine, who left East Florida for the Bahamas and other British Caribbean islands when rule by Spain resumed in 1783, returned to their former estates a decade later. The historian Edward E. Baptist writes of migrants to Middle Florida whose "fascination with the sweet staple underscored their interest in becoming a part of a world of trade, commerce, and power that transcended regional and even national boundaries." Expecting to become as rich as the sugar titans in Jamaica, planters on the Atlantic coast and in Middle Florida invested heavily in machinery for crushing cane and boiling juice to manufacture sugar crystals.[13]

Kingsley was one of those planters. George Gibbs, married to Kingsley's sister Isabella, stated in 1823 that Kingsley "attained perfection" as a sugar cultivator. Gibbs wrote that Kingsley harvested a surplus of cane that year, which he intended "to sell . . . for seed," but "having then no works of his own to manufacture it, sent a sloop load of it to the mills of Mr. Carnochan" to be processed into sugar. By 1829 Kingsley had acquired a mill to press juice from the cane, boiling kettles, and a furnace, and was able to ship fifty hogsheads of sugar from White Oak Plantation, each weighing in excess of a thousand pounds.[14]

A letter Kingsley wrote in 1830 to the editor of the *Southern Agriculturalist* describing the "process of Manufacturing and Clarifying Sugar" confirms that he was engaged in processing brown crystal sugar on a large scale. Kingsley's letter addressed a problem encountered at plantations where cooler days and nights and the threat of autumn freezes delayed the maturation of cane and required special processing techniques. Kingsley learned those techniques from the Marquis des Fougeres, a former French consul to Charleston who swore loyalty to Spain and became a resident of East Florida. Kingsley and the Marquis met at St. Augustine in 1818 and discussed planting practices perfected in Martinique.[15]

It is not likely that Kingsley installed the expensive machinery necessary to manufacture sugar for export at Fort George, where cane was generally planted in small plots to produce molasses and brown sugar for consumption by residents of the island only. Kingsley's nephew Kingsley Beatty Gibbs, the owner of Fort George Island from 1840 to 1843, planted between three and eight acres in sugarcane, and his highest annual yield was only 260 gallons of syrup and 600 pounds of sugar. It was at White Oak Plantation in Nassau County that Kingsley installed the expensive milling machinery.[16]

In Florida, the practice of sugar planting was to fell trees on fallow land, trim and burn branches and brush, and use the ash residue for fertilizer. Stumps were left in the fields, drains were dug, and the soil was laid up in furrows to plant "seed" cane for seeding. Horse-drawn plows were used when practical, but often the work was done by hand with shovels and hoes.[17]

Roughly eight of every ten cane stalks harvested were sent to the mill to be crushed for juice, while the two remaining stalks were cut into pieces called "seeds" to be used in the next year's planting. The "seeds" were "banked" in plowed furrows and covered with dirt as protection against freezes. During the second year the cane roots sprouted again and were known as "ratoons." In Florida, cane was harvested for four or five years, after which the field was returned to nature for a period of years and new fields were prepared.[18]

Planting began in early February. Shoots began to push through the soil by the end of March, a sure signal that the monotonous work of hoe-weeding around the stalks would be needed three times before October, when the cane harvest began. Slaves advanced on the fields carrying machetes to cut the stalks and trim leaves sharp enough to cut a novice worker. Throughout the three- or four-month harvest ordeal, male slaves cut cane and hauled it to the mill, while others (often women and boys) sorted seed cane and carted loads to be banked in furrows for a future crop. The other slaves were divided into several work groups and tasked variously with cutting and hauling wood from the forest that heated the boiler kettles, minding the furnace, hauling away the bagasse, feeding and tending animals, butchering hogs and beef, and other activities. While sugar making was under way, most of the workers were involved and the hours were long and exhausting.

Preparatory work at the mill started in the weeks before October. Carpenters removed and rounded the wooden mill rollers and refurbished the other mill machinery. Oxen had to be broken to plod in the endless circle, turning the wheel that powered the crushers. Axe men felled trees for the lumber used by carpenters to make the tongues, wheels, axles, and rails for the mule-drawn carts that hauled the cane to the mill. Stacks of firewood were hauled to replenish supplies at the furnaces. Troughs of cypress wood were fashioned to transmit juice from crusher to boiler kettles. Cisterns were constructed of cypress to capture molasses that drained from cooler troughs. Coopers constructed dozens of hogshead barrels that were filled with granulated brown sugar crystals.

Experienced sugar makers checked the temperature of the juice as it boiled and condensed, adding lime juice and wood ash at the appropriate time to clarify the liquid. Scum and impurities that floated to the surface were skimmed off, and the clarified juice was ladled from kettle to kettle as it evaporated and condensed to a syrupy mixture that was transferred to long wooden "cooler" vats. Within twenty-four hours the thin layers of the mixture would crystallize and the granules were "potted" in hogsheads that were carted to a "draining" room. Here, rows of hogsheads topped with boards to retain heat and further the evaporation process were placed over drains that carried the runoff (molasses) to cisterns. Eventually, hogsheads weighing between one thousand and twelve hundred pounds were hauled to the wharf and loaded on ships.

Sugar making was deemphasized at White Oak in the 1830s. Prices paid for sea island cotton had recovered from a steep downturn in the 1820s, and north Florida planters had learned from a series of early freezes that relying on sugar for income carried risks. Small fields of cane were subsequently planted at White Oak and Fort George Island, but the manufacture of syrup and sugar was limited to amounts needed to supply residents of the plantations. Cultivation of sea island cotton and rice became the principal focus of Kingsley's planting operations.

Kingsley's most ambitious project between 1816 and 1821 was the restoration of White Oak Plantation. Located twenty-five miles from the Atlantic Ocean on the St. Marys River, White Oak was first developed in 1768 when East Florida was a British colony. In that year, Governor James Grant conveyed a tract of land known as White Oak to Andrew Way, a rice planter in South Carolina who became a deputy surveyor of lands in the new British province. Way chose for himself a tidal freshwater marsh situated where the St. Marys and the Little St. Marys joined, with adjoining fertile hammock land. On May 22, 1771, the tract was conveyed to Jermyn Wright, a South Carolina planter. Wright's slaves finished the clearing, ditching, damming, rice gates, and canals that alternately drained and irrigated the rice fields. The plantation thrived until 1776, when rebels from Georgia breached the levees and destroyed the fields. All of the buildings were burned to the ground.[19]

The White Oak fields were idle for the next four decades. Spanish governors granted small tracts of land in the vicinity to settlers, but the border region at the northeast corner of Florida—the haunt of lawless bandits since the closing years of the American Revolution—continued to be turbulent and unsafe. Kingsley received a land grant of 1,000 acres at White Oak in 1814, and between 1816 and 1819 he purchased four smaller adjoining tracts for a total of 2,125 acres.[20]

Kingsley moved slaves to the property in mid-1816, and within five years it had been transformed into one of the premier plantations in East Florida. The names and ethnic origins of the workers responsible for this

FIGURE 9. A contemporary aerial view of the rice field at White Oak Plantation, located at the junction of the St. Marys River and its tributary, the Little
St. Marys River, in Nassau County, Florida. Constructed in the 1760s by enslaved Africans, destroyed in border warfare during the American Revolution,
and restored by slaves owned by Zephaniah Kingsley, this field was abandoned
more than a century and a half ago. It is remarkable that the dikes and canals
have survived countless storms and the ravages of time. Image by Michael J.
Canella, www.aerial-photo.com, for Florida History Online, www.unf.edu/
floridahistoryonline.

achievement are not known, but the core of the workforce was the group
of seventy-nine Africans transported from Pongo River in Guinea, West
Africa, that Kingsley acquired in 1816 from the estate of the deceased John
Fraser. In 1812 an overseer described them as "prime Africans" who had
been in Florida "three to four years" and were experienced planters.[21]

Clearing the two-decade growth from the dormant fields at White Oak
began under Kingsley's direction in 1816. No buildings, tools, or machinery existed at the tract, and as the lawless nature of the region continued,
startup work suffered several interruptions. In 1818, Kingsley traveled to
Charleston to purchase Ceceem, Bella, Tomba, and Duramame from the

estate of Samuel Gale, another American planter with a slave-trading business on the Pongo River in West Africa. As late as January 1821, Kingsley complained that three robberies had recently been committed at his "precariously situated" property and that he was searching for an overseer who could establish "a very respectable *military* establishment." Undaunted by the threat of robberies, Kingsley continued to invest in White Oak. By mid-1821 the agricultural fields had been restored and planted, and dwellings and farm buildings had been constructed. The restored dikes and canals of the rice field were so well constructed that they are still visible on contemporary aerial photographs and accessible via Google Earth.[22]

Only a few months after the work was completed, Kingsley advertised White Oak Plantation for sale in the Charleston *City Gazette*. White Oak was promoted as an "excellent and healthy" plantation located on a "permanently fresh" body of water. Large oceangoing ships could sail from the Atlantic all the way to the wharf at White Oak. The property consisted of "about 2000 acres, of which 400 are low rich hammocks, 600 well timbered, thrifty cattle range and good for cultivation, and 1000 acres of rich river swamp, 250 acres of which is well banked and drained." The working hands were cultivating "Cotton, Corn, Sugar and Rice" and had constructed a "Gin House, Cotton House, Barns, [and] Dwelling Houses." Prospective buyers were advised that the "Scaffolding, Trunks, &c. are new and mostly cypress" in the rice field. Kingsley boasted of the "excellence of the soil," the already installed "Negro Houses" and "excellent fences, machinery and other conveniences for cleaning Cotton on a large scale."[23]

It is not known why Kingsley sought a buyer for White Oak. The exchange of flags between Spain and the United States had taken place the previous July, and American troops were expected to curb violence along the St. Marys River. Only eight months before, he had predicted that "we shall be more fixed & less liable to misfortunes" after the American takeover. Perhaps it was Kingsley's recognition of the enormous potential for profit the plantation represented that persuaded him to take the property off the market. An early history of Florida described White Oak under Kingsley's ownership as so productive it "produced crops of the value of ten thousand dollars in one year. In 1829 he made five thousand bushels of rough rice, fifty hogsheads of sugar, besides a large quantity of cotton, corn, peas, and potatoes."[24]

In 1830 Kingsley employed four white men at White Oak who supervised 185 enslaved black men, women, and children, approximately 85 of whom were in their prime laboring years. The head overseer was Kingsley's future son-in-law John S. Sammis, a migrant to Florida from Dutchess County, New York. The overseers resided alongside the river in an octagonal wood-frame building with a thirty-eight-foot-wide foundation of tabby slabs poured perpendicular to the ground. Parts of the foundation slabs remain in place today.

East of the dwelling and alongside the river, tabby buildings were constructed for plantation artisans. Dozens of large pieces of tabby still lie beneath the trees and brush, extending for more than two hundred feet. The buildings accommodated the carpenters who manufactured barrels for rice and sugar, blacksmiths who forged barrel hoops, hoes, and other agricultural tools, and wheelwrights who fashioned wheels and axles for wagons. The footings for a large wharf can still be seen beneath the eroding riverbank between the tabby debris and the levees of the rice field.[25]

Approximately sixty feet back from the river is the ruin of a rectangular tabby foundation that was once a rice-pounding mill. No visible evidence can be found of the two-story wooden structure that was formerly situated above the foundation. However, the twelve-inch-thick tabby exterior walls still stand three feet above the ground and measure thirty-two by twenty feet. The walls were originally poured on a base of twelve-inch-square cypress logs that are still beneath the surface of the moist ground. The walls enclose several parallel trenches, six feet deep, each with tabby floors, that accommodated the gears, pulleys, and belts that conveyed power from a detached steam engine to the pounding machinery on the floors above. No traces of the machinery are visible at the site.

A series of four tabby structures stand east of the foundation, extending in a straight line toward a canal at the edge of the rice field. The first is a ground-level platform that adjoins the foundation wall. Approximately twenty-four feet further east is a slightly taller solid tabby platform, measuring eight feet long and three feet wide, placed beside a ditch that no longer has a flow of water. Twenty-four feet beyond the ditch is a third tabby structure that stands two and one-half feet tall. The final structure is a four-foot-tall tabby pillar measuring eight by three feet at the base. It has notches built into the crown to accommodate abutting ends of wood planks, and it stands next to the furthest west canal of the rice field.

The function of the tabby structures was to facilitate production at harvest time, which usually began in September. Workers went into the fields with hand scythes to cut the stalks and gather them into bundles to stand until dry. The bundles were then loaded onto flat barges and floated from the fields to the waterside pillar, where they were heaped on carts and rolled down an incline of plank fixed atop the tabby pillars and platforms until they reached the mill foundation. The bundles were pitched onto a belt that led to the top floor of the mill house, where threshing and pounding began. The end product, pounded rice kernels, was loaded into barrels on mule-drawn wagons that were backed into the mill house. When a measure of twenty bushels of rice filled a barrel, coopers sealed it with lids and metal hoops and the wagon was moved to the nearby wharf.[26]

John Lee Williams's report that the 5,000 bushels of rice (approximately 250 barrels, each weighing approximately 600 pounds) harvested at White Oak in 1829 was "rough rice" implies that Kingsley had not installed a mill and was selling his harvests as "rough" or "unhulled" rice. That may have been the case for the first few harvests, but by 1826 he had installed a rice mill. The foundation of that mill stands at the property today.

"Rough rice" referred to the head of the grain that had been separated from the stalk in a manual process known as threshing. Workers, usually women, beat (threshed) the stalks with a flail until the grains fell off and were collected in "fanner" baskets and were "winnowed" by tossing the contents in the air to let wind blow chaff away. The kernels were packed in barrels and sold as "rough rice" to merchants in Charleston or Savannah, where commercial mills finished the processing.

If further processing occurred at plantations that lacked mills, the next step was labor intensive and known as "hulling." It was generally done by slave women, who used wooden clubs to pound and roll rice kernels placed in the bottom of a hollowed-out log. This pestle-and-mortar procedure removed the hull that coated the exterior of the kernel. The hulled brown rice, while nutritious, spoiled quickly and did not command the high price that planters received for "white rice," which required further milling to remove the bran layer and rice germ.

Late in the eighteenth century planters began installing rice-pounding mills powered by the tidal action of rivers adjoining their rice fields. This lessened burdens on labor and increased profits for planters, but required sizable capital investments. The water mills were subsequently replaced by mills powered by more efficient steam engines. According to a government surveyor, Kingsley had invested in a rice-pounding mill for White Oak by at least 1826.[27]

An additional reminder of Kingsley's time at White Oak is the ruin of another structure located approximately one hundred yards away from the St. Marys. It is six feet high and constructed of tabby. All four walls are standing, although the roof and rafters have vanished; the lack of window openings suggests that it was used as a storage building. Today it is surrounded by a very high and imposing security fence and is part of a natural-setting habitat for the conservation of cheetahs. The White Oak Conservation Center, established in 1982 by philanthropist Howard Gilman and conservation biologist John Lukas, is today one of the world's premier facilities for preservation of endangered animal species.

The storage building was once part of an industrial complex that included a cotton gin described by Kingsley as capable of "cleaning Cotton on a large scale," a sugar mill, furnace and pans for boiling cane juice, barns for storing hogsheads of sugar and bales of cotton, more barns, and stables for oxen, horses, and mules. White Oak was a major plantation with an industrial center that would have been correspondingly large, complex, busy, and noisy.

Upriver from the industrial complex and the overseer's dwelling, Kingsley established a residential village for the enslaved laborers. The setting was beside the St. Marys at a place where the river takes a ninety-degree turn to the north before bending back again in a westerly direction. Several early maps pinpoint the location on the property.[28]

For the next fifteen years White Oak Plantation produced bumper crops of rice. In 1844 the rice harvest exceeded 8,000 bushels (377 barrels) and sold for $6,942 ($250,000 in today's currency values). Between 1845 and 1856, the last year for which data was available, the average number of enslaved laborers at White Oak Plantation was 147, twice the number at the next-largest plantation in Nassau County.[29]

At Kingsley's plantations slaves worked full days from Monday through Friday, and one-half of Saturday. For the rest of the weekend they were spared labor demands and permitted limited autonomy in their affairs. Rations of cornmeal, peas, beans, and sometimes pork or fish were dispensed on Saturdays. Food was cooked by the slaves in the cabins, and they supplemented rations with the produce of their own family gardens or with wild game and fish from the island's forests and surrounding waters.

The work routine was regulated by a "task system" that was similar in application to common practices in the coastal regions of South Carolina, Georgia, and Florida. Kingsley Gibbs, one of Zephaniah's nephews, learned plantation management while living at Fort George Island. In 1838 Gibbs purchased the island from Kingsley. On October 5, 1841, Gibbs wrote: "No work done today, as all the people have it to gather their *own* crop. It is a rule which we have, to give all the negroes one day in the spring to plant, and one day in the fall to reap, and as there is a rule on Sea Island plantations fixing the tasks required each day to be done, it occurs, during the long days in summer, that the hand is generally done with his task by 2 p.m., often sooner, so they have abundance of time to work their *own* crop, fish &c. &c."[30]

This description may exaggerate leniency. According to Ira Berlin and Philip D. Morgan, owners extracted as much labor as possible each day whether they used the gang or task system. Even the strong and capable workers who could finish their tasks by midafternoon, as Gibbs stated was the norm, would be compelled "to assist others—spouses, parents, children, and friends—in completing their work, keeping all in the fields late into the day and making a mockery of the independence tasking promised."[31]

Without specific evidence, it is not possible to judge whether Gibbs's assessment of the length of the workday at Fort George Island is accurate. He learned plantation and slave management from his uncle, Zephaniah Kingsley, who stated that his goal was to "excit[e] ambition by cultivating utility, local attachment, and moral improvement among slaves," which implies a reasonable labor expectation. He acknowledged the necessity of providing an environment wherein slaves were "discreetly restrained under the Patriarchal system," but if they were treated humanely it was possible "to neutralize the spirit of disaffection which necessarily results from every unequal distribution of privileges," and the result would be an agricultural surplus and a wealthy slave owner.[32]

Kingsley told his overseers where to plant and when to begin and end planting, and then he authorized them to conduct daily operations. The overseers delegated authority to enslaved drivers, who assigned each slave a specific task and inspected to ensure that the work was completed. If properly completed, the slave's obligation to labor was ended for the day. At Fort George Island, where cultivation of cotton was the main income producer, there were several weeks each year that tasks related to either planting, picking, sorting, or ginning of that product were assigned to nearly all able hands on the plantation. When looking at the totality of assignments over an entire year, it is clear that slave labor assignments in northeast Florida were remarkably varied.

In January it was not unusual for a group of men, women, and older boys and girls to be tasked with sorting and ginning cotton picked in previous months, while another group of men cut and burned brush and prepared a new field for planting. Yet a third group was busy planting a four-acre plot with seed cane. Kingsley planted approximately three hundred acres in cotton at Fort George Island.

January was also a time for butchering hogs, potting sugar, bottling syrup, and, if the weather was cooperative, setting out the first of the fruit trees to be planted during the year. Preparing land for planting continued in February and was generally finished by the end of March. Men and women worked with broad hoes to lay up furrows and add fertilizer before the seeds were planted.

During February and March, more land was prepared. If the weather was warm enough, slip potatoes (yams or sweet potatoes), seed potatoes (Irish potatoes), arrowroot, guinea or seed corn, and sweet corn could be planted. Men tasked to plow and plant in the groves shared the advantage of working amid blossoming peach, apricot, nectarine, and orange trees. Throughout these months, carpenters were busy repairing houses, crafting canoes and oars, hammering out bean arbors for gardens, and making fence rails and wagon wheels.

Warmer temperatures in April and May meant that a large variety of garden produce could be planted without fear of frost. Lima beans, string beans, peas, pumpkins, melons, cashews, squashes, and more Irish and slip potatoes were planted at plantations all over northeast Florida, sown in open fields and even in the groves after horse plows had gone through. Cereal grains planted at this time included rye, millet, and several varieties of corn planted with beans and field peas. Slaves routinely received weekly rations of corn, beans, and peas throughout the year.

At the end of April a day was designated when no work assignments were given. Gibbs wrote in his journal on April 30, 1842: "No work today. As is usual, all the people have today to plant their own crops." The next day, however, tasks were again assigned.

By late May and throughout June, corn plants needed weeding, either by men and women working with hoes or by horse-drawn plows. Cotton plants were in blossom and in need of weeding, with intensifying monotony as temperatures climbed into the nineties. It was normal to experience numerous rainy days in June, which provided an opportunity to plant more peas and potatoes, both the slip and Irish varieties. The constantly hot days and nights in July intensified the growing cycle and endless weeding assignments. By the end of July, corn stalks were stripped for fodder to feed the animals.

Cotton plants needed continued weeding throughout July and August, which became increasingly burdensome due to the intense heat and the prevalence of red bugs in the fields. Caterpillars were also a menace: Kingsley Gibbs once tasked men to dig a ditch between fields in an attempt stop the advance of caterpillars from one field to the next.

Journal entries reading "all hands picking cotton" and "hands stripping cotton" became frequent in August, sometimes lasting into December. It was more common, however, for drivers to divide the labor force and assign a variety of tasks: stripping fodder from corn plants, carting stalks and ears of the corn to storage bins, weeding potato fields, and planting trees. Carpenters worked on cart bodies and wagon wheels, cut clapboards to repair roofs, built dwellings and barns, made gates for ox and horse pens, and completed dozens of other projects.

The diversity of tasks assigned at northeast Florida plantations seems endless. Animals had to be fed, shod, bridled, saddled, yoked, and hitched to carts and wagons. Colts born in Fort George pastures in the spring were later "broke" for riding or for draft work. Hogs and beef were slaughtered, the meat preserved with salt or ground into sausages and smoked. When cattle were butchered, tallow was saved to make candles. Butchering hogs was preceded by boiling wood ash to make potash lye, which was boiled with the lard rendered from hog fat to produce soap. Corn was cracked, ground into flour, and distributed as rations. Women spun and wove the cotton fibers and made clothing, later mending and washing them. Kingsley, his relatives, the overseers, and visitors demanded that food be prepared, chamber pots emptied, and living quarters cleaned.

For five and one-half days each week, twelve months every year, slaves at Kingsley's plantations worked at their assigned tasks. Once these were completed, they often engaged in work of their own choosing: carpentry or manual labor projects for wages, tilling plants in their family gardens, raising corn to sell to their owner, tending fowl or hogs, and hunting and fishing. The only breaks from routine came in April and October, when, as Kingsley Gibbs stated: "It is a rule which we have, to give all the negroes one day in the spring to plant, and one day in the fall to reap." A well-deserved day off, but work nonetheless.

After a year of such labor, the following journal entry recorded by Gibbs conveys the relief and joy felt throughout the slave quarter: "This is Christmas Day, and a very cold one it is, got the Beef for the people yesterday, and gave out *double* allowance of corn, and salt also, so that the negroes could feed their holiday visitors of course no work for *anybody*." Christmas was a five-day holiday at Fort George Island, nearly a week without labor tasks being imposed. On December 30 Gibbs wrote: "The Holidays are now over. The negroes well tired out and now must begin in earnest for another year."

11 "The Door of Liberty Is Open to Every Slave Who Can Find the Means of Purchasing Himself"

From Spanish to American Race Relations

Zephaniah Kingsley had been a slaveholder in Florida for nearly two decades when the American flag was raised over St. Augustine on July 10, 1821. During those years he became convinced that white men became sickly and perished when they labored in the heat of Florida's weather. In a pro-slavery tract written in 1828, Kingsley asserted that the semitropical coastal zone of the southern states was "unfavorable to the health and production of white people." To prosper under these conditions, it was necessary for whites to command the labor of black slaves, "as it is evidence that the darkness of complexion here is a measure of capacity for endurance of labor." The dilemma, Kingsley recognized, was the risk of violence and rebellion that inevitably accompanied coercing the labor of enslaved Africans. Just and humane treatment of slaves reduced but did not eliminate that risk; the most effective deterrent was a three-caste social structure wherein liberal emancipation laws encouraged the growth of a middle caste of free people of color who identified with the interests of the white slave owners.[1]

During the second Spanish governance of East Florida, Spain's attention and resources were directed to wars in Europe and independence revolutions in its colonies. The colony's governors, out of necessity, had depended on free black militia companies and Indian allies to supplement a weak military garrison. Recognizing these geopolitical realities, East Florida planters generally embraced Spain's liberal manumission policies, believing they would produce an essential middle caste that would unite with whites to defend against foreign invaders and help control the slave population.

Significant economic and political conditions were joined with Catholic doctrine and Spanish law and custom to shape the three-caste race policies in East Florida.

Free blacks attended schools, worked as artisans and laborers, and became landowners and slave owners. Catholic priests baptized slave children, sanctified their marriages, and recorded the events in parish registers. Spanish law prohibited owners from separating families by selling husbands and wives and children apart. Miscegenation was not prohibited by law, and the children born of such unions were often freed, acknowledged, and educated by their white fathers. Slaves were also freed by government and by their owners for meritorious acts or for military service. They could initiate their own manumission proceedings under the Spanish principle of "coartacion"—the right to freedom through self-purchase—and could appeal to the courts if owners refused to cooperate. Blacks also served in militias without facing formal discrimination and demeaning prohibitions.[2]

The 1794 case of Philip Edimboro, a slave of the wealthy planter and merchant Francisco Xavier Sánchez, is telling. As father to eight mulatto children, Sanchez might have been expected to show sympathy to a slave seeking freedom, but self-interest led him to obstruct the initiative. Edimboro appealed to the governor, who conducted an inquiry and prescribed conditions for self-purchase. As a free man, Edimboro became the owner of land and slaves and a member of the free colored militia.[3]

The American planters who migrated to Florida after 1821 viewed the three-caste system with distrust and alarm. Their experience was with a two-caste social structure—a white ruling class and black slaves—and they viewed free blacks as inherently inferior and prone to incite slave insurrections. In Georgia and South Carolina, laws passed to control slaves also applied to free blacks. The American two-caste system of slavery, with its harsh and rigid racial dimensions, minimized in law the possibility of emancipation. Conflict over race policies between holdover Spanish-era settlers and the incoming Americans was inevitable.

Kingsley experienced this conflict firsthand in 1823 when he was appointed to the Legislative Council of the new Territory of Florida by President James Monroe. He served on the council for a single term, and during that session he participated in debates over future race and slavery policies. Efforts by council members to institutionalize a two-caste system were thwarted in that first term, but several discriminatory laws aimed at restricting the activities and rights of slaves were enacted in the 1824 session. The council later focused on restricting the activities of free African Americans in Florida. In debates, council members blamed free people of color for creating discontent among slaves, and used these accusations to bar them from entering Florida. Rights of assembly and free speech were restricted. The right to carry firearms was restricted in 1825 and 1828 and was taken away entirely in 1833. Free blacks were barred from voting, serving on juries, and testifying against whites in court proceedings.[4]

Particularly vexing to Kingsley was a law that prohibited interracial marriage and made children of interracial couples ineligible to inherit their parents' estates. White men found guilty of fornicating with African American women could be fined up to one thousand dollars and stripped of their civil and political rights. Head taxes were levied on all free black males over fifteen years of age, and supplemental taxes were assessed in subsequent years by both state and municipal governments.[5]

Kingsley was outraged when the council moved aggressively to outlaw manumission. A law implemented in 1829 required owners to pay a fee of $200 for each person emancipated (in excess of $7,000 today) and to post a security bond equal to the value of the slave. The bond was liable to forfeiture if the person freed did not permanently leave Florida within thirty days. Freedmen found in noncompliance could be seized by a sheriff and sold back into slavery. Free blacks already in the general population could be sold into slavery to satisfy debts or fines arising from misdemeanor convictions, including nonpayment of head taxes. In 1842 all free blacks were required to place themselves under a white guardian.[6]

Free blacks tried to block passage of the discriminatory laws, and later they protested enforcement. In St. Johns County they petitioned the territorial council in 1823, wrote letters to newspaper editors, and sought justice in the courts. St. Augustine resident Robert Brown's 1824 letter to the *East Florida Herald* is compelling. Calling himself a man of "common sense" born in East Florida and a landowner, Brown asked his white neighbors about the precedent for the $8 annual poll tax St. Johns County levied on free blacks at age fifteen (whites paid only $1, beginning at age twenty-one). He was told "such is the case in Georgia, an old and well regulated state." Other neighbors felt the laws were justified because whites provided more services to the government than free blacks. Brown conceded it was true that free blacks had none of the burdens that came with "elections and legislation" but pointed out they were forbidden to participate in self-government. "If we have none of the burdens of jurors neither are we tried by our peers. If we have none of the cares, labours, responsibilities and dangers of civil and military offices neither have we any of their profits and honors. . . . It is not that we would not take our part . . . and glad of the opportunity of doing so but we are declared so far degraded as to be rendered incapable. They would have us to pay for the degradation that has been laid on us."[7]

While Brown was writing to the local newspaper, a prominent St. Augustine family challenged the newly enacted county poll tax laws in court. In November 1824, James Clarke, a free black, petitioned the St. Johns County Court seeking termination of the "discriminatory and unconstitutional" poll tax. On November 20 the *East Florida Herald* reported that Judge Joseph L. Smith "has decided in favour of the petitioner" and ruled the county poll tax unconstitutional.[8]

Supporters of the tax took their case to the legislative council, and in 1828 a territorial law was passed authorizing county and municipal governments to impose poll taxes on free blacks. Undeterred, Clarke again challenged the law's constitutionality. This time, his brothers George, Joseph, John, and William were co-plaintiffs, and their white father, George J. F. Clarke, was the principal supporting witness.[9]

Kingsley joined in the efforts to deter the rush of legislation against free blacks. His 1826 "Address to the Legislative Council of Florida" justified enslavement of black men and women as "the most permanent and indestructible of all forms of property." The "Address" also contained two political messages: first, slavery could be defended against attacks by abolitionists and the "zealots of colonization" only by treating slaves with "justice, prudence, & moderation"; and second, liberal emancipation laws were necessary to persuade free people of color to be "interested in preserving peace and good order among the slaves and being firmly attached to the side of whites by having the same Interest."[10]

Two years later, disturbed by the continuing legislative assault on the rights of free people of color, Kingsley refined and lengthened his "Address" and published it as a brief proslavery tract, *A Treatise on the Patriarchal, or*

Co-operative System of Society. The historian Eugene Genovese has called the *Treatise* "an extraordinary booklet" in which Kingsley "forcefully asserted that no society could expect to sustain itself without a measure of slavery in some form, but he no less forcefully asserted that class, not race, provided the bedrock of social relations."[11]

Enslaving Africans and coercing their labor was fraught with danger, Kingsley cautioned, as "very few People will labour to a greater extent than . . . necessities oblige." Even though "instances of disturbance or revolt are rare," the possibility of violence was ever present and must be avoided by sensible precaution and enactment of wise and practical public policy. For individual planters, Kingsley recommended a just, humane, and patriarchal system of labor, while being aware that "slaves in all cases will require more or less constraint." The public policy Kingsley recommended was passage of laws that would encourage emancipation and promote the growth of a class of "free people of Color" who could be trusted to ally with the ruling class of white slave owners. "Color and common origin renders the slaves perfectly tractable & obedient and such is the entire confidence between all the cast[e]s that you will hardly find a hall door locked in the night on any of the . . . plantations" in the West Indies colonies.[12]

"The door of liberty is open to every slave who can find the means of purchasing himself," Kingsley wrote. "It is true, few have the means, but hope creates a spirit of economy, industry, and emulation to obtain merit by good behavior, which has a general and beneficial effect." The statement has been interpreted by some as a hoax, an inducement to good behavior with false promises of freedom, while others have considered it evidence that Kingsley was a lenient slave master. It is therefore important to question whether Kingsley implemented in reality the self-purchase policies he touted in print.

The evidence found in court records in the northeast Florida counties where Kingsley owned slaves clarifies that his promise of self-purchase was not a hoax. He emancipated a surprising number of slaves, and after his death his son George and his acknowledged wife, Anna Madgigine Jai, followed his policy and fulfilled his promises. Slaves at Kingsley's plantations were permitted to acquire and control personal property, including provisions crops, poultry, and hogs, which could be sold and the cash saved to apply toward self-purchase. After daily work assignments were completed satisfactorily, and during weekend hours when no work was required, Kingsley's slaves were permitted to work at extra projects to earn income that could be used to buy freedom. His self-purchase policy was not necessarily evidence that he was a lenient or kind slave master; it was instead a measure that minimized the threat of rebellion and enabled him to amass money. For Kingsley, self-purchase was a policy that created a free middle caste that became the "grand chain of security by which the slaves are held in subordination." To sustain slavery it was necessary to create a caste of "free people of color, whose persons, properties, and rights are protected by law, which enables them to acquire and hold property in their own name, and allows the free children of quarteroons by a white man, to be white by law. By this link, they become identified with the whites on one side and with the slaves by descent on the other; a connexion which perfectly cements the three castes of which the whole nation is composed."[13]

In 1833 Kingsley penned a "Memorial to Congress" that was signed by eleven other former Spanish Florida planters, all fathers of mixed-race children. In forceful language, the petition denounced the "nostrums of political quackery" and the prejudices of the territorial assembly, and reminded members of Congress that in Spanish Florida and "in all Spanish countries," free people of color were "admitted to most of the rights of Spanish subjects especially to the natural and inherent right of legal protection from which they are now excluded." The rights of free people of color should not be "extinguished at once by intolerance and persecution or any other moral or political fanaticism."[14]

The memorial denounced race discriminatory taxes and cruel laws that made it possible for free blacks to be "sold as slaves for life if they [free blacks] should be too poor to pay these odious and unequal taxes." Particularly obnoxious to the petitioners was an 1829 law considered a threat to the "paternal obligations and ties of natural affection which have existed for years past by imposing a fine of one thousand dollars with the penalty of disfranchisement upon every White person who is *suspected* of having a connexion with a coloured woman." Members of Congress were implored to repeal the "cruel, unnecessary and most impolitic laws."[15]

The petitioners were as unsuccessful with Congress as they had been with the Florida legislative council. The legal framework for a two-caste social structure was in place by 1829, and the laws were strengthened over time. Influential Spanish subjects who remained in Florida under American governance withdrew to their plantations but carried on their business and family affairs much as they had under Spanish rule. In the first two decades of the territorial period, Kingsley and other holdovers from the Spanish era constituted the dominant group among the major slave owners in northeast Florida. They owned the best land, often in large blocks situated on the principal waterways; possessed economic power; and held key political offices as delegates to the territorial legislature, justices of the peace, sheriffs, clerks of court, and judges. As a result of their accumulated wealth and influence, the holdover planters were able to ignore the new restrictive laws on race.

The main form of wealth in northeast Florida was enslaved property. According to the 1830 census of Duval County, 1,018 African Americans were held in bondage by eighty-eight owners. One-third of all heads of households owned a slave or slaves, but only forty-seven individuals had slaveholdings in excess of five, and nearly all were holdovers from the Spanish era. Wealth and power generated influence with sheriffs and court officials.[16]

Anti-miscegenation statutes were ignored, as were the manumission prohibitions of the 1829 law. Kingsley and other white men lived openly with black women and their mixed-race families. Court officials issued emancipation papers without receipt of security bonds and without enforcing the mandatory thirty-day emigration provision. Judges and sheriffs upheld the validity of emancipation papers despite the obvious contravention of the 1829 law. Even after their mortal influence expired, owners emancipated slaves through their wills.

In 1830 more than one-third of Florida's 844 free people of color lived in three northeast Florida counties: 172 in St. Johns, 46 in Nassau, and 86 in Duval. Over the next thirty years those numbers were reduced to 82 in St. Johns County, increased to 55 in Nassau County, and nearly doubled in Duval County to 171. Kingsley was an important reason the numbers increased in Duval and Nassau Counties, partly because he emancipated the children he fathered, and their mothers, but also because he liberated slaves who paid him one-half their appraised value.[17]

Kingsley's beliefs and practices were shared by other planters in northeast Florida. Francis Richard, a refugee sugar planter from Haiti, left a will providing for his white son, Francis, but also for his large "colored" family. Richard wrote in his will that his "colored children will soon all reside in the Island of Hayti." Only some of those children moved to Haiti; others remained in northeast Florida. His daughter, Cornelia Richard, married John Taylor, a white planter, and managed a large Duval County estate after her husband's death. Fortune Richard owned a 370-acre farm on Little Pottsburgh Creek. John Richard was a successful blacksmith in Jacksonville until 1862, when he joined the Union army.[18]

Joshua Hickman, another Spanish-era settler, also permitted slaves to purchase freedom. After his death in 1837 it was discovered that Bella, Sally, Josiah, and Tena had been making self-purchase payments to Hickman for several years. When the estate received $50 from Bella and Sally, they were emancipated. After receiving $101.37 to complete the payments and "account for his freedom," Josiah was manumitted. Tena was not so fortunate. In October 1842, after having paid $92 toward her purchase price, Tena was sold at auction—along with four others—to settle a claim against the Hickman estate.[19]

John F. Brown left instructions for executors to free three of his twenty-seven slaves following his death in 1835. In 1842, Mary Hobkirk, the daughter of a Spanish-era planter, made unusual provisions in her will to provide protection for three of her slaves. Charlotte was to "be sold to some good master of her selection." Harry was also to be sold, with "his father Harry King of St. Marys [a free black] to have the preference among the purchasers." Hagar was to be sold "for a trifling sum not exceeding $75, on condition that as soon as she, or any for her shall pay to the purchaser the sum of money for which she is sold she shall be free, her own slave and the property of no one."[20]

George J. F. Clarke's life represents the classic statement on the three-caste system of race relations in Spanish Florida. Born in British St. Augustine in 1774, Clarke remained when Spanish rule resumed. In 1797 he purchased and emancipated Flora and the infant Philis, the first of their eight children. A widower by 1821, Clarke settled in St. Augustine near his children, who by then were educated and respected citizens and landowners.[21]

By the time of his death in 1836 Clarke had another slave family. His will left most of his wealth to his first eight children, but the most valuable property was to be sold and the money used to purchase and emancipate

Hannah, his second wife, and her four children. Clarke wanted his family moved from Fernandina to a "small snug house and lot" in St. Augustine where his children could be educated. All excess funds were to go to Hannah.[22]

From the settlement of a claim against the U.S. government, Clarke wanted $2,000 invested "in healthy grown negroes, and conveyed to said Hannah and her children," because "the hire of negroes in these southern countries [is] the most lucrative sane and simple investment of property that can be found." Hannah's brother Antonio was "to be among the first slaves purchased."

To Clarke, slavery lacked a harsh racial dimension; it was an unfortunate and temporary legal circumstance that an economic transaction could terminate, and the freed person could merge into society. That happened with Clarke's first family; he willed the same for Hannah and her children. Clarke followed the three-caste race policies of the Spanish era, but in 1836 Florida was no longer Spanish. For Clarke's second family to gain freedom under U.S. territorial law, local officials would have to ignore the law. That happened: Hannah Clarke and her children were freed, and then settled in Florida even though it was a violation of the mandatory migration provision of the 1829 emancipation law.[23]

Judging from extant northeast Florida county records, Hannah Clarke's path to freedom was trod by other enslaved persons. Several dozen emancipations occurred in the 1830s and 1840s; all violated terms of the 1829 anti-manumission law passed by the territorial council. Until the 1850s, sympathetic public officials in northeast Florida, generally holdover planters from the Spanish era, ignored the new laws and permitted the more flexible mores and folkways of the previous government to continue extralegally. Newly freed persons stayed in northeast Florida, in violation of the 1829 law that mandated emigration within thirty days.

Although Kingsley objected to the imposition of a two-caste racial structure, he continued as a slave and plantation owner in Florida until his death in 1843. Throughout his remaining years he was a keen observer of debates in the legislative council, but he withdrew from active personal involvement in governance issues. He focused instead on managing his slave plantations and acting out a role he created for himself as patriarch of a large and unique free colored family. The role he aspired to was one he described in *Treatise on the Patriarchal*: a "just, conscientious, and humane master . . . who provides for the physical wants of his servants, his wife and children, in health, sickness and old age." His slaves lived in nuclear family units and regulated their own family and cultural lives. They worked under a task system supervised by enslaved drivers who received preferential treatment but lived as part of the slave community, often interrelated by marriage and kinship. The special privileges the drivers received bound them to Kingsley and focused their attention on managing labor and maintaining social order.

The workweek at Kingsley's plantations consisted of five and one-half days of labor tasks assigned by the drivers. When the tasks were completed, the laborers had the rest of the day to do as they wished, with reasonable limits, and with minimal supervision. They could engage in extra work for wages, raise grain, animals, or fowl for sale, or use the time for recreation, fishing, or tending their own gardens. Kingsley said that after receiving provisions allowances in the afternoon on Saturdays, "their time was usually employed hoeing their corn, and getting their supply of fish for the week. Both men and women were very industrious. Many of them made twenty bushels of corn to sell." That individual slaves had twenty bushels of corn suggests that Kingsley made small plots of land available in addition to the personal "kitchen" gardens they cultivated in the open areas between the tabby family dwellings. In this he may have been influenced by his travels in the West Indies, where planters allocated small plots of less productive lands to slaves, who raised provisions crops and sold excess produce at local markets.[24]

The income earned by slaves from extra labor projects or from the sale of produce, fowl, and small animals was their own to keep, either for personal use or for application toward self-purchase of freedom. Kingsley allowed self-purchase for one-half of appraised value, believing that the possibility of freedom minimized the risk of violence and rebelliousness, and he put that belief into practice. He also staffed his outlying properties with small numbers of slave families he trusted and whom he believed would work without supervision by a white overseer. Living and working independently served as a further incentive for accumulation of earnings for self-purchase and as preparation for freedom.

Kingsley's Florida landholdings were anchored on the north by White

Oak Plantation on the St. Marys, the border between Florida and Georgia. From there to his primary residence at Fort George Island was a journey by water of approximately fifty miles. To reach his most southerly plantation, Drayton Island in Lake George, Kingsley traveled upriver (south) on the St. Johns for another 150 miles. When he traveled between Fort George and Drayton Islands, he passed by two dozen other properties he owned.

White Oak and Fort George were intensively cultivated and populated with large numbers of slave families, white managers, and enslaved black drivers. In contrast, the distant settlements to the south were either rented to other planters or were less intensively cultivated and sparsely populated by small numbers of trusted slave families. These properties were visited periodically by Kingsley or his representative to deliver supplies and collect agricultural produce.[25]

At Drayton Island, Kingsley planted provisions, cotton, and groves of "China oranges" soon after he purchased the island. In subsequent years the groves required seasonal laborers to maintain, harvest, and pack the fruit for export, but it was not necessary to have a large workforce there throughout the year. Nor was it necessary to employ a white manager on a permanent basis. Consequently, the small number of families on the island worked independently, tended three separate groves, packed the fruit for export, planted small fields of cotton and cane, and worked in the forest. In general, the slave families tended their own "kitchen" gardens, grew corn and other crops in small personal fields, and raised chickens and other fowl, hogs, and cattle to sell or barter for personal income. Such residential and labor arrangements are strikingly reminiscent of the lives of slaves who lived as proto-peasants in the Caribbean Islands that anthropologist Sidney W. Mintz has explored in a series of insightful studies.[26]

During the Second Seminole War (1835–42), Jacksonville and St. Augustine newspapers printed accounts of events at Drayton Island. In December 1835 a team of loggers employed by the Palmer and Ferris Company to cut live oak trees reported that "one of Kingsley's negroes, left on the Island in charge of the improvements there," entered the loggers' camp to warn of an impending attack by Seminole warriors. The loggers fled downriver to a safer location and returned a week later, only to flee again when they encountered a Seminole war party. As they fled, they passed "the northern point of the Island near to the shore" where Kingsley's plantation dwellings were in flames. "The Negroes had some days before left the Island," the *Jacksonville Courier* reported. "Doubtless everything like a habitation is destroyed."[27]

Within a year of the raids Kingsley returned to Drayton Island with twenty slaves, confident that hostilities had ended. He was mistaken. St. Augustine's *East Florida Herald* reported on June 22, 1837, that "three negroes belonging to Z. Kingsley, Esq. arrived at Picolata yesterday, from Drayton Island, near Lake George, who report that they saw Indian fires all around them, and that they left for fear of capture. It is feared the remainder, seventeen in number, have been captured by the Indians as they have not been since heard of."[28]

Kingsley reestablished the settlement a few months later and planted another round of crops. Seminole warriors returned in July 1839 and forced the slaves to flee again. According to the Charleston *Southern Patriot*, "the plantation of Mr. Kingsley, near Lake George, was abandoned by his negroes, they having been compelled to fly from the Indians—the Indians told the negroes that they could leave the plantation, and they would gather the crop."[29]

Analysis of documents related to Kingsley's less intensively populated and cultivated properties expands understanding of his diverse management practices. In December 1832 he transferred title to a thousand-acre tract in St. Johns County known as Buena Vista to his son George. The tract was located east of the St. Johns River across from Palatka. The transfer of title included ownership of the three enslaved families residing there: Solomon and June and their three children, Dick and Mary and their four children, and Elliebo and Polly and their two children. Other than occasional visits by Kingsley or his agent, the three families apparently lived and worked independently cultivating small fields of cotton and packing oranges for export. In addition, they worked for themselves after daily tasks were completed in an effort to earn money for the self-purchase of freedom.[30]

In 1844, the year after Kingsley's death, an inventory of his property listed the slaves by family. Missing from the list are the three families identified on the 1832 title transfer. It is known that Elliebo and his family were among fifty-three slaves liberated by Kingsley in 1836 and 1837 and transported to Haiti to work as indentured laborers at the estate acquired by George

Kingsley. Solomon, June, Dick, and Mary are not named on subsequent inventories of Kingsley's human property or on records related to members of his extended family. Their names are not found on the Schedule of Free Persons on the 1850 and 1860 censuses of the northeast Florida counties. One possible explanation is that they, like Elliebo and Polly, chose self-purchase through indenture contracts in Haiti.[31]

Ironically, the eldest son of Elliebo and Polly, George Elliebo, benefited from his former owner's Florida estate as a result of his marriage in Haiti to Anatoile Kingsley, the eldest daughter of George Kingsley. The wedding occurred after George Kingsley's death in 1846, despite the objections of the bride's mother, the widowed Anatoile Vauntravers Kingsley. A provision in George Kingsley's will entitled his daughter Anatoile to a one-sixth portion of her father's estate, and because the Zephaniah Kingsley estate was still being probated at the time of George's death, Anatoile also received a portion of her grandfather's Florida estate.[32]

In December 1832 Kingsley transferred title to Deep Creek Plantation, a thousand-acre tract located east of the St. Johns and north of today's East Palatka, to "Anna Madgigine Kingsley." Thirteen slaves were living on the property at the time. Lindo (living alone), Abdalla and Bella and their four children (Jim, Elsey, Ann, and Patty), Cato and Dorchas and their child, and Quala and her two children were deeded to Anna Kingsley.

The names of Cato and Dorchas do not appear on the 1844 inventory of Kingsley's human property or on other subsequent documents. It is presumed that during the intervening years they were manumitted. It is possible they were among the laborers transported to Haiti.

The other adults named on the 1832 deed were among the slaves listed on the 1844 inventory of the deceased Kingsley's property. Lindo had formed a family by then and was living with a wife, Sophy, and three children. Abdalla and Bella were living with two children. Qualla was identified as a single parent living in a family unit with two daughters, Letitia and Victorine. Titles to all three families were confirmed to Anna Kingsley in 1846, when they were moved to the plantation of John Sammis, Anna's son-in-law, and also her agent and guardian. Qualla and her children are not found in subsequent records. However, the families of Lindo and Sophy and of Abdalla and Bella can be traced as far as the 1860 census, where they are identified as free black residents of Duval County. Anna Kingsley, and also George

Kingsley and John Sammis, honored Zephaniah Kingsley's self-purchase pledge after his death.[33]

It is difficult to objectively evaluate Kingsley's patriarchal system. The evidence is limited and subject to a variety of interpretations. Kingsley did, however, emancipate numerous slaves by self-purchase, beginning as early as 1811 when he freed the slave manager at Laurel Grove Plantation, Abraham Hanahan. Between 1811 and 1828 Kingsley also emancipated Hanahan's wife, Sophy Chidgigane, and four of their daughters. The most remarkable example of self-purchase carried out by Kingsley occurred in the late 1830s, when he liberated more than fifty slaves who agreed to indenture labor contracts binding them to work for two to nine years at an estate on the north shore of Haiti (today in the Dominican Republic) he purchased for George Kingsley. When Kingsley proclaimed that "the door of liberty is open to every slave who can find the means of purchasing himself," he meant it as more than a cruel and deceptive hoax. The possibility of emancipation was real for slaves owned by Kingsley.

The possibility of self-purchase of freedom, however, did not eliminate slave disobedience and rebelliousness. In *Treatise on the Patriarchal*, Kingsley juxtaposed what he proposed to be blissfully peaceful relations at Laurel Grove Plantation with the unruly behavior, thieving, and intractability among some of the "new negroes" he purchased after 1813. At Laurel Grove, Kingsley asserted, "perfect confidence, friendship, and good understanding reigned between us," but at Fort George Island he experienced difficulty maintaining control. He blamed the problems on a "minister [who] got among them" and the resultant "superstition (by some called religion) among negroes, whose ignorance and want of rationality rendered them fit subjects to work upon." Even punishment "had no effect; it only made it worse."[34]

It is an ambiguous passage in which Kingsley idealizes and embellishes his experiences at Laurel Grove, and seems to vent anti-African biases. It is more likely that he was describing reactions common to any people enslaved in a new land where they were confronted by alien languages and cultural norms. Kingsley, not a religious man, denied the passage was a rant against religion, yet it can be interpreted that way. Whatever the motivation, the passage makes it clear that enslaving human beings has always been fraught with problems and dangers.[35]

12 | "In Trust for Flora Hanahan Kingsley and Her Son Charles"

Kingsley as Patriarch

It is difficult to imagine that a man who never married but fathered numerous children by several different women, all of whom were his teenage slaves when the initial sexual relations occurred, would consider himself a family man. Yet, Zephaniah Kingsley Jr. thought of himself as the patriarch of a very large family encompassing the slaves he owned, his own mixed-race children, and their African mothers. He was kind and attentive to the needs of his widowed mother, Isabella Kingsley, in her later years. He assisted George Gibbs, the husband of his sister Isabella, when Gibbs experienced setbacks in business, provided housing accommodations for his sisters and their families, and served as a surrogate parent for their children during long residences at his home on Fort George Island. He employed his nephews, Kingsley B. Gibbs and Charles J. McNeill, and left them generous bequests in his will. The biracial children he fathered were freed, educated, and provided with property and protection, as were their mothers. Late in his life, worried that his biracial family would be victimized by Florida's discriminatory racial policies, Kingsley arranged the purchase of a 32,000-acre plantation in Haiti for George Kingsley and his family and for the families of his children by Anna Jai, Flora Hanahan, and Sarah Murphy. There may have been chapters of his life story that he came to regret, but he continued to think of himself as a just and humane patriarch of a very large family.

The curtains of Kingsley's family life were surprisingly open for a head of household who lived in scandalous defiance of the mores and laws of the society around him. Kingsley made no attempt to conceal his convention-challenging sexual relationships with enslaved African women. He was never formally married, in either a civil or religious ceremony, or at least a record of such a union has not been found. He did, however, father children by several enslaved women, for which abundant evidence can be found in Spanish colonial records, parish records of the Roman Catholic Church in St. Augustine, the St. Johns County deed books, and his Last Will and Testament in the archives of the Duval County Probate Court.

Choosing a label that fits the family relationships between Kingsley and the mothers of his children is a challenge. No label fits comfortably, although polygamy comes close. Kingsley had more than one spouse at one time, but not as the result of a religious or civil ceremony. The relationships resemble common-law marriage, but that term infers that other people recognize the involvement of two persons in a marital relationship in the absence of a formal ceremony. It is hard to imagine that Kingsley's first joining with teenagers like Munsilna or Anna was by mutual consent, which is generally recognized as a requirement for common-law marriage. It is tempting to label the relationships serial monogamy, since Kingsley moved from one young woman to another younger woman, fathering children in the process. But the relationships were not short term. Kingsley's relationships with Munsilna, Anna, and Flora lasted for decades, and he assumed familial responsibilities.[1]

Kingsley was an all-powerful figure on a large slave plantation, and his potential choices for sexual partners were many. He owned the teenage women who became the mothers of his children. For them to have refused his initial sexual overtures is unlikely. What is known is that the children and the mothers were freed and that they lived in separate dwellings with their children, in matrifocal and consanguineal family households, although Kingsley was an ongoing—if intermittent—presence in all of their lives.[2]

Anna Jai, the first of the African women Kingsley emancipated, exercised a special authority in his life and plantation affairs. That fact is made clear from his acknowledgment of her special status in his July 1843 Last Will and Testament: "she has always been respected as my wife, nor do I think that her truth, honor, integrity, moral conduct or good sense will lose in comparison with anyone." A relationship between Zephaniah and Anna lasted for nearly four decades, until his death, and resulted in four children and numerous grandchildren, although the closeness of the bond varied over the years. In addition to freedom, property, and praise, Anna received a sizable bequest in Kingsley's will.[3]

Kingsley managed the plantations, while Anna managed household activities and food preparation at the owner's dwellings at Laurel Grove Plantation and Fort George Island. According to reports, Anna inspected the health of the workers each day, nursed illnesses and injuries, and became involved in managing the plantation when Kingsley was not present. In a July 1842 interview, Kingsley described Anna as "a fine, tall figure, black as jet, but very handsome. She was very capable, and could carry on all the affairs of the plantation in my absence, as well as I could myself. She was very affectionate and faithful and I could trust her."[4]

Anna also directed the labor of her own slaves at Fort George Island. She owned between eleven and fifteen slaves in Florida from 1812 through the 1850s. During the years she lived in Haiti her slaves were placed under the supervision of her son-in-law John S. Sammis. In 1860 she owned only Julia, Elizabeth, Joe, and Polly, ranging in age from nine to seventeen years.[5]

At Fort George Island, the residence for Anna and her children was the two-story dwelling located seventy feet south of the house occupied by Zephaniah. According to Hannah Rollins, whose husband, John Rollins, purchased Fort George Island in 1868, a walkway lined with oleander and crepe myrtle trees led from Anna's house to the south porch of the main house. Built circa 1820, the two-story dwelling constructed for Anna Jai was of tabby brick downstairs and wood frame above. Downstairs, two rooms were for food preparation and cooking and a third was a combination parlor and sitting room. The second story had bedrooms on alternate sides of the stairway landing, the north room occupied by Anna, the south by the children.[6]

A visitor to Fort George Island in 1836 or 1837 described the grounds in the owner's complex as "a perfect garden, laid out in parks, arbors and flower beds." A later owner of Fort George Island reminisced that in 1868 a "fine grove of old and prolific lemon trees" stood west of the "Ma-am Anna" house, along with a small grove of orange trees and a flower garden. A thick hedge of bitter-sweet orange trees screened a small cemetery with "narcissus, jonquils, old rose bushes and a very tall date palm tree" growing amid the upright markers. The identity of the individuals interred in the cemetery is unknown, as the markers were uprooted in the late nineteenth century and placed horizontally under a thick layer of dirt. Directly south of the "Ma-am Anna" house stood a large well and a "grove of purple and white fig trees." East of the house was a large group of banana trees, several large orange trees and crepe myrtle trees, and a "well with sweep and bucket."[7]

Kingsley's dwelling house and Anna's house were both surrounded by fences when Hannah Rollins first saw them in 1868. An avenue extended eastward from the lawn south of the main house to the northeast corner of the island. Large and beautiful cedar trees lined each side of that avenue. An avenue of laurel oak trees led to the stables. An 1850s survey map shows the outline of additional small buildings east of the main house and beside the cedar avenue.[8]

George, Martha, and Mary Kingsley, the children of Anna and Zephaniah, were ages eight, six, and four when they arrived at Fort George Island in 1814. John Maxwell Kingsley was born there in 1824. Their half sister Fatimah Kingsley, only a few months older than George, lived nearby in a separate dwelling with her mother, Munsilna McGundo. Fatimah's three younger siblings are not mentioned in the Fort George Island documentation, but it is assumed they also resided in Munsilna's dwelling.

"Tutors have attended them from infancy," a traveler wrote of Kingsley's children after visiting Fort George Island in 1836. He added: "the girls have been taught music and dancing, the modern languages and polite literature." Late in his life, with most of his children and grandchildren living in Haiti, Kingsley attempted unsuccessfully to bring tutors from the United States to provide for their education. His daughters Martha and Mary, after they married and became plantation mistresses, employed tutors from northern states to board at their plantations and teach their own children. After the Civil War, Mary Kingsley Sammis and her husband donated land and money for a school to educate all children living near their residence.[9]

In early January 1829, a memorable religious ceremony was celebrated at Fort George Island. Father Edward Mayne, a priest from the St. Augustine parish, stopped at Kingsley's plantation while conducting his annual visitation to the distant farms and plantations to administer the sacrament of baptism. The Irish-born priest encountered unusual circumstances as he toured the province representing Christ on earth, but it is doubtful he presided over another occasion that presented such a confusing mixture of races and cultures and tangled lines of kinship, marital, and extramarital relationships.

If the Irish priest had prior knowledge of Kingsley's lifestyle, he would have been aware that the plantation patriarch was not formally married yet lived openly with several women who had given birth to his children. Kingsley was described by contemporaries as a learned man who traveled widely and accumulated unforgettable experiences, and who enjoyed entertaining visitors at his frontier home. Nevertheless, the thought of an Irish Catholic priest who had taken a vow of celibacy dining with an outspoken nonbeliever who equated Christian doctrines with superstition and once said that attending Quaker meetings helped him contemplate his best business deals is evocative.

Father Mayne baptized four children the following day. The first was four-year-old John Maxwell Kingsley, born on November 22, 1824, to "Zephaniah Kingsley . . . and the free black Ana M. Kingsley, native of the Coast of Africa." John Maxwell's seventeen-year-old mixed-race sister, Mary Kingsley, and his white uncle, Zephaniah Charlton Gibbs, stood beside him as godparents. By sponsoring the child at baptism, they pledged to nurture him and ensure his spiritual well-being in the event of the death or incapacity of his parents.

John Maxwell's niece, Mary Martha Mattier, was the second child baptized. Mary Martha was born free on June 13, 1827, to Fatimah McGundo Kingsley, Zephaniah's twenty-one-year-old mulatto daughter, and a white planter named Luis Mattier. Mary Martha was sponsored for baptism by her aunt, Martha Kingsley (John Maxwell's sister and Fatimah's half sister), and a wealthy white planter, José Maria Ugarte.

Mary Martha's mother and father were not married. In fact, Mattier was married to Priscilla Mattier, a white woman and the mother of Luis's other children. Mary Martha's mother, Fatimah, was John Maxwell's half sister, who had been born into slavery as the child of Munsilna McGundo, an enslaved African owned by Zephaniah Kingsley. He later freed Fatimah and Munsilna.[10]

Waiting in line to approach the impromptu baptismal font that Father Mayne had arranged were the sponsors of two infant children of enslaved Africans owned by Zephaniah Kingsley. Elizabeth Kingsley Wyly was carried forward by Martha Kingsley and her older brother, George Kingsley.

Elizabeth was born on October 18, 1828, to the black slave parents Quala Kingsley and Samuel Wyly (Kingsley). The last child brought to the font that day was Federico, born on November 29, 1828, to the black slave parents Mary and William Kingsley. Federico was sponsored by Mary Kingsley, Anna and Zephaniah's daughter, and a white man from a prominent Florida family, Samuel Fatio.[11]

Kingsley was sixty-three years old on the day his son and granddaughter were baptized in January 1829. He had become a wealthy man, the owner of thousands of acres of prime plantation properties and several hundred slaves. Always a controversial figure because of his unorthodox views on race and family arrangements, Kingsley nevertheless commanded respect as a man of substantial intellect, and his wealth translated into significant power and influence in the region. Scrutiny of his activities in the early 1830s, however, reveals that he was not only troubled by the trends in Florida politics but, more important, he was in the process of making major life changes.

One writer has posited that Kingsley was troubled at the time because *Treatise on the Patriarchal* had generated opposition and "his character and allegiance . . . had come into question" because of "a particularly damaging public scandal." The scandal was the result of an arrangement he made with a federal marshal to employ fifty-six African survivors of a shipwreck near the Florida Keys. Armed Spanish slavers reclaimed 400 of the Africans from American authorities and sold them in Cuba, but 121 were brought to St. Augustine until arrangements could be made to transport them to Liberia. Kingsley was in need of labor at the time and welcomed the opportunity to rent additional workers at two dollars a month plus room, board, and clothing. In this account, Kingsley is charged with "horrid treatment" of the Africans, and it is alleged that residents of the area were vitally interested in the incident and viewed it as a "damaging public scandal." The anthropologist and historian Jean B. Stephens investigated the same incident and concluded it was a "folk tale and not historical fact." Key West historian Gail Swanson has worked tirelessly to track down the records of this incident and found that it was more than a "folk tale," but she offers no evidence that Kingsley abused the workers. The evidence, it must be said, does not substantiate accusations of "horrid treatment."[12]

The same author draws attention to a second incident he claims was even "more damaging to Kingsley's reputation." Kingsley had circulated a petition in late 1830 intended to persuade President Andrew Jackson to replace William P. Duval as governor of the Territory of Florida. Duval retaliated with an attack that mocked Kingsley as a "learned, didactic, and patriarchal friend of Africa . . . who carries in his pocket the poems of the immortal Horace" but who "also cherishes in his bosom his *ebony wife*." Duval ridiculed Kingsley for advocating racial intermarriage in his "amalgamation pamphlet" (*Treatise on the Patriarchal*), and he sparred with Kingsley supporter Joseph M. White, the Florida territorial delegate to Congress. White described Kingsley as "a classical scholar, who would consider it a degradation to be put on a footing with governor Duval in point of intellect, or education." The public jousting no doubt amused newspaper readers in Tallahassee, but to conclude it was "a political battle that ended with . . . [Kingsley] in the losing faction and his published racial views the source of national ridicule" overemphasizes limited and parochial evidence. Kingsley was generally disdainful of public opinion and critical of political infighting.[13]

Other issues weighed on Kingsley's mind at the time. He had initiated a sexual relationship with another of his teenage slaves, Flora Hanahan, who had given birth to a son named Charles on November 15, 1828 (fathered by Kingsley). Flora was emancipated before Charles was born. On the manumission document Kingsley described her as "a mulatto-colored woman of twenty years of age, a native of Florida."[14]

Flora's mother was Sophy Chidgigane, emancipated by Kingsley three days before Flora was freed. Sophy was one of the enslaved African teenagers Kingsley purchased at Havana and carried to Laurel Grove with Anta Madgigine Ndiaye in 1806. Sophy and Anna Jai were natives of Jolof, in Senegal, West Africa, and were possibly "shipmates" during their time of terror crossing the Atlantic aboard a slave ship. Sophy became the wife of Abraham Hanahan, the enslaved plantation manager at Laurel Grove freed by Kingsley in 1811. The circumstances were, even for Kingsley, complicated.[15]

Kingsley's relationship with Flora marked a departure from his previous patterns in that he moved away from Fort George Island to cohabitate with her at New Hope Plantation, a 350-acre property located on the east bank of the St. Johns and the north shore of Goodbys Creek. A deed to the property was conveyed on June 26, 1829, to his nephew Zephaniah C. Gibbs and his brother-in-law George Gibbs, to be held "in trust for Flora Hanahan Kingsley and her son Charles." On July 20, 1831, the property was conveyed back to Kingsley and deeded to Flora and her children as "tenants in common." By that time Flora had given birth to a second child, James Kingsley, born on October 14, 1830. Three more children were born to Flora and Zephaniah at New Hope Plantation: Sophia on September 27, 1833, William on January 5, 1835, and Osceola on January 15, 1837. Roxana Marguerite Kingsley was born on February 21, 1842, at Puerto Plata, Haiti (now Dominican Republic). Kingsley moved Flora and her children there in November 1841.[16]

Kingsley contracted with his son-in-law John S. Sammis to build a new house at New Hope. Sammis boarded there while the house was being built and helped supervise work in corn, cotton, and provisions fields and the orange grove. The frame of the house was assembled with lumber cut at Kingsley's sawmill at St. Johns Bluff and Sawmill Creek and rafted to Goodbys Creek. Work on the house was completed by two of Kingsley's slave carpenters, Carpenter Bill and his assistant Bonafi.[17]

In court testimony given in August 1877, Sammis said he moved from New York to Florida in 1828 and met Flora in 1829. While he lived at New Hope, Sammis observed that "Kingsley and Flora cohabitated as man and wife." Kingsley "slept in her room and he frequently told witness [Sammis] that the plaintiffs [James, William, and Osceola Kingsley] were his children." When Flora and the children left New Hope in 1841 to live in Haiti, Sammis testified, Kingsley "went there with them and their mother, Flora Kingsley, at the same time." In the opinion of John Sammis, Flora was "an honest woman and was true to Zephaniah Kingsley."[18]

It may have been during the years that Kingsley was with Flora at New Hope that Susan Philippa Fatio L'Engle began visiting Anna Madgigine Jai at Fort George Island. Susan, the daughter of Francis Philip Fatio Jr., had probably come to know Anna when they were both living at Fernandina during the Patriot insurgency. She later married a West Point graduate and army officer, John L'Engle, and settled into the life of the wife of a planter and sawmill owner. A brilliant and intellectually curious woman, Susan Fatio L'Engle was intrigued by the free black woman she called "the

FIGURE 10. Portrait of Osceola Kingsley, born in 1837 at the Goodbys Creek farm deeded to Flora Hanahan Kingsley by Zephaniah Kingsley. Osceola, the son of Flora and Zephaniah, relocated with his mother and siblings to a home at Puerto Plata and a farm at Bergantin in today's Dominican Republic in 1841. He became a national hero during the war for independence from Spain and was buried at Bergantin. The image is treasured as the only known image of a child of Zephaniah Kingsley. It is a copy of a portrait, oil on canvas, loaned to the author by an anonymous benefactor. Working from the original, Mr. Tony Lébron, a resident of the Dominican Republic, skillfully re-created the portrait. A copy is in the collection of the Kingsley Plantation at Fort George Island.

African princess" and arranged visits to Fort George Island during which they "went off together to the princess's rooms, and talked, and drank cold tea together." In *The Summer of the Great-Grandmother*, Madeleine L'Engle, the great-granddaughter of Susan Fatio L'Engle, has left an endearing account of the visits that is based on memories passed down through the generations of Fatios and L'Engles.[19]

The oral legend of these visits presents Anna as a lonely woman who felt "ostracized by both whites and blacks" and "nearly died of homesickness." Instead of Zephaniah living in the house next to hers, George Kingsley and his white wife, Anatoile, had moved into the main dwelling and assumed control of plantation affairs, possibly eclipsing Anna's authority of nearly thirty years. Her daughters had recently married white men, Martha to Oran Baxter and Mary to John S. Sammis, and had moved away from Forth George Island. Anna was left at Fort George with only John Maxwell, not yet ten years of age. Zephaniah's visits to Fort George Island were occasional; he was living with a much younger woman and was again fathering children.

The trust deed Kingsley executed for Flora and Charles Kingsley was the first of many property transfers filed in courthouses between 1829 and 1836. Kingsley was one of East Florida's most powerful citizens at the time and was able to provide a web of protection for his family members. But he had marked his sixty-fifth birthday on December 4, 1830, and he knew his influence would expire soon after his death. The numerous property transfers were part of a plan to protect his family from the harsh racial policies the legislative council was rushing to implement in the Territory of Florida. For a man who supported Spanish policies that encouraged owners to manumit slaves and incorporate them into a three-caste racial society, the American policies that judged all persons of color, whether free or enslaved, as members of an inferior race and unworthy of freedom was both appalling and alarming. In a society composed of only two castes, free whites and enslaved blacks—with no place for free persons of color—Kingsley's black and mixed-race family was consigned to a degraded status and would be in continual danger of reenslavement.

The Kingsley family had some immunity, since residents of Spanish Florida at the time of cession to the United States received special legal protections under terms of the Adams-Onis Treaty. But Kingsley could never be sure how the territorial courts would interpret the new laws. If one of his children forgot to pay the discriminatory head taxes and failed to pay the resulting court fine, he or she could have been subjected to enslavement. John Maxwell was born after Florida was ceded to the United States, as were Kingsley's children born to Flora Hanahan and all of his grandchildren, which meant they lacked treaty protection and were potentially subject to the harshest penalties of the laws. Wealth and influence could shield the family for a few years, but the future was ominous. By deeding property to his children, Kingsley was acting to ensure their future physical and economic security.

In 1829, Kingsley entrusted management of Fort George Island to his eldest son, twenty-two-year-old George Kingsley. On May 5, 1831, George married a white woman of French ancestry, Anatoile Françoise Vauntravers, and one month later a trust deed was executed assigning title to Fort George Island to him in exchange for ten dollars in cash and "further consideration and affection, and ten years of service." The timing suggests a wedding gift from an indulgent father, but important obligations accompanied the deed. The first "consideration" was a mandate that "Anna Madgigine Kingsley, mother of George, shall possess and have the use of her house and whatever ground she may desire to plant during her life." The second was a proviso that "Munsilna McGundo and her daughter Fatimah [Zephaniah's child], shall possess the use of her house and four acres of land—also rations during life."[20]

Kingsley deeded several other valuable properties to George, beginning in December 1832 when he transferred title to his 1,000-acre Buena Vista Plantation, along with the three slave families in residence there. Four years later, George received title to an adjoining 600-acre tract known as Orange Grove (also known as Buena Vista Point). Again in 1836, George was deeded San Jose, a 300-acre tract in Duval County also known as Yellow Bluff, and Drayton Island, a 2,000-acre property in Lake George in Putnam County.[21]

Kingsley deeded valuable properties to his daughters by Anna, Martha and Mary. Martha Beatrice Kingsley, born in 1809, married Oran Baxter, a native of Cold Spring, New York, who moved to Florida circa 1830. In 1831 Kingsley gave Martha a 350-acre tract named Naranjal (Orange Grove) de San Jose. Later he transferred title to a 347-acre property in today's Arlington neighborhood known as St. Isabel Plantation to Martha and Oran Baxter. Thirty-six slaves were employed on that property in 1840, also a gift from Martha's father. By 1860 Martha was one of the wealthiest residents of Duval County. Although her husband died in 1847 and left her responsible for his substantial debts, she had met the obligations by 1854, in part by hiring her slaves to her creditors. She had also increased the number of slaves she owned to forty-eight. Four years later, her real estate holdings were valued at $5,000 and her personal property, including slaves, at $27,500.[22]

Mary Kingsley, born in 1811, married John S. Sammis, a native of Dutchess County, New York, who became a Florida resident in 1828. Sammis was a skilled carpenter, shipbuilder, and planter who worked as an overseer at Kingsley's White Oak Plantation before he and Mary were married. In 1831 Kingsley gave Mary and her husband title to Little San Jose (also known as Ashley's Old Field). The thirty-six slaves reported as property of John S. Sammis on the 1840 census of Duval County were almost certainly the result of the assistance and generosity of his father-in-law. John and Mary Sammis raised a large family and accumulated thousands of acres of land, a water-powered sawmill, and sixty-six slaves by 1850. In 1860 the value of their real estate and personal property was judged to be more than $100,000.[23]

In 1832 Kingsley added security to Anna Kingsley's leasehold at Fort George Island with a transfer of title to Deep Creek Plantation, a 1,000-acre tract in St. Johns County located immediately north of Buena Vista. Kingsley stated that the deed transfer was in payment of $2,500 in wages due to Anna and for "faithful services during twenty five years." Included in the transfer were the thirteen "Negro slaves" living there at the time. Anna also owned a 125-acre tract located in today's Mandarin and a 225-acre plot at Dunn's Creek that had been granted to her by the Spanish government to compensate for her losses in 1813.[24]

In addition to providing his children and their mothers with financial security through gifts of real estate and slaves, Kingsley obligated his son George to act in a capacity similar to a guardian for seven children: "the three slave children of Sophy Chidgigane who now live with their mother at Camp New Hope on the St. Johns River, the three slave children of Munsilna McGundo, and Salina, the daughter of Yellow Hannah." No further record of Salina and Yellow Hannah has been found, but for the other six children the transfer of title is perplexing because they were already free persons of color. The "three slave children of Sophy Chidgigane," for example, were Ana Juana, Josefa Ana, and Patty, whom Kingsley had emancipated in 1819 and 1823. The statement that the children were living with their mother at Camp New Hope meant they were living at the home of Sophy's eldest daughter, Flora Hanahan, at a property deeded to Flora in 1829. It also meant that Sophy was living with her two grandchildren, Charles and James Kingsley, the sons of Flora and Zephaniah Kingsley.

Identifying Munsilna McGundo's children as slaves is equally perplexing. Kingsley could not have meant to count Munsilna's daughter Fatimah as a slave, as she was his eldest child, born in February 1807 and emancipated in 1811. A record has not been found for Munsilna's emancipation, but in all other known circumstances involving Kingsley's procreation of children by slave women, he emancipated the mothers as well as the children.[25]

It is difficult to imagine that Munsilna had not been a free woman for many years before 1831, when Kingsley inserted the command on the deed to Fort George Island that Munsilna and Fatimah "shall possess the use of her house and four acres of land—also rations during life." The "three slave children of Munsilna McGundo" mentioned on the 1832 deed for Buena Vista Plantation were undoubtedly free at the time, since all children born to free black women were free at birth, and were probably living at Fort George Island in the house Kingsley set aside for Munsilna.

The unusual contingency clause on the 1832 deed transfer should be considered an obligation imposed on an eldest son who had been favored with a gift of the largest portion of the father's accumulated property. In return, George Kingsley was expected to assume the role of patriarch and family guardian in the event of his father's absence or death. One way white fathers could protect their mulatto children from harsh racial laws was to deed them to a trusted relative or friend when death was imminent, and pray that the recipient would act as guardian and permit them to live as if they were free. Placing the children of Sophy and Munsilna under the proxy ownership of George Kingsley was a way to protect them from discrimination and possible enslavement in the event of Zephaniah's death and the expiration of his protective web of wealth and influence. George was a free person of color, but he would command significant financial resources; his father had seen to that.

By the mid-1830s, Kingsley had distributed valuable real estate to members of his family. He had also provided them with deeds to even more valuable properties, enslaved men and women, as is proven by the following list of the ten individuals who owned the largest numbers of slaves in Duval County in 1846. The tax assessor counted 1,758 slaves, owned by 160 individuals. Few owners, however, held large numbers: the median slaveholding was five, only nineteen persons owned twenty or more, and ten owned thirty-two or more:

1. John H. McIntosh — 169
2. H. B. Sadler — 120
3. Zephaniah Kingsley — 89
4. John Houston — 54
5. James Plummer — 48
6. George Kingsley — 46
7. John S. Sammis — 45
8. Oran Baxter — 42
9. Kingsley B. Gibbs — 32
10. Michael Hearn — 32

The amount of wealth in human property in Duval County concentrated in the hands of five persons in one extended family is striking. In 1846, Zephaniah and George Kingsley, John S. Sammis and Oran Baxter (married to Kingsley's daughters), and Kingsley B. Gibbs (his nephew) were each among the ten largest owners of slave property in the county. Together, they owned 254 slaves. When the eleven slaves owned by Anna Kingsley are added in, six persons in Kingsley's family network owned 15 percent of all slaves in Duval County.[26]

In addition to distributing title to land and slaves to family members during the first half of the 1830s, Kingsley attempted to terminate his duties as executor of the John Fraser estate and close out his business affairs in Florida. An August 1832 notice in a St. Augustine newspaper alerted area residents that Kingsley planned to be absent from Florida for a few weeks and that Kingsley Gibbs and John Sammis were authorized to act as his attorneys until he returned. He also announced that he would be residing in Nassau County in the near future and that he intended to dispose of all his property and "leave the [Florida] territory."[27]

Kingsley and Phillip R. Yonge had been appointed executors of the John Fraser estate following his death by drowning in 1813. They successfully petitioned to stop the Spanish colonial governor from confiscating and selling Fraser's assets, with the proceeds assigned to the treasury rather than the decedent's heirs. The testamentary proceeding was still ongoing when the

Territory of Florida was created, and the executors were immediately subjected to lawsuits filed by Fraser's sister, Ann Fraser Robertson, who had moved from Scotland to St. Augustine, and his daughters, Elizabeth Fraser Skelton and Mary Ann Fraser Curtis, residents of Guinea, West Africa. Kingsley continued to manage the assets of the estate, renting property, making reports to the probate court, and arranging payments to the heirs. In 1829, acting as executor for the estate, Kingsley sued Benjamin Chaires for illegally cutting two thousand live oak trees and one thousand other valuable trees from Fraser's Greenfield Plantation on the San Pablo and St. Johns Rivers. The suit was settled in 1832, with the defendant ordered to pay nearly $20,000 for rent of the plantation and the timber, and for damages.[28]

In 1833 Kingsley settled a lawsuit filed against him by the Fraser heirs, who were demanding payment for the eighty-nine slaves Kingsley purchased from the Fraser estate in 1816. Kingsley redeemed his obligation by agreeing to pay the heirs $20,250 plus interest in three annual payments and by agreeing to mortgage White Oak Plantation and "fifty healthy Negro slaves" as security. When the debt was satisfied in April 1836, Kingsley asked the judge of probate to close out the estate. He announced in the St. Augustine *Florida Herald* that he had "adjusted his accounts" and would ask the court for "a full and final settlement and for discharge." The judge refused to honor the motion, asserting that the Fraser claim for losses suffered during the Patriot insurgency had never been settled by the U.S. government and that one asset was outstanding. That asset was the mortgage for the seventy-nine slaves purchased from the Fraser estate by Philip R. Yonge, the second executor of the estate. Yonge had never paid legatees for the slaves he acquired from the estate in 1816. Therefore, the case file remained active for several more years, and Kingsley continued to be involved until the day of his death.[29]

Kingsley had decided by this time that an extraordinary action might become necessary to protect his mixed-race family from the increasingly discriminatory race policies of the Florida territorial government. At some time in the early 1830s, he became interested in emigration to another country as a possible way to provide that protection. The exact events and influences that led to this decision are uncertain. What is known is that during the same years Kingsley was attempting to secure the future of his family through gifts of land and slaves, he was studying the writings of advocates for colonization and traveling to northern cities to listen to speeches by abolitionists.

The hysterical fear of slave rebellion that spread through the South after the 1831 Nat Turner rebellion in Virginia may have convinced Kingsley that providing his family with deeds to plantations and slaves might not be sufficient protection in the future. The Second Seminole War (1835–42) provoked even greater racial hysteria and xenophobia in Florida. Blacks fighting alongside Indian warriors terrified Florida slaveholders. Implacable foes in combat, the Black Seminoles conspired in attacks on plantations before escaping to remote forest and wetland retreats. The historian Larry E. Rivers has described the first three years of the war as "a massive slave revolt." St. Augustine residents were alarmed in 1836 when they learned that slaves residing in the town had conspired with free blacks and Seminole Indians in a raid on a nearby plantation. Jacksonville's militia leaders, suspecting that "internal enemies" lurked in their own black population, gave orders to keep all slaves and free blacks not directly supervised by owners or guardians under armed detention. The Jacksonville newspaper warned that the "tragic scenes of Hayti" could be repeated in Jacksonville and that abolitionists were plotting to "deluge our country with blood." Free African Americans faced rigid restrictions: anyone attempting to "teach any colored person to read or write" could be severely punished. Kingsley's resolve to move his family out of harm's way was reinforced by these events.[30]

Direct evidence of Kingsley's attitude toward the Seminole War is ambiguous. During his first decade in East Florida he had traded with the Seminoles through his mercantile operation at Laurel Grove. The July 1812 Seminole raid that resulted in the destruction of that plantation and the abduction of more than forty of his African slaves may have soured his outlook on Native Americans. In the late 1820s he was still complaining to government officials that the abducted slaves had never been returned to him, blaming corrupt government-appointed Indian agents. Perhaps his opposition to Andrew Jackson's Indian policies influenced his choice of names for two of his sons, both born in 1837. His son by Flora Hanahan was named Osceola, one of the most militant and anti-American of the Seminole leaders. The second son was the child of another teenage slave woman owned by Kingsley, an African-born woman named Sarah Murphy. The child was named Micanopy, after the hereditary chief of the Alachua bands of the Seminole who refused to move to the reservation land set aside by government in 1832.[31]

By 1839 Kingsley was still opposed to the government's war policies, and he was alarmed by the devastating impact the war was having on planting and commerce throughout Florida. His own distant plantations on the St. Johns were particularly vulnerable to Seminole raiders. His properties on the lower St. Johns were less affected because of the presence of U.S. soldiers in Duval County and the ease of access to open shipping lanes to Savannah and Charleston. However, the war had intensified the effects of the panic of 1837 for Floridians, driving down land values and causing financial ruin for many planters.

In a January 1839 letter to Secretary of War Joel R. Poinsett, Kingsley denounced the "present state of misery and suffering" and complained that "expenditure of public money has nearly doubled the price of manual labor and of everything else . . . and has nearly annihilated the value of real property by which National prosperity is estimated." He advised Poinsett to end the war as soon as possible and to rely on "the ordinary increase of population . . . to expel the present Indian Inhabitants from Florida at some future period of time." Kingsley urged Poinsett to make "peace upon the best and cheapest terms" even if it meant granting the Seminoles a "permanent residence within specified limits and upon certain conditions which we know . . . would certainly be broken on their part. With peace there is still time to settle the Country so thickly this spring and summer, as to set all future fears of Indian disturbance at rest. They would then petition to be removed and we could dictate such terms as were most economical." One year of peace would bring enough American settlers to more effectively "crowd out and displace the Indians from E. Florida than Five years war with any premium [government incentives of free land] that could reasonably be offered."[32]

Between 1830 and 1835 Kingsley traveled to northern cities to attend lectures by abolitionists and advocates of colonization for America's free blacks and slaves. The lecture tours by the Englishman E. S. Abdy in 1833–34 and by George Thompson in 1834–35 are examples. Kingsley met with Abdy in New York and Philadelphia and invited him to visit Fort George Island before returning to England. Abdy declined the invitation but was impressed by Kingsley's "remarkable intelligence" and thought him "one of the most benevolent men, though a slave-holder, I ever met."[33]

One year later, Kingsley attended lectures by George Thompson, a more controversial and provocative abolitionist, whose tour between August 1834 and November 1835 included stops at cities in Massachusetts, New York, Maine, and Pennsylvania. Thompson's extremist positions raised howls of protest and serious threats on his life that led to cancellation of some of his speeches. The abolitionist Lydia Maria Child was surprised to hear Kingsley say in an 1842 interview that "he likes the abolitionists" and was a "prodigious admirer of George Thompson. . . . 'My neighbors call me an abolitionist . . . I tell them that they may do so, in welcome; for it is a pity they shouldn't have *one* case of amalgamation to point at.'" It remains unclear whether Kingsley was teasing Ms. Child or ridiculing his neighbors for hypocrisy.[34]

Kingsley was well read on the motivations and policies of abolitionists, especially those who advocated colonization as a means to end slavery in America or to eliminate free people of color from the general population. The historian Daniel Stowell carefully elucidates Kingsley's numerous references to colonization advocates in each edition of *Treatise on the Patriarchal*. Kingsley came to embrace colonization only reluctantly, realizing that three-caste race policies in support of slavery would never be accepted by his fellow slaveholders in Florida. Once Kingsley came to that position, however, he argued against choosing Canada or Mexico as a place of refuge and stated passionately that colonizing former slaves in Africa would be a "sad alternative of submitting to a condition worse than slavery" and would condemn them to live "where sickness, privations and barbarity must soon put an end to all their troubles." Settling former American slaves in Africa would be impossibly expensive and would engender the resentment of Africans "whom they must displace . . . ; [their] lives must be sacrificed to famine or resentment at the despotic nod to cruelty and superstition."[35]

If not Africa, then in what country could free people of color settle where their lives would be enhanced rather than endangered, and where they could prosper through hard work and intelligence? Kingsley had visited all of the potential sites in Africa and in the Western Hemisphere being touted for colonization. He was convinced "a great opportunity was lost of colonizing more rationally at the late evacuation of the Spanish part of Saint Domingo, where there would have been ample room for all the colored people of the U. States, within five days sail of Charleston." But that was in 1828, when Kingsley was still trying to convince Floridians, and Americans, of the merits of a patriarchal system of slavery and of the need to pass liberal laws to encourage manumission and grant rights to free people of color.[36]

By 1835 Kingsley had changed his mind. He had been persuaded that the possibility of a three-caste racial policy in Florida had ended with the departure of the Spanish colonial government, and he was determined to find a place where his "colored and natural children" could be safe. Kingsley had determined that "the illiberal and inequitable laws of this Territory will not afford to them and to their children that protection and justice, which is due in civilized society to every human being." Consequently, he decided his children should relocate "to some land of liberty and equal rights, where the conditions of society are governed by some law less absurd than that of color." Haiti, the only free black republic in the Western Hemisphere, still loomed in Kingsley's mind as a safe haven for his family. In early September 1835 he set sail for Puerto Plata on the north shore of Haiti to investigate conditions in a land he had not visited in two decades.

13 The "Island of Liberty" and Kingsley's Final Journeys

During the summer of 1835, Kingsley traveled to

Haiti to determine the truth of President Jean-Pierre Boyer's boast that the former French colony synonymous with sugar and slavery had become an "Island of Liberty." Reports in the abolitionist literature had been positive, but Kingsley knew that the slave rebellion which drove away the French and transformed Saint-Domingue into Haiti, the first free black republic in the Western world, had also devastated the economy and laid waste to much of the countryside. Kingsley planned to travel westward along the northern coast from the former Spanish colony of Santo Domingo to Port-au-Prince. He knew the cities and countryside well from his previous journeys to purchase coffee, but on this adventure he was searching for a large and fertile tract where his biracial family could live in freedom and prosperity.

The journey was routed through New York City, where firms with convenient transportation and commercial connections to Haiti were based. Kingsley also planned to meet with George H. Evans, editor of the *Working Man's Advocate*, to arrange publication of a series of letters he anticipated writing while touring Haiti. If he decided that the only free black republic in the Western Hemisphere was indeed an "Island of Liberty," he intended to publicize that fact and attract other free colored migrants. The *Working Man's Advocate*, with its proven audience among abolition societies, would serve Kingsley's purposes well.

Evans had four years earlier published "Prejudice against Color," written by a "Free Colored Floridian," in which Florida's "colored people" were urged to consider emigration to "Mexico as a place of safety and permanent refuge." The anonymous author deplored "the general prejudice or fashionable jealousy against complexion or difference of color, which seems singularly predominant in all our States: even so far as to neutralize or rather to hostilize [sic] the whole colored population of the Union." Equating prejudice with ignorance, the writer argued for equal protection under the law and public acceptance of free people of color. The underlying tone of the letter implied that reason would prevail over ignorance, but in the event that discrimination intensified, free people of color were encouraged to consider emigration to a new homeland where the government "offers an ample guarantee against prejudice or injustice to every settler." Canada offered such a guarantee, but "the extreme coldness of the climate" lessened its attractiveness, whereas Mexico possessed a more genial climate and a government whose constitution and laws "recognize no difference of merit on account of color," and its citizens "are mostly colored and entirely free from all prejudice against complexion."[1]

A critical reading of the letter indicates that George Kingsley was the author. Only twenty-four years old, newly married, and already a plantation and slave owner, George Kingsley seems an incongruous spokesperson for emigration of free people of color. Advocacy of emigration and colonization was contrary to his father's published opinions, and Evans was an unlikely ally for slaveholders. Evans was an abolitionist and a radical agitator for labor reform and free land for white workingmen, and a supporter of Andrew Jackson's attacks on elites and aristocracies. In the aftermath of the 1831 Nat Turner rebellion in Virginia, Evans condemned the violence but triggered a furious response in the slaveholding states when he argued that the desire for freedom was the real reason the rebels rose in arms.[2]

A more compatible publisher for George Kingsley's letter would have been the Quaker abolitionist Benjamin Lundy, whose *Genius of Universal Emancipation* promoted nonviolent tactics. Lundy had, as early as 1815, organized antislavery societies and worked tirelessly for abolition causes. During the 1820s and 1830s he encouraged former slaves to consider emigration as a solution to their plight in a racist country. After a brief editing partnership with William Lloyd Garrison, during which the two men praised Haiti as a potential haven for free colored emigrants, Lundy changed his endorsement to Mexico's Texas province as a homeland. Garrison, of course, became the nation's leading advocate for immediate abolition and opposed all plans for colonization. He condemned members of the American Colonization Society as bigots who advocated emigration to Liberia and as pro-slavery racists who wanted to eliminate free people of color in the United States.[3]

Zephaniah Kingsley also opposed plans for emigration to Africa, Canada, and Mexico, but unlike Garrison, he was pro-slavery and a missionary for humane and patriarchal treatment of slaves. Instead of abolishing slavery, Kingsley advocated liberal manumission laws and the granting of rights to free people of color as a means to buttress the institution. By 1835, however, he had lost confidence in the possibility of persuading Florida slaveholders to accept a three-caste racial society and was willing to investigate the potential of Haiti as a sanctuary. He knew that letters published in the *Working Man's Advocate* would reach a wide audience.

During the New York meeting, Kingsley promised to send travel letters with "a true description of what I saw in my progress through this Island of Liberty." Evans published the letters in the *Working Man's Advocate* and later republished them in a pamphlet titled *The Rural Code of Haiti*. He prefaced the first letter with an endorsement: "The statements of the writer may be implicitly relied on."[4]

Kingsley arrived at Puerto Plata on September 4, 1835. His seventieth birthday would occur before he returned to Florida, and yet he was about to engage in an undertaking that would try the endurance of young and healthy men. Kingsley noted ships in the harbor waiting to depart with cargoes of mahogany logs and tobacco bales, and a town of "pretty . . . one story houses" similar in size to St. Augustine. In the surrounding countryside he found "waving cocoa nut and majestic palm trees, growing on the gently rising plain . . . between the town and the mountain . . . majestically rising behind it, to the height of three thousand feet, and richly covered with trees to the top."[5]

For ten days, Kingsley examined the soil, small farms, crops under cultivation, and "rich, uncut forests" as he rode on horseback across the coastal plain to the summit ridges of the mountain. Everywhere he traveled, Kingsley said, he was greeted with a "hearty welcome" by the "black and poor colored people" living on small rural farms in peaceful abundance and with "natural kindness of heart, which sustains their practical moral merit of character." It was unlike any other country he had observed, a land of "perfect freedom and equality without law or restraint; yet no one trespasses upon . . . decorum and politeness." He experienced no anti-white prejudice, prompting the observation that if prejudice was not supported by laws, it "soon melts, and is dissolved by our moral relations, if let alone, like any other legal privilege."

Americans familiar with Kingsley's arguments in *Treatise on the Patriarchal* must have been puzzled by what they read in his letters from Haiti. The author still held more than one hundred men and women in bondage in rural Florida, and he had written that slave drivers and a caste of free colored allies were necessary to keep the slaves under control. The overwhelmingly African-born population of Haiti, in Kingsley's telling, had only recently been liberated from slavery, yet they had created a nation free from penury, crime, cruelty, and racial prejudice.

Kingsley's next letter to Evans was written on September 29 from Cap Haitien, also on the north shore of the island. In two weeks, accompanied by a guide and another man, Kingsley had ridden "a distance of two hundred miles or more," through "a rich alluvial valley" with the remains of stone buildings at former sugar plantations where trees had grown up in the former cane fields. The coastal plain and valley were interrupted by two mountain ridges that extended to the ocean. He praised the soil's fertility and agricultural produce and assessed the herds of cattle and "flocks of sheep and goats" as "the finest" he had ever seen. He had ridden the entire distance without coming upon a "tavern or public house on the whole road," taking lodging whenever and wherever it was convenient and finding each time "not only a friendly welcome, but genteel and fashionable accommodations. No tale of robbery or personal insult could be heard of."[6]

From Cap Haitien, Kingsley and his companions rode west and south to Gonaïves, a journey of sixty-five miles. They examined the ruins of plantations that still lay idle thirty years after the revolutionary violence ended, and passed near the opulent palace of Sans-Soucie, built circa 1810 for the Haitian dictator Henri Christophe (the palace was destroyed by an earthquake in 1842). He was favorably impressed by the harbor at Limbé, the valley of Camp Cog, and the small one-family coffee farms in thickly wooded surrounding hills, the "lively village of Plaisance, with its . . . fertile fields and well stored gardens of fruit and vegetables," and the mahogany forests adjoining the Artibonite River.[7]

From Gonaïves, Kingsley boarded a small coasting vessel bound for

Port-au-Prince. During his two days and three nights aboard the vessel, Kingsley was entertained by the laughter and good humor of the Haitian women and the musical talents and war stories told by their men. They landed at Port-au-Prince on Sunday, October 11, in time to observe "their great market and parade day" and witness the bounteous array of provisions arriving aboard small craft and the "innumerable horse and jackass loads of all kinds of tropical fruit and country produce, chiefly conducted by women." Kingsley mused that he had traveled more than three hundred miles through the interior of a country experiencing "the persecution and open war now carrying on against them in the United States" feeling often "humbled and ashamed at the undeserved respect and deference with which I, as a white man, was everywhere treated and received."

On the following Sunday, Kingsley was granted "a long and familiar interview with President [Jean-Pierre] Boyer." Kingsley judged the president to be "a very intelligent and sensible man . . . of great integrity and patriotism." He posed a series of questions to the president and the phalanx of generals surrounding him, and was told he would receive answers in a mailed response composed after the relevant government statutes were consulted.

To this point, Kingsley was confident that Haiti was a safe and suitable refuge for his biracial family and other free people of color. "The price of land is extremely low," he wrote, and consequently it was possible to purchase "superb and costly old plantations, with all their improvements and imperishable buildings of brick and stone, together with their valuable mill streams and water privileges convenient to towns . . . for a small part of what the improvements alone would cost." The only impediment he foresaw to Haiti's emergence as a powerful and wealthy nation was a shortage of capital for investment.[8]

Kingsley booked passage for New York in late October. On November 13 he posted another letter to Evans that included a response to the inquiries Kingsley had posed to President Boyer. The response was in the form of a letter written by the Honorable B. Ingenac, secretary general of the Republic of Haiti. Kingsley learned that persons of African descent could migrate to Haiti as long as they registered with a justice of peace upon entering the country. Thereafter, they could locate wherever they wished and could purchase land from government or private individuals after completing a mandatory one year's residence. Slavery was forbidden, but emigrants could bring indentured laborers if contractual arrangements were declared upon entry and the indentures swore they agreed to the terms and had signed the contracts of "their own free will." Terms of indenture were limited by Haitian law to a maximum of nine years, and children could be bound to indenture contracts by their parents or guardians until they reached the age of majority (twenty-one years). Neither emigrants nor their indentured laborers were required "to do military duty as regular soldiers of the Republic," although citizen proprietors were required to join the national guard of their home district.[9]

Satisfied with the answers, Kingsley returned to Florida. George Kingsley returned title to Fort George Island to his father and began plans to become the leader and resident manager of a Haitian settlement that would be titled in his name. Six of Kingsley's slaves were emancipated and signed to indenture contracts binding them to work under George's direction for a maximum term of nine years. The families of the men departing for Haiti would remain in Florida until houses were erected and the first round of land clearing and planting was completed. In October 1836, Kingsley, his son George, and six indentured men cast off for Haiti on a ship loaded with provisions, tools, seeds, cuttings for citrus and other fruit trees, clothing, and other necessities. At Puerto Plata, a "minister of finance" arranged for rental of a valuable tract of land known as Mayorasgo de Koka—previously granted on January 1, 1832, to Theodore J. Heineken but vacant at the time the Kingsleys arrived—to George Kingsley on December 24, 1836.[10]

Kingsley penned an invaluable account of the founding of the colony that was printed in abolitionist publications and widely disseminated in North America. He wrote that he left for Haiti with his son, "a healthy colored man of uncorrupted morals, about thirty years of age, tolerably well educated, of very industrious habits, and a native of Florida, together with six prime African men, my own slaves, liberated for that express purpose." After registering with Haitian officials at Puerto Plata, the group traveled eastward along twenty-seven miles of the north shore until they reached Mayorasgo de Koka, which Kingsley renamed Cabaret (today Cabarete). It was a "thickly timbered" property that stretched inland from the sea across a fertile coastal plain to the crest of the mountains. Kingsley returned to Florida in mid-November 1836. Progress reports mailed by his son indicated

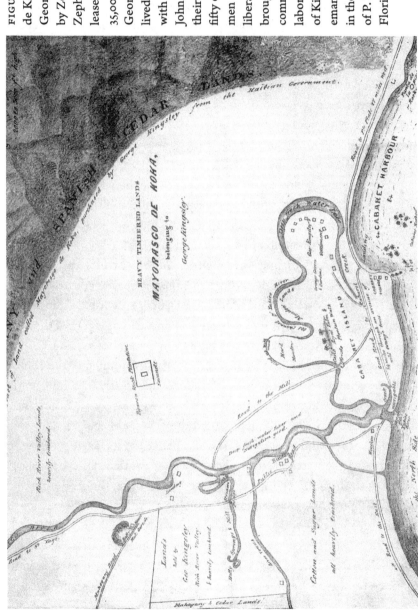

FIGURE 11. "Mayorasgo de Koka, belonging to George Kingsley," drawn by Zephaniah Kingsley Jr. Zephaniah arranged the lease and purchase of this 35,000-acre tract for his son George. Anna Jai Kingsley lived here from 1838 to 1846 with her sons George and John Maxwell Kingsley and their families. More than fifty of Kingsley's enslaved men and women were liberated in Florida and brought to this agricultural community as indentured laborers. Descendants of Kingsley and of the emancipated slaves still live in the area. Map courtesy of P. K. Yonge Library of Florida History.

that by January 1837 trees had been felled and enough land cleared to permit planting of "sweet potatoes, yams, cassava, rice, beans, peas, plantains, oranges, and all sorts of fruit trees."[11]

In October 1837 Kingsley purchased "a coppered brig of 150 tons" and sailed from St. Marys, Georgia, to his son's settlement. Passengers were George Kingsley's wife, Anatoile, and her children, and the wives and children of the six enslaved men Kingsley liberated in 1836. Also aboard were "two additional families . . . all liberated for the express purpose of transportation to Haiti, where they were all to have as much good land in fee as they could cultivate, say ten acres for each family and all its proceeds." The "servants" were also guaranteed to receive "one-fourth part of the net proceeds of their labor from my son's farm, for themselves; also victuals, clothes, medical attendance, &c., gratis, besides Saturdays and Sundays, as days of labor for themselves, or for rest, just at their option."[12]

The brig arrived at Cabarete in early November 1837. Only twelve months before, Kingsley had left a frontier settlement where his son and six African men were felling trees and building shelters. He now found the laborers in "good health" and their personal fields "overflowing with the most delicious variety and abundance of fruits and provisions." They had constructed "good comfortable log houses all nicely white-washed" in preparation for the arrival of their families, and had each cleared and planted "five or six acres of land." Already, they had harvested surpluses of "rice, corn, potatoes, sugar cane, fowls, peas [and] beans" to sell at local markets and had accumulated savings of "thirty to forty dollars apiece."

Kingsley's son farmed on "a larger scale," the advantage gained from six indentured servants working five days a week on his improvements. "Commodious dwelling[s]" and a variety of farm and utility buildings had been constructed at the proprietor's compound. In nine months, "three crops of corn of twenty-five bushels to the acre" and bountiful supplies of "high land rice" had been harvested from George Kingsley's fields. Cotton planted in March was fifteen feet tall, and fields of yams, cassava, and sweet potatoes were thriving. The sweet orange cuttings brought from Florida had been budded on wild orange trees found on the property and were already flowering.

For the next three months Kingsley remained at the settlement, helping build "a new two story house" and assisting with several other projects. In February he traveled to Port-au-Prince for another meeting with President Boyer, and was gratified by "a favorable answer" to his son's petition requesting permission to "own in fee simple, the same tract of land upon which he then lived as a tenant," a tract of thirty-five thousand acres. Boyer ordered a survey of the land and a deed of ownership to be granted in George Kingsley's name (whites were barred from citizenship and land ownership in Haiti). The land was surveyed and valued at $3,000, or, in Kingsley's words "about ten cents an acre."[13]

In February 1838, Kingsley returned from Haiti fired with a passion—as he later told Lydia Maria Child—"to do great things for Haiti." His enthusiasm may explain why he sent a report to the editor of the *Christian Statesman*, a publication sponsored by the American Colonization Society (ACS). Kingsley had been outspoken in opposition to policies favored by the ACS: separation of the races, the idea that free people of color inspired slave rebellions, and removal of freedmen and women by colonizing them in Liberia. ACS publications reached a wide audience, and the pragmatic Kingsley wanted favorable publicity for his colonization venture in Haiti. Once Kingsley decided that Haiti was indeed an "Island of Liberty" and his family could prosper at Cabarete, he worked avidly to promote colonization. In addition to his free colored sons and daughters and their mothers, he also transported to Haiti a number of unrelated free colored persons and several dozen slaves liberated prior to departure.[14]

Kingsley delegated his plantation affairs in Florida to overseers while he shuttled back and forth to Haiti and to New York and other American coastal cities on behalf of emigration to Haiti. When in Florida, an inordinate amount of his time was devoted to legal matters and to bringing a satisfactory conclusion to the still outstanding claims against the U.S. government dating all the way back to 1812–14. His own large claim for the destruction of Laurel Grove Plantation was pending before the Treasury Department, and his last obligation as executor of the John Fraser estate was to settle an even larger claim for the destruction of Fraser's two plantations.

From his old residence at Fort George Island, Kingsley began in the latter months of 1838 to organize a large-scale emigration of free persons of color to Haiti. He hired his nephew Charles J. McNeill as overseer at Fort George, hired another overseer at San Jose, and a third at Drayton

Island. His Laurel Grove and White Oak plantations had previously been sold. In March 1839 he mortgaged Fort George Island and forty slaves to his nephew Kingsley B. Gibbs and to Ralph King, Gibbs's brother-in-law and business partner.[15]

On August 9, 1839, the *Boston Recorder* reported that Kingsley had departed the St. Johns River in Florida on July 20 aboard the "brig America" headed for Haiti with "nearly 100 free colored and some white passengers of that neighborhood. They were mostly of the useful and laborious classes of this community," farmers, craftsmen, and "some first rate ship builders and other mechanics, intending to settle near Port au Plate, under the patronage of Mr. Kingsley, a Florida planter, who wishes to transfer their industry to his own fertile lands in Hayti."[16]

Anna Kingsley and her son John Maxwell Kingsley were among the passengers. Anna's two daughters, Martha Baxter and Mary Sammis, were married to wealthy white men and secure enough to remain in Florida. Upon arrival at Cabarete, Anna and John Maxwell moved into a dwelling at George Kingsley's settlement alongside Cabaret Creek. Kingsley descendants in Haiti still repeat stories of "the African Princess" walking the short distance from the settlement to the beach at Cabaret Harbor, where she had a second dwelling with a patio that extended to the water. In the family legend, a tall and dignified woman with long hair and long gold jewelry walked to the beach each morning attended by a servant. In an 1842 interview, Zephaniah described Anna as "a fine, tall figure, black as jet, but very handsome. . . . I have fixed her nicely in my Haitien colony."[17]

Sarah Murphy and her son Micanopy Murphy Kingsley also left Florida in 1839 for a new life in Haiti. According to baptismal records of the Catholic Church of Puerto Plata, Sarah gave birth to a daughter, Altagracia Kingsley, on January 1, 1840. On September 19, 1842, Kingsley appeared before Leandro Garcia, a notary public at Puerto Plata, to acknowledge paternity of Altagracia and Micanopy Murphy Kingsley, the latter born in Florida on February 1, 1837. Kingsley also acknowledged Micanopy as his son in his Last Will and Testament.[18]

A reliable history of immigration to Haiti by Dr. Jose Augusto Puig Ortiz asserts that approximately two thousand free persons of color migrated to the Puerto Plata area in the nineteenth century. Puig Ortiz posits that 157 families came from Florida, in addition to fifty-three individuals brought to a "feudal enclave" near Puerto Plata at "Cabarete (Sosúa) y El Batey (Sabaneta de Yasica)" by Zephaniah Kingsley. Dr. Puig Ortiz underestimated the number brought by Kingsley when he combined forty-two indentured laborers (slaves who were liberated prior to emigrating) and a biracial family of eleven persons. The three "esposas" and their children that Dr. Puig Ortiz counted as Kingsley's family (Anna Jai, Flora Hanahan, and Sarah Murphy) consisted of at least fourteen persons, and he apparently overlooked Munsilna McGundo, and possibly one or more of her children. The respected local historians Neit Finke and Pablo Juan Brugal said in interviews that they inspected government records, since lost, that documented the arrival of Munsilna McGundo at Puerto Plata.[19]

Abraham Hanahan resettled in Haiti as well. Since his birth in Charleston in the household of Kingsley's father, Abraham and Zephaniah were associated in numerous capacities until the latter's death in September 1843. It is assumed that Abraham's wife, Sophy Chidgigane Hanahan, and possibly one or more of their younger children also migrated to Haiti.[20]

The departure date for the expedition cited in the *Boston Recorder*, July 20, 1839, matches relevant circumstances and fits within the schedule of Kingsley's journeys to and from Haiti. It also occurred at a time when the numbers of free persons of color in Florida dropped precipitously. Between 1830 and 1850 the population of free persons of color in northeast Florida's three coastal counties—Duval, Nassau, and St. Johns—declined by one-third, from 304 to 207, while the slave population increased by one-third, from 2,814 to 4,176, and total population increased by one-third, from 5,959 to 9,012. Among the free colored persons known to have traded lives in Duval County for the Puerto Plata area of Haiti are Ana Taylor and Marta King, and also Adelaida Richard, Teresa Richard, and Teresa's five children. From Nassau County, Samuel Cooper, the son of a white planter and an emancipated woman of color, migrated to Puerto Plata. Free colored emigrants from St. Johns County included Francisco Clarke, a carpenter, and Joseph C. Clarke, who became a merchant at Puerto Plata. That these individuals left Florida and settled in Haiti is proven by Dominican Republic census data and the careful research of Dr. Puig Ortiz, but it is not known if they migrated in July 1839 under the direction of Kingsley.[21]

Teresa Richard's emigration closely matches the account in the *Boston*

Recorder. Teresa's five children (Luis, Miguel, Cornelia, Cristina, and Josefina) were identified at Puerto Plata as the children of Francis Richard II, who acknowledged in his Last Will and Testament that he was their father. Richard's own father, born in France, became a planter at Saint-Domingue before the slave rebellion forced him to flee with his family to Spanish East Florida in 1791. Francis Richard II became a planter in East Florida and was granted nearly seventeen thousand acres by the Spanish government. For several years he operated a water-powered sawmill in what is today the Arlington neighborhood of Jacksonville. In 1837 he made arrangements in his will for bequests to his legitimate white son and to his "colored children, Fortune, Fernando, Cornelia, Anne, Francis (aka Pardo), John, Josephine, Genevieve, Teresa and her children Lewis, Michael and Christiana." He wrote that his "colored children will soon all reside in the Island of Hayti in the West Indies," and directed that if his legitimate son "should die leaving no heirs, the slaves and the income thereof herein mentioned as given and bequeathed to him be divided in specific property as nearly as can be among my colored children before mentioned and shipped to them in the said Island of Hayti." Richard also bequeathed $500 for "Eve a colored woman" and directed that his slaves "Harry, Prince and Elizabeth and her issue" be given to Teresa, "a free colored woman now residing in the Island of Hayti." In November 1839, the time of Richard's death, Teresa and her children, and possibly Eve and one or two others mentioned in Richard's will, had already emigrated to the Puerto Plata region. Richard and Kingsley had known each other for years and had cooperated on various projects. The circumstances, therefore, support the possibility that Teresa and her children may have participated in a group emigration venture sponsored by Kingsley.[22]

Kingsley B. Gibbs, the new proprietor of Fort George Island, wrote in his journal in March 1840: "Mr. Kingsley is now planting at San Jose on the St. Johns, and occasionally [St.] Augustine & Ft Geo are favored with a visit." Kingsley returned to Haiti soon after Gibbs entered the diary notation. A port-of-entry record documents Kingsley arriving at New York City from Puerto Plata on July 22, 1840, aboard the ship *America*, the same vessel that had departed the St. Johns River for Haiti on July 20 of the previous year.[23]

Contemporary newspaper evidence indicates that Kingsley continued to recruit emigrants for Haiti. In November 1840 the *Baltimore Sun* published an appeal to "free people of color of the United States" to consider emigrating to George Kingsley's settlement at Cabarete in Haiti rather than to Africa or the British West Indies. The article was not attributed to Kingsley, but internal evidence leaves little doubt that he was the author. "Industrious farmers who are not afraid of work" and individuals with $100 to purchase land were urged to call at the office of "Charles Collins, of Franklin Square" in New York City to view a pamphlet "with a more particular description" and to make arrangements for a voyage "to Port Plate this fall" or to "wait until the spring, when a vessel will be hired to carry out such emigrants." Collins, a Quaker abolitionist and a prominent New York grocer, had promoted emigration to Haiti since 1824, when President Boyer sent him 50,000 pounds of coffee to pay for transportation costs of black American emigrants.[24]

According to Kingsley, his son's estate at Cabarete was from the outset a harmonious and prosperous endeavor, with the laborers sharing in the profits and acquiring land of their own. Inland from the beach and harbor, a coastal plain of rich soil supported sugar and cotton production, citrus groves, corn and vegetable gardens, and cattle grazing. From its source in the heavily timbered mountains enclosing the coastal plain, the Yasica River wound through the tract on its route to the ocean. Trees cut in the rich mahogany and cedar forests were floated down streams that connected the Yasica River to a sawmill owned by George Kingsley. Lumber was transported to the harbor at Puerto Plata for shipment to Europe and the United States. The residential quarter for George's family and his mother, Anna, and brother, John Maxwell, was along Cabaret Creek at the point where it became a deep freshwater lake. The creek flowed easterly beyond the settlement through orange groves, gardens, a royal palm and plantain walk, meadows, and cane fields before merging with the Yasica River.

In a conversation with Lydia Maria Child, Kingsley described "Mayorasgo de Koka" as located "in a fine, rich valley, heavily timbered with mahogany all around, well watered, flowers so beautiful, fruits in abundance, so delicious that you could not refrain from stopping to eat. . . . My son has laid out good roads, and built bridges and mills; the people are improving, and everything is prosperous." In response to Ms. Child's accusation that he held the laborers in "a sort of qualified slavery" and that he "may sell them again," Kingsley vigorously denied the charge.[25]

A reader of Ms. Child's report wrote to the *Emancipator and Free American* with his own account of a visit to George Kingsley's settlement in the winter of 1837–38. Zephaniah was not present, but "his son, a good-looking, apparently intelligent mulatto," welcomed the visitors and led them on a tour of the property and the improvements. The anonymous letter writer was impressed by the progress made thus far and stated that the elder Kingsley's praise of the property was "entirely free from exaggeration." Concerning Child's accusation that the laborers were kept in "a sort of qualified slavery," the visitor commented: "what he says of their not being chattels, or legally liable to sale, is perfectly true. The laws of Haiti allow no property in man, and no service for life, or for an indefinite period." He felt the conditions of servitude at Cabarete fell short of the standards of life of a New England farm laborer, but he was emphatic in his belief that "Geo. Kingsley was not a slaveholder, nor his workmen slaves." While at the plantation, the visitor witnessed a dispute between the proprietor and "some of his hands, about the terms of their contract." To settle the dispute, "appeal was made to the authorities of the island, not to the summary decision of the cart whip. And all the way from Port au Platte . . . the commandant rode out to hear the parties discuss the grievance and adjust the difficulty."[26]

Ralph Higginbotham, a commercial agent employed by the U.S. Department of State, made inquiries in Port-au-Prince between October 1838 and January 1839 after hearing stories of a man named Kingsley, "a gentleman from Florida who came here some little time since with many people, formerly his slaves." General B. Ingenac assured Higginbotham that Kingsley's former slaves were indentured laborers in Haiti and that they were guaranteed rights of citizenship and shares of the proceeds of the estate. In Haiti, the general said, indenture contracts were limited by law to a maximum of nine years, and land ownership was restricted to persons of African descent. Higginbotham agreed with Kingsley that Haiti was far superior to Africa as an emigration destination: "The climate and everything connected with this country would be in their favor. . . . This country can support *ten* millions of inhabitants, and here no ground is lost, it can be cultivated to the very summit of the mountains."[27]

For much of 1841, Kingsley was back in Florida. In April, Kingsley Gibbs wrote in his journal: "Mr. Kingsley often visits us, as I have a great deal to do for him as his attorney, particularly in the claim for losses in 1812. He now fears that he will have to assign my mortgage and bond . . . for the purchase of this Island and 40 negroes." On November 15, 1841, Gibbs wrote: "Mr. Kingsley sailed for Hayti today."[28]

Kingsley, age seventy-seven at the time, traveled with Flora Hanahan and her four sons (Charles, James, William, and Osceola) on this journey. A daughter, Roxana Marguerite Kingsley, was born to Flora at Puerto Plata on February 21, 1842. Kingsley had returned to Florida before Roxana's birth, but on his next journey to Haiti he testified before a notary public at Puerto Plata on September 19, 1842, that he was Roxana's father and that he was the father of Flora's four sons. This record establishes that Flora and her sons were living at Puerto Plata prior to February 21, 1842.[29]

Kingsley stayed only briefly in Haiti on this journey. He returned to Florida on January 8, 1842, stopping at Fort George Island on his way to San Jose Plantation. Kingsley Gibbs recorded in his diary: "Mr. Kingsley returned up the river and the weather like Spring." On May 24 Kingsley stopped again at Fort George Island to release Gibbs's "Bond and Mortgage and take back twenty-eight Negroes." One week later, on May 31, Gibbs noted that "Mr. Kingsley Sailed for Hayti in the brig Virginia." It was Kingsley's seventh trip to the "Island of Liberty" in seven years, and it would be his final journey to Haiti.[30]

Kingsley stayed at Puerto Plata and Cabarete for five months on this journey, returning to the United States in November, just one month shy of his seventy-eighth birthday. During previous visits, Kingsley had arranged family dwellings for Flora Hanahan and Sarah Murphy at Puerto Plata and for Anna Kingsley at Cabarete. In 1842 he secured rural tracts of land for Flora at Bergantin and for Sarah Murphy at Jamao in Moca Province. Anticipating that he was nearing the end of his days, he called family members together before departing Haiti to draw up a partition of lands and responsibilities in the event of his death. The children were told "to love and respect one another," and the older children were urged to "look after the younger ones and for their best interests." George was named the patriarch of the family and assigned a guardian's responsibility for the minor children. The land was partitioned into four parts, with two assigned to George, one to John Maxwell, and one to be divided among Flora's children

(Charles, James, William, Osceola, and Roxana) and Sarah's son Micanopy. The mothers were told they would not inherit land, but they could enjoy the proceeds and live in comfort. Kingsley strongly encouraged them to not return to the United States.[31]

During Kingsley's absence from Florida in 1842, Gibbs continued to advance Kingsley's claim before Judge Isaac H. Bronson for damages suffered in 1812–13 during the Patriot insurgency. He also represented Kingsley regarding the claim for damages of the plantations of the deceased John Fraser, for which Kingsley was still the court-appointed executor. Gibbs met with Judge Bronson in St. Augustine and also traveled to Darien and Doboy Island, Georgia, to meet with Philip R. Yonge, the other executor of the Fraser estate in Florida. Yonge refused to cooperate, saying he wanted nothing "more to do with that Estate."

In October, Judge Bronson concluded deliberations on the Fraser claim and awarded payment of $157,140 for damages. Kingsley was still in Haiti when the decision was reached, but notification was dispatched and he booked passage on a ship bound for Philadelphia, arriving on November 10, 1842. A customs officer recorded the arrival of passenger "Kingsley, Z. age 75, a farmer of U.S. nationality" aboard the schooner *Caroline*, Henry Harper, master, inbound from Port-au-Prince. From Philadelphia, Kingsley traveled to the Office of the First Comptroller of the Treasury, Washington, D.C., to meet with Gibbs and Brigadier General Joseph M. Hernandez, Florida's former territorial delegate. Kingsley had appointed Hernandez the lead attorney.[32]

On December 8, Gibbs wrote: "finally Mr. Kingsley was paid $157,140 and at 5 p.m. Mr. K., Genl. Hernandez & self left for New York" with warrants for that amount in U.S. stock. The two attorneys were paid handsomely for their services: $5,000 to Gibbs and $15,000 to Hernandez. By the end of December all three men had returned to Florida and commenced negotiations with Samuel L. Burritt, attorney for Fraser's sister, Ann Robertson. Her lawsuit, intended to disinherit Fraser's widow and five children, had been resolved with an award of eight slaves and a one-third interest in the entire estate to Ann Robertson. John Fraser limited his two siblings to a combined total of $8,800, yet his sister Ann managed to garner a one-third share of a fortune intended for his African heirs.[33]

On January 20, 1843, Robertson received "$35,000 in Government

6[%] . . . stock, redeemable in 1862." Gibbs wrote in his journal: "We have a good deal of trouble, but the matter is now settled and the money paid, so far as Mrs. R is concerned." Gibbs immediately turned his attention to Kingsley's Patriot War claim: "I have a great deal of writing to do for Z. K., as his claim [for damages at Laurel Grove] is now before the Judge [Bronson], and I have to collect evidence to sustain it, and he calls me often away on many matters of his own."[34]

One matter of importance that Kingsley was working on was revising and filing his Last Will and Testament. A careful reading of his will indicates that some of the terms had been written a few years before it was witnessed and filed at the Duval County Court House on July 20, 1843. The will is another indication that Kingsley was planning carefully for his final departure and that his concerns were first and foremost for the future of his extended biracial family.[35]

The will begins with bequests for the sons of his sisters, Isabella Gibbs and Martha McNeill. Kingsley B. Gibbs received the schooner *North Carolina* and 1,000 acres of land at Twelve Mile Swamp in St. Johns County. The adjoining 1,000 acres of land at Twelve Mile Swamp were bequeathed to George Cooper Gibbs. Charles J. McNeill was left 62½ acres at Beauclerc Bluff in Duval County, 300 acres "at the head of six mile creek (Saw Mill Creek)" in St. Johns County, a "negro woman Betsey[,] Peggy the daughter of Nancy and all their children and issue," and a horse and saddle.

Kingsley next instructed his executors to pay his legal debts and convert the remaining property (including whatever the U.S. government awarded in settlement of his Patriot War claim) into money. That pot of money was to be divided into twelve equal shares: one each for his nephews Kingsley B. Gibbs and Charles J. McNeill in compensation for any future claims that might levy against the estate, one for Anna Kingsley, two for John Maxwell Kingsley, four for George Kingsley, two for "Flora H. Kingsley her heirs or assigns," and one for "Micanopy the son of Sarah M. Kingsley, should he live until the years of discretion."

The eighth proviso in the will directed his executors: "whenever I may happen to die [ensure] that my body may be buried in the nearest, most convenient place without any Religious ceremony whatever, and that it may be excused from the usual indiscreet formalities and parade of washing, dressing &c., or exposure in any way, but removed just as it died to the common burying ground."

In the ninth and tenth provisos Kingsley wrote: "Should I leave any Slaves, I earnestly recommend to my Executors not to separate the families by selling them individually without their consent, if to be avoided." He also directed executors to "allow to any of my slaves the privilege of purchasing their freedom at one half the price of their valuation, on consideration of their migrating to Hayti, if they cannot be allowed to stay as free in this territory."

Kingsley acknowledged that he was the father of the children of Flora H. Kingsley and Sarah Murphy, but he made it plainly evident that Anna Madgigine Jai had been the most important woman in his life. He referred to her several times as "my wife," and he wrote: "nor do I know in what light the law may consider my acknowledged wife, Anna Madgigine Jai, as our connubial relations took place in a foreign land, where our marriage was celebrated and solemnized by her native African customs altho' never celebrated according to the forms of Christian usage; yet she has always been respected as my wife and as such I acknowledge her, nor do I think that her truth, honor, integrity, moral conduct or good sense will lose in comparison with any one."

In a passage intended as advice to his and Anna's married daughters, Martha Baxter and Mary Sammis, Kingsley wrote: "I do also solemnly enjoin my colored and natural children, that seeing the illiberal and inequitable laws of this territory will not afford to them and to their children that protection and justice, which is due in civilized society to every human being: Always to keep by them a Will, ... legally executed, directing the disposal of their property after their death until they can remove themselves and properties to some land of liberty and equal rights, where the conditions of society are governed by some law less absurd than that of color. This I strongly recommend."

In addition to completing his Last Will and Testament, Kingsley worked with Gibbs and Hernandez throughout the spring and summer of 1843 hoping to pressure Judge Bronson to reach a final decision on his Patriot War claim. Kingsley grew weary of the tedious delays and on August 12, 1843, informed Hernandez of his plan to "proceed to the North in a week or so with a view of making some arrangements for a trip to the West Indies for a short time." Rather than proceed directly to Haiti, Kingsley booked passage to New York City. He was a traveler with a purpose, and he carried an inordinate amount of money with him.[36]

On arriving in New York, Kingsley contacted merchant firms and ship captains who conducted trade at establishments along the Pongo and Nunez Rivers in West Africa, where the last of John Fraser's heirs resided. It was Kingsley's intention to fulfill his final obligation as executor to his deceased friend and fellow slave trader by sending the funds remaining in Fraser's Florida estate to his daughters in Africa. Kingsley deposited $55,000 in U.S. Treasury bonds with the firm of Hussey and Mackey. The firm's proprietor, George F. Hussey, was a commerce merchant with years of experience trading at West Africa and the Caribbean. Hussey and Mackey owned ships engaged in the West African trade and also commissioned cargoes with Captains Enoch R. Ware and Obid Carey, whose stops included Victoria on the Nunez River, where Elizabeth Fraser lived with her husband, William Skelton, and at Falangia on the Pongo River, where Mary Ann Fraser lived in a common-law relationship with Thomas Gaffery Curtis. Like Elizabeth and Mary Ann Fraser, Skelton and Curtis were European-educated and successful traders, born of African mothers and European fathers who settled in West Africa to make their fortunes from the slave trade.[37]

When the funds from the Fraser estate were secured with Hussey's firm, Kingsley's personal obligation had finally and honorably been fulfilled. Kingsley had fretted for years about unscrupulous attempts to divert estate funds into undeserving hands. In 1819, under Spanish law, and again in the early years of American rule, Kingsley had contested the attempts by Fraser's sister, Ann Robertson, to disinherit Fraser's African son and daughters. In 1821 Kingsley urged his attorney, Joseph M. Hernandez, to act like a "guardian and defender of those helpless orphans." He wanted Hernandez to be bound by "honor & duty to do *all* in your power to *correct* such impious attempts to overturn & trample upon the most sacred document known amongst men & the solid guarranty [*sic*] we have for our industry in this life." Hernandez was ordered to "oppose any measures that may tend to invalidate the Will or Rights of Fraser's children."[38]

Their efforts to protect the rights of the African legatees were only partially successful. Kingsley was forced by court order to pay one-third of the estate proceeds to Ann Robertson. Over time she received more than $50,000 from her brother's estate, and in her own will she bequeathed funds to an orphanage, a church, a church school, a missionary society, and to her own daughter. It is an ironic commentary on the times that a woman described as "a pious Christian lady" bequeathed to her daughter and Christian organizations beneficent portions of a fortune derived from the sale and labor of enslaved Africans that Fraser had intended for the exclusive use of his own Anglo-African children, and that his surviving daughters were in the 1840s residing in Africa still engaged in the purchase and sale of enslaved Africans. Kingsley's experience with the Fraser case prompted his worry that his own biracial children would be disinherited by a sibling after his own death. It was more than casual conversation when he told Lydia Maria Child in 1842 that in the event of his death it was "likely enough . . . my heirs would break my will."[39]

Kingsley arranged the voyage with the Caribbean merchant John Lamotte, whose firm traded with George Kingsley's settlement at Cabarete. Troubling issues continued unresolved at home in Florida, including his claim for damages suffered during the Patriot insurgency and the fate of more than eighty slaves at his plantations. This was to be his final Haitian journey, a time to say farewell to his children and their mothers.[40]

Kingsley never boarded the ship. The captain instead sailed to Puerto Plata with sad news for the Kingsley family. On September 13, 1843, at age seventy-eight, the man who had been a maritime merchant, slave trader, planter, pro-slavery theorist, advocate for amalgamation, and founder of a colony in Haiti as a refuge for his biracial family and for other free people of color in America, suffered a heart attack and died in New York City. He was buried, not in a common burial ground as his will directed, but in a Quaker cemetery in the plot next to his mother's final resting place.

14

"To Do Good in This World We *Must* Have Money"

The Kingsley Legacy

In 1842, journalist and abolitionist Lydia Child urged Kingsley to liberate his slaves before he died to avoid the potentially "dreadful risk" and "cruel chances of slavery" they might be subjected to under a less benevolent owner. Kingsley acknowledged that he was troubled by the thought but said his desire to "do great things for Haiti" could only be accomplished "by keeping them in slavery a few more years" in order to generate profits from his Florida plantations. "All we can do in this world is to balance evils," he told Child, and "to do good in the world, we *must* have money."[1]

One year later, Kingsley was dead. Eighty-four men, women, and children in Florida remained on the bondage side of Kingsley's scale of justice. He had filed his Last Will and Testament with the Duval County Circuit Court only two months before his death, but the document was silent regarding emancipation of his remaining slaves. His only concession was a directive to the executors of his estate: "It is my will and I do hereby authorize my Executors not to separate the families but to allow to any of my slaves the privilege of purchasing their freedom at one half the price of their valuation, on consideration of their migrating to Hayti, if they cannot be allowed to stay as free in this Territory."[2]

Judge William Crabtree authorized John H. McIntosh and Albert G. Philips to conduct an inventory and appraisal of Kingsley's personal property and slaves. The inventory filed on March 13, 1844, valued Kingsley's schooner, the *North Carolina*, his plantation equipment, provisions, livestock, and miscellaneous property at $2,101. In striking contrast, the eighty-four slaves were valued at $29,979 (more than one million dollars in today's currency). In addition, estate executors Kingsley B. Gibbs and Benjamin A. Putnam reported to the court stocks and bonds, outstanding loans made to local planters, and miscellaneous real estate holdings valued at more than $60,000.[3]

Kingsley had confided to Child that after his death one of his relatives would likely challenge his will. As predicted, Martha Kingsley McNeill filed a petition with the Duval County Clerk of Court seeking to invalidate her brother's will and to disinherit the designated heirs. The basis of the challenge was that Anna Kingsley was "a negress" and that George Kingsley, John M. Kingsley, Flora Kingsley, Sarah Murphy, and Micanopy Kingsley were "mulattoes and each a slave of Zephaniah Kingsley" until they "voluntarily and of their own free will and accord" migrated to Haiti, disqualifying them from returning to Florida, where territorial law barred their entry. Even if they had remained in Duval County, according to the petitioner, they were legally classified as "coloured" and were therefore barred from inheriting property. The petition also demanded that estate executors "prohibit emancipation for any reason," which would have the effect of denying self-purchase of freedom to Kingsley's slaves.[4]

While Martha McNeill's court challenge was pending, attorneys representing Anna Kingsley and her son George Kingsley filed separate petitions claiming ownership of, and seeking recovery of, more than fifty of the slaves listed on the 1844 inventory. In addition, they called for a distribution to the legatees of the funds held by the estate executors.

Judge Crabtree ruled positively on the petitions filed by the Kingsleys. Nine slaves were awarded to Anna Kingsley and transferred to the plantation of John Sammis, located in today's Arlington neighborhood of Jacksonville. Sammis was Anna's son-in-law as well as the agent for her slaves. George Kingsley's claim to forty-seven slaves was also upheld by the judge. Since Zephaniah had transferred title to San Jose Plantation to George several years before, the slaves awarded to him remained there.

In a controversial motion of her petition, Anna Kingsley insisted that Charles J. McNeill, the son of Martha Kingsley McNeill, be dismissed as overseer at San Jose and that the land and slaves be rented to other planters. She contended that operating the plantation under an overseer was producing less revenue than could be gained from renting the land and slaves separately to other planters. After an extensive investigation that

FIGURE 12. Portrait of Martha Kingsley McNeill, the youngest sibling of Zephaniah Kingsley Jr. The painting is by Samuel Waldo and William Jewett, circa 1834. Martha, married to Dr. Daniel McNeill of Wilmington, North Carolina, was the mother of Charles Johnston McNeill, who lived with his uncle Zephaniah at Fort George Island for many years and served as one of the overseers. Martha was also the mother of Anna Matilda McNeill Whistler, and grandmother of the acclaimed artist James Abbot McNeill Whistler. Readers who have viewed Whistler's portrait *Arrangement in Grey and Black, No. 1*—better known as *Whistler's Mother*—will notice the resemblance between Anna Matilda and her mother. Image courtesy of the Wadsworth Atheneum Museum of Art, Hartford, Connecticut, and Art Resource, New York City.

included deposing several prominent local planters, Judge Crabtree ruled against the motion out of concern that overwork, harsh treatment, and decline in the health of the enslaved men and women would inevitably result if they were rented out, as well as the suffering that slave families would experience from separations. McNeill was replaced as overseer at San Jose, though whether by dismissal or resignation is not known.[5]

With both Anna Kingsley and George Kingsley residing in Haiti, John S.

Sammis represented their interests in Florida. George Kingsley consulted with a New York attorney on the feasibility of reestablishing residency in Florida, but before that could happen he drowned in a shipwreck on the Atlantic in late February 1846. He had filed a Last Will and Testament in Puerto Plata, dated February 14, 1846, that was entered into probate in Haiti and in Florida following his death. His mother, "Anna Nyai Kingsley," was promised "the full enjoyment of her possessions at Cabaret [in Haiti]." To his lawful children and his wife, Anatoile V. Kingsley, he bequeathed all of his rights and titles to land in Haiti and the United States. About those rights and titles he wrote: "My land titles are regulated by an agreement between me and my Father in which all his children are mentioned and I wish the same to be carried out fully by my Brother, Mother, and Wife, and all of my rights in the United States." The terms of that agreement, which must have been specified in a notarized document, cannot be found in court records in Florida or the Dominican Republic.[6]

Only a few days after the death of George Kingsley, on March 2, 1846, newly elected Circuit Court Judge Farquhar Bethune entered a judgment on Martha McNeill's lawsuit. The court's ruling upheld the validity of Kingsley's 1843 will and declared that Zephaniah Kingsley's "colored" heirs and legatees were thereafter eligible to inherit his estate. Martha McNeill's subsequent appeals to Florida's higher courts for a reversal of the decision also failed.[7]

Following the court ruling, and no doubt influenced by the death of her eldest son, George, Anna Kingsley decided to forgo her comfortable living arrangement in Haiti and return to live in Florida. Her former home at Fort George Island was no longer available to her, as Zephaniah had sold the property and moved to San Jose Plantation in the last years of his life. She returned to Duval County in 1846 and participated aggressively in matters related to the Kingsley estate. She probably resided with one of her daughters, Martha Baxter or Mary Sammis, until purchasing Chesterfield, a twenty-one-acre farm located on the east bank of the St. Johns River midway between the Sammis and Baxter plantations.[8]

On August 21, 1846, Anna Kingsley petitioned the Circuit Court for a distribution of assets to the legatees. The executors filed an accounting in September listing a balance of nearly $60,000 that included securities, outstanding loans, real estate, and human property. Judge Crabtree ordered the real and personal property sold at auction on January 1, 1847, with the proceeds distributed to the heirs.[9]

Zephaniah Kingsley's estate proceedings remained active in the Duval County courts for many years, augmented by loan and interest payments, and greatly supplemented when his long-pending claim for damages suffered during the Patriot War of 1812–14 was finally settled for $78,000. Beginning in 1846, each of the legatees designated in Kingsley's will, including those in Haiti, began receiving payments of thousands of dollars.[10]

On January 1, 1847, and February 1, 1848, all of the slaves named on the 1844 inventory of Zephaniah Kingsley's estate that had not been bequeathed to legatees or claimed by heirs with approval of the Circuit Court were sold at auction. Charles McNeill inherited Kingsley's "negro woman Betsey, and Peggy the daughter of Nancy, and all their children and issue." Betsy, her children Celeste, John, and Emma, and Peggy and her daughters Eliza and Nancy were moved from San Jose Plantation to Reddy's Point, a small farm in Arlington that McNeill purchased from the Kingsley estate for $200. When that occurred, however, it resulted in a violation of Kingsley's well-known policy of not separating slave families. Peggy and her children had been living in a family unit at San Jose with a man named Hannibal as head of family. McNeill mitigated the grievance in 1848 by purchasing Hannibal and reuniting that family. McNeill also purchased Peggy's mother, Nancy, and sister Chloe, reuniting three generations of one family.[11]

Judge Crabtree's ruling that nine slaves listed on the 1844 inventory belonged to Anna Kingsley unintentionally resulted in the separation of two families. Abdalla and Bella had been deeded to Anna Kingsley in 1832, along with their three children, Amy, Elsey, and Jim. By 1844, however, two of the children had matured and married: Jim to Becca, the daughter of one of the slave carpenters, and Elsey to Sam, one of the plantation drivers. Because Judge Crabtree had previously confirmed ownership of Sam and Becca to George Kingsley, they remained at San Jose when Elsey and Jim were moved to Anna Kingsley's farm in response to the court order.[12]

The January 1, 1847, court-ordered auction of Kingsley's property also resulted in family separations. A woman named Julia Ann and a child born after 1844 were purchased by Samuel Houston, moving Julia Ann away from a San Jose household headed by Prince, property of the estate of the deceased George Kingsley. Nanny and her children (Sylvia, Jacob, Adam, and Edwin) were purchased by John H. McIntosh and moved to his Ortega Plantation. Andrew, husband of Nanny and father of her four children, remained at San Jose. In the third family separation resulting from this auction, Charles McNeill of Reddy's Point was high bidder for Comba, who is listed on the 1844 inventory as the wife of Cooper Dick, who remained at San Jose.[13]

At this same auction, John Sammis called out the high bid of ten dollars for an elderly family, Toby and Patty, and soon thereafter emancipated them. A census taker making rounds in 1860 found "Toby Kingsley" living alone in a dwelling located close by the Sammis residence. He was ninety years old, a free black man, and a native of Africa. Patty was apparently deceased by then.[14] Sammis also reunited a slave family as a consequence of his purchase of Sophy and her children: Labo, George, Phillip, Joe, and Polly. The husband of Sophy and father of her children was Lindo, who had previously been confirmed by Judge Crabtree as property of Anna Kingsley and moved to her farm. Sammis moved Sophy and her children to his nearby plantation, thus reuniting them with Lindo.[15]

Lindo represents an example of a slave of Zephaniah Kingsley who was able to purchase freedom for himself and his wife, Sophy. For years, Lindo raised corn in a personal garden to sell to overseers and worked at extra projects after completing his assigned tasks, applying earnings toward self-purchase of freedom. Anna Kingsley honored her deceased husband's commitment and emancipated Lindo. John Sammis permitted Lindo to purchase Sophy's freedom. Two children born to Sophy after the emancipations were free at birth.

Lindo is identified on the 1860 Census of Duval County as a free black man, age fifty-five, living in a dwelling on the Sammis property. Sophy, age forty, was living in the same dwelling, along with John, age five, and Iradina, age three. All in the family were identified as free, black, and born in Florida.

Anna Kingsley liberated Abdalla and Bella during the 1850s. The 1860 Census of Duval County records them as living in a dwelling close by the residence of Lindo and Sophy. They were each sixty years old, natives of Africa, living in close proximity to the slave community at the Sammis plantation, where their daughter and grandson, Elsey and Stephen, and their son Jim resided. At the February 1, 1848, auction of the property of the deceased George Kingsley, John Sammis had purchased Elsey's husband, Sam, and Jim's wife, Becca, reuniting two family units.[16]

Among the male slaves listed as living alone on the 1844 inventory of Kingsley's property was a man named Romeo, whose $650 valuation was among the highest assigned. Born at Fort George Island, Romeo was moved to San Jose Plantation after Kingsley sold Fort George in 1839. According to testimony in an 1846 court inquiry before Judge Crabtree, Romeo became rebellious after Kingsley died. John Sammis testified that the overseer, Charles McNeill, "had some trouble with the negroes after Mr. Kingsley's death. I know some of them ran away in the fall of 1843 and the winter of 1844. I know the negroes refused to obey his orders. He sent for some of his neighbors. Two of the negroes ran away. One of them he had flogged." McNeill was so incensed at Romeo, one of the runaways, that he offered "a twenty dollar reward [for his capture], dead or alive, and employed George Hagins to hunt Romeo with bull dogs."[17]

Sammis was away from Florida when McNeill's troubles with the slaves occurred, but when he returned he persuaded McNeill to call off Hagins and his dogs. Sammis promised to find Romeo and return him to the plantation if McNeill agreed to "not beat him cruelly . . . and punish the boy [only] in my presence." Sammis told Judge Crabtree that McNeill was "a man of very excitable temperament" but that he had calmed by the time Sammis returned Romeo to San Jose. McNeill "gave him a talking and did not whip him. He then said the Negroes might do as they pleased, he would not whip them."

When the February 1848 auction of George Kingsley's property was held, Romeo's name was missing from the list of slaves offered for sale. He had self-purchased freedom and was known as Romeo Murray, a river pilot of sufficient skill to navigate a major Union troop transport during the American Civil War. When the *Maple Leaf* was destroyed by Confederate underwater explosives in 1864, Romeo Murray was the pilot aboard the vessel.[18]

Another of Kingsley's slaves, a driver named Sam, also caused trouble for McNeill after Kingsley died. Sam was approximately thirty years old at the time and had formerly been highly reliable. The trouble with Sam ended when McNeill restored him to his old driver position. According to Sammis, "McNeill told me that Sam was such a good driver he saved him the trouble of going into the field much." Sammis recognized the driver's merit and purchased him at the 1848 auction of George Kingsley's property, an action that reunited the family of Sam and Becca.[19]

The most compelling self-purchase account in the post-Kingsley years involves an African-born man known as Carpenter Bill, whose skills were well known in the area. Planter James McDonald testified in 1846 that he "hired the Negro Carpenter Bill" after obtaining permission from Charles McNeill. McNeill "allowed Bill the privilege of hiring his own time at certain seasons. . . . He was worthy of the privilege because of . . . [his good example] and use upon the place." When demand lessened at San Jose, McNeill permitted Carpenter Bill to work for McDonald. "Bill brought a Negro man named Bonafi with him as a 'journeyman' carpenter," McDonald testified, but "Bill was the chief workman. They were at three different periods with me, in all thirty-one and one-half days. . . . I paid Bill $1 per day. Bill settled with Bonafi what he thought proper."[20]

On the 1844 inventory of Kingsley's human property at San Jose Plantation, Carpenter Bill and his wife, Hannah, are identified as the parents of five children: Frank, Lavinia, Alonzo, Marianne, and Bill. The estate appraisers valued the family at $3,605, which meant that under Kingsley's policy of self-purchase of freedom for one-half the appraised value, Bill needed $1,803 to free the family.[21]

At compensation of $1 per day earned during only some seasons of each year, minus the amount passed on to Bonafi, Carpenter Bill's challenge of saving the amount required to purchase freedom for his family of seven seems insurmountable. Hannah and the children may have earned extra money by making clothing, cultivating corn, raising poultry or livestock, or working at miscellaneous projects. The challenge would still have been immense and would have demanded a lengthy and determined commitment.

On October 19, 1844, thirteen months after Zephaniah's death, George Kingsley authorized a deed of manumission for "Carpenter Bill and wife [Hannah] and daughter [Marianne]." Their children—Frank, Lavinia, Alonzo, Becca, and Bill—were still property of George Kingsley, and some were mature and choosing marital partners. Becca had already married Sam and become the mother of Stephen. Lavinia had married Mike, one of two sons born to Kingsley's slaves Genoma and Jenny, and become the mother of Larry.[22]

On February 1, 1848, the personal estate of the late George Kingsley was sold at public auction in front of the Duval County Courthouse on Forsyth and Market Streets in Jacksonville. Forty slaves were sold that day, including three of Carpenter Bill's children. Sammis managed to purchase Sam, which reunited the plantation driver with Becca and Stephen, and he was high bidder for Elsey, thereby reuniting her with her mate, Jim, and locating her near the residence of her free black parents, William Kingsley and Hannah.[23]

Near the end of the auction a man in the crowd shouted out the high bid of $400 for an eight-year-old black child named Alonzo. It was Carpenter Bill who stepped forward to claim the purchase. Less than four years after his emancipation, the black man known now as William Kingsley had saved enough from his earnings to purchase freedom for his son Alonzo.

The free black carpenter was not able to outbid William G. Christopher for Mike and Lavinia and their infant child Larry. Bids for the family ended at $1,300, a sum well beyond the means of a former slave who had only recently been emancipated and who had already purchased freedom for himself and three others in his family. Christopher also purchased San Jose Plantation at the auction, which meant that Lavinia remained there, several miles away from her parents' residence at the Sammis plantation. Carpenter Bill's eldest son, Frank, is not found in records of the Kingsley estates after 1846. Bill, the youngest in the family, is also missing from the records.

The story of William Kingsley is an inspiring example of a responsible man with ambition, discipline, talent, and devotion to family. He was born in Africa circa 1790, captured in a raid, and brought to Florida on a slave ship. While a slave of Kingsley he married Hannah, who was also born in Africa and brought to Florida as a slave. William and Hannah raised five children in slavery. Their willingness to work extra hours after fulfilling the tasks demanded by the plantation drivers, and to faithfully save earnings over several years to apply toward multiple purchases of freedom, shows heroic dedication to family and to freedom. In 1850 a census taker found a free black couple, William and Hannah Kingsley, natives of Africa, living in a household on the Sammis plantation with their free black daughter, Marianne, age thirteen, born in Florida.[24]

Ten years later another census taker stopped at the Sammis residence and found six consecutive households occupied by free persons of color.

The names of the six heads of household were Alonzo Phillips, Toby Kingsley, Mary Williams, Maria Kingsley, Lindo Kingsley, and Abdallah Kingsley. The head of household number 530 was Alonzo Phillips, age twenty. Alonzo, the eight-year-old slave child purchased by his father at auction in 1848, had taken the last name Phillips in freedom, and in 1860 he shared a household with his seventy-year-old father, William Kingsley. His mother, Hannah, was not listed and is presumed to have died by then. The head of household number 532 was Mary Williams, age twenty. Sharing the dwelling were Rebecca, thirty-five, Hannah, six, and Nelly, two. It may be only a striking coincidence, but it suggests that Carpenter Bill and his wife, Hannah, were the parents of Mary and Rebecca (Marianne and Becca) and the grandparents of Hannah and Nelly.[25]

It is not a coincidence that these dwellings were located near the residence of Zephaniah Kingsley's daughter Mary and her husband, John Sammis. Although Sammis owned a large number of slaves, his plantation had for sixteen years provided employment and protection for free blacks who had previously been slaves of Zephaniah Kingsley. The wealthy and influential Sammis had arranged their emancipation papers with the Duval County Clerk of Court and had ensured that they were not seized by the sheriff and sold back into slavery, as was possible under Florida law. Sammis then served as legal guardian to the freed persons.[26]

The 1844 inventory of Zephaniah Kingsley's estate contains a listing of twenty slave families and four slaves living alone. Kingsley included in his will a clear and firm order that his slave families not be separated, yet all but seven of the families experienced some form of separation. Between 1844 and 1848 the slave community listed on the 1844 inventory was divided four times, twice by court order and twice by sale at auction. For some families the separation was temporary, as in the example of Charles McNeill's actions discussed above, and other families were reunited by John Sammis and Anna Kingsley. Nevertheless, 65 percent of the family units on the 1844 inventory of Kingsley's human property experienced the agony of family separation during a four-year period. This was a common experience among slaves in the United States, where no laws existed to protect the sanctity of slave families. When an owner died, slaves lived in fear of being sold away from their loved ones.[27]

The family of Bonafi, the assistant to Carpenter Bill, and his wife, Mary, was severely victimized by separation. In 1844, estate appraisers valued Bonafi and Mary and their eight children (Beck, Scipio, Louis, Esther, George, Tena, June, and Sarah) at $4,620. Two more children, Selena and Abram, were born between 1844 and 1848. Bonafi and Mary suffered the pain and indignity of losing four children to four different owners: Beck to Moses Barber, Scipio to Doctor Randolph, Lewis to Jacob Martin, and Tenah to George Kingsley's widow, Antoinette V. Kingsley. Sammis purchased Bonafi, Mary, and their other six children at the February 1, 1848, auction of George Kingsley's property.[28]

Duval County planter Moses Barber purchased four young enslaved men at the February 1848 auction: Jeffrey, Beck, Napoleon, and Cooper Dick. Each of the slaves was from a different family. Barber also purchased Monroe (aka Hard Times), who was the brother of Jeffrey. The brothers went to Barber, but their parents, Tamba (a blind man) and Cootah, and a third brother, Thomas, were sold to William Braddock.

Child had warned Kingsley in 1842 of the "cruel chances of slavery" his slaves could be exposed to if he failed to liberate them. She thought his response was evasive and that he was "altogether unaccountable," but in fact he revealed to her the major concern of his adult years. "To do good in this world," Kingsley said, "we *must* have money." Without slaves, he would not be able to make the money in Florida he needed to "do good" for his family in Haiti. For nearly all of his adult years Kingsley made his money from either buying and selling slaves or from working slaves on his Florida plantations. Measured in contemporary currency values, Kingsley accumulated millions of dollars, and nearly all of it came from enslaving Africans. "To do good" meant doing good for Kingsley, his children, and their mothers.

It is also true that Kingsley was concerned about the welfare of his slave families. He advocated humane treatment of slaves, the sanctity of slave families, a task system of labor, liberal emancipation policies, self-purchase of freedom, and guaranteed rights and a protected middle-caste position in society for free people of color. As discussed previously, Kingsley acted on those principles and was considered a humane slave owner. He was also a pragmatic businessman who knew that his race and slavery policies increased his financial gain and provided allies for the small class of ruling whites. Providing incentives for slaves, as the examples of Carpenter Bill and Driver Sam proved, produced benefits for their owners.

Supporting a liberal emancipation policy, however, did not mean that Kingsley was an abolitionist. Instead, he was proslavery to the end of his life. He was not a racist, but neither was he an abolitionist. Slaves were a means to make money, and money meant "good" for Kingsley and his extended family. The driving force of Kingsley's adult life was a quest for financial security, perhaps as a result of witnessing the misfortunes experienced by his father during the turbulent years before and after the American Revolution. Kingsley was an adolescent in Charleston during that revolution, and he encountered danger and uncertainty in subsequent decades as a maritime merchant when the Atlantic world experienced the shocks and violence of the French Revolution and its overseas manifestations.

Uncertainties abounded for a life lived in the Age of Revolution. As a child, Kingsley witnessed the king's army and American patriots contending for control of Charleston. As a young mariner he faced daily danger at sea, lost ships and cargoes to privateers, and survived a lengthy incarceration in Martinique by the British navy. He was a witness to the violence of the slave rebellion in Saint-Domingue and the mind-numbing horror and violence of the Atlantic slave trade. His life was almost ended when he was shot and stabbed in a senseless shipboard attack by a drunken ship captain and crew at Fernandina harbor. During the War of 1812, when British soldiers burned Washington, D.C., Seminole warriors allied with the Spanish governor of East Florida applied the torch to Kingsley's three settlements at Laurel Grove Plantation. Life and fortune remained a risky game of chance in the aftermath of the so-called Patriot War as violent gangs of brigands looted and burned settlements throughout northeast Florida. Uncertainties abounded, but through it all Kingsley aggressively sought economic security through the sale and forced labor of enslaved Africans and the acquisition of thousands of acres of planting land in Florida. By 1820, with the stability that came with the American flag, it is clear that Kingsley was building an enviable fortune.

At the end of his life, with his own fortune secured, Kingsley turned his attention to protection of his extended family by providing them with gifts of plantations and slaves. Events in the 1830s, however, convinced Kingsley that the increasingly discriminatory race policies in Florida represented a potentially insurmountable threat to the freedom and security of his black and mixed-race wives and children. He arranged a haven for them by purchasing (in the name of his eldest son) a huge agricultural estate in the free black Republic of Haiti (today on the north shore of the Dominican Republic). He emancipated more than fifty of his slaves and transported them to Haiti to work at his family's estate under terms of indenture with the promise of wages and tracts of land.

In the aftermath of Kingsley's death, his son George Kingsley, his "wife" Anna Jai Kingsley, daughters Mary Sammis and Martha Baxter, son-in-law John S. Sammis, and nephew Charles J. McNeill all honored his commitments to self-purchase of freedom, liberal emancipation policies, and the sanctity of slave families. After George's death in 1846, the other four families lived in close proximity in a rural enclave in what is today the Arlington neighborhood of Jacksonville. That rural enclave was unique in antebellum Florida. From the Sammis residence east of the St. Johns River at the merger of the Arlington River, to Charles McNeill's farm at Reddy Point, a distance of seven miles along the St. Johns, much of the waterfront property was owned by members of the extended family of the late Zephaniah Kingsley. Sammis owned 8,000 acres of land and operated a water-powered sawmill. In 1854 he owned eighty-five slaves. Less than two miles to the north, Anna Kingsley's 21-acre farm was worked by fifteen slaves. Adjoining her to the north was the 300-acre St. Isabel Plantation of Martha Kingsley Baxter, a widow and the owner of forty-eight slaves in 1840. Charles McNeill lived nearby at a 350-acre farm known as Reddy's Point, with a biracial wife, nine children, and sixteen slaves.[29]

In addition to the 164 slaves residing at these properties, more than seventy free persons of color resided at fifteen separate households located in this rural enclave. The majority of the free blacks had been slaves emancipated by Kingsley or were the children of those freed persons. Only in the towns of St. Augustine and Pensacola, both colonial capitals under Spanish governance, could free black communities of comparable numbers be found as late as 1860. This rural community flourished during the 1840s and 1850s, a time of increasingly virulent race hysteria that prompted many free blacks to move away from Florida. Free black population numbers in Florida remained relatively static from 1830 to 1860, increasing from 844 to only 932, while decreasing as a percentage of total population from 2.4 percent to 0.6 percent. During these same years the total population increased fourfold, from 34,730 to 140,424. In St. Johns County, free blacks numbered 172

FIGURE 13. Portrait of Emma Baxter Mocs, grandchild of Zephaniah Kingsley and Anna Jai Kingsley. Emma's parents were Martha Kingsley Baxter and Oran Baxter, the latter a native of Cold Springs, New York. Widowed in the 1840s, Martha hired Joseph Mocs, a refugee of the failed 1848 revolution for independence in Hungary, as music teacher for her children. Emma, at age nineteen, married Mocs, age thirty, in 1858. This is the only known likeness of a grandchild of Zephaniah and Anna Kingsley. Image courtesy of David P. Stair.

in 1830 and declined to 82 in 1860 (from 7 to 3 percent of total population), with more than 90 percent residing in St. Augustine. In Nassau County, 86 percent of the county's 55 free blacks resided in the town of Fernandina. The free black population of Duval County, however, increased from 86 in 1830 to 180 in 1860, while the percentage living in towns decreased from 73 to 48 percent over those same years.[30]

It should not be forgotten, however, that the economic security of Anna Kingsley, John and Mary Sammis, Martha Baxter, and Charles McNeill was based on the continuation of slavery. These families followed Zephaniah Kingsley's slavery and emancipation policies, and they shared his proslavery views as well. These four mixed-race families controlled much of the land and financial resources in the area during the 1850s, and they depended heavily on enslaved men and women to produce their wealth. By 1860 they had determined that the secession hysteria of the 1850s was heading toward disunion and war and that slave property was no longer a safe investment. When a census taker came to their residences in 1860, only a handful of enslaved domestic servants were found in the dwellings where a few months before 164 slaves had resided. The heirs and legatees of Zephaniah Kingsley had converted their human properties to cash and were making plans to move with their families to the free states in the North.[31]

In 1860 Anna Kingsley owned only four slaves, all between the ages of nine and seventeen. Charles McNeill owned one slave, a sixty-year-old woman. From forty-eight slaves in 1854, Martha Baxter had only four adult slaves in 1860, probably domestic servants, and eight slave children remaining on her property. Martha Baxter was still a wealthy woman, with real estate valued at $5,000 and a personal estate worth $52,000, and she had begun investing in real estate in and near Jacksonville's business district.[32]

At the Sammis residence the decline in slave numbers between 1854 and 1860 is startling, from eighty-five to zero. Some slaves were undoubtedly emancipated, but Sammis is known to have transported slaves to New Orleans to sell to Louisiana sugar planters who were confident that slavery would last indefinitely. Many decades later an elderly woman in Duval County remembered the day in early 1860 when the Sammis slaves packed their belongings and boarded a ship at the wharf on Pottsburgh Creek. Ophelia Moore had been a young slave then; she was still alive in the 1930s and able to recall the events of that day. She remembered standing on the riverbank watching as a ship passed by carrying the Sammis slaves down the St. Johns River and away from Florida. It is likely the ship also carried slaves owned by Anna Kingsley, Martha Baxter, and Charles McNeill.[33]

One person who was aboard that ship was able to confirm Ophelia Moore's recollection. A Jacksonville newspaper reporter came to the Arlington home of Esther Lottery in 1925 after hearing she was one hundred years old and a former slave. Esther was unable to remember her exact date of birth but stated that she was born at Fort George Island and moved with her family to San Jose Plantation, where she was living when Zephaniah Kingsley died. Esther was one of ten children born to the carpenter Bonafi and his wife, Mary. Purchased by Sammis at the February 1, 1848, auction in front of the Duval County Courthouse, she married an enslaved man named Quash Lottery before the day in 1860 when the slaves were shipped to Louisiana. At the slave market in New Orleans, Esther and Quash Lottery were purchased by John Pratt, the owner of a country estate at Bellevue near New Orleans. After the war they returned to Duval County and were given a small tract of land by Mary and John Sammis.[34]

The heirs and legatees of Zephaniah Kingsley who lived in Duval County in the 1850s shared his views on race and slavery. Together, they were responsible for the creation of a free colored community in their rural enclave east of the St. Johns River. Like their patriarch, they were proslavery and believed in the need for financial security to protect against the uncertainty of life in turbulent times. Having lived through a decade of intense race hysteria and discrimination toward free persons of color, and with their eyes fixed on the possibility of a war between the free and slave states, the Kingsley, Sammis, Baxter, and McNeill families traded human property for money. Seeking financial security as protection in a divided nation, they agreed with their departed patriarch, Zephaniah Kingsley: "To do good in this world we *must* have money."

Appendix A

Forty-Five Slaves Lost, July 1812, at Laurel Grove and Drayton Island

Andrew son of Polly, a boy	7 to 8 years old
Jacob a prime Eabo Negro	30
Camilla, his wife, a Rio Pongo, prime	25
Jim (same as the above)	7 to 8
Bob, a New Calabar, prime	28
Molly his wife (same)	26
Sammy (same)	7 to 8
Prince, a New Calabar, prime	32
M Badie, his wife (same)	26
Charlotte (same)	8 to 9
Barbara (same)	6 to 7
Peggy (same)	4 to 5
Toby (same)	2 to 3
Jack, a Zinguibari, carpenter, very prime	30
Tamassa, his wife, very prime	28
Ben (same)	8 to 9
M Toto (same)	6 to 7
Molly (same)	4 to 5
Rose (same)	2 to 3
Philip, a Calabari, prime	35
Tibi his wife (same)	28
Boy Badja (same)	8 to 9
Martin M Guinda	26
Jenny, Zinguibari, prime	28
Billy (same)	4 to 5
Hannah, daughter of old Rose	8 to 9
Bruchy, Eabo nation, prime,	36
Adda his wife (same)	30
July (same)	8 to 9
Dick (same)	6 to 7
Hannah (same)	4 to 5
Aibo, a Calabari	40
M Sooma, Carpenter, a Zinguibari	28
Eliza, his wife (same)	26
Boy March (same)	7 to 8

(continued)

Mike, son of old Jenny	8 to 9
Jun, a Calabari, driver, very prime	34
Anobia, his wife, very prime	28
Charles, a SooSoo, very prime	24
Old Paul, Eabo nation	48
Cabo Mouse, sailor, very prime	26
Value	$20,500
Morton, blacksmith, very prime, killed	1,000
Peter, driver, manager, mechanic, killed	1,000
Pablo, 45 years old, abducted at Drayton Island	500
Juan, a SooSoo, 30 years old, abducted at Drayton Island	500

Source: Petition of Zephaniah Kingsley Jr. to Honorable Raymond Reid, Judge of the Superior Court, East Florida Claims, Zephaniah Kingsley Jr., B131, F16, Claims, 1843, St. Augustine Historical Society Research Library, St. Augustine, Florida.

Appendix B

Inventory of Zephaniah Kingsley's Estate at San Jose Plantation, March 13, 1844

Men	Women	Children	Average value	Total
José	Penda	Mira, Nacebo, Mary*, William	$333	$1,998
Carpenter Bill	Hannah	Frank, Lavinia, Alonzo, Marianne, Bill*	$515	$3,605
Carptr Bonafi	Mary	Beck, Scipio, Louis, Esther, George, Tena, June, Sarah*	$462	$4,620
Lindo	Sophy	Labo, George, Philip	$360	$1,800
Jenoma	Jenny	Mike, Augustus	$275	$1,100
	Betty	Patty, Jenny	$283	$849
	Qualla	Letitia, Victorine	$212	$636
Horse Bill	Yamba	Bolivar	$250	$750
Abdalla	Bella	Paul, Annie	$312	$1,248
Tamba	Couta	Monroe, Jeffrey, Thomas	$285	$1,425
Prince	Julia Anne		$550	$1,100
Sam	Elsy		$550	$1,100
Jim	Becca		$550	$1,100
Hannibal	Peggy	Eliza, Nancy	$375	$1,500
Andrew	Nanny	Jacob, Silvia*	$300	$1,200
	Tamasa	Rose, Jack, David*	$237	$948
Brutus	Nancy	Chloe, Joe	$275	$1,100
Toby	Patty		$100	$200
Cooper Dick	Comba		$150	$300
Romeo			$650	$650
David			$550	$550
Dick			$650	$650
	Betty	Celeste, John, Emma	$275	$1,100
	Old Rose		$150	$150
Total Value of Slave Property				$29,679

Schooner North Carolina, $500; Flat & Boats, $250	$750	
Carts, Wagons & c., $30; Plantation Tools, $ 32	$62	
Arms $50, Books $7	$57	
40 Head of Cattle, $140; 7 mules, $420	$560	
1 horse, $65; 4 horses, $120; Harness, $30; 1 Saddle, $12	$227	
Corn, $375; 150 gallons of molasses, $30; 600 lbs. Sugar, $40	$445	

(*continued*)

Total Value of Other Personal Property	$2,101
Aggregate Value of Personal Estate & Slaves	$31,780
Appraisal by Jno [John] H. McIntosh, Albert G. Philips	

Note: *Infants

Source: Probate File 1203, Zephaniah Kingsley, Duval County Courthouse.

Appendix C

Slaves Claimed by George Kingsley from the Estate of Zephaniah Kingsley Jr.

No.	Names of Slaves in Families	Average Value/Total Value
Negroes claimed by George Kingsley with their valuation in the appraisement of the estate of Zephaniah Kingsley, deceased		
8	Carpenter Bill, Hannah, Frank, Becca, Lavinia, Alonzo, Mariane, Bill*	($515/$4120)
10	Carpenter Bonifay, Mary, Beck, Scipio, Louis, Esther, June, George, Tenah, Sarah*	(462/4620)
6	Jose, Penda, Mira, Nacebo, Mary*, William	(333/1998)
5	Coota, Tamba, Jeffry, Hard Times, Thomas	(285/1425)
4	Genoma, Jenny, Mike, Augustus	(275/1100)
3	Rose, Jack, David*	(237/711)
3	Horse Bill, Yamba, Bolivar	(250/750)
1	Old Rose	150
1	Andrew	300
1	Hannibal	375
1	Davy	550
1	Sam	550
1	Romeo	650
1	Prince	550
1	Tamassa	237
(47 total)		($18,086 total value)
Negroes included in the appraisement in the possession of John S. Sammis Esquire, who claims them as the attorney in fact of George Kingsley		
3	Betty and her children Patty & Jenny	(283/849)
2	Genoma & Jenny	not valued here.

Source: Probate File 1205, George Kingsley, Duval County Courthouse.

Note: Those marked * are not mentioned on the declaration filed against the executors but are assumed to be children of the women therein named.

Appendix D

Slaves Recovered by Anna Kingsley from the Estate of Zephaniah Kingsley Jr.

No. in Family	Names of the Negroes	Average/Total Value
1	Lindo	360
3	Qualla, Letitia, Victorine	212/636
3	Abdalla, Bella, Amy	312/936
1	Elsey	550
1	Jim	550
9		$3,032

Stephen, son of Elsey, born since the appraisement.

Source: Probate 1203, Zephaniah Kingsley, Duval County Courthouse.

Appendix E

Account of Sales of Property, Sold at Auction, January 1, 1847

Nancy and Chloe	(sold to Charles McNeill)	$350
Comba	(sold to Charles McNeill)	$80
Julia Ann and child	(sold to Samuel Houston)	$500
Nanny, Sylva, Jacob, Adam, Edwin	(sold to John H. McIntosh)	$1,060
Sophy, Labo, George, Phillip, Joe, Polly	(sold to John S. Sammis)	$1,210
Toby, Patty	(sold to John S. Sammis)	$10
William	(sold to John S. Sammis)	$305
Dick	(sold to George Gibbs)	$385

Source: Probate File 1203, Zephaniah Kingsley, Duval County Courthouse.

Appendix F

Inventory of the Real and Personal Estate of George Kingsley

- A tract of land situated in Orange County known as Drayton Island, containing about 1700 acres.
- A tract of land known as Forrester's Point, in St. Johns Co. containing 600 acres.
- A tract of land situated in St. Johns County, known as Buena Vista containing one thousand acres.
- A plantation situated in Duval County, containing 300 acres & known as the San Hose Plantation.
- 450 bushels corn valued at seventy five cents $337.50
- 300 bushels potatoes at twelve&one/half cents $37.50
- Sale of oranges in the hands of O. Wood $338.75
- one sextant, one chart, one map called The Coast Pilot, special legacy from his father $50
- one surveyors compass (part of said legacy) $10

Total $773.75

The following slaves to wit:

Rebecca	500	Lavinia	500
Alonzo	450	Mary	350
Selina	150	Sarah	150
Beck	400	Napoleon	150
Cooper, or Dick	50	Bonafi	700
Scipio	550	Lewis	550
Easter	350	June	300
George	250	Tenah	200
Cootah	100	Tambah (blind)	0
Jeffrey	650	Monroe (aka) Hard Times	600
Thomas	350	Hosea	700
Penda	200	Almira	500
Nassebo	300	Helena	250
William	200	Horse Bill	250
Yamba	50	Bolivar	350
Jenoma and Jenney	0	Mike	600
Augustus	600	Sam	700
Romeo	650	Prince	350
		Total	$13,773.75

Source: Probate File 1205, George Kingsley, Duval County Courthouse.

Appendix G

Account of the Sale of the Personal Estate of George Kingsley, February 1, 1848

José, Penda, Almyra, Nassebo, Eleanor, William, family	(Purchased by William H. King)	$2,000
Bonafi, Mary, June, George, Sarah, Selina, Abram, Easter, family	(Purchased by John S. Sammis)	$2,000
Sam	(Purchased by John S. Sammis)	$650
Rebecca	(Purchased by John S. Sammis)	$575
Mike, Lavinia, & infant Larry, family	(Purchased by William G. Christopher)	$1,300
Horse Bill, Yamba, Bolivar, family	(Purchased by Charles J. McNeill)	$650
Jeffrey, Beck, Napoleon, Cooper Dick (family)	(Purchased by Moses Barber)	$1,525
Tamba (blind), Cootah, Thomas, family	(Purchased by William M. Braddock)	$150
Scipio & Old Rose	(Purchased by Doctor Randolph)	$660
Lewis	(Purchased by Jacob Martin)	$600
Monroe	(Purchased by Moses Barber)	$585
Hannibal	(Purchased by Charles J. McNeill)	$500
Augustus and Jenoma, family	(Purchased by John Jones)	$590
Davy	(Purchased by John D. Braddock)	$505
Prince	(Purchased by J. McDonald)	$350
Alonzo	(Purchased by William Kingsley)	$400
Tenah	(Purchased by A. V. Kingsley)	$200
Total		**$13,240**

1 surveyors compass to Thomas Ledwith	$5
1 sextant, 1 Coast Pilot & a lot of maps to J. Forman	$20
145 bushels potatoes at $.18&3/4 to W. H. King	$27.19
72 gallons syrup at $.33 to J. Johnson	$23.76
400 pounds sugar at 4 cents per to J. S. Sammis	$16
1 cart to J. S. Sammis	$10
4 plows to J. S. Sammis	$3
1 dozen hoes to J. S. Sammis	$2
9 axes to J. S. Sammis	$5
3000 pounds fodder to W. H. King	$20
300 bushels corn at 65 cents to P. Cox	$195

(*continued*)

600 bushels corn at 65 cents to J. S. Sammis	$390
30 gallons syrup at 33 cents to J. S. Sammis	$9.90
Rent of San Jose Plantation to January 1, 1849, to W. H. King	$80
Total	**$806.85**
Grand Total	**$14,046.85**

Source: Probate File 1205, George Kingsley, Duval County Courthouse.

Notes

Abbreviations

BSP	Buckingham Smith Papers, New York Historical Society
DCC	Duval County Courthouse, Jacksonville, Florida
DNA	Danish National Archives, Copenhagen
EFC	East Florida Claims, RG 217, Settled Treasury Accounts, NARA-CP
EFP	East Florida Papers, LC (index online at PKY)
FSA	Florida State Archives, Tallahassee
JH	James Hamilton
JHP	James Hamilton Papers, Perkins Library, Duke University
LC	Library of Congress, Washington, D.C.
NADR	National Archives of the Dominican Republic, Santo Domingo
NARA-CP	National Archives and Records Administration, College Park, Maryland
NARA-W	National Archives and Records Administration, Washington, D.C.
NCC	Nassau County Courthouse, Yulee, Florida
NSARM	Nova Scotia Archive and Records Management, Halifax
PKY	P. K. Yonge Library of Florida History, University of Florida, Gainesville
PWC	Patriot War Claims, SAHSRL
RG	Record Group
SAHSRL	St. Augustine Historical Society Research Library
SCDAH	South Carolina Division of Archives and History, Columbia
SCL	South Caroliniana Library, University of South Carolina, Columbia
SJCC	St. Johns County Courthouse, St. Augustine, Florida
SPLG	Spanish Land Grant Claims, FSA (online at *Florida Memory*)
WPA	Works Projects Administration. Historical Records Survey, Division of Community Service Programs. *Spanish Land Grants in Florida*, Tallahassee.
ZK	Zephaniah Kingsley Jr.

Introduction

1. ZK, "Address to the Legislative Council of Florida on the Subject of Its Colored Population," State Library of Florida, Tallahassee, 1926.

2. ZK, *Treatise on the Patriarchal*, from Stowell, *Balancing Evils Judiciously*, 41.

3. Child, "Letter from New York (1842)," from Stowell, *Balancing Evils Judiciously*, 107–8.

4. Last Will and Testament, Probate file 1203, ZK, DCC.

5. Child, "Letter XXIII."

Chapter 1. The Kingsley Family, Charleston, and the American Revolution

1. Kingsley testified in 1784 that he "went to Charleston in the year 1770 [and] carried over goods" to become a colonial merchant. See Zephaniah Kingsley, Loyalist Examination, February 27, 1784, in "Transcripts of the American Loyalist Examinations and Decisions," RW 3169, Volume 52, 488–95. Department of Archives and History, Columbia, South Carolina.

2. For the store on Bedon's Alley, see *South Carolina Gazette*, January 31, 1771, and August 23, 1773; and Poston, *The Buildings of Charleston*, 51–54, 80–84, 155–60. For the postwar fate of Loyalists Charles Johnston and his partners see G. Palmer, *Biographical Sketches*; K. R. Coker, "Punishment of Civil War Loyalists," 342, 440, 505; and Chesnutt, *Papers of Henry Laurens*, 6:219n, 7:277n, 8:255n, 9:439n, 10:16, 54, 57–60, 13:276n.

For sibling relationship of Isabella Johnston Kingsley and Charles Johnston see "The Correspondence of James McNeill Whistler, 1855–1903," edited by MacDonald et al., which includes Tourziari, "The Correspondence of Anna McNeill Whistler, 1855–1880," online edition, University of Glasgow, http://www.whistler.arts.gla.ac.uk/correspondence. Anna Matilda Whistler (AMW) was the daughter of Dr. Daniel McNeill and Martha Kingsley McNeill, the youngest daughter of Isabella Kingsley and Zephaniah Kingsley Sr. AMW married George Washington Whistler and was the mother of the artist James Abbot McNeill Whistler. See AMW to Margaret (last name not given), August 1867, number 08180, in which she identifies "my mother's cousin Miss [Anna] Johnstone . . . now 80 years of age . . . and her devoted niece Mrs. Corbett." Anna Johnstone was one of six children born to Charles and Mary Mackenzie Johnston. Her siblings were Robert Mackenzie, Charlotte, Katherine (married to James Macbeth), Marion (married to Peter Porcher Jr.), and Mary (married to Josiah Sturgiss). Margaret Corbett was the daughter of Marion Johnston Porcher. Widowed at age twenty-five, she resided at South Bay Street, neighbor to her aunt, Anna Johnston, on property inherited from Charles Johnston. See also AMW to Jane Wann, July 24, 1867, 06530, AMW to James H. Gamble, March 26, 1857, 06482, February 4, 1858, 06494, May 7, 1858, 06496, and August 27, 1867, 06532, and AMW to Margaret, December 23–24, 1864, 11479, and Leonora W. Gibbs to Mrs. James C. McDiarmid, March 3, 1929, GB 0247 Ms Whistler G22.

Charles Johnston purchased lots on South Bay Street from his father-in-law, Robert Mackenzie, one of four developers of the White Point area at the south end of Charleston, and built homes for family. See Webber, "Marriage and Death Notices." Mary Corbett's only child was a daughter, Elizabeth, who married Polydore Duclos and resided in New York City. See also Will of Charles Johnston, June 1, 1803, proved

April 2, 1804, Will Book D (1800–1817), page 443; Will of Marion Porcher, widow, June 10, 1811, proved April 23, 1812, Will Book E (1800–1817), page 262; and Will of Charlotte Johnston, August 1, 1861, Charleston County Public Library, 68 Calhoun Street, Charleston, South Carolina. For residential addresses see Hagy, *City Directories for Charleston, South Carolina.*

3. Their marriage license lists Isabella Johnston as twenty-four years old, "a spinster" (not previously married) and a resident of the Parish of St. Mary-le-Bow, and Zephaniah as twenty-seven, a "linnen draper" (cloth merchant) and a resident of the Parish of All Hallows, Bread Street. The Reverend Brooke Heckstall, Church of England, presided at the ceremony, Mary Mallat and William Johnston witnessed. See Bannerman, *The Registers of St. Mary le Bowe,* 370, and Microfilm Roll 4999, "St. Mary LeBow Parish Registers: Marriages, 1754–1794; and Banns 1754–1831," at Corporation of London's Guildhall, London. For a more complete document see the Marriage Licence (Bond) for Zephaniah Kinsley [*sic*] and Isabella Johnston, 28 September 176[3], issued by the Vicar General of the Archbishop of Canterbury, Lambeth Palace Library, London.

4. See Nicholson, *Bygone Lincolnshire*; Rigby, "'Sore Decay' and 'Fair Dwellings'"; Bowden, "Wool Supply and the Woollen Industry"; P. Thompson, *History and Antiquities of Boston*; and Hostettler, "Local History in Lincolnshire." Kingsley, reared a Quaker, moved to London, where genealogist D. J. Steel estimates Quakers were "particularly strong in textile trades." See Steel, *Sources for Nonconformist Genealogy,* 602–3, and Hudson, "A Suppressed Chapter in Quaker History." For the cloth industry in London see Earl, *Making of the English Middle Class,* 8, 87, 94–95, 107. See also Darcy, *Encouragement of the Fine Arts,* 7–10.

5. See M.1, Militia Lists of 1771, Bristol Record Office, compiled by Dr. Aul Glennie, Department of Geography, University of Bristol, and Bristol Trade Directory, 1768, in Pinney Papers, University of Bristol Library. For Port of Bristol and Atlantic trade, see K. Morgan, "Bristol and the Atlantic Trade."

6. K. Morgan, "Shipping Patterns"; Dresser, *Slavery Obscured.*

7. See records of marriages and births, Quaker Meeting of Bristol, 1762–1782, BMO SF/A7, Society of Friends, Bristol and Frenchay, and SF/A7/1, Illustrations of discipline 1666–1808. See also SF/A8, Certificates of Removals 1760–1790, and SF/A5, Testimonies of Minutes of Disunion of the Men's Meeting of Bristol, from 1762–82. See also Birth Record Registers, Temporary MSS, 933, Lincolnshire's Friends' Registers, 1618–1837, Vol. 1, Births and Marriages. Friends Library, Friends House, Euston Square London. Originals are at Lincolnshire Record Office, Lincolnshire Archives, Lincolnshire County Council, Lincoln, England.

Isabella Johnston Kingsley, 1737–1814, and Charles Johnston, 1732–1804, were brother and sister. In family legend Isabella is the daughter of Lady Katherine Melville, a descendant of Henry Dundas, the first Marquis of Melville and the Lord Advocate of Scotland; her father is Sir William Johnstone, Marquis of Annandale, Earl of Hartfell and Chief of his clan. Flattering antecedents, but no credible evidence supports the legend. She was more likely the daughter of Robert Johnston and Catherine Melville, born in 1837 at Fireside, Scotland, immediately north of Annan in the Dumfries and Galloway region of southwest Scotland. Her mother is believed to have been the daughter or the niece of John Melville, a steward or a factor at one of the estates owned by the Duke and Duchess of Buccleugh. Isabella Johnston Kingsley died in New York on December 14, 1814, at age seventy-seven. She was buried at the Quaker cemetery at Houston Street in New York City. See endnote 2 above, and Macbeth, *An Abstract of a Genealogical Collection*, 16-17, 25–27, and "Scottish Old Parochial Register Indexes, Baptisms and Marriages, prior to 1855," Society of Genealogists, The National Library and Education center for Family History, Barbican, London. See also Henshaw and Marshall, *Encyclopedia of American Quaker Genealogy*, 2:193. The flattering family legend is in Margaret Gibbs Watt, *The Gibbs Family*. A Sir William Johnstone (1663–1720) was First Marquess of Annandale, deceased prior to Isabella's birth, and his three sons all died unmarried. See Burke, *A Genealogical History*, 299–302; Sir Walter Fraser, *The Annandale Family Book of the Johnstones*; Alexander Johnston, *General Account of the Family of Johnston*; Johnstone, *History of the Johnstones*; and T. B. Johnston and Robertson, *Historical Geography of the Clans of Scotland*.

Zephaniah Kingsley Sr. was the grandchild of Quakers, born on April 11, 1734, at Leake, Lincolnshire, to Elizabeth Wright and Benjamin Kin[g]sley. His siblings were Benjamin, George, Jeremiah, and Martha Kingsley, born at Sibsey, Friskney, and Hogsthorpe, all in Lincolnshire. See Temp MSS, 933, Lincolnshire's Friends' Registers, 1618–1837, Vol. 1, Births and Marriages. See also Digest Registers: Births, 1733/4-11-12 (823/32), and Marriages, 1724/4-23 (833/112), at the Library of the Religious Society of Friends, Friends House, Euston Square, London.

8. *Gentleman's Magazine*, December 1768. In North America it was the French and Indian War. Bailyn, *Ideological Origins*, is still essential for conflicts between Britain and the colonies. See also Christie, *Wars and Revolutions*, 80–99; Black, *A System of Ambition*; Brewer, *Sinews of Power*; Anderson, *Crucible of War*.

9. Ernest, "Currency Act," and Sosin, *Agents and Merchants*. For Bristol see Minchinton, "Stamp Act Crises," "Political Activities of Bristol Merchants," and "Bristol—Metropolis of the West." See also K. Morgan, "Bristol and the Atlantic Trade."

10. The burial ground by Old Park Meeting House was used by several Quaker meeting houses. The record is at Friends House Library, Euston Street. See also B. Holmes, "Haunts of the London Quakers," 210–13 and 336–37.

11. The migration figures are from P. M. G. Harris, *The History of Human Population*, 2:191–94. See also DuPlessis, "Cloth and the Emergence," and Nash, "Organization of Trade and Finance."

12. In 1771 Charleston's rice exports exceeded 130,000 barrels; in 1775 more than one million pounds of indigo dye was sent abroad. Sellers, *Charleston Business*, 10–20; W. J. Fraser, *Charleston*, 98–168; and Edgar, *South Carolina*, 204–25.

13. W. J. Fraser, *Charleston*, chapter 3.

14. See Webber, "Extracts from the Journal of Mrs. Ann Manigault" and "William Hort's Journal."

15. Webber, "Extracts from the Journal of Mrs. Ann Manigault," 18 n. 68.

16. Quaker birth records, cited earlier in note 7.

17. Dillwyn, "Diary of William Dillwyn," 29–35 and 73–78. See also Webber, "Records of the Quakers in Charleston."

18. W. J. Fraser, *Charleston*, 96–168; Edgar, *South Carolina*, chapter 10.

19. Rogers, "The Charleston Tea Party," and Lambert, *South Carolina Loyalists*, 22–23. See also Godbold and Woody, *Christopher Gadsden and the American Revolution*, and McDonough, *Christopher Gadsden and Henry Laurens*.

20. *South Carolina Gazette*, November 21, 1774; Lambert, *South Carolina Loyalists*, 65.

21. W. J. Fraser, *Charleston*, 138–41.

22. *South Carolina Gazette*, February 1, 1771. Gillespie also ran a night school at his home on Bay Street.

23. W. J. Fraser, *Charleston*, 135.

24. Rogers, *Charleston in the Age of the Pinckneys*, 86.

25. Donnan, "Slave Trade into South Carolina"; K. Morgan, "Slave Sales in Colonial Charleston."

26. Berkeley and Berkeley, *Dr. Alexander Garden*, 29–58.

27. *South Carolina Gazette,* May 31, 1773: all eight ships sailed from West African ports. K. Morgan, "Slave Sales in Colonial Charleston," is useful on imports and sales, as is W. J. Fraser, *Charleston*, 98–168. See also J. Bennett, "Charleston in 1774," 179–80.

28. Graham to Grant, September 11, 1769, James Grant of Ballindalloch Papers, Governorship Series, Microfilm roll 18, 327–30, National Archives of Scotland, Edinburgh.

29. *Charleston Courier*, April 28, 30, May 1, June 6, 26, all 1806.

30. W. J. Fraser, *Charleston*, 143–48.

31. For date of birth see "The Correspondence of James McNeill Whistler: The On-line Edition," University of Glasgow, 2004–2007, www.whistler.arts.gla.ac.uk/correspondence/. I thank Mr. Everette McNeill Kivette of Burnsville, North Carolina, for information on the McNeill/Gibbs/Kingsley families.

32. Edgar, *South Carolina*, 226–29, and W. J. Fraser, *Charleston*, 148–50.

33. Kingsley's testimony, February 27, 1784, in Coke, "Memorial of Zephaniah Kingsley."

34. Ibid.

35. Searcy, *Georgia-Florida Contest*; W. J. Fraser, *Charleston*, 157–59; Edgar, *South Carolina*, 231–33. For the siege see Borick, *A Gallant Defense*.

36. John Peebles Diary, February 8–June 1780, SCL.

37. *South Carolina Gazette*, August 23, 1780. See also Lambert, *South Carolina Loyalists*, 191–93.

38. See Coke, "Memorial of Zephaniah Kingsley." See also W. J. Fraser, *Patriots, Pistols and Petticoats*, 132–33; Lambert, *South Carolina Loyalists*, 188, 192–93; McGowen, *British Occupation of Charleston*, 83; and A. S. Brown, "James Simpson's Reports on the Carolina Loyalists."

39. Edgar, *South Carolina*, 233–37.

40. W. J. Fraser, *Charleston*, 166–67. Persons sentenced to "amercement" could retain property by paying fines.

41. See Coke, "Memorial of Zephaniah Kingsley." Records of sales of Kingsley's land are in "Account of Sales, 1782–1783," Commissioners of Forfeited Estates, records of the Comptroller General, SCDAH. See also K. R. Coker, "Punishment of Civil War Loyalists," 349–53.

42. *Royal Gazette* (Savannah), April 30, 1782. See also Hagy, *City Directories for Charleston, South Carolina*, 2. See also Carne to Rolleston, October 12, 1780, Samuel Carne Papers, SCL. A city directory for 1782 lists "Kingsley & Taylor, Merchants, [at] 16 Broad Street," the property purchased by Kingsley in 1775. Taylor, also a Loyalist, managed to stay in Charleston.

43. Coke, "Memorial of Zephaniah Kingsley," 96–97.

44. Lambert, *South Carolina Loyalists*, 253–54; and Edgar, *South Carolina*, 237–40.

Chapter 2. New Brunswick Years

1. *Felix Farley's Bristol Journal*, February 1, 1783. See also January 18, February 1, 17, April 12, 1783. Vanderhorst to Laurens, February 4, 1783, is from Chesnutt, *Papers of Henry Laurens*, 16:139–40.

2. Mrs. Christian Barnes, Letterbook, September 22, 1783, LC. See also Nash, "Organization of Trade and Finance," 87–90. See also Kingsley to House of Representatives, November 6, 1784, SCDAH, 1785-49-01, H343-01. As late as 1788, Kingsley still owed money to Graham Johnston Co., a British firm with colonial branches. See Troxler, "The Migration," 325.

3. The Petition of Isabella Kingsley to the S.C. House of Representatives, January 28, 1783, Charlestown, SCDAH, 1783-343-01. For the August 5, 1782, and June 1783 sales of Kingsley's property see K. R. Coker, "Punishment of Civil War Loyalists," 350.

4. Abbott to White, July 27, 1784, and Kingsley to White, September 3, October 4, 1784, Gideon White Family Papers, NSARM.

5. Kingsley to the House of Representatives of the State of South Carolina, November 6, 1784, SCDAH, 1785-49-01.

6. Ibid.

7. Ibid. Isabella Kingsley petitioned again in 1807, seeking compensation for dower rights. It was rejected. See Committee Report, Petition of Isabella Kingsley, December 12, 1807, SCDAH, 165005/1807/00046.

8. *South Carolina Gazette* (Charleston), August 27, 1783. To clarify, the announcement does not specifically identify Zephaniah Jr. as the passenger, but it is doubtful that at age fourteen, his brother George would have been returning from London. It is possible that Zephaniah Jr. was returning from attending school in England. The unidentified nephew was likely Charles Johnston's son Mackenzie.

9. E. C. Wright, *Loyalists of New Brunswick*, 298.

10. Ibid., passim; Troxler, "The Migration," 105–46. For pre-Loyalist migration see

Bailyn, *Voyagers to the West*, 361–429. For Winslow see Condon, "The Loyalist Community in New Brunswick."

11. Moore, *Loyalists*, 183–223.

12. White to Thomas Melish, August 3, 1784, Shelburne No. 300, Gideon White Papers, NSARM.

13. *The World and Fashionable Advertiser*, September 14, 1784. See also Moore, *Loyalists*, 197.

14. MacNutt, *New Brunswick*, 65–66.

15. *Royal Gazette and New Brunswick Advertiser*, July 23, 1785, April 11, May 9, 16, November 14, 1786, March 20, 1787.

16. First quote is from the *Royal Gazette and New Brunswick Advertiser*, December 18, 1787; second quote is from *St. John Gazette and Weekly Advertiser*, January 16, 1789.

17. E. C. Wright, *Loyalists of New Brunswick*, 298. For the petition see University of New Brunswick Memorial Volume, University of New Brunswick Library, Fredericton; and MacNutt, "The Founders and Their Times," University of New Brunswick, no date.

18. Power of Attorney, Kingsley Sr. to Cathcart and Mowatt, June 1785, S38-1, F3, Correspondence, Hazen Collection of Ward Chipman Papers, 1783–1824, New Brunswick Museum, Saint John, New Brunswick.

19. For the property transactions see Petitions to Governor Carleton, The Carleton Papers, Public Archives of Canada, microfilm roll 367, Deed Book A, Registry Office of Kings County, 2–3, Hampton, New Brunswick; Kingsley file, University Archives, University of New Brunswick; Beyea, "History of French Village," unpublished manuscript, 66, New Brunswick Museum. The Kingsley sisters sold the Hammond River acreage to Nathaniel Golding on November 1, 1811, for £400 sterling. The deed was acknowledged at New York City before Thomas Barclay, British Consul General for the Eastern States of America.

20. *Royal Gazette and New Brunswick Advertiser*, April 11, 1786. Legends regarding the Gibbs and Kingsley families are found in Watt, *The Gibbs Family*.

21. Troxler, "The Migration," 135.

22. T. C. Holmes, *Loyalists to Canada*, 25–26. The reference to the *True Briton* is from the *St. John Gazette and Weekly Advertiser*, September 12, 1788, as cited by Troxler, "The Migration," 136. Assistance from Philadelphia was in July 1787.

23. Mather Byles to Edward Winslow, April 11, 1786, Winslow Papers, volume 5, no. 33, University of New Brunswick Archives and Special Collections, Fredericton, New Brunswick. For the *True Briton*, see the *Royal Gazette and New Brunswick Advertiser*, September 4, 1787. See also May 9, 1786, for Collins as master of the *New Hope* at Saint John, from London. Kingsley may have acquired the *True Briton* from his brother-in-law, Charles Johnston. In the mid-1770s, Johnston, John Simpson, and Edinburgh merchant John Forrest Jr. were owners of the *Briton*, a vessel of 200 tons built in South Carolina in 1773 that sailed between Charleston and London. The name may have been changed in 1778 after the vessel was seized by a privateer, condemned, and sold to new

owners under the new name *Hope*, then returned to the original owners by a British admiralty court. See Chesnutt, *Papers of Henry Laurens*, 9:439n, and 13:276n; *South Carolina Gazette*, September 19, 1774; and Olsbert, "Ship Registers," 224.

24. Between 1777 and 1833, correspondence in the Gideon White Papers, NSARM, documents two generations of the White family's involvement in trade between Halifax and Jamaica. See item 41, vol. 498, and item 1292, vol. 955. For the *Argo* see G. S. Brown, *Yarmouth, Nova Scotia*, 203–6, and J. R. Campbell, "A History of the County of Yarmouth." For Kingsley Sr.'s residency in Fredericton see advertisements in the *Royal Gazette and New Brunswick Advertiser*, January 13, 1789; *St. John Gazette and Weekly Advertiser*, January 16, March 20, 1789; and ZK Sr. File at University Archives, University of New Brunswick.

25. References to Kingsley's finances are in Hazen, "Collection of Ward Chipman Papers, 1783–1824," New Brunswick Museum; Mather Byles, Letter Books, Number 4, 1784–1786, Winslow Papers, University of New Brunswick Archives and Special Collections, Fredericton; and White Family Papers, MG 1, vol. 947, nos. 296, 309, and 319, NSARM.

26. MacNutt, *New Brunswick*, 68–78.

27. Wylly to Chipman, July 18, 1791, Ward Chipman Papers, Hazen Collection, New Brunswick Museum. For Wylly see Riley, *Homeward Bound*, 172–77, and Lawrence, *The Judges of New Brunswick*, 56–57.

28. For the move to Wilmington, see ZK to James Hamilton, May 1, July 20, 1801, JHP. For Kingsley's visits at Wilmington see Fouts, "Abstracts from Newspapers of Wilmington, North Carolina, 1765–1775 and 1788–1799," vol. 1, 74. I thank Ms. Beverley Tetterton for this information. See also McDiarmid, "Whistler's Mother," unpublished biography, typescript, Special Collections, Glasgow University Library, Glasgow, Scotland. The mother of the artist James McNeill Whistler was Anna McNeill Whistler, Martha Kingsley's daughter. For Isabella Gibbs see Watt, *The Gibbs Family*.

29. There is the possibility that Kingsley Jr. changed his residence from St. John, New Brunswick, to Yarmouth, Nova Scotia. See G. S. Brown, *Yarmouth, Nova Scotia*, 168, 203–6, 327. For Kingsley as captain of the *Argo* at the port of Charleston, see M. H. Jackson, *Privateers in Charleston*, 17 n. 26, 128–29; and *City Gazette and Commercial Daily Advertiser* (Charleston), March 29, October 21, 1793. Zephaniah Kingsley Sr. is presumed to have died circa 1792. Hereafter, Zephaniah Kingsley Jr. will be identified without the suffix.

30. For Kingsley's oath of loyalty at Charleston see Holcomb, *South Carolina Naturalizations*, and M. H. Jackson, *Privateers in Charleston*, 128–29, but see also ibid., 17 n. 26, and *City Gazette and Commercial Daily Advertiser*, October 21, 1793. For Kingsley's Danish "Burger Brief" (oath of loyalty) at St. Thomas, DNA, RA, GTK, Udskrift af St. Jan og St. Thomas, Søpasprotokoller, 1788–1807. Kingsley swore an oath of allegiance to Spain at St. Augustine, East Florida, on September 24, 1803. See EFP, Oaths of Allegiance, 1793–1804, page 104.

Chapter 3. "My Saddle Bags Loaded with Specie"

1. *City Gazette and Commercial Daily Advertiser,* February 23, 1791, and October 21, 1793, and *Georgia Gazette,* February 23, March 29, 1792.

2. M. H. Jackson, *Privateers in Charleston,* 17, 26, 118, 128–29. See also *City Gazette and Commercial Daily Advertiser,* October 21, 1793; Alderson, *The Bright Era,* 126–28; P. C. Coker, *Charleston's Maritime Heritage,* 131–35.

3. See the excellent introductory essay in Dubois and Garrigus, *Slave Revolution in the Caribbean.*

4. Scott, "'Negroes in Foreign Bottoms.'"

5. Fulwar Skipwith to Secretary of State, May, 1, October 1, 1793, St. Pierre, Martinique, and July 6, 1793, Fort Republic, Martinique, T431, Vol. 1, Roll 1, June 26–October 24, 1831, Martinique, and David M. Clarkson to Secretary of State, May 11, June 14, 1793, January 15, March 7, April 30, 1794, Christiansand, St. Eustatius, T236, Vol. 1, Roll 1, May 11–March 23, 1828, St. Eustatius, RG 59, Consular Despatches, Department of State, NARA-CP.

6. *City Gazette and Commercial Daily Advertiser,* November 7, 23, 1793. Charleston city directories list Johnston as a merchant and/or planter with residences at White Point in 1782, Lamboll's Lane in 1790, No. 3 Lamboll Street in 1794, 1796, and 1800. His children resided on South Bay Street as late as 1855. See Hagy, *City Directories for Charleston.*

7. Geggus, "Jamaica and the Saint Domingue Slave Revolt, 1791–1793," 219–33.

8. See Alderson, *The Bright Era,* 54–73.

9. Ibid., 54–57.

10. Ibid., 74–92, and Alderson, "Charleston's Rumored Slave Revolt."

11. See *City Gazette and Commercial Daily Advertiser,* February 27, 1797. For Penman see also Jervey, "Items from a South Carolina Almanac"; and Dobson, *Directory of Scots in the Carolinas,* 262.

12. J & E Penman & Company Daybook, 1794, 45, 73–74, 82, 89, 93, 101, 175, SCL.

13. Holcomb, *South Carolina Naturalizations.*

14. For maritime law see Holmbert, "The Acts, Orders in Council, & c. of Great Britain [on Trade], 1793–1812."

15. See the 1793 entries in the John Smith and Company Letter Books, Volume III, Maryland Historical Society, Baltimore.

16. St. Eustatius, April 30, June 14, 1793, U.S. Consular Despatches, RG 59, T236, Roll 1, NARA-CP. See also David M. Clarkson to Secretary of State, January 15, 1794, and Fulwar Skipwith to Secretary of State, March 7, 1794, ibid. See also Sherman, "Orders in Council"; Fewster, "The Jay Treaty"; Smelser, "The Passage of the Naval Act of 1794"; and Keith, "Relaxations in British Restrictions."

17. See "Statement by 40 Owners," GRE/A/382b, Grey Volumes, Earl Grey Papers, 1st Earl [Grey], Department of Paleography and Diplomatic, Archives and Special Collections, Palace Green Library, Durham University Library, U.K. Courtesy of Michael R. Harkness, archivist.

18. Shallcross to Secretary of State, April 9, 1794, St. Vincent, T327, Vol. 1, Roll 1, April 9, 1830–November 3, 1830, Antigua, RG 59, Consular Despatches, Department of State, NARA-CP. See also Fewster, "The Jay Treaty."

19. Shallcross to Secretary of State, April 7, 1794; and "Statement by 40 Owners."

20. Shallcross to Secretary of State, May 20, 1794, T327, Vol. 1, Roll 1, April 9, 1830–November 3, 1830, Antigua, RG 59, Consular Despatches, Department of State, NARA-CP. See also March 28, June 28, 1794.

21. Shallcross to Secretary of State, May 20, 1794, Antigua. On July 4, 1794, Shallcross sent a gossipy report: "the traitor [Benedict] Arnold came out to Guadeloupe to speculate in the plunder. He was taken by the French on their landing, has been confined three weeks but made his escape in a hen coop" on the deck of a ship.

22. Shallcross to Secretary of State, June 20, August 14, 1794, ibid.

23. September 1, 1794, Letter Book Entry, John Smith and Company Letter Books.

24. See Duffy, *Soldiers, Sugar, and Seapower*. For Jay's Treaty see Fewster, "The Jay Treaty"; J. Charles, "The Jay Treaty"; and Estes, *The Jay Treaty Debate*.

25. Dubois and Garrigus, *Slave Revolution in the Caribbean*. See also Dubois, "'The Price of Liberty.'" For an excellent study of Guadeloupe port cities and population, see Pérotin-Dumon, "Cabotage, Contraband, and Corsairs," 58–86.

26. Dubois, *A Colony of Citizens*, 241–46.

27. *City Gazette and Commercial Daily Advertiser*, June 28, 1794. For schooner *Polly* see Penman & Co. Daybook, 1794, 89 & 99, SCL. For George Kingsley see *City Gazette and Commercial Daily Advertiser*, June 4, September 24, 1794. Charles Johnston owned a one-half interest in "a schooner *Polly*" at his death in 1804. See Inventory of Charles Johnston, Esquire, May 16, 1804, Inventories and Appraisement Book, 1783–1851, Charleston County, South Carolina, L10136, Microfilm Roll CH 007, page 260 DZ 194638, SCDAH. See also *City Gazette and Commercial Daily Advertiser*, November 5, 1795.

28. The two schooners named *Polly* captured at St. Pierre were out of Providence, Rhode Island, and Newburyport, Massachusetts. See "Statement by 40 Owners."

29. John Smith and Co. Letter Book, Volume III, March 26, 1795.

30. The *Georgia Gazette* (Savannah), June 30, 1796, reprinting news from Charleston. Essequibo, Demerara, and Berbice are now British Guyana. See R. T. Smith, *British Guiana*, chapter 2. See also da Costa, *Crowns of Glory*, 46; de Vries, "The Dutch Atlantic Economies"; Berka, "Citizens of St. Eustatius, 1781"; and especially Drescher, "The Long Goodbye."

The *Columbian Museum* (Savannah) issue of September 30, 1796, reprints a favorable account of Hugues by a ship captain from Boston who was brought into Point-au-Petre by a privateer from Guadeloupe.

31. *City Gazette and Commercial Daily Advertiser*, January 17, 31, February 27, March 29, September 25, 1797.

32. Stowell, *Balancing Evils Judiciously*, 31–32.

33. Ibid., 39–75.

34. For troop losses see Geggus, "Slavery, War, and Revolution," 24–25. See also "Unidentified Citizen of Saint Domingue, Extracts of Minutes of a General Meeting of West Indies Planters and Merchants at a London Tavern," November 8, 1791, Folio 109, Additional Manuscripts 38351, British Library, London. For a differing opinion see Major General G. Forbes's comments on the necessity to recruit thousands of former slaves to fight for the British by offering freedom after five years of military service. Forbes had become convinced that "blacks in this climate must be conquered by blacks." Forbes to Lt. General Ralph Abercromby, December 10, 1795, February 23, 1796, Additional Manuscripts 39,824, Letterbook of Major General G. Forbes, 1795–1796, British Library. For General Leclerc's comments see Dubois, *Avengers of the New World*.

35. Popkin, *Facing Racial Revolution*; Geggus, *Slavery, War, and Revolution*; Dubois, *Avengers of the New World*; Garrigus, *Before Haiti*.

36. Carolyn E. Fick writes that the free people of color "owned one-third of the colony's plantations, one-quarter (over 100,000) of the slaves, and one-quarter of the real estate" and "may even have exceeded . . . [the numbers] of whites." See Fick, "The French Revolution in Saint Domingue," 56, 71 n. 13.

37. Dubois and Garrigus, *Slave Revolution in the Caribbean*, 30. To grasp the complex and enormously difficult steps leading Sonthonax and Polverel to the general emancipation decree, see the comprehensively researched study by Popkin, *You Are All Free*, 257–88.

38. Geggus, *Slavery, War, and Revolution*; Buckley, *The Haitian Journal of Lieutenant Howard*, 28. For Biassou after Saint-Domingue see Landers, *Atlantic Creoles*, 55–94.

39. Garrigus, "Blue and Brown."

40. Garrigus, *Before Haiti*, 269–72, 283–87.

41. Ibid., 284–85.

42. Dubois, *Avengers of the New World*.

43. For the undeclared war see Ellis, *Passionate Sage*, 28–29, 76, and DeConde, *The Quasi-War*. For American vessels seized by French vessels see G. H. Williams, *The French Assault on American Shipping*. See also M. Palmer, *Stoddert's War*.

44. Silas Talbot to Timothy Pickering, February 5, September 27, October 4, 11, 12, 17, November 7, 19, 1796, January 21, May 7, 1797, Dispatches from United States Consuls in Kingston, Jamaica, 1796–1906, RG 59, T31, Roll 1, NARA-W; Joseph Blakely to Secretary of State, May 13, 1799, RG 59, T55, Roll 1, Volume 1, Dispatches, Santiago de Cuba, May 31, 1799–December 27, 1836. Blakely said French privateers lurked just outside the harbor and in the bays on the south shore of Cuba.

45. Kingsley's Danish "Burger Brief" at St. Thomas, DNA, RA, GTK, Udskrift af St. Jan og St. Thomas, Søpasprotokoller, 1788–1807.

Chapter 4. Shifting Loyalties

1. For Kingsley's loyalty oath to Denmark see DNA, GTK, Udskrift af St. Jan & St. Thomas Sópasprotokoller, 1788–1807. April 12, 1804, Danish Sea Pass. On June 5, 1795,

Captain George Kingsley registered at the port of Christiansted, St. Croix. See Rigsarkivet, Copenhagen, West Indian Passport and Citizenry Registers, Christiansted, St. Croix, 1794–1805, DNA. For the danger U.S. ships encountered in the Caribbean see Josiah Blakely to Secretary of State, May 13, 1799, November 1, 1801, April 10, 1804, July 1, 1805, RG 59, T55, Records of the Department of State, Consular Dispatches, St. Yago, Cuba, Roll 1, Volume 1, NARA-CP.

2. Highfield, "The Danish Atlantic"; Holsoe, "The Origin, Transport, Introduction and Distribution of Africans on St. Croix." See also "A Brief History of the Danish West Indies, 1666–1917," DNA, at http://www.virgin-islands-history.dk/eng/vi_hist.asp.

3. Scott, "Crisscrossing Empires," 129.

4. Nissen, *Reminiscences*, 31–51.

5. Trollope, *West Indies and Spanish Main*, 2, 8, 235–36. See ZK to JH, February 28, 1805, Liverpool, England, and ZK to JH, January 10 and April 11, 1802, JHP. For George Kingsley's loyalty oath see West Indian passport and citizenry registers, Christiansted Police Station, Registers of persons arriving and leaving, 1794–1805, DNA.

6. Highfield, "The Danish Atlantic," 16. See also Nørregard, *Danish Settlements in West Africa*, 1–20; and Feldbaek, "Danish Trading Companies."

7. Green-Pedersen, "Scope and Structure." The estimate is from Statistical Appendix, table 1, 178. Green-Pedersen estimates re-exports of 70,000 slaves from 1733 to 1807. See also Green-Pedersen, "History of the Danish Negro Slave Trade," and Highfield, "The Danish Atlantic and West Indian Slave Trade."

8. Green-Pedersen, "Scope and Structure," 151, 159–60, and table 7, "Transit Trade at St. Thomas," 185. Danish ships transporting slaves directly from Africa to Charlotte Amalie between 1777 and 1789 carried an average of 366 men and women. See also Green-Pedersen, "Colonial Trade under the Danish Flag" and "Economic Considerations behind the Danish Abolition."

9. It would have been possible to complete one, possibly two, voyages to Africa during these months, depending on the destination and how quickly the human cargo was purchased and loaded. Svend E. Holsoe found evidence of Danish ships completing voyages to and from the coast of Africa in the vicinity of Cape Verde and Gorée Island in ten to fourteen weeks. See, for example, the ships *Valentin* in 1796 and the *Favourite* in 1799 and 1800, in VL, St. Thomas, Bytings Protokol, 1796–1798, January 3, 1797, f. 20, no. 453VJ1796; February 21, 1799, and June 19, 1799, nos. 589VJ1799/1015VJ1799; and December 30, 1799, and April 9, 1800, nos. 952VJ1799, 371VJ1800, 752VJ1800, 585VJ1800, all from DNA. Courtesy of Svend E. Holsoe. I also benefited from Dr. Holsoe's unpublished "Slave Carrying Vessels between the Danish West Indies and Gorée and/or Cape Verde" (1994). See also Eltis, "A Brief Overview of the Trans-Atlantic Slave Trade." Eltis writes: "a few ships sailing from Upper Guinea could make the passage to the Americas in three weeks," compared to two months for ships departing all regions of Africa.

10. See RA, GTK, Udskrift af St. Jan & St. Thomas Søpasprotokoller, 1788–1807, October, 1799, June 1800, July 1800, January 1801 (all Danish Sea Passes), DNA. See also

Garrigus, *Before Haiti*, 269–72, 283–87. Firms like the Philadelphia-based Ball, Waddrop and Jennings operated branches at St. Eustatius, St. Thomas, and St. Croix and conducted commerce in Saint-Domingue and Charleston. See the William Ball Family Papers, Pennsylvania Historical Society, Philadelphia.

11. G. H. Williams, *The French Assault*, and Dubois, *Avengers of the New World*.

12. ZK to JH, May 1, 1801, Port-au-Prince, Haiti, JHP. See also Dubois, *Haiti*, 35–38.

13. The British occupation came after Denmark joined Russia and Prussia in the League of Armed Neutrality in protest of Britain's blockade and seizure of neutral Danish ships in the Baltic Sea and the West Indies. On March 28 a British fleet arrived with four thousand marines. The occupation ended on February 16, 1802. See Dookhan, *History of the Virgin Islands*.

14. ZK to JH, June 13, 1801, JHP. For the quarantine policy see McMillin, *Final Victims*, 110.

15. ZK to JH, July 20, October 4, 1801, January 10, 1802, JHP.

16. ZK to JH, July 20, 1801, JHP. The outstanding debt continued to torment him for months. See, for example, ZK to JH, New York, October 4, 1801.

17. Gibbs to JH, Wilmington, August 17, 1801, JHP.

18. U.S. Consul Reports, Havana, RG 59, Consular Dispatches from United States Consuls in Havana, 1793–1906, M 899, Roll 1, December 1, 1783–October 2, 1807: Vincent Gray to Madison, October 29, 1802. All Havana, Cuba, NARA-CP. See also John Norton to James Madison, January 20, March 17, 1802, ibid.

19. Fitzsimmons Letter Book, typescript, Vol. 1, June 5, 1800, June 1, 1802, Christopher Fitzsimmons Papers, SCL. Skelton was a British-born African slave trader married to an African woman and settled in today's Republic of Guinea. His son, also William Skelton, continued in the slave trade, married the biracial daughter of the Scot slave trader John Fraser, settled at Bangalan on the Pongo River, and married an African woman. See Schafer, "Family Ties That Bind," and Mouser, *American Colony on the Rio Pongo* and "Baltimore's African Experiment."

20. Fitzsimmons Letter Book, February 26, June 30, 1803, SCL.

21. Ibid., October 15, 17, 1803.

22. ZK to JH, January 10, 1802, St. Thomas, JHP. For the location of Hamilton Plantation see Ferguson, *The John Couper Family*, 66–67.

23. See Norton to Madison, January 20, March 17, 1802, and Gray to Madison, October 29, 1802 (all Havana, Cuba), U.S. Consul Reports, Havana, RG 59, Consular Despatches from United States Consuls in Havana, 1793–1906, M 899, Roll 1, December 1, 1783–October 2, 1807, NARA-CP.

24. ZK to JH, January 10, 1802, St. Thomas, JHP. The file in the Green-Pedersen private archive (DNA) suggesting an 1801 African voyage by Kingsley aboard the *Superior* does not contain confirming evidence. Bowers, of the *Commerce*, is identified in Fitzsimmons Letter Book, Volume 1, entry for November 9, 1799, SCL.

25. The three voyages are in West Indian passport and citizenry registers, Chris-

tiansted Police Station, Registers of persons arriving and leaving, 1794–1814, DNA. I thank Svend E. Holsoe for this data.

26. For Kingsley and the *Superior* see RA, Notorial Protocol [St. Thomas] [TB 34], 1804–1806, and RA, VRR, Toldregnskaber, Nr. 7, 1802, Liquidations Beregning, DNA. For Captain Callen and the *May* see BPP/ST61 1971: 31, 435, and RA, VL, VI Regering, Toldregnskaber, Nr. 11, and Nr. 7, both 1802, 'Liquidations Beregning,' f. 1, DNA. See also RG 55, Box 509, Xsted Antegnelser 1802, 79 Post, Outgoing no. 17, NARA-CP. For Bonny & Bight of Biafra see Lovejoy and Richardson, "'This Horrid Hole.'" See also Lovejoy, *Transformations in Slavery*, 59–60, 102–4, and H. S. Klein, *The Atlantic Slave Trade*, 62–64.

27. GTK, Udskrift af St. Jan & St. Thomas Sópasprotokoller, 1788–1807, February 20 to July 20, 1802, DNA. For John Souffraine see Green-Pedersen, "Colonial Trade under the Danish Flag."

28. Eltis, "Volume and Structure"; H. S. Klein, *The Atlantic Slave Trade*, 130–60; Kiple and Higgins, "Mortality Caused by Dehydration"; and Thomas, *The Slave Trade*, 421–23.

29. For Kingsley at Havana on the *Superior*, see H. S. Klein, "Slave Trade to Havana."

30. ZK to JH, Havana, Cuba, March 14, 1802, JHP.

31. ZK to JH, March 27, 1802, and Gibbs to JH, April 11, 1802, JHP.

32. See Gibbs to JH, April 11, 13, 1802, JHP.

33. ZK to JH, May 16, 1802, St. Croix, JHP. See also ZK to JH, March 27, 1802, Havana, JHP.

34. Cusick, "East Florida Papers Oaths of Allegiance," vol. 2.

Chapter 5. "Fortune Is Neither to Be Won by Prudence nor Industry"

1. Cusick, "East Florida Papers Oaths of Allegiance," vol. 2; Landers, *Black Society*, 73–75. See also J. B. Miller, "The Struggle for Free Trade," and WPA, *Spanish Land Grants in Florida*, vol. 1. Pesos and dollars were equal in value. For British sterling multiply by 4.4. My conversion is based on newspaper evidence and samples of commodity prices in Florida estate inventories, excluding slaves and land values. I concluded that $1 in 1815 is worth $35 today. Derks, "Composite Commodity Price Index," 2, sets the value of $1 in 1860 at $30.838 in 1989.

2. Cusick, "Across the Border," 280–83, 286–89. See also S. Johnson, "Climate, Community, and Commerce"; Knight, *Slave Society in Cuba*, 6–11; Paquette, *Sugar Is Made with Blood*, 36.

3. For Clarke see Wyllys, "The East Florida Revolution," citing The Case of United States v. Ferreira, printed in Senate Miscellaneous Documents, 36th Congress, 1st sess. (1859–1860), 17–18. See also Landers, *Black Society*, 82, 238. Sandbars and shallow water at the entrance to the Matanzas River off St. Augustine forced heavily burdened vessels to load and off-load cargoes offshore, thus minimizing ship traffic there.

4. For immigration see Cusick, "East Florida Papers Oaths of Allegiance."

5. Ibid. For Fraser see Schafer, "Family Ties That Bind."

6. Landers, *Black Society*, 82–83, 161, 238–39.

7. Ibid., 174–79, 276–77. For naturalization of Fraser-owned ships see Fraser to Governor, September 2, 1809, R81, Section 44, and same to same, November 16, 1809, R149, Section 76, EFP. For Fraser's request for admission of 110 slaves at Amelia Island for use at his plantation see Fraser to Governor, April 28, 1810, R133, Section 70, EFP. Fraser plantations are inventoried in testamentary proceedings, February 15, 1814, R145, Section 71, EFP. George Long's testamentary file is February 15, 1814, Section 71, EFP. Regarding prize ships see Behrendt, "Markets, Transaction Cycles, and Profits," 176–78.

8. For advice on property Kingsley may have called on two longtime residents, John Leslie, a partner in the Panton and Leslie Company, and George J. F. Clarke, a planter and land surveyor. For Clarke see Landers, *Black Society*, 99, 239–44, and Schafer, "'A Class of People Neither Freemen Nor Slaves,'" 596–97.

9. See testamentary proceedings, William Pengree, June 18, 1794, R136, Section 71, and Rebecca Pengree, February 18, 1804, R139, Section 71, EFP. The Pengree property consisted of three contiguous tracts: Bueno Suceso, Monte de Laureles, and Puente de Laurel. For British development of the property see Schafer, *William Bartram*.

10. The tax records were researched by Dr. Svend E. Holsoe and communicated by personal correspondence. I thank Dr. Holsoe for this generous assistance.

11. For Hanahan see testimonies of Rebecca E. Read and John M. Bowden in East Florida Claim, Abraham Hanahan, Records of the Superior Court of East Florida, Box 124, Folder 24, SAHSRL and and Claim of Zephaniah Kingsley, Superior and Circuit Court Records, Box 131, Folder 16, SAHSRL. A Hanahan household bordered the Kingsley home in Charleston.

12. See the Notarial Protocol St. Thomas, 1804–1806, f. 178; GTK, Udskrift af St. Jan & St. Thomas Sópasprotokoller, 1788–1807, April 1804; and Seapass, no. 11, March 1800, VI., St. Thomas, Bytings Protokol, 585VJ1800 & 752VJ1800, all DNA. Again, I thank Dr. Holsoe for this documentation.

13. For arrival in St. Augustine see ZK to Governor, November 25, 1803, Section 44, and May 5, 1804, R133, Section 70, both EFP. See also ZK to Governor, June 30, 1804, R80, Section 44, EFP.

14. ZK requests admission, June 15, 1804, R133, Section 70, and June 25, 1804, R80, Section 44, both EFP.

15. The *Gustavia* was apparently named after the town of that name at Sweden's Caribbean colony, St. Barthélemy. See Ekman, "Sweden, the Slave Trade and Slavery," and Lavoie, Fick, and Mayer, "A Particular Study of Slavery."

16. For the *Gustavia* at Liverpool see Entry no. 4186, *Lloyd's List*, January 22, 1805. I thank Stephen Behrendt for bringing this source to my attention. See also Cameron and Crooke, *Liverpool*, 1–10. See also Mackenzie-Grieve, *The Last Years*, 12–20; Richardson, Schwarz, and Tibbles, *Liverpool and Transatlantic Slavery*, 1–13; and Richardson, "Slavery and Bristol's 'Golden Age.'"

17. Behrendt, "Markets, Transaction Cycles, and Profits"; Richardson, Schwarz, and Tibbles, *Liverpool and Transatlantic Slavery*, 1–13; K. Morgan, "Liverpool's Dominance";

Rediker, *The Slave Ship*, 53–55; Richardson, "Shipboard Revolts," 69–92; and Small-wood, *Saltwater Slavery*, 72–74, 142.

18. ZK to JH, February 28, 1805, Liverpool, JHP.

19. Eltis and Richardson estimate that 40 percent of the slaves entering the Atlantic slave trade between 1595 and 1867 came from this region. See their "The 'Numbers Game' and Routes to Slavery" and "West Africa and the Transatlantic Slave Trade." See also H. S. Klein, *The Atlantic Slave Trade*, 70–71, 196.

20. Alpers, *The East African Slave Trade*, 12. In 1804, Alexander McClure returned to Charleston from a voyage to the "East-Indies" with "seeds of useful plants" acquired at Mozambique, including the "valuable" seed of "Bourbon Cotton" then in great demand with English buyers. He also brought exotic birds, wine, and "a sow with pig of the Chinese breed of hogs." See *Charleston Courier*, July 16, 1804.

21. Bowers to JH, March 30, 1805, Liverpool, JHP.

22. For the Petit-Goâve debt see Samuel Campbell to JH, Baltimore, March 1805, JHP.

23. ZK to JH, February 28, 1805, Liverpool, JHP.

24. Ships traveling south along the coast of West Africa faced stiff currents and winds south of the Zaire River. The more westerly route was the course of least resistance, but careful piloting was needed after ships passed Bahia and turned east, lest northerly wind and currents forced them north along the Angola coast. See J. C. Miller, *Way of Death*, 318–24, and Thomas, *The Slave Trade*, 413–14.

25. First quote is from Gibbs to JH, November 15, 1805, relaying news from ZK to Gibbs, August 1, 1805. Second quote and those that follow are from ZK to JH, Cape of Good Hope, August 8, 1805, JHP.

26. For seasonal winds and currents see McMillin, *Final Victims*, 104. For historical maps that label the East African coast "Zanguebar," see "Le Zanguebar Tiree de Sanut &n c./ Partie du Zanguebar ou Sont les Costes d'Ajan et d'Abix & c. Amsterdam: N. Sanson, 1700; and "COTE DE ZANGUEBAR," in Vaugody, *Atlas Portatif Universel*. Both maps can be seen online at www.swaen.com/antique-map-of.php?id+9600. See Machado, "A Forgotten Corner," 17–18, and "Without Scales and Balances," 254–88. See also Beachey, "The East African Ivory Trade," 169; and H. S. Klein, *The Atlantic Slave Trade*, 67–71. "Zanguebar" had been used by mariners since at least the seventeenth century.

27. Newitt, *A History of Mozambique*, 247–48; Alpers, *The East African Slave Trade*, 4–9, and *Ivory and Slaves*, 209. See also Nicholls, *The Swahili Coast*, 80–90, 212–13.

28. Newitt, *A History of Mozambique*, 247–48; Sheriff, *Slaves, Spices and Ivory in Zanzibar*, 42; Alpers, *The East African Slave Trade*, 17.

29. Sheriff, *Slaves, Spices, and Ivory in Zanzibar*, and Harries, "Slavery, Social Incorporation and Surplus Extraction," 313–14. It is doubtful the *Gustavia* dropped anchor at Zanzibar, since that island's dominance in the slave trade came after the Napoleonic Wars ended in 1811. The explosive growth of spice plantations explains the massive purchases of captives in the nineteenth century.

30. ZK, *A Treatise on the Patriarchal*. "M'Choolay Moreema" has not been identified. It may have been on a route from Mozambique or Tanzania on the east and Angola on the west that converged at Kazembe-Lunda, located east of and between Lake Tanganyika and Lake Malawi.

31. I thank Professor Douglas R. Egerton for personal correspondence (November 11, 1996) with information that verifies Gullah Jack's fifteen-year residence at Charleston.

32. A Kenyan living in Miami made the identifications of the Kamba names. I thank Dr. Svend E. Holsoe for conducting the interview. Claim of ZK, Account no. 88515, RG 217, EFC. See also MC 31, PWC. The quotations used with "M Sooma" and other names are meant to recapture the way they were written on the document.

33. Based on H. S. Klein, *The Atlantic Slave Trade*, 93–95, 142, 148, 150; Thomas, *The Slave Trade*, 409–30; and Smallwood, *Saltwater Slavery*, 44–46. In West Africa yams were often purchased as subsistence for the Africans.

34. H. S. Klein, *The Atlantic Slave Trade*; Thomas, *The Slave Trade*.

35. Richardson, "Shipboard Revolts," 72–75.

36. The above composite is drawn from Rediker, *The Slave Ship*, passim, and Christopher, *Slave Ship Sailors*, 174–80, 187–89. The quotation from John Newton is in *Thoughts on the African Slave Trade*, taken here from Rediker, *The Slave Ship*, 241.

37. For Newton see "Publications of the House of Commons," borrowed here from Christopher, *Slave Ship Sailors*, 186; Thomas, *The Slave Trade*, 311. For numbers of slaves embarked on the *Gustavia* see Eltis, "'Voyages: The Trans-Atlantic Slave Trade Database': Voyage 25457, Gustavia (1806), US flag, 300 ton ship, owned by Spencer John Man. Total embarked: 332. Arrived Charleston: 250." The number debarked was likely 258. For sharks see Rediker, *The Slave Ship*, 37–40, and for studies of disease and mortality based on surgeon's journals see ibid., 273–76, 285, and H. S. Klein, *The Atlantic Slave Trade*, 150–57.

38. Gibbs to JH, New York, November 15, December 27, 1805, February 26, April 15, 1806, JHP.

39. Eltis and Richardson, "A New Assessment of the Transatlantic Slave Trade."

Chapter 6. Family Ties

1. ZK to William Allen, April 21, 1806, from Tybee Island, James Hamilton Papers, Hargrett Rare Book and Manuscript Library, University of Georgia Libraries, Athens. The quarantine facility was first utilized in 1767. The Sullivan's Island quarantine station near Charleston was transferred to James Island and not operative in April 1806. See "Atlantic Slave Trade to Savannah," *The New Georgia Encyclopedia*, at www.georgiaencyclopedia.org/nge.

2. *Jacksonville Courier*, April 30, 1806.

3. Ibid., May 6, June 26, 1806.

4. Ibid. On June 2 the *Courier* announced that "a part of the cargo of the Ship

Gustavia, having undergone the vaccine, and now in perfect health" was available for purchase. For the *El Pele* (also recorded as *El Pepe*) see R114 B270 and R147 B323, EFP.

5. ZK to JH, February 28, 1805, JHP.

6. For records of the *Esther* at Charleston see the *Charleston Courier*, August 11, 1806, and McMillin, *Final Victims*, 67, 99–100. For the *Esther* at Havana see the *Courier*, September 23, 1806. For the ship's cargo see Klein, "Computerized data on Slave Ships Arriving at Havana, 1790–1821." For Kingsley at Havana in 1806 see R97 B231 J18 and R172 B231 N21; for Havana to Florida voyage see R163 B350 U4, all EFP.

7. For more on Munsilna McGundo and Fatimah Kingsley see chapter 13 of the present volume.

8. For a more complete version of Anna Kingsley's life see Schafer, *Anna Madgigine Jai Kingsley.*

9. In an unpublished paper presented at the Anna Kingsley in Senegal Historical Conference held March 11, 2000, at Gorée Island, historian Mbaye Guèye called these years a period of great crisis for all of Senegambia. For Jolof, Kajoor, and the other Wolof states, see Guèye, *L'Esclavage au Sénégal*; Barry, *Senegambia and the Atlantic Slave Trade*; Diouf, *Le Kajoor*. See also Searing, *West African Slavery*; Curtin, *Economic Change in Precolonial Africa*; Lovejoy, *Transformations in Slavery*; and Robinson, "The Islamic Revolution of Futa Toro." Victoria Bomba Coifman was my guide to the history of Jolof in Senegal. See "History of the Wolof State of Jolof until 1860," and "The Pre-Nineteenth Century Political Tradition of the Wolof." Also of value is Charles, "A History of the Kingdom of Jolof (Senegal), 1800–1890"; Klein, "Servitude among the Wolof and Sereer of Senegambia"; and "Women and Slavery in the Western Sudan." For the upper Senegal Valley, see Becker, "Conditions écologiques," and Becker and Martin, "Kayor et Baol: Royaumes sénégalais et traite des esclaves au dix-huitième siècle." See also Robinson, "The Islamic Revolution of Futa Toro." For Wolof Culture, see David P. Gamble, *The Wolof of Senegambia.*

10. For the horse trade and Saharan-based merchants see Webb, *Desert Frontier.* Barry, *Senegambia and the Atlantic Slave Trade*, discusses the destructive impact of European trade on West African society. For the destruction and relocation of rural villages and transformation of housing styles in Jolof see Brahim Diop, "Traite Negriere et Cadres de View dans le Pays Wolof," and Barry, *Le royaume du Waalo.*

11. E. A. Charles, *Jolof Kingdom.* See also Searing, *West African Slavery and Atlantic Commerce*, 10–12. See also Victoria Bomba, "History of the Wolof State of Jolof until 1860" and "The Pre-Nineteenth Century Political Tradition of the Wolof." For related events in Trarza and Brakna and for Portuguese involvement see Barry, *Senegambia and the Atlantic Slave Trade*, and Robinson, "The Islamic Revolution of Futa Toro."

12. For Kajoor see Diouf, *Le Kajoor*, and Barry, *Senegambia and the Atlantic Slave Trade*, 44. Barry sees the Kingdom of Kajoor from 1677 as "a perfect example of *ceddo* power" and of the "ubiquitous violence" spread throughout the region. See Webb, *Desert Frontier*, 70–72, 76–81, 88–96, for horses and cavalry states in the Senegambia.

Exchange prices were generally fifteen to thirty captured slaves for every horse. In the early years of trade in Sengambia, Portuguese traders sold horses. For the tyeddo see Diouf, *Le Kajoor,* and Searing, *West African Slavery and Atlantic Commerce.*

13. Maxwell, "Answer to the Questions Proposed by his Majesty's Commissioner for Investigation of the Forts and Settlements in Africa," January 1, 1811, Original Correspondence of the Secretary of State, Colonial Office, Series 267, vol. 29, National Archives, Kew.

14. Diop, "Les villages Désertés du Sénégal" and "Traite Négrière."

15. Searing, *West African Slavery and Atlantic Commerce,* 155–62.

16. The conclusion that raids continued into Jolof is from Diouf, *Le Kajoor.* I thank Dr. Diouf for an oral interview conducted in November 1994 in Dakar. See also Searing, *West African Slavery,* and Barry, *Senegambia and the Atlantic Slave Trade,* for the religious wars. See also M. A. Klein, "Servitude among the Wolof and Sereer of Senegambia." Slaving raids were generally mounted between October and April, after the annual June-to-September rainy season ended and the muddy roads leading to the interior had dried. For discussion of temperature and climate see Webb, *Desert Frontier,* chapter 1. My own observations are similar, based on visits to Senegal in 1970, 1994, and 2000.

17. Colonel Lloyd to Secretary of State, August 16, 1805, and May 23, 1806, Original Correspondence of the Secretary of State. Series 267, vol. 29, Colonial Office, National Archives, Kew. See Diouf, *Le Kajoor;* Benoist and Camara, *Gorée: The Island and the Historical Museum;* Searing, *West African Slavery and Atlantic Commerce,* 93–128; also Wadstrom, *Observations on the Slave Trade,* vol. 1, for a contemporary account by a Swedish traveler. Slave coffles stopped at Rufisque, an important market town on the mainland where an agent representing the Damel of Cayor supervised slave sales. Gorée (from the Dutch word for "good harbor"), had been home to slave merchants since the middle of the fifteenth century. Portuguese nationals controlled the island until 1627, followed by Dutch traders, then French, and English between 1800 and 1817.

18. *Signares* (from the Portuguese word for "dame," *senhora*) were important merchants at Gorée for several generations. Europeans arrived without wives and formed semi-official liaisons with African women, then returned to Europe leaving their businesses under control of their African mates, who became female heads of "canoe companies" that dominated coastal trade and island commerce. James Searing, in *West African Slavery and Atlantic Commerce,* characterizes the *signares* as pioneer business women who provided European merchants with a wide range of services, produce, and supplies of slaves purchased at mainland markets. The families of mulatto merchants who descended from the *signares* became the essential middle-level arbiters in the slave trade to Gorée and St. Louis. See also G. E. Brooks, "The Signares of Saint-Louis and Gorée."

19. I believe Anta's place of origin was Jolof; James Searing, an expert on the slave trade in Senegal, considers Kajoor more likely and any of the Wolof states a possibility.

The Senegalese historians Mbaye Gueye, Penda Mbow, and Mamadou Diouf agree that it was Jolof. I thank them and Professor Boubakar Barry for guiding me through the complex history of Senegal.

20. Monteil, "Le Dyolof et Al-Bouri Ndiaye."

21. This interview was conducted by Ms. Peri Francis, a descendant of Anna Kingsley who lives in Atlanta, Georgia. I thank her for our conversations in July and October 1999.

22. My own interviews with Mr. Cisse in March 2000 were inconsequential. However, I arranged for Mr. Sy to conduct additional interviews. Mr. Sy communicated the results to me in a May 19, 2000, letter from Dahra, Senegal.

23. Mr. Sy and Mr. Cisse accompanied me to Yang Yang, along with my wife, Joan Moore, and Dr. Jane Landers, of Vanderbilt University.

24. Ababacar Sy to the author, May 19, 2000. See Leyti, "Le Doloff et ses Bourbas," and Monteil, "Le Dyolof et Al-Bouri Ndiaye."

25. The ships with all-male cargoes were both named the *Esther*, one owned by Kingsley and flying a U.S. flag, the other under the flag of Denmark. For Wright's departure from Charleston see *Charleston Courier*, August 11, 1806. See also McMillin, *Final Victims*, 67, 99–100. For Kingsley and the *Esther* in Havana see *Charleston Courier*, September 23, 1806, and Captain Henry Wright, October 21, 1806, R133, Section 70, and October 24, 1806, R166, Section 85, EFP. For ships and slave cargoes arriving at Havana see the exceedingly important database in H. S. Klein, "Slave Trade to Havana."

26. Ship manifest declared at the U.S. Consulate, Havana, Cuba, October 10, 1806, in R97 B231 J18 and R172 B231 N21, EFP.

27. Manumission of Anna Kingsley, March 4, 1811, R172, B376, EFP. Translation by James Donlan.

28. The essay first appeared in the journal as Letter XXIII (July 7, 1842) of "Letters from New-York" and was published in 1843 as a book with the same title. See Child, *Letters from New-York*, from Letter XXIII (July 7, 1842), 96–102.

29. Probate file 1203, ZK, DCC.

30. Benjamin, "The Sea Islands," 844. For Kingsley legends see Corse, *The Key to the Golden Islands*; Dodge, "An Island by the Sea"; Benjamin, "The Sea Islands"; May, "Zephaniah Kingsley, Nonconformist"; C. E. Bennett, "Zephaniah Kingsley, Jr."; and Cabell and Hanna, *The St. Johns*, 160–73. Kingsley's description of Anna Jai is in Child, *Letters from New-York*, 98.

The most recent fantasy legend posits Kingsley in 1804 searching for a wife using services of an African matchmaker residing on Pongo River in today's Republic of Guinea. It also claims that Anta Ndiaye was brought to Pongo River, trained for hostess duties in Florida, married to Kingsley, and transported later to join her husband at Havana, presumably for a belated honeymoon cruise to Florida. See Wu, "Manumission of Anna." For a more realistic understanding of the Pongo River slave traders and their families see the exhaustively researched and definitive study by Bruce L. Mouser, *American Colony in the Rio Pongo*.

31. Claim of ZK, PWC, and Superior and Circuit Court Records, Box 131, Folder 16, SAHSRL.

32. For the homestead see Claim of Anna Madgigine alias Kingsley, Box 20, File K-9, PWC.

33. The most insightful study is Landers, *Black Society in Spanish Florida*.

34. For examples of black overseers see Schafer, "'A Swamp of an Investment'?" For Gibbs's efforts to hire a manager see Gibbs to Hamilton, November 4, December 27, 1805, and January 18, 1806, JHP.

35. ZK to Richard Carnochan, February 24, 1807, JHP. The cotton was consigned to Benjamin Gray of Liverpool. ZK to JH, May 24, 1807, JHP. For arrival of the *Zibra* (possibly *Libra*) at St. Thomas, see RA, Protocol over andomne reisende fra 3 Marts 1805 tdil Marts 1810, St. Thomas, DNA. I am again indebted to Dr. Svend Holsoe for sending a photocopy of this document. For Kingsley's arrival at Amelia Island in command of the *San Juan* (aka the *Welaka*), see Justo Lopez to Enrique White, March 24, 1808, R59, Section 32, EFP. For failed efforts to hire a white overseer for Laurel Grove see ZK to JH, January 10, George Gibbs to JH, February 17, 1808, and ZK to Richard Carnochan, May 4, 1808, all in JHP.

36. Account of all Foreign Vessels Clearing Outwards, Naval Office, Saint Thomas, from June 10, 1808, to December 30, 1808, Inclusive. Colonial Office 259/2. Copy at NARA-CP.

37. See Bolster, *Black Jacks*.

38. For further detail see Schafer, *Anna Madgigine Jai Kingsley*, chapter 4.

39. For the consular reports see RG 59, Consular Despatches from United States Consuls in Havana, 1793–1906, M 899, Roll 1, December 1, 1783–October 2, 1807: October 16, December 20, 1803, February 11, April 10, 28, 1804, NARA-CP.

Chapter 7. Laurel Grove Plantation, Slavery, and East Florida's Booming Economy

1. Documentation exists for imports of seventy-four slaves, but witnesses stated that Kingsley had eighty to one hundred "fully taskable hands" plus children and others unable to work.

2. The incident is documented in R125 B28902 document 1810, no. 4, EFP.

3. Ibid., Testimony of George Cook, July 19, 1810.

4. Ibid., Testimony of Andrew Maclean, July 19, 1810.

5. Ibid., Craig to White, June 22, 1810.

6. Ibid.

7. Ibid., June 23, 1810.

8. Ibid., Testimony of Abraham Hanahan, not dated.

9. Ibid., Tribunal to Gov. White, July 31, 1810.

10. Landers, *Black Society*, 207–9, 217, 220.

11. Ibid., 24–30, 76–80.

12. Landers, "Rebellion and Royalism." See also Landers, *Atlantic Creoles*, chapter 2; Geggus, "Slavery, War and Revolution"; Sidbury, "Saint Domingue in Virginia."

13. See M. Mullin, *Africa in America*, chapter 9; G. W. Mullin, *Flight and Rebellion*, 140–63; Chaplin, *Anxious Pursuit*, chapter 8; Kulikoff, "Uprooted Peoples"; P. Morgan, "Black Society in the Lowcountry."

14. Cusick, "East Florida Papers Oaths of Allegiance."

15. Schafer, "'A Class of People Neither Freemen nor Slaves'" and "Family Ties That Bind." See also Parker, "Men without God or King," and Weber, *The Spanish Frontier*, 265–301.

16. Cusick, *The Other War of 1812*, chapter 3, and Weber, *The Spanish Frontier*, chapter 10.

17. Kingsley's Patriot War claim identifies the manager as John Ashton.

18. Ibid. See also Patriot War claim of Abraham Hanahan, Box 124, Folder 24, Superior Court Files, SAHSRL. During the Patriot insurgency of 1812–14, Hanahan was taken prisoner by U.S. troops and put to work as a river pilot. In 1816 he received a land grant of fifty acres near Buena Vista. See also WPA, *Spanish Land Grants*, Confirmed Claims, vol. 4, 279.

19. Records of the Superior Court, District of Northern Florida, SAHSRL; and Case of ZK, MC31, PWC, SAHSRL; "Petition to Honorable Raymond Reid, Judge of the Superior Court," Superior Court Files, Box 131, Folder 16, SAHSRL; Claim of ZK, Account no. 88415, RG 217, EFC. See also Cusick, *The Other War of 1812*.

20. "Petition to Honorable Raymond Reid." See also Account no. 88415, Claim of Zephaniah Kingsley, RG 217, NARA-CP.

21. Pesos and dollars were then equal in value; one pound British sterling was worth 4.4 pesos. My study of prices in newspapers and probate records led to the conclusion that $1 in 1812 equals $30 to $35 today. Derks, "Composite Commodity Price Index," 2, values $1 U.S. in 1860 at $30.838 in 1989.

22. J. Bartram, "Diary of a Journey"; W. Bartram, *Travels*; and Schafer, *William Bartram*, chapter 1.

23. See Original Spanish Land Grant Files, John H. McIntosh, RG 599, FSA.

24. See Thornton, *Africa and Africans*, 72–97, and P. Morgan, "Cultural Implications of the Atlantic Slave Trade."

25. Berlin and Morgan, *Cultivation and Culture*, 1–45, and Campbell, "As 'A Kind of Freeman.'"

26. In *Treatise on the Patriarchal*, note 13, Kingsley says that many of his slaves came from Africa. I thank George E. Brooks for the personal correspondence (August 1, 1998) on Cabo Mouse. See also Brooks's recent book which combines many of his important contributions: *Western Africa and Cabo Verde*.

27. A Kenyan living in Miami, identified M'Sooma. I am indebted to Dr. Svend E. Holsoe for conducting the interview.

28. The census can be seen at the P. K. Yonge Library.

29. See Weber, *The Spanish Frontier*, chapter 12.

30. Landers, *Black Society*; Cusick, *The Other War of 1812*; Marotti, "Negotiating Freedom." See also Marotti, *The Cana Sanctuary* and *Heaven's Soldiers*. I thank Dr.

Marotti for sending a copy of his doctoral dissertation. It became my invaluable research guide at the National Archives.

31. Hoffman, *Florida's Frontiers*, 207–42.

32. For McIntosh see Claim of John H. McIntosh, Account no. 85731, RG 217, EFC, and Claim of John H. McIntosh, MC31, PWC.

33. Claim of Spicer Christopher, Account no. 84647, and Claim of Lewis Christopher, Account no. 86381, RG 217, EFC. For the 1811 inventory see Spicer Christopher testamentary proceedings, July 14, 1811, R143, Section 71, EFP. See also Cusick, "East Florida Papers Oaths of Allegiance." The deathbed inventory was by Spanish soldiers pursuing Spicer Christopher Jr., charged with shooting and wounding a postal agent. See Romero to Governor White, February 4, 1811, R126, Section 65, EFP.

34. Kingsley's remarks are in Claim of Philip Dewees, Account no. 80150, RG 217, EFC.

35. Landers, *Black Society*, 171–72, and Landers, "Francisco Xavier Sánchez." See also Claim of Francis X. Sanchez, Account no. 74969, RG 217, EFC. For Fatio see Parker, "Success through Diversification."

36. Holcomb, *South Carolina Naturalizations*, 93; and Court of Admiralty for the District of South Carolina, Microfilm 1183, Roll 1, p. 11, NARA-CP. Phenda, formerly married to Thomas Hughes Jackson, was widowed in 1798. See WPA, *Spanish Land Grants*, Unconfirmed Claims, vol. 1, 119, and Confirmed Claims, vol. 3, 141–45. Bruce L. Mouser, whose research is essential for this region of West Africa, believes that Phenda was Baga or Susu, which would have given Fraser a family connection for local trade. See Mouser, "Trade and Politics in the Nunez and Pongo," "Trade, Coasters, and Conflict," and "Landlords-Strangers." See also Schafer, "Family Ties That Bind," and Robertson versus Yonge and Kingsley, Records of the Superior Court of East Florida, Box 156, File 59, SAHSRL; Thomas Napier Papers, SCL; and Claim of John Fraser, Account no. 85766, RG 217, EFC. For the possibility that Kingsley purchased slaves at Bangalan see Griffin, *Odyssey of an African Slave*, 17, 31.

37. Charleston merchant Paul Cross recorded purchases of slaves, ivory, and gold in the Rio Pongo vicinity circa 1780. See Paul Cross (d. 1784) Papers, SCL. Irving is mentioned often in the Napier Papers. See also Thomas Powell to Governor Zespedes, R15 B37, EFP. R81, B133 and B134, are especially useful for ship "naturalizations." See also Fyfe, *History of Sierra Leone*, 61, 203. For the final months of slave imports at Charleston, see Stevens, "'To get as many slaves as you can,'" 187–96, and advertisements in the *Charleston Courier*, 1803–8.

38. WPA, *Spanish Land Grants*, Unconfirmed Claims, vol. 1, 119, and Confirmed Claims, vol. 3, 141–45. For names of ships and owners see List of ship owners, 1808, R84, Section 45, EFP.

39. Claim of John Fraser, MC31, PWC. See also Robertson versus Yonge and Kingsley, Records of the Superior Court of East Florida, Box 156, File 59, SAHSRL, and Thomas Napier Papers, SCL.

40. Claim of John Fraser, Account no. 85766, RG 217, EFC.

41. Ibid. The amended claim for Greenfield and Roundabout was for $291,284; the amount awarded was $157,146 (54 percent).

42. For Fraser see Schafer, "Family Ties That Bind."

43. Paquette, *Sugar Is Made with Blood*, 105.

Chapter 8. "Left by the Patriots a Perfect Desert"

1. The first quote is from ZK to Hernandez, June 21, 1817, JHP. The second is Kingsley's testimony in United States v. Ferreira, printed in Senate Miscellaneous Document, No. 55, 36th Congress, 1st sess. (1859–1860), page 24.

2. The definitive study of the Patriot War is Cusick, *The Other War of 1812*. See also Landers, *Atlantic Creoles*, 110–19, and Owsley and Smith, *Filibusters and Expansionists*, 61–81.

3. Weber, *The Spanish Frontier*, 281, 297–98. See also Joslin, *West Florida Controversy*, 388–403, and McAlister, "Pensacola during the Second Spanish Period."

4. Unless otherwise noted, discussion of the Patriot War in this chapter is based on Cusick, *The Other War of 1812*.

5. Kingsley's account is from his testimony in Claim of Philip Dewees, Account no. 80150, RG 217, EFC; and *United States Appellants v. Francis P. Ferreira, Administrator of Francis Pass, Deceased*, Supreme Court of the United States No. 197, Senate Misc. Document No. 55, 36th Congress, First Session (Washington, D.C.: George W. Bowman, 1860).

Cusick, *The Other War of 1812*, 161–62, and 331 n. 45, identifies the Patriot campsite as the residence at William Craig's plantation. He also gives April 5 as the date for the encounter, which I believe is a mistake. Kingsley gave several accounts of the incident, each with slightly different details. Claims of James Cashen and Francis Philip Fatio Sr., Account nos. 82920 and 76455, RG 217, EFC.

6. Cusick, *The Other War of 1812*, 141–52.

7. ZK to JH, April 1, 1812, JHP.

8. Kingsley lost forty-one men, women, and children at Laurel Grove and two men at Drayton Island.

9. ZK to JH, August 12, 1812, JHP.

10. Cusick, *The Other War of 1812*, 222, 339 nn. 32 and 33. See also Claim of ZK, Account no. 88415, RG 217, EFC, and Abraham Hanahan, Box 124, File 24, Records of the Superior Court of East Florida, SAHSRL.

11. Newnan to Smith, October 11, 13, 1812, and John Floyd to Smith, October 25, 1812, Letterbook of Thomas Adams Smith, 1812–1837, Western Historical Manuscript Collection, 1029, State Historical Society of Missouri. From Thomas Adams Smith (1781–1864) Papers (1798–1864), Microfilm copy at PKY. The letters were written at Laurel Grove Plantation.

12. Smith to ZK, February 2, 1813, Smith Letterbook, from Cusick, *The Other War of 1812*, 342 n. 37.

13. The petition was dated April 9, 1813. The wording and sentiment concerning the

Spanish free black militia seems out of character for Kingsley. Self-preservation, especially from threats by Patriot rebels, may have been his motive. See Cusick, *The Other War of 1812*, 260–61, and 343 n. 5, for first quote, and 263, and 343 n. 9 for the second.

14. For examples of destruction see Claim of Farquhar Bethune, Account no. 73008, RG 217, EFC. See also Claims of Farquhar Bethune and Andrew Atkinson, MC31, PWC, especially the testimony of Joseph Simeon Sanchez in the Bethune claim.

15. Atkinson to Kindelán, October 18, 1813, enclosing Buckner Harris to Captain Andrew Atkinson, R62 B149 F12, EFP.

16. Llorente to governor, November 5, 8, 12, 1813, R12, Section 2, and R62, Section 32, and Llorente to governor, March 15, 1814, R62, Section 32, all EFP.

17. ZK to Governor Kindelán, November 25, 1813, Fernandina, from Papeles de Cuba 1790, Archivo General de Indias, Seville, Spain. I thank Jane Landers for sending a copy of this document.

18. Ibid.

19. Ibid.

20. Ibid. For the rejection see William Lawrence to Governor, December 2, 1813, and Kindelán to Apodaca, November 28, 1813, both in R62, Section 32, EFP.

21. Cusick, *The Other War of 1812*, 286. The account that follows is from Schafer, *Anna Madgigine Jai Kingsley*, chapter 4.

22. For the site of Anna Jai's homestead see Schafer, *Anna Madgigine Jai Kingsley*, 35–37. See also Claim of Anna Madgigine alias Kingsley, File 58, MC 31, PWC 1812–1846.

23. Reports of Thomas Llorente (October 25, November 24, 26, 27, December 13, 17), R62, Section 32, EFP.

24. Moreno to Llorente, November 24, 1813, enclosed in Llorente to Kindelán, November 26, 1813, R62, Section 32, EFP. Unless otherwise noted, remaining quotations in this section come from this source.

25. Llorente to Kindelán, November 26, 27, 30, December 13, 17, 1813, all R62, Section 32, EFP.

26. Llorente to Kindelán, December 13, 17, 1813, R62, Section 32, EFP.

27. Ibid., December 13 and 17, 1813.

28. For McIntosh to Madison and Monroe see Cusick, *The Other War of 1812*, 213, 247, 262–63. For McIntosh's views on amnesty and the sale of Fort George Island see "Communication," *National Intelligencer*, July 2, 1823, Washington, D.C. For sale of Fort George Island see Clarke to McIntosh, January 23, 1817, R166, Section 81, and R174, Section 92, EFP. See also Patrick, *Florida Fiasco*, 56–57, 259–68, 300–302; Wildes, "The McIntosh Family." Kingsley purchased Fort George for $7,000 in 1817. McIntosh returned to Florida, and the U.S. Treasury awarded his heirs $127,580 for property damages.

29. "Case of John H. McIntosh," Patriot War Claims, U.S. Treasury Department Records, FSA. McIntosh said that "every building except the dwelling house" was burned and that even the locks on the doors of the dwelling were stolen.

30. See correspondence between Llorente and Kindelán in February 1814, R62, Sec-

tion 32, and Navarro to Governor, May 2, 24, 1814, R75, Section 40, EFP. For the launch see Navarro to Governor, October 1, 1814, R75, Section 40, EFP.

Chapter 9. "Like a Turtle without a Shell"

1. Kindelán to Apodaca, August 20, September 23, 1814, R12, Section 2, EFP. See Cusick, *The Other War of 1812*, 287–91, for the Harris-led invasion of Alachua.

2. The Prosecution of Zephaniah Kingsley for Wounding Pilot Genaro Gray, November 26, 1814, R126, Section 65, EFP. I thank Manuel Lebron, a descendant of Zephaniah Kingsley and Anna Kingsley, for translating this long file. For the *Providencia* see Kingsley to Governor, December 19, 1815, R150, Section 76, EFP.

3. For conflict between Ribera and Fernandina merchants see Carlos Seton to Governor, December 23, 27, 1814, R65, Section 34; Kindelán's response is in December 12, 1814, R12, Section 34; Ribera's refusal to surrender command is in Puente to Governor, December 31, 1814, R65, Section 34, all in EFP.

4. Morriss, *Cockburn and the British Navy*, 115–20; Bartlett and Smith, "A 'Species of Milito-Nautico-guerilla-plundering warfare.'"

5. Bullard, *Cumberland Island* and *Black Liberation on Cumberland Island*. See also Hickey, *The War of 1812*, 281–99.

6. The eighteen hundred liberated includes deaths after arrival. See Morriss, *Cockburn and the British Navy*, 116–20.

7. Brabo to Governor, January 26, February 3, 1815, R165, Section 81; Pangua to Governor, June 24, 1815, R165, Section 68; Kindelán to Apodaca, February 5, 1815, R13, Section 2; Juan Jose de Estrada to Juan Ruiz de Apodaca, December 22, 1815, R13, Section 2; all EFP.

8. For detailed discussion of John Fraser and his African family, and Kingsley's involvement in his probate estate, see Schafer, "Family Ties That Bind."

9. Fraser to Governor, September 2, 1813, R62, Section 2, and Apodaca to Governor of East Florida, February 8, 1814, R5, Section 1, both EFP. John Couper rented the slaves.

10. ZK, *Treatise on the Patriarchal*, from Stowell, *Balancing Evils Judiciously*, 63 n. 6.

11. Kingsley to Kindelán, January 23, 1815, R165, Section 81, and January 26, 1815, R174, Section 92; Kindelán to Cockburn, January 31, 1815, R174, Section 192; Cockburn to Kindelán, February 13, 1815, R174, Section 92; all in EFP.

12. See correspondence between Kingsley and Governor Coppinger in John Fraser testamentary proceedings, February 15, 1814, R145, Section 71, EFP.

13. Ibid., Fraser testamentary proceedings. For Kingsley's desire to protect the inheritance rights of Fraser's widow and children and his willingness to defend his own honorable intentions, see ZK to Hernandez, January 16, 19, 28, 30, 1821, BSP.

14. ZK to Hernandez, June 16, 1815, BSP. In 1815, ninety slaves escaped from Mosquito Inlet to Apalache. See Kindelán to Apodaca, February 22, 1815, R13, Section 2, EFP.

15. For weapons distributed at Apalachicola, see Owsley and Smith, *Filibusters and*

Expansionists, 103–17 and 210 n. 5. See also Landers, "Slave Resistance," and Mulroy, *Freedom on the Border*.

16. Covington, "Negro Fort"; Owsley and Smith, *Filibusters and Expansionists*, 103–17; Boyd, "Events at Prospect Bluff"; Patrick, *Aristocrat in Uniform*, 24–36.

17. ZK to Hernandez, Amelia, June 16, 1815, BSP.

18. Ibid.

19. ZK to Mitchell, September 13, 1816, Telamon Cuylor Collection, Hargrett Rare Book and Manuscript Libraries, University of Georgia Libraries, Athens. I thank Jim Vearil for bringing this letter to my attention.

20. Ibid. See also John Whitehead to Mitchell, February 12, and William Gibson to Mitchell, September 7, 1816, both in Cuylor Collection.

21. Doyle to John Innerarity, Prospect Bluff, January 28, 1817, in Boyd, "The Panton, Leslie Papers," 313. Panton and Leslie Co. operated three trade stores on the Apalachicola. See also Hawkins to Peter Early, December 13, 1814, Cuylor Collection.

22. Owsley and Smith, *Filibusters and Expansionists*, 141–63; Mahon and Weisman, "Florida's Seminole and Miccosukee Peoples"; Knetsch, *Florida's Seminole Wars*, 21–41. See also J. L. Wright, "A Note on the First Seminole War.."

23. See Adams to Jackson, April 2, 1821, in Moser et al., *Papers of Andrew Jackson*, 5:25–26. See also C. Brown, "Tales of Angola," 11.

24. The two men had a close working relationship and were related by marriage: Jane "Ahkohkee" McIntosh married William Simpson Mitchell. First quote is from Carrier, "Black Seminoles, Maroons and Freedom Seekers," 1; second quote is from C. Brown, "Tales of Angola," 11.

25. Child, "Letters from New York.—No. 30," from Stowell, *Balancing Evils Judiciously*, 111.

26. Landers, *Black Society*, 70–71; Parker, "Men without God or King." See also Corbitt, "'The Return of Spanish Rule," 47–48, and Hill, "George J. F. Clarke."

27. Hill, "George J. F. Clarke"; Coppinger to Morales, November 7, 1816, R65, Section 34, and Coppinger to Clarke, April 30, 1820, R63, Section 32, EFP.

28. Charles Seton and George J. F. Clarke to Coppinger, July 22, 1816, enclosed in Coppinger to Jose Cienfuegos, July 22, 1816, R13, Section 2, EFP.

29. ZK to Hernandez, June 21, 1817, BSP.

30. Ibid.

31. Ibid. Support for Coppinger is in Bushnell, *La República de las Floridas*, 7–18.

32. ZK to Hernandez, June 21, 1817, BSP.

33. Ibid.; see also Lowe, "American Seizure"; Owsley and Smith, *Filibusters and Expansionists*, 118–40; and Heckard, "The Crossroads of Empire." I thank Professor Philip M. Smith for sending a copy of the latter.

34. T. F. Davis, *MacGregor's Invasion*. For Mitchell's dismissal see African Case Proceedings, 1818–1821, Ad Hoc Collection: 00864, 00865, 00866 Georgia State Archives, Morrow. Accessible also via Georgia's Virtual Vault: http://cdm.sos.state.ga.us/ or by http://cdm.sos.state.ga.us/cdm4/search.php?cisoroot+all.

35. Lowe, "American Seizure," 23.

36. P. C. Brooks, *Diplomacy and the Borderlands.*

37. For the rumors see Schafer, *Anna Madgigine Jai Kingsley*. Coppinger suspected that Kingsley and other St. Johns River planters purchased slaves from the pirates. See Coppinger to Jorge Clarke, May 13, 1819, R63, Section 32, EFP.

38. ZK to Hernandez, January 16, March 30, 1821, BSP.

Chapter 10. "Discreetly Restrained under the Patriarchal System"

1. Kingsley also owned town and water lots at Fernandina and St. Marys, Georgia, and a town lot and a small tract on Maria Sanchez Creek at St. Augustine. See SPLG, Confirmed and Unconfirmed volumes, FSA; Archibald Abstracts of Deeds, DCC, and deed records at Clay, St. Johns, Nassau, and Putnam Counties in the respective county courthouses. See also the executor's annual reports to the probate judge, Probate file 1203, ZK, DCC.

In 1832 Zephaniah owned 6,300 taxable acres of land in St. Johns County. In 1845 and 1846 executors of his estate claimed 7,043 acres in the same county. By the mid-1830s he had sold his Nassau County real estate. See also county tax rolls at Florida Library, FSA.

2. ZK, *Treatise on the Patriarchal*. Kingsley's eighteen-page booklet was first published in 1828, with revised editions appearing in 1829, 1833, and 1834. Throughout this work I have relied on Stowell, *Balancing Evils Judiciously*.

Kingsley received a 16,000-acre land grant in 1816 from Governor Coppinger in return for promised construction of a water-powered sawmill on McGirt's Creek. The bounds of the property were Doctors Lake on the south, John H. McIntosh's Ortega property on the north, and extending west from Kingsley's Laurel Grove Plantation to encompass a tract of five square miles (16,000 acres) that included today's Kingsley Lake. Kingsley testified that he began constructing the dam for the mill pond but that unsettled conditions in the province in 1816 forced him to discontinue the project temporarily. The U.S. government rejected the claim. See U.S. v Kingsley, 37 U.S. 476: Volume 37, 1838, or Justia.com: US Supreme Court Center, http://supreme.justia.com/us/37/476/case.html. I thank Dr. Frank Marotti for sending me a photocopy of the complete file.

3. There were no interior stairways to the second story. Stowell, *Timucuan Ecological and Historic Preserve*, 67–78; Wood, *Jacksonville's Architectural Heritage*, 309–23. For McQueen see McQueen, *Letters of Don Juan McQueen*. Hanna B. P. Rollins's observations are from "Ft. George Island," an undated manuscript written circa 1904, Kingsley Plantation Office. See also Wilson, "Notes Concerning the Old Plantation." A special thank-you to Carol Davis Clark.

4. Spalding's essays are in *Southern Agriculturalist*, for example, December 1830, Part I, 617–23. Janet Gritzner has argued that the tabby tradition originated in Senegal: "Tabby in the Colonial Southeast." While traveling in Senegal, I viewed ancient tabby structures between Dakar and Portudal.

5. Wood, *Jacksonville's Architectural Heritage*, 318. See also Vlach, "Not Mansions."

6. ZK, *Treatise on the Patriarchal*, from Stowell, *Balancing Evils Judiciously*, 50, 69–70.

7. Description of the gardens and fruit trees is from Wilson, "Notes Concerning the Old Plantation." See also Benjamin, "The Sea Islands," and Rollins, "Ft. George Island," Olin Library, Rollins College, Winter Park, Florida.

8. Stowell, *Timucuan Ecological and Historic Preserve*, 73.

9. Diop, "Traite Négrière" and "Les villages désertés du Sénégal."

10. I am grateful to Dr. Sidi Camara of the Ministry of Education, Senegal, for these observations, for assistance with the Anna Kingsley in Senegal Conference in March 2000, and for initiating correspondence with the former president of Senegal, Abdou Diouf.

11. Fretwell, *Kingsley Beatty Gibbs and His Journal*. For temporary slave housing see Schafer, *Governor James Grant's Villa* and "'Yellow Silk Ferret Tied Round Their Wrists.'"

12. J. L. Williams, *Territory of Florida*, 44, 57, 135–36, 195–96.

13. Baptist, *Creating an Old South*, 20–21; Siebert, "The Early Sugar Industry"; Schafer, "'A Swamp of an Investment'?" See also Schene, "Robert and John Grattan Gamble"; Paisley, *Red Hills of Florida*; Wayne, *Sweet Cane*.

14. Gibbs's statement was in *East Florida Herald* (St. Augustine), March 23, 1823. William Carnochan was the owner of "The Thicket," a major sugar plantation and rum distillery.

15. Z. Kingsley Jr., "Process of Manufacturing." The Marquis had plantations on Halifax River and Black Creek. See Wayne, *Sweet Cane*, 66–67; Hooper, *Early History of Clay County*, 106, 123, 219–20, 263.

16. At Fort George Island, archaeologist James Davidson recently uncovered remains of an octagonal tabby foundation.

17. Labor routine is based on journals of Farquhar Bethune and Kingsley Beatty Gibbs. See also Wayne, *Sweet Cane*; Follett, *Sugar Masters*, 4–22; and Sitterson, "Ante-Bellum Sugar Culture" and "Financing and Marketing."

18. Schene, "Sugar along the Manatee" and "Robert and John Grattan Gamble."

19. Claim of Jermyn Wright, Parliamentary Claims Commission: East Florida, Treasury 77, Piece 18, Folio 14, National Archives, Kew, England. Jermyn Wright migrated to South Carolina in 1729. His brother, Sir James Wright, was twice appointed royal governor of Georgia.

20. Zephaniah Kingsley, Land Claims, Box 18, 19, and 20, Confirmed Claims, SPLG, FSA (online at *Florida Memory*). The smaller tracts were purchased from Burrows Higginbotham, James Martinelly, Robert Hutchinson, and William Hobkirk.

21. Claim of John Fraser, Account no. 85766, RG 217, EFC.

22. Bill of Sale, January 18, 1818, Probate of Samuel Gale, Charleston, SCDAH. Carney, *Black Rice*; Coclanis, *Shadow of a Dream*; Littlefield, *Rice and Slavery*; P. D. Morgan, *Slave Counterpoint*; Chaplin, *Anxious Pursuit*.

23. ZK to Hernandez, January 16, 1821, BSP; *City Gazette and Commercial Daily Advertiser* (Charleston), November 24, 28, December 26, 1821.

24. J. L. Williams, *Territory of Florida*, 135–36.

25. Sammis was wed to Mary, second daughter of Anna Jai and Kingsley. The 1840 U.S. Census of Duval County lists Sammis and Mary Kingsley living with five "free-colored" children, and Sammis as the owner of thirty-six slaves. See also David H. Burr's April 5, 1850, re-survey of the original lines marked for Kingsley's White Oak Plantation in 1826, in Township Maps, Surveyor Field Notes, Township 4 North, Range 25 & 26 East, pages 102–5, FSA. The originals are in 49/9.7, Records of Florida Land Offices, Records of the Bureau of Land Management, RG 49, 1685–1993. NARA-CP. http://data.labins.org/surveydata/landrecords/GLO/search.cfm.

I first viewed the tabby ruins in the early 1980s courtesy of Mr. Wallace Prince, superintendent. I thank Mr. John Lukas, superintendent of White Oak Plantation and president of the White Oak Conservation Center, for many subsequent visits.

26. The foundation, platforms, and pillars still stand.

27. Early maps show a run of water close to the east wall of the mill. It appears too small to power a rice mill.

28. Mr. Wallace Prince said the tabby dwellings were bulldozed to clear the site for a home for Sondra and Charles Gilman Jr. Charles Gilman, president of the Gilman Paper Company from 1967 to 1982, purchased White Oak in the 1960s and chose the site to take advantage of the river view, the constant breezes from the east, and the near absence of mosquitoes. The house was recently demolished and replaced by an open-air pavilion and boat dock. In a September 2011 telephone conversation, Sondra Gilman said she did not see ruins of buildings at the site prior to building the home she designed.

29. The Horace S. Pratt Estate, Inventory and Appraisal of Estates, 1831–1867, Book A, 56–57, 197–98, 237–40, 274, 282–83, Camden County Courthouse. See also the Nassau County censuses for 1840 and 1850 and tax roll data for the years 1845–56. The plantation agent was C. M. Caldwell of St. Marys, Georgia.

30. Fretwell, *Kingsley Beatty Gibbs and His Journal*. The summary of labor tasks is based on three years of Gibbs's entries, supplemented by the more complete journal recorded in 1830–33 by St. Johns River planter Farquhar Bethune. Florida Historical Society Library, Cocoa, Florida.

31. Berlin and Morgan, *Cultivation and Culture*, 15. See also P. D. Morgan, "Task and Gang Systems."

32. ZK, *Treatise on the Patriarchal*, from Stowell, *Balancing Evils Judiciously*, 42, 71–72.

Chapter 11. "The Door of Liberty Is Open to Every Slave Who Can Find the Means of Purchasing Himself"

1. ZK, *Treatise on the Patriarchal*, from Stowell, *Balancing Evils Judiciously*, 41–43.

2. Landers, *Black Society*, 214–20.

3. Ibid., 149–58, and Chappell, "A Report on the Documentation." There is now an expansive scholarship on this subject. The most relevant are Landers, *Black Society*; Berlin, *Slaves without Masters*; Tannenbaum, *Slave and Citizen*; H. S. Klein, *Slavery in the Americas*; Cohen and Greene, *Neither Slave Nor Free*; Foner, "The Free People of Color"; M. Harris, *Patterns of Race in the Americas*; Fields, *Slavery and Freedom on the Middle Ground*; Knight, *Slave Society in Cuba*; Genovese, *Roll, Jordan, Roll*; Degler, *Neither White Nor Black*.

4. Stowell, *Balancing Evils Judiciously*, 6.

5. Ibid. See also Schafer, "'A Class of People Neither Freemen Nor Slaves'"; C. Brown, "Race Relations in Territorial Florida"; Garvin, "The Free Negro in Florida"; T. Bates, "The Legal Status"; J. J. Jackson, "The Negro and the Law"; Morris and Maguire, "Beginnings of Popular Government"; Martin, *Florida during the Territorial Days*, 25–47; W. G. Davis, "The Florida Legislative Council, 1822–1838"; Lisenby, "The Free Negro in Antebellum Florida"; May, "Zephaniah Kingsley, Nonconformist"; C. E. Bennett, "Zephaniah Kingsley, Jr."

6. L. A. Thompson, *Florida Laws, Statutes*, 533; J. F. Smith, *Slavery and Plantation Growth*, 119–21; Ellsworth and Ellsworth, *Pensacola*, 45–46; Barr and Hargis, "The Voluntary Exile." The 1845 census of St. Johns County was reported in the *St. Augustine News*, February 27, 1846.

7. *East Florida Herald* (St. Augustine), October 23, 1824.

8. Ibid., November 20, 1824.

9. Ibid., March 25, 1829; James F. Clarke v. Francis J. Avice, Records of the Superior Court, St. Johns County, 1829, Box 129, File 103, SAHSRL; and Martin, *Florida during Territorial Days*. See also George W. Clarke v. State of Florida, January 12, 1846, Records of the Circuit Court, St. Johns County, Box 98, File 58, SAHSRL.

10. ZK, "Address," from Stowell, *Balancing Evils Judiciously*, 27–35.

11. Ibid., 39–75. See also Genovese, "Foreword," in ibid., xi–xiii.

12. Ibid., 28–29.

13. ZK, *Treatise on the Patriarchal*, from Stowell, *Balancing Evils Judiciously*, 44–45; *East Florida Herald* (St. Augustine), June 7, 1823.

14. Carter, *Territorial Papers*, 3:800–802.

15. Ibid.

16. Manuscript returns of the Fifth, Sixth, Seventh, and Eighth United States Census (1830–1860), Clay, Duval, Nassau, and St. Johns Counties (population schedules: free and slave). Clay County split off from Duval in 1858.

17. Ibid. Total population of these counties increased from 6,019 to 13,722, while the free black population only increased from 304 to 308. Free black percentage of total population declined from 5 to 2 percent. Slave percentages also declined, from 47 to 38 percent, as whites in the region increased from a minority status in 1830 to 60 percent of the population in 1860.

18. For examples see Probate files 1203, ZK, and 1205, George Kingsley, DCC; Deed Book B, page 93, Book F, page 324, and Book I-J, 328, SJCC. See Puig Ortiz, *Emigracion*,

32, 53, 117–18. For Richard's August 19, 1837, will see Probate 1756, DCC. Richard's free black mistress, Teresa, their children Lewis, Michael, and Christiana, along with Josephine (all named in his will), migrated to Puerto Plata, Dominican Republic. See also *Florida News*, December 19, 1845, March 5, 1847; Schafer, "Freedom was as Close as the River."

19. Probate file 850, Joshua Hickman, DCC (August 29, 1837). For sale of Tena see *Florida Republican*, January 3, 1850.

20. Probate files 79 and 853, DCC.

21. Hill, "George J. F. Clarke."

22. For the Clarke family see Marotti, "Negotiating Freedom"; George Clarke, biographical folder, SAHSRL; PWC, MC 31, Folder 48, SAHSRL.

23. See St. Johns County Censuses, 1830–1860, for the Clarke family.

24. ZK, *Treatise on the Patriarchal*, from Stowell, *Balancing Evils Judiciously*, 69–70.

25. For a possible model see ZK's remarks concerning a South Carolina planter who divided slaves among several plantations where "all the cotton raised . . . belonged to the owner" and "all the hogs, corn, and provisions . . . belonged to the negroes, who might do with it as they pleased." Ibid., 71–72.

26. For China oranges see *St. Augustine News*, May 22, 1834; Mintz, "Slavery and the Rise of Peasantries" and "From Plantations to Peasantries in the Caribbean"; Cratan, *Empire, Enslavement*, 282–305.

27. *Jacksonville Courier*, December 17, 1835.

28. *East Florida Herald* (St. Augustine), June 22, 1837. I thank Mark Little for bringing this source to my attention.

29. *Southern Patriot* (Charleston), July 22, 1839. Sammis traveled to Drayton Island until 1848. See Probate file 1205, George Kingsley, DCC.

30. St. Johns County Deed Record, ZK to George Kingsley, December 20, 1832. Record of orange exports is in Probate file 1205, George Kingsley, DCC.

31. The Kingsley estate at Mayorasgo de Koka on the north shore of Haiti (now the Dominican Republic) is discussed in chapter 14.

32. Probate file 1205, George Kingsley, DCC. The mother's objection is part of the family legend told to the author at Puerto Plata, Dominican Republic, by descendants and local historians Nate Finke and Pablo Brugal.

33. See Deed Book, SJCC, December 21, 1832. Also recorded in Book of Conveyances, No. 32, February 1894 to December 1894, Office of Circuit Court, Putnam County Court House, Palatka, Florida.

34. ZK, *Treatise on the Patriarchal*, from Stowell, *Balancing Evils Judiciously*, 70–71.

35. Ibid., 53.

Chapter 12. "In Trust for Flora Hanahan Kingsley and Her Son Charles"

1. For Wolof culture and polygamous marriage patterns see Schafer, *Anna Madgigine Jai Kingsley*. For a contrary interpretation see Fleszar, "The Atlantic Mind."

2. In a clumsy attempt to define Kingsley's sexual and family unions, I drew on R. T.

Smith, "The Matrifocal Family," 121–44, and Soliene de González, "The Consanguineal Household and Matrifocality."

3. Deed to Deep Creek Plantation, Deed Book K, SJCC. See also Will, Probate file 1203, ZK, DCC.

4. Child, "Letters from New York," from Stowell, *Balancing Evils Judiciously*, 109. Mary Kingsley, daughter of Anna Jai, wife of Sammis, testified that her daily routine was to check the workers' health every day, presumably following her mother's practices.

5. See Will, 1860, Probate file 1210, Anna Kingsley, DCC, and census and tax roll evidence cited earlier.

6. The Anna Jai house was in disrepair when Rollins arrived in the late 1860s, after serving as a stable and henhouse. Former slaves told Mrs. Rollins the building was once the residence of "Maum Hannah," meaning Anna Kingsley. See also Wilson, "Notes Concerning the Old Plantation," 4.

7. For the visitor see Notes of an Invalid, No. 9, "The Rich Mr. K. with His Black Consort and Offspring," *Christian Register and Boston Observer*, September 30, 1837. Hannah Rollins objected to having a cemetery within sight of her residence and had it leveled and covered with dirt.

8. Ibid. Hannah Rollins described the fence around the main dwelling as a white paneled fence of two boards and capped posts, and called the cedar avenue the "Sandfield Road." She said a tabby smokehouse, or possibly a jail, was located east of the main house near the cedar avenue. The 1851 map shows the outline of possible foundations for buildings. Recent field investigations by Dr. James Davidson have confirmed the existence of foundations.

9. See Wilson, "Notes Concerning the Old Plantation"; Dodge, "An Island by the Sea"; and Benjamin, "The Sea Islands." For the visitor to the island see Notes of an Invalid, No. 9. This is also the source of the racist description of Anna Jai as the "sooty spouse . . . as strongly scented as a musk-rat . . . [and] as ugly as pictures of the king of sinners." The author also wrote that George Kingsley was present and managing at Fort George Island during the visit, when he was in fact in Haiti.

Zephaniah Kingsley told Lydia Maria Child of being thwarted when trying to hire a tutor for his children in Haiti. See her "Letter from New York," in Stowell, *Balancing Evils Judiciously*. For tutors at the homes of Martha Baxter and Mary and John Sammis, see Duval County censuses for 1850, 1860, and 1870.

10. Cathedral Parish Records, Baptisms (microfilm roll 3, entry 650, January 30, 1829), SAHSRL. See also Gannon, *Cross in the Sand*, 139–49.

11. It is possible that Quala and Mary were among the slaves emancipated by Kingsley. See the 1860 Duval County Census of free persons of color for Mary Kingsley and her children. Samuel Wyley may have been one of the Kingsley slaves emancipated and transported to Haiti to work as an indentured laborer at George Kingsley's estate.

12. Fleszar, "The Atlantic Mind," 149–51. Kingsley allegedly intended to employ the "recaptured" Africans at deepening the channel of the inland waterway. See James

Gadsden to Chief Engineer, December 31, 1829, July 10, 1830, and Joseph White to Martin Van Buren, March 10, 1831, in Carter, *Territorial Papers*, 24:312–13, 426–28, 508. See also Swanson, *Slave Ship Guerrero*, and Stephens, "Zephaniah Kingsley and the Recaptured Africans."

13. Fleszar, "The Atlantic Mind," 151–54. For the quotation see Stowell, *Balancing Evils Judiciously*, 109.

14. Flora's date of manumission is March 20, 1828. The birth date for Charles Kingsley comes from a grave marker at a cemetery in Puerto Plata, Dominican Republic. I thank Peggy Fried for sending me a copy of a photograph of the marker, and Manuel Lebrón and his parents, Sondra and Tony Lebrón, for touring the cemetery with me. The word order in the quote was rearranged for clarity.

15. On her manumission record, Sophy is described as "a woman of Jalof, thirty-six years of age, about five feet high, black complexion" freed "for faithful services." See Deed Book, SJCC.

16. For birth records of James and Sophia Kingsley see Marriage License and Baptism Records, Box No. X, Records prior to establishment of Diocese of St. Augustine. Parish Records, St. Joseph's Church Archives, Mandarin, Jacksonville, Florida.

17. Archibald Abstracts, DCC, Book B, 10 and 12 (June 26, July 20, August 15, 1831); *Florida Herald* (St. Augustine), August 9, 1832. Testimony of John Sammis in William, James and Osceola Kingsley v. John and Adele Broward, Records of the Superior Court, July 8, 1876, establishes that Kingsley resided off and on with Flora at New Hope Plantation from 1832 until she moved to Haiti in 1842. See also Marriage License and Baptismal Record, Box X. I was provided copies of baptismal records for a child born to Flora and Zephaniah in Puerto Plata, Dominican Republic, by Mr. Pablo Juan Brugal. Copies of Kingsley's acknowledgment of his children by Flora, and also his child, Micanopy, by Sarah Murphy, were sent by Peggy Fried, a descendant of Kingsley and Sarah Murphy.

18. Sammis's testimony is from Kingsley v. Broward, the Circuit Court, 4th Judicial Circuit of Florida, Duval County. James, William, and Osceola Kingsley, sons of Flora and Zephaniah and residents of the Dominican Republic, were the plaintiffs; John and Adele E. Broward were the defendants. From Rainey, *Cases Argued and Adjudged*, 19:722–47.

19. L'Engle, *Summer of the Great-Grandmother*.

20. Archibald Abstracts, Book C, 20, 405-C-1 (July 20, 1831). The May 5, 1831, marriage occurred at St. Johns Bluff, a Zephaniah Kingsley property, and was performed by Justice of the Peace Samuel Kingsley (kinship, if any, unknown). See Shaw, Duval County Florida Marriages, 1823–1867, Book O, DCC.

21. Buena Vista is Deed Book I & J, 388 (December 20, 1832); Orange Grove is Book M, 231 (August 9, 1836); Drayton Island is Book M, 232 (August 10, 1836), all SJCC.

22. Schafer, *Anna Madgigine Jai Kingsley*, 94–95.

23. Archibald Abstracts: Book B-76 & 176; Book E-61, DCC.

24. Deed Book I & J, 389 (December 21, 1832), SJCC.

25. Kingsley authorized Joseph Hernandez to "settle with Don Horatio Dexter for the

salvage of free Fatimah," captured by brigands during the Patriot insurgency. See ZK to Hernandez, January 16, 1821, BSP.

26. Duval County Tax Roll, 1846, Florida State Library, FSA. The list was compiled three years after Kingsley's death; his slaves were under control of executors.

27. *Florida Herald* (St. Augustine), August 9, 1832.

28. ZK versus Benjamin Chaires, Civil Action, St. Johns County, Superior Court Files, Box 131, Folder 17, May 19, 1829, SAHSRL.

29. Zephaniah Kingsley and William and Elizabeth Skelton, et al, Indenture, September 21, 1833, Deed Book K, 89–97, SJCC.

30. Rivers, *Slavery in Florida*, chapter 10. See also C. Brown, "Race Relations in Territorial Florida." Mahon, *History of the Second Seminole War,* is still the balanced and classic source on the war. Porter, *The Black Seminoles*, is excellent concerning black warriors. See also *Jacksonville Courier*, August 7, September 3, 17, October 8, 1835.

31. See Mahon, *History of the Second Seminole War,* chapter 6; Covington, *The Seminoles of Florida*, chapter 4. For accusations of corruption see ZK to Joseph M. White, January 14, 1828, Letters Received by the Office of Indian Affairs, Florida 1827–1831, RG M234, Microfilm Roll No. 287, Exposures 182–86. NARA-W. I thank Jim Vearil for this source.

Osceola Kingsley was born on January 14, 1837, at Goodbys Creek, Micanopy was born on February 1, 1837, probably at Fort George Island. See Leandro Garcia, notary public, Puerto Plata, Dominican Republic, September 19, 1842, NADR. I thank Peggy Fried for copies.

32. ZK to Poinsett, Fort George Island, January 29, 1839, Letters Received by the Office of Adjutant General, 1822–1860, Main Series, 190 K-L, 117, 1839, Microcopy 567, RG 94, NARA-W. I thank Jim Vearil for this source.

33. Abdy, *Journal of a Residence*, 2:71, 267.

34. Rice, "The Anti-Slavery Mission." See Child, *Letters from New York*, from Stowell, *Balancing Evils Judiciously*, 111–12.

35. Stowell, *Balancing Evils Judiciously*, 18–19, 33–34, 54–55, 73–74; Pamphile, "Emigration of Black Americans to Haiti." See also Pamphile, *Haitians and African Americans*. Charles Collins, a New York City merchant with ties to Kingsley, represented the Haitian government as an immigration recruiter. James Redpath established a Haitian Emigration Bureau in Boston. For emigration to Haiti see Dixon, *African Americans and Haiti's Emigration*; Hunt, *Haiti's Influence*; Burin, *Slavery and the Peculiar Solution*.

36. Kingsley's Will, Probate file 1203, July 20, 1843, DCC.

Chapter 13. The "Island of Liberty" and Kingsley's Final Journeys

1. *Working Man's Advocate*, October 1, 1831, in Stowell, *Balancing Evils Judiciously*, 76–81.

2. Earle, *Jacksonian Antislavery*, 27–37.

3. See Dillon, *Benjamin Lundy*, and Mayer, *All on Fire*.

4. *Rural Code* is reprinted in Stowell, *Balancing Evils Judiciously*, 87–101.

5. ZK to Evans, Puerto de Plata, Haiti, September 13, 1835, ibid., 87–90.

6. ZK to Evans, September 29, 1835, ibid., 91–93.

7. ZK to Evans, Port-au-Prince, circa October 26, 1835, ibid., 93–98. The date is uncertain, written in diary form with introductory paragraphs followed by entries dated October 11, 17, and 26. Kingsley may have posted the letter after returning to New York. Letter 4 is dated New York, November 13, 1835. Letter 3 was printed on November 21, 1835.

8. Letter 3, Port-au-Prince, dated October 12, 1835, but covering entries through November 26. Ibid., 93–98.

9. November 13, 1835, ibid., 98–101.

10. Leasehold is recorded on "Survey and Plan, Register of Lands, Puerto Plata, May 23, 1838, Book 92, page 2, NADR. I thank Peggy Fried, a descendant of Sarah Murphy and Zephaniah Kingsley and their child Micanopy, for sending a copy. See also ZK to Gurley, June 30, 1837, in Stowell, *Balancing Evils Judiciously*, 102–6.

11. ZK to Gurley, June 30, 1837.

12. Ibid.

13. Ibid. See also note 10 above.

14. See Burin, *Slavery and the Peculiar Institution*.

15. Fretwell, *Kingsley Beatty Gibbs and His Journal*, 11.

16. *Boston Recorder*, August 9, 1839, from Fleszar, "The Atlantic Mind," 164–65.

17. The exact date is not known. I interviewed numerous Kingsley descendants and others residing in the Dominican Republic, including Sondra LeBron and her son Manuel, who descend through John Maxwell Kingsley's line. Kingsley's description of Anna is from Child, "Letter from New York," in Stowell, *Balancing Evils Judiciously*, 109. The timing is right, but the assertion that Anna was on that vessel is my speculation.

18. Peggy Fried found the baptismal record in September 1998, along with Kingsley's registration and acknowledgment of paternity of Micanopy before the public scribe at Puerto Plata. See also Puig Ortiz, *Emigracion*, 88.

19. Puig Ortiz, *Emigracion*, 11–12, 33–50, 67–69. I interviewed Finke and Brugal at Puerto Plata in December 1994.

20. Abraham Hanahan and John Maxwell Kingsley witnessed George Kingsley's Will at Puerto Plata on February 14, 1846. See Probate file 1205, George Kingsley, DCC.

21. See census data for Duval, St. Johns, and Nassau Counties, 1830–1850; Puig Ortiz, *Emigracion*, 110, 117, 118.

22. Puig Ortiz, *Emigracion*, and the Will of Francis Richard II, dated August 19, 1837, in Probate file 1756, DCC. Richard died in November 1839. Most of his "colored children" remained in Florida. John Olson carefully analyzed the Richard probate file.

23. Fretwell, *Kingsley Beatty Gibbs and His Journal*, 15. Passenger Lists, Port of Entry Records, New York, NARA-W.

24. *Baltimore Sun*, November 11, 1840; Pamphile, *Haitians and African Americans*, 41; and Fanning, "Haiti and the U.S.," 90–91, 136–42.

25. See Mills, *Letters from New York*, 114, for Child's account of her interview with Kingsley, first published in the July 7, 1842, issue of the *National Anti-Slavery Standard*.

26. "Kingsley's Plantation," *Boston Emancipator and Free American*, September 1, 1842.

27. Higginbotham to Forsyth, October 26, November 12, 15, December 15, 1838, January 7, 1839, Consular Dispatches from United States Consuls, Haiti, RG 59, T 330, Roll 1, February 1797–December 15, 1838, and Roll 2, Volumes 1 and 2, January 1839–1850, NARA-CP. See also the fascinating travel accounts in RG 59, Consular Dispatches, Santo Domingo, T56, Roll 1, Volume 1, June 1837–September 1854.

28. Fretwell, *Kingsley Beatty Gibbs and His Journal*, 20–24.

29. Sophia Hanahan Kingsley, born September 27, 1833, at Goodbys Creek, did not make the journey to Haiti. Her name is missing from subsequent records, indicating her probable death prior to November 1841. The date of Flora's emigration is easily confused. Kingsley's will, dated July 20, 1843, states that Flora was residing at Camp New Hope at that time. Apparently, the will was written earlier but not filed until that date. John Sammis testified in 1883 that Flora and her sons moved to Haiti prior to 1843. See Kingsley et al. v. Broward, 19 Florida 772 (1883), FSA. A copy of Kingsley's will is in Probate file 1203, DCC. I thank Peggy Fried for sending me a copy of Kingsley's testimony before the Dominican notary public and for sending other important documents.

30. Fretwell, *Kingsley Beatty Gibbs and His Journal*, 25–28.

31. Peggy Fried to author, September 10, 14, 1998. See also "Agricultural Directory, Principal Owners of Fincas," Census of Puerto Plata, 1919, NADR, courtesy of Ms. Fried.

32. Passenger Lists of Vessels arriving at Philadelphia, 1800–1882, Philadelphia, Microfilm 960, Roll 75, NARA-W; Fretwell, *Kingsley Beatty Gibbs and His Journal*, 30–31.

33. Fretwell, *Kingsley Beatty Gibbs and His Journal*, 31.

34. Superior Court Records 156/59, SAHSRL. The compromise is in Gould to Napier, January 17, 1843, November 16, 1846, P/1407 (July 1804–December 1857), Napier Papers, CLUSC. See also Gibbs, *Journal*, January 12, 20, 31, 1843.

35. Probate file 1203, ZK, DCC.

36. ZK to Hernandez, August 12, 1843, BSP.

37. See Doggett, *Supplement*, 1845; *New York Morning Herald*, July 19, 22, September 11, 1830, October 16, 1844, February 26, 1845.

38. ZK to Hernandez, January 16, 1821, BSP.

39. Child, "Letters from New York," in Stowell, *Balancing Evils Judiciously*, 111. John Fraser and his African family are discussed at length in Schafer, "Family Ties That Bind." In addition, see two manuscript collections discovered after "Family Ties" was published: Mary Ann Fraser, et al, vs Philip R. Yonge, No. 272, 1846–1851, Box 4, Folder 3, Gregory Yale Papers, 1828–1871, University of California Library, Department of Special Collections, Manuscripts Division; and The John Fraser Estate Collection, 1823–1873, Manuscripts, M-2678f, William M. Clements Library, University of Michigan, Ann Arbor. For a more detailed discussion of Kingsley's Florida family in the years after his death, see Schafer, *Anna Madgigine Jai Kingsley*, chapters 7, 8, 9. See also Deed Book K, 89–97, SJCC. Elizabeth and Mary Ann Fraser, and Robertson, divided $20,250 minus attorney fees. The John Fraser Estate Collection contains letters that supplement my analysis in "Family Ties That Bind." Napier negotiated funds from Burritt to send to Skelton. There are plaintive letters written to W. W. Campbell between 1853 and 1857 from the

aging and twice-widowed Skelton, victimized by an African Lothario, a clever swindler named Bollibinyah, and by a Mr. Gabbidon. Skelton relocated to Tombo Island (today Conakry, Guinea) and was fleeced of her inheritance.

40. Kingsley deposited $15,000 with Lamotte's firm, probably the legal commission he received as executor of Fraser's estates for three decades.

Chapter 14. "To Do Good in This World We *Must* Have Money"

1. Child, "Letter XXIII." 141–50. I changed the order of quotations but left meaning and intent intact.

2. See "Last Will and Testament," ibid., 116–21.

3. Probate file 1203, ZK, DCC. Cash, stocks, bonds, and mortgages were reported annually.

4. See Records of the Superior Court, Box 131, File 16, SAHSRL, for the most complete account of the lawsuit. See also "Answer to Petition of Anna Kingsley; Response of Benjamin A. Putnam and Kingsley B. Gibbs, September 5, 1846," File 2, Papers Concerning the Will of Zephaniah Kingsley, 1844, 1846, in M878-020, FSA; Probate file 1203, ZK, DCC; Broward vs. Kingsley (19 Florida 722), Supreme Court of Florida, Tallahassee; and Claim of ZK, PWC, Records of the Superior Court, SAHSRL. For an attorney's assessment see May, "Zephaniah Kingsley, Nonconformist." Martha McNeill added names of her children: William Gibbs McNeill, Catherine McNeill Palmer, Anna McNeill Whistler, and the daughters of her sister, Isabella Kingsley Gibbs: Isabella Gibbs King and Sophia Gibbs Couper. None of the co-petitioners resided in Florida: one was in St. Petersburg, Russia, another in New Orleans, and yet another, Sophia Gibbs Couper, asked the judge to remove her name from the lawsuit, writing: "I never wished or intended to have anything to do with the litigation of the will." See also the February 20, 1846, entry by Judge William F. Crabtree, "Revocation of the Probate of the Last Will and Testament of Zephaniah Kingsley," Judge's Order Book, DCC.

5. Historians have generally seen free black slave owners as benevolent individuals purchasing their own family members to protect them from slavery. Anna Kingsley's petition shows instead a desire to maximize profit. See Berlin, *Slaves without Masters*, 273; Woodson, *Free Negro Owners of Slaves*, 42. Koger, *Black Slaveowners*, 80–86, found "colored masters" in South Carolina to whom "slaves were merely property to be purchased, sold or exchanged."

6. Probate file 1205, George Kingsley, DCC. James Johnson, "History of Zephaniah Kingsley," typescript, circa 1940, WPA, Florida Room, Jacksonville Central Library, has notes from letters George Kingsley wrote to John Sammis (originals are missing). Johnson's narrative contains serious errors. The shipwrecked vessel was the *Frank Henry*. Profitability at Mayorasgo de Koka had declined by the time Anna returned to Florida. A revolt drove the black Haitian rulers from the eastern portion of the island, and the former Spanish rulers returned until an independence movement led to the creation of independent Dominican Republic. The Kingsley properties were in the main zone of

violence during these events. In addition, timber resources at the estate were depleted and laborers drifted away from the estate. See Pons, *The Dominican Republic*, chapters 7–10.

7. March 2, 1846, Judge's Order Book, DCC.

8. The farm, part of the Branchester Tract, purchased in January 1847 from James and Sarah Acker, is today part of the Jacksonville University campus. In June 1847, Anna sold Deep Creek Plantation in St. Johns County. An additional property east of Dunn's Lake granted in 1816 by the Spanish government was never cultivated. In 1851 it reverted to the State of Florida for "default of taxes." See the Archibald Transcript of Duval County Deeds, DCC. For Deep Creek see Deed Book I–J, SJCC, December 21, 1832, p. 389. For the tax default see the December 12, 1851, Deed Book P, p. 250.

9. Gregory Yale represented Anna Kingsley before Judge Crabtree. See Yale to Crabtree, August 24 and September 7, 1846. On February 1, 1847, Crabtree ordered K. B. Gibbs and Benjamin Putnam, executors, to distribute assets to the heirs.

10. Signed receipts, Probate file 1203, ZK, DCC.

11. Ibid. and appendixes A, B, D, and F. See also Probate file 1205, George Kingsley, DCC.

12. See appendixes C and F.

13. See appendix E.

14. 1860 Census of Duval County.

15. See the recollections of Henry Adams, a slave owned by Francis Richard who slept with his slave wife and family in the Sammis slave quarter and walked to work at his owner's property. Schafer, *Anna Madgigine Jai Kingsley*, 77, 90–93.

16. Ibid. See also appendix G.

17. Probate file 1203, ZK, DCC.

18. For Romeo Murray and the *Maple Leaf* see Schafer, *Thunder on the River*, 204–17.

19. Ibid. Sam and Elsy are listed as a family on the 1844 Inventory (appendix B). On the 1847 inventory (appendix F) Sam was valued at $700, the highest value assigned. Sam's rebelliousness may have been the result of being separated from his wife and child.

20. Probate file 1203, ZK, DCC.

21. See appendix B.

22. Probate file 1205, George Kingsley, DCC.

23. See appendix G.

24. Census of Duval County, 1850.

25. Ibid., 1860.

26. Alonzo H. Phillips became a merchant in Jacksonville and enlisted as a private in Company A, Twenty-first United States Colored Infantry, on June 13, 1863. Promoted to commissary sergeant, he returned to Jacksonville in 1865 and settled in Chaseville on land formerly Martha Baxter's until his death on April 9, 1931. See Schafer, *Thunder on the River*, and Alonzo's enlistment in pension record number 839,934, NARA-W. Bonafi's son George Gaston Napoleon served in the Twenty-fifth United States Colored Troops. He volunteered in February 1864 at Philadelphia. After the war he and his father were

given land by Mary and John Sammis. See also S. P. Bates, *History of the Pennsylvania Volunteers*, 1026–30.

27. The female-headed families of Qualla (two children) and Tamassa (three children) are not found in 1844.

28. See appendixes A, E, and F.

29. My census tallies differ from the official numbers. Free persons of mixed-race backgrounds were counted as white or black or mulatto, depending on the census taker and on the gender and social standing of the head of household. In 1850 and 1860 the census lists Mary Sammis and her children as white even though she was the daughter of an African woman and a white man. Mary's sister, Martha Baxter, along with the Baxter children, were listed as white in 1850 and mulatto in 1860. My tally includes nonwhites in the following households: John S. Sammis, Alonzo Phillips, Toby Kingsley, Mary A. Williams, Maria Kingsley, Lindo Kingsley, Abdallah (Kingsley), Martha B. Baxter, Joseph Mocs, Anna M. Kingsley, Elizabeth King, Cornelia Taylor, George Hagins, John B. Richard, and Charles J. McNeill. Census takers sometimes omitted persons. Albert Sammis, son of John S. Sammis and Albert's mother, freed slave Antoinette (later Antoinette Payne), were not listed. For consistency, Clay County, carved from Duval County in 1858, is counted with Duval for 1860.

30. See *Population of the United States in 1860*, and the tables in Berlin, *Slaves without Masters*, 46–47, 136–37. See also Barr and Hargis, "The Voluntary Exile," 3–5; Garvin, "The Free Negro in Florida"; St. Johns County Census, 1860; L. A. Thompson, *Florida Law, Statutes*, 533; J. F. Smith, *Slavery and Plantation Growth*, 119–21; Ellsworth and Ellsworth, *Pensacola*; and Barr and Hargis, "The Voluntary Exile," 3–14. For the 1845 Florida State Census, see the *Jacksonville News*, February 27, 1846. See also Cathedral Parish Records, microfilm roll 3, Colored Baptisms (November 23, 1848), SAHSRL. Land purchase is in Archibald Transcripts, Book G, 16 (January 1847), and 285 (July 5, 1854), DCC.

31. *St. Johns Mirror* (Jacksonville), May 2, 1861. In June 1861 Sammis sold his rural properties to Margaret J. Mosely for $1. Mosely returned them after the war. See Archibald Abstracts, DCC, entries for March 6, 27, 1873.

32. Duval County Census, 1860, slave schedules; Duval County Tax Rolls, FSA; Anna Kingsley's Will, dated April 24, 1860, is reprinted in Schafer, *Anna Madgigine Jai Kingsley*, 129–31.

33. Ophelia Moore was interviewed by James Johnson, Works Progress Administration. For the New Orleans slave market see W. Johnson, *Soul by Soul*. Records of emancipations in Duval County were lost in fires.

34. "Sammis Slaves Are Still Alive," *Florida Times-Union*, June 21, 1925. Pratt arranged Esther's return as reward for securing his family's treasures from Yankee troops. After Lottery died, Esther remarried a Bartley. Bonafi chose the surname Napoleon after 1865. See appendixes A, B, C, F.

Bibliography

Primary Sources

Account of Foreign Vessels Clearing Outward. Naval Office, Saint Thomas, from June 10, 1808, to December 30, 1808. Colonial Office [Britain] 259/2. Copy at National Archives, College Park, Maryland.

Account of Sales, 1782–1783, Commissioners of Forfeited Estates. Records of the Comptroller General. South Carolina Division of Archives and History, Columbia.

African Case Proceedings, 1818–1821, Ad Hoc Collection: 00864, 00865, 00866. Georgia State Archives, Morrow.

Agricultural Directory, Principal Owners of Fincas, 1919 Census of Puerto Plata. National Archives, Dominican Republic, Santo Domingo.

Archibald Abstracts of Historical Property Records, 1821–1901. Duval County Courthouse, Jacksonville, Florida.

Ball, William, Family Papers. Pennsylvania Historical Society, Philadelphia.

Baptism and Marriage License Records, Box X, Cathedral Parish Records prior to establishment of Diocese of St. Augustine. St. Joseph's Church Archives, Mandarin, Florida.

Barnes, Christian, Papers. Manuscripts Division, Library of Congress, Washington, D.C.

Bethune, Judge F[arquhar], Diary. Florida Historical Society Library, Cocoa, Florida.

Birth Record Registers, Temporary MSS, 933, Lincolnshire's Friends' Registers, 1618–1837, Volume 1, Births and Marriages. Volume 2, Burial Records. Copy at Friends House Library, Euston Street, London.

Black Baptisms, Cathedral Parish Records, St. Augustine. St. Augustine Historical Society Research Library, St. Augustine, Florida.

Book of Conveyances, no. 32. Office of the Circuit Court, Putnam County Courthouse, Palatka, Florida.

Bristol Trade Directory. 1768. Copy in Pinney Papers, Special Collections, University of Bristol Library, Bristol, England.

Callen, Captain Patrick. Customs Accounts, St. Thomas, November 7, 1802. Danish National Archives, Copenhagen, Denmark.

Carleton, Thomas, Papers. Public Archives of Canada, Toronto.

Carne, Samuel, Papers. South Caroliniana Library, University of South Carolina, Columbia.

Certificates of Removals, 1760–1790; Testimonies of Minutes of Disunion of the Men's Meeting of Bristol, 1762–1782. Friends House Library, Euston Street, London.

Chipman, Ward, Papers, 1783–1824. Hugh T. Hazen Collection. New Brunswick Museum, Saint John, New Brunswick, Canada.

Citizenship and Birth Registry, Puerto Plata, September 19, 1842. National Archives, Dominican Republic, Santo Domingo.

Clarke, George W. v State of Florida, January 12, 1846. Records of the Circuit Court, Box 98, File 58, St. Augustine Historical Society Research Library.

Clarke, James F. v Francis J. Avice, 1829. Records of the Superior Court. Box 129, File 103, St. Augustine Historical Society Research Library, St. Augustine, Florida.

Consular Dispatches from United States Consuls, Haiti, Record Group 59, T 330, Roll 1, February 1797-December 15, 1838, and Roll 2, Volume 1 and 2, January 1839–1850. Account of all Foreign Vessels Clearing outwards. Naval Office, Saint Thomas, June 10, 1808 to December 30, 1808. National Archives, College Park, Maryland.

Consular Dispatches from United States Consuls, Havana, 1793–1906. Microfilm 899. Roll 1. December 1, 1783-October 2, 1807. Record Group 59, T55, Records of the Department of State. National Archives, College Park, Maryland.

Consular Dispatches from United States Consuls, Santo Domingo. Record Group 59, T56, Roll 1 Volume 1, June 1837–September 1854. National Archives, College Park, Maryland.

Consular Dispatches from United States Consuls, St. Yago, Cuba, Roll 1, Volume 1, Josiah Blakely to Secretary of State, May 13, 1799, November 1, 1801, April 10, 1804, July 1, 1805. Record Group 59, T55, Records of the Department of State. National Archives, College Park, Maryland.

Court of Admiralty for the District of South Carolina, Microfilm 1183, Roll 1. Record Group 59, T57. National Archives, College Park, Maryland.

Cross, Paul, Papers. South Caroliniana Library, University of South Carolina, Columbia.

Cuylor, Telamon, Collection. Hargrett Rare Book and Manuscript Library, University of Georgia Libraries, Athens.

Danish West Indies Sea Passes, April 1804. West Indian Passport and Citizenry Registers, St. Thomas, March 1805–March 1810. Danish National Archives, Copenhagen, Denmark.

Deed Book A, Registry Office, Kings County, Hampton, New Brunswick, and Public Archives of Canada, Toronto.

East Florida Claims. Claims for Losses during the Operation of American Troops in East Florida, 1812–1813. Record Group 217, Settled Miscellaneous Treasury Accounts, September 6, 1790–September 29, 1894, Office of the First Auditor, Records of the Accounting Officers of the Department of the Treasury. National Archives, College Park, Maryland.

East Florida Papers, 1783–1821, the local government archive of Spanish East Florida. Library of Congress, Washington, D.C. An online searchable Index to the East Florida Papers is at the P. K. Yonge Library of Florida History, University of Florida, Gainesville.

Fitzsimmons, Christopher, Papers, 1799–1956. Letter Book, Vol. 1. South Caroliniana Library, University of South Carolina, Columbia.

Forbes, Major General G. Letter Book, 1795–1796. Additional Manuscripts, Number 39,824. British Library, London.

"Founders' Petition of 1785." Archives and Special Collections, University of New Brunswick, Fredericton, Canada.

Fouts, Raymond Parker, comp. "Abstracts from Newspapers of Wilmington, North Carolina, 1765–1775 and 1788–1799." New Hanover County Public Library, Wilmington, North Carolina.

Fraser, John. Estate Collection. William L. Clements Library, University of Michigan, Ann Arbor.

Gale, Samuel. Probate File 1818: Bill of Sale, January 18, 1818, Charleston, S.C. South Carolina Division of Archives and History, Columbia.

Gibbs, Kingsley, Petition. East Florida Claims. 33rd Congress, 1st Session. Senate. Executive Document number 82. Report of the Secretary of the Treasury and the Attorney General, and Senate Document 468. 29th Congress. 1st Session: National Archives, College Park, Maryland.

Grant, James. James Grant of Ballindalloch Papers, Governorship Series. National Archives of Scotland, Edinburgh.

Grey, General Charles [1st Earl Grey], Papers. "Statement by 40 Owners," GRE/A/382b, Department of Paleography and Diplomatic, Archives and Special Collections, Palace Green Library, Durham University, England.

Hamilton, James, Papers. Hargrett Rare Book and Manuscript Library, University of Georgia Libraries, Athens.

———. Perkins Library, Duke University, Durham, North Carolina.

Hanahan, Abraham. Patriot War Claim. Records of the Superior Court of East Florida, Box 124, Folder 24. St. Augustine Historical Society Research Library, St. Augustine, Florida.

Hickman, Joshua. Probate File. Records of the Probate Court. Duval County Courthouse, Jacksonville, Florida.

"A History of French Village on the Kennebecasis, Kings County, New Brunswick," unpublished manuscript by Andrew Sherwood Beyea, 1923. University of New Brunswick Library, Archives and Special Collections, Fredericton, New Brunswick, Canada.

Holsoe, Svend E., comp. "Slave Carrying Vessels between the Danish West Indies and Gorée and/or Cape Verde." Typescript, unpublished, 1994.

Johnston, Charles. Estate Inventory, May 16, 1804. Inventory and Appraisement Book, 1783–1851, Charleston County, South Carolina. Charleston Public Library.

Judges' Order Books. Probate Court: Book A: 1846–1866. Book B: 1866–1878. Duval County Courthouse, Jacksonville, Florida.

Kingsley, Anna. Patriot War Claim. Collection MC 31, St. Augustine Historical Society Research Library, St. Augustine, Florida.

———. Probate File 1210. Records of the Probate Court. Duval County Courthouse, Jacksonville, Florida.

Kingsley, George. Oath of Loyalty, June 5, 1795. West Indian Passport and Citizenry Registers, Christiansted, St. Croix, 1794–1805. Danish National Archives, Copenhagen, Denmark.

———. Probate File 1205. Records of the Probate Court. Duval County Courthouse, Jacksonville, Florida.

Kingsley, Isabella. Petition to the Legislature. Committee Report. December 12, 1807. South Carolina Division of Archives and History, Columbia.

———. Petition to the South Carolina House of Representatives, January 28, 1783. South Carolina Division of Archives and History, Columbia.

Kingsley, Z[ephaniah], Jr. "Address to the Legislative Council of Florida on the Subject of Its Colored Population." State Library of Florida, Tallahassee, 1926.

———. Oath of Loyalty, October 9, 1798, St. Thomas. West Indian Passport and Citizenry Registers, 1788–1807. Danish National Archives, Copenhagen, Denmark.

———. Probate File 1203. Records of the Probate Court. Duval County Courthouse, Jacksonville, Florida.

———. Records of the Superior Court of East Florida, Box 131, Folder 16. St. Augustine Historical Society Research Library, St. Augustine, Florida.

Kingsley, Zephaniah v Benjamin Chaires, Civil Action, St. Johns County, May 19, 1929. Records of the Circuit Court. Box 131, Folder 17, St. Augustine Historical Society Research Library. St. Augustine, Florida.

Kingsley, Zephaniah, Sr. File of Papers. University of New Brunswick Library, Archives and Special Collections, Fredericton, New Brunswick, Canada.

———. Loyalist Examination. South Carolina volumes from the New York Public Library. Transcripts of the American "Loyalist Examinations and Decisions," February 27, 1784.

———. Petition to the House of Representatives of the State of South Carolina, November 6, 1784. South Carolina Division of Archives and History, Columbia. From Parr Town, River Saint Johns, Nova Scotia.

Letters Received by the Office of Adjutant General, 1822–1860. Main Series: 190 K-L, 1839. Record Group 94, Microcopy 567. National Archives, College Park, Maryland.

Letters Received by the Office of Indian Affairs, Florida 1827–1831, Record Group M234, Microfilm Roll no. 287, Exposures 182–86. National Archives, College Park, Maryland.

Marriage and Birth Records, Quaker Meeting of Bristol, 1762–1782, Illustrations of discipline 1666–1808, Society of Friends, Bristol and Frenchay, SF/A7/1. Bristol Record Office, copy at Friends Library, Euston Street, London.

Marriage License: Zephaniah Kinsley [sic] and Isabella Johnston, 28 September 1763. Lambeth Palace Library, London, England.

Marriage Records. Clerk of Court's Office. Duval County Courthouse, Jacksonville, Florida.

Mary Ann v Philip R. Yonge, 1846–1851, in Yale, Gregory, Papers, 1828–1871, Box 4, Folder 3. Manuscripts Division, Department of Special Collections, Research Library (Charles E. Young), University of California Los Angeles.

McIntosh, John H. Patriot War Claim. Collection MC 31, St. Augustine Historical Society Research Library, St. Augustine, Florida.

Napier, Thomas, Papers. South Caroliniana Library, University of South Carolina, Columbia.

Papeles de Cuba, 1790. Archivo General de Indias, Seville, Spain.

Patriot War Papers and Patriot War Claims, 1812–1846. MC 32, St. Augustine Historical Society Research Library, St. Augustine.

Peebles, John, Diary, February 8–June 26, 1780. South Caroliniana Library, University of South Carolina, Columbia.

Penman, James and Edward, Company Daybook, 1794. South Caroliniana Library, University of South Carolina, Columbia.

Pratt, Horace S., Estate Inventory. Inventory and Appraisal of Estates, 1831–1867. Book A. Camden County Courthouse, Woodbine, Georgia.

Property Records, Nassau County, Florida. Deed Books A, B, C. Nassau County Courthouse, Yulee, Florida.

Property Records of St. Johns County, Florida. Deed Books A, B, C, D, E, F, G, H, I, J. St. Johns County Courthouse, St. Augustine, Florida.

Records of Florida Land Offices, Records of the Bureau of Land Management, Record Group 49 (49/9.7), 1685–1993. Florida State Archives, Tallahassee. http://data.labins.org/surveydata/landrecords/GLO/search.cfm.

Registers of Persons Arriving and Leaving Christiansted Police Station 1794–1805. Christiansted, St. Croix. Danish National Archives, Copenhagen, Denmark.

Richard, Francis. Probate File. Records of the Probate Court. Duval County Courthouse, Jacksonville, Florida.

Robertson, William and Ann, v. Philip R. Yonge and Zephaniah Kingsley, Records of the Superior Court of East Florida, Box 156, File 59. St. Augustine Historical Society Research Library, St. Augustine, Florida.

"Scottish Old Parochial Register Indexes, Baptisms and Marriages, prior to 1855." National Archives of Scotland, Edinburgh.

Smith, Buckingham, Papers, 1613–1941. New York Historical Society Library, New York.

Smith, John, Company Letter Books, Volume III, 1774–1821. Maryland Historical Society, Baltimore, Maryland.

Smith, Thomas Adams, Papers. Letterbook, 1812–1837. Western Historical Manuscript Collection, Number 1029. State Historical Society of Missouri, Columbia. Copy at P. K. Yonge Library of Florida History, University of Florida, Gainesville.

Spanish Land Grant Claims, Confirmed and Unconfirmed Volumes, S 991 RG 000599, United States. Board of Land Commissioners. Florida State Archives, Tallahassee.

"St. Mary LeBow Parish Registers: Marriages, 1754–1794; Banns 1754–1831." Microfilm Roll 4999. British Archive, Kew, England.

Survey of White Oak Plantation, Nassau County. U.S. Township Maps, Surveyor's Field Notes: Township 4 North, Range 25 & 26 East, pages 102–5. Florida State Archives, Tallahassee.

Tax Records, Duval County, Florida, 1846–1860, 1866–1869, 1872–1875, 1876–1877. Florida State Archives, Tallahassee.

Tax Records, Nassau County, Florida, 1845–1869. Florida State Archives, Tallahassee.

"Unidentified Citizen of Saint Domingue, Extracts of Minutes of a General Meeting of West Indies Planters and Merchants at a London Tavern," November 8, 1791. Additional Manuscripts 38351, Folio 109. British Library, London.

United States, Appellants v. Francis P. Ferreira, Administrator of Francis Pass, Deceased. Supreme Court of the United States no. 197, Senate Misc. Document no. 55, 36th Congress, First Session. Washington, D.C.: George W. Bowman, 1860.

United States v. Kingsley, 37 U.S. 476: Volume 37, 1838. Justia.com: US Supreme Court Center. Http://supreme.justia.com/us/37/476/case.html.

West Indian passport and citizenry registers. St. Thomas Police Station. Registers of persons arriving, 1805–1899. Danish National Archives, Copenhagen, Denmark.

White, Gideon, Family Papers. Nova Scotia Archives, Halifax, Nova Scotia.

Will Books D and E, Charleston County Public Library, 68 Calhoun Street, Charleston, South Carolina.

Winslow Family Papers: Mather Byles Letter Books, Number 4, 1784–1786. Archives and Special Collections, University of New Brunswick Library, Fredericton, New Brunswick, Canada.

Wright, Jermyn, East Florida Claim. Parliamentary Claims Commission: East Florida. Treasury 77, Piece 18, Folio 14. National Archives, Kew, England.

Newspapers

Baltimore Sun
Boston Emancipator and Free American
Boston Recorder, August 9, 1839
Charleston Courier
Christian Register and Boston Observer
Christian Statesman, June 30, 1837
City Gazette and Commercial Daily Advertiser (Charleston)
Columbian Museum (Savannah)
East Florida Herald (St. Augustine)
Felix Farley's Bristol Journal
Florida Herald (St. Augustine)
Florida News (Jacksonville)

Florida Republican (Jacksonville)
Gentleman's Magazine
Georgia Gazette (Savannah)
Jacksonville Courier
National Anti-Slavery Standard
New York Morning Herald
Royal Gazette (Savannah)
Royal Gazette and New Brunswick Advertiser (St. John)
Saint John Gazette
South Carolina Gazette
Southern Agriculturalist
St. John Gazette and the Weekly Advertiser
St. Augustine News
Southern Patriot (Charleston)
Working Man's Advocate (New York)
World and Fashionable Advertiser (London)

Secondary Sources

Abdy, E. S. *Journal of a Residence and Tour in the United States of North America, from April, 1833, to October, 1834*. Vol. 2. London: John Murray, 1835.

Alderson, Robert J. *The Bright Era of Happy Revolutions: French Consul Michel-Ange-Bernard Mangourit and International Republicanism in Charleston, 1792–1794*. Columbia: University of South Carolina Press, 2008.

———. "Charleston's Rumored Slave Revolt of 1793." In *The Impact of the Haitian Revolution in the Atlantic World*, ed. David P. Geggus, 93–111. Columbia: University of South Carolina Press, 2001.

Alpers, Edward E. *The East African Slave Trade*. Nairobi, Kenya: Historical Association of Tanzania, Paper no. 3, 1967.

———. *Ivory and Slaves: Changing Pattern of International Trade in East Central Africa to the Later Nineteenth Century*. Berkeley: University of California Press, 1975.

Anderson, Fred. *Crucible of War: The Seven Years War and the Fate of Empire in British North America*. New York: Random House, 2000.

"Atlantic Slave Trade to Savannah." *The New Georgia Encyclopedia*, at www.georgia encyclopedia.org/nge.

Bailyn, Bernard. *The Ideological Origins of the American Revolution*. Cambridge: Harvard University Press, 1967.

———. *Voyagers to the West: A Passage in the Peopling of America on the Eve of the Revolution*. New York: Knopf, 1986.

Bannerman, W. Bruce, ed. *The Registers of St. Mary le Bowe, Cheapside, All Hollows, Hosey Lane, and of St. Pancres, Soper Lane, London. Part II, Marriages*. London: Publication of the Harleian Society (Vol. XLV), 1915, p. 370. Copy at Guildhall, London, Printed Books Division.

Baptist, Edward E. *Creating an Old South: Middle Florida's Plantation Frontier before the Civil War*. Chapel Hill: University of North Carolina Press, 2002.

Barr, Ruth B., and Modeste Hargis. "The Voluntary Exile of Free Negroes of Pensacola." *Florida Historical Quarterly* 17 (July 1938): 3–14.

Barry, Boubacar. *Le royaume du Waalo: Le Sènègal avant la conquête*. Paris: Èditions Karthala, 1985 (revised edition of a 1972 original edition).

———. *Senegambia and the Atlantic Slave Trade*. Cambridge: Cambridge University Press, 1998.

Bartlett, C. J., and Gene A. Smith. "A 'Species of Milito-Nautico-guerilla-plundering warfare': Admiral Alexander Cochrane's Naval Campaign against the United States, 1814–1815." In *Britain and America Go to War: The Impact of War and Warfare in Anglo-America, 1754–1815*, ed. Julie Flavell and Stephen Conway, 173–204. Gainesville: University Press of Florida, 2004.

Bartram, John. "Diary of a Journey through the Carolinas, Georgia, and Florida, 1765–66." Ed. Francis Harper. *Transactions of the American Philosophical Society*, new series, vol. 33, pt. 1, pp. 1–55. Philadelphia: American Philosophical Society, 1942.

Bartram, William. *Travels Through North and South Carolina, Georgia, East and West Florida, the Cherokee Country, the Extensive Territories of the Muscogulges or Creek, and the Country of the Chactaws; containing an account of the Soil and Natural Productions of those regions, together with observations on the Manners of the Indians*. Philadelphia: James and Johnson, 1791.

Bates, Samuel P. *History of the Pennsylvania Volunteers, 1861–1865*. Vol. 5. Harrisburg, Pa.: R. Singerly, State Printer, 1871.

Bates, Thelma. "The Legal Status of the Negro in Florida." *Florida Historical Quarterly* 6 (January 1928): 161–68.

Beachey, R. W. "The East African Ivory Trade in the Nineteenth Century." *Journal of African History* 8, no. 2 (1967): 269–90.

Becker, Charles. "Conditions écoligiques, crises de subsistence et histoire de la population à l'époque de la traite des esclaves en Sénégambie (dix septième-dix-huitième siècle)." *Canadian Journal of African Studies* 20, no. 3 (1986): 357–76.

Becker, Charles, and Victor Martin. "Kayor et Baol: Royaumes sénégalais et traite des esclaves au dix-huitième siècle." *Revue francaise d'histoire d'outre-mer* 62, no. 228 (1975): 270–300.

Behrendt, Stephen D. "Markets, Transaction Cycles, and Profits: Merchant Decision Making in the British Slave Trade." *William and Mary Quarterly*, 3rd ser., 58, no. 1 (2001): 171–204.

Benjamin, Samuel G. W. "The Sea Islands." *Harpers New Monthly Magazine*, November 1878, 839–61.

Bennett, Charles E. "Zephaniah Kingsley, Jr." In *Twelve on the River St. Johns*, 89–113. Jacksonville: University of North Florida Press, 1989.

Bennett, John. "Charleston in 1774 as Described by an English Traveler." *South Carolina Historical and Genealogical Magazine* 47 (July 1946): 179–80.

Benoist, Father Joseph Roger, and Abdoulaye Camara, comps. *Gorée: The Island and the Historical Museum*. Dakar, Senegal: Historical Museum of Gorée, 1993.

Berka, Norman F. "Citizens of St. Eustatius, 1781." In *The Lesser Antilles in the Age of European Expansion*, ed. Robert L. Paquette and Stanley L. Engerman, 223–38. Gainesville: University Press of Florida, 1996.

Berkeley, Edmund, and Dorothy Smith Berkeley. *Dr. Alexander Garden of Charles Town*. Chapel Hill: University of North Carolina Press, 1969.

Berlin, Ira. *Generations of Captivity: A History of African-American Slaves*. Cambridge: Harvard University Press, 2003.

———. *Slaves without Masters: The Free Negro in the Antebellum South*. New York: New Press, 1976 and 2007.

———. "Time, Space, and the Evolution of Afro-American Society on British Mainland North America." *American Historical Review* 85 (1980): 44–78.

Berlin, Ira, and Philip D. Morgan, eds. *Cultivation and Culture: Labor and the Shaping of Slave Life in America*. Charlottesville: University of Virginia Press, 1993.

———, eds. *The Slaves' Economy: Independent Production by Slaves in the Americas*. London: Frank Cass, 1991.

Black, Jeremy. *A System of Ambition: British Foreign Policy, 1660–1793*. London: Longman, 1991.

Bolster, W. Jeffrey. *Black Jacks: African American Seamen in the Age of Sail*. Cambridge: Harvard University Press, 1997.

Bomba, Victoria. "History of the Wolof State of Jolof until 1860, including comparative data from the Wolof state of Walo." Ph.D. diss., University of Wisconsin, Madison, 1969.

———. "The Pre-Nineteenth Century Political Tradition of the Wolof." *Bulletin de l'institute fundamental d'Afrique noire*. Série B, Sciences humaines, 36, no. 1 (January 1974): 1–13.

Borick, Carl P. *A Gallant Defense: The Siege of Charleston, 1780*. Columbia: University of South Carolina Press, 2003.

Bowden, P. J. "Wool Supply and the Woollen Industry." *Economic History Review*, n.s., 9, no. 1 (1956): 44–58.

Boyd, Mark F. "Events at Prospect Bluff on the Apalachicola River, 1808–1818." *Florida Historical Quarterly* 16, no. 2 (October 1937): 55–96.

———. "The Panton, Leslie Papers: Letter of Edmund Doyle, Trader." *Florida Historical Quarterly* 17, no. 4 (April 1939): 312–18.

Brewer, John. *The Sinews of Power: War, Money, and the English State, 1688–1783*. Cambridge: Harvard University Press, 1990.

Brooks, George E. "The Signares of Saint-Louis and Gorée: Women Entrepreneurs in Eighteenth Century Senegal." In *Women in Africa*, ed. Nancy Hafner and Edna Bay, 19–44. Stanford: Stanford University Press, 1976.

———. *Western Africa and Cabo Verde, 1790s–1830s: Symbiosis of Slave and Legitimate Trades*. Bloomington, Ind.: Author House, 2010.

Brooks, Philip C. *Diplomacy and the Borderlands: The Adams-Onis Treaty of 1819*. Berkeley: University of California Press, 1939.

Brown, Alan S. "James Simpson's Reports on the Carolina Loyalists, 1779–1780." *Journal of Southern History* 21, no. 4 (November 1995): 513–19.

Brown, Canter. "Race Relations in Territorial Florida, 1821–1845." *Florida Historical Quarterly* 73 (January 1995): 287–307.

———. "Tales of Angola: Free Blacks, Red Stick Creeks, and International Intrigue in Spanish Southwest Florida, 1812–1821." In *Go Sound the Trumpet! Selections in Florida's African American History*, ed. David H. Jackson Jr. and Canter Brown Jr., 5–21. Tampa: University of Tampa Press, 2005.

Brown, George S. *Yarmouth, Nova Scotia: A Sequel to Campbell's History*. Boston: Rand Avery Co., 1888.

Buckley, Roger Norman, ed. *The Haitian Journal of Lieutenant Howard, York Hussairs, 1796–1798*. Knoxville: University of Tennessee Press, 1985.

Bullard, Mary R. *Black Liberation on Cumberland Island in 1815*. DeLeon Springs, Fla.: E. O. Painter, 1983.

———. *Cumberland Island: A History*. Athens: University of Georgia Press, 2005.

Bullion, John L. *A Great and Necessary Measure: George Grenville and the Genesis of the Stamp Act, 1763–1765*. Columbia: University of Missouri Press, 1982.

Burin, Eric. *Slavery and the Peculiar Solution: A History of the American Colonization Society*. Gainesville: University Press of Florida, 2005.

Burke, Sir Bernard. *A Genealogical History of the Dormant, Abeyant, Forfeited and Extinct Peerages of the British Empire*. London: Harrison, 1866.

Bushnell, David, comp. *La República de las Floridas: Texts and Documents*. Mexico City: Pan American Institute of Geography and History, 1986.

Cabell, James Branch, and A. J. Hanna. *The St. Johns: A Parade of Diversities*. New York: Farrar & Rinehart, 1960.

Cameron, Gail, and Stan Crooke, *Liverpool—Capital of the Slave Trade*. Liverpool: Picton Press, 1992.

Campbell, John. "As 'A Kind of Freeman'? Slaves' Market-Related Activities in the South Carolina Up Country, 1800–1860." In Berlin and Morgan, *Cultivation and Culture*, 243–74.

Campbell, The Reverend John Roy. "A History of the County of Yarmouth, Nova Scotia." Saint John, N.B.: J. & A. McMillan, 1876.

Carney, Judith A. *Black Rice: The African Origins of Rice Cultivation in the Americas*. Cambridge: Harvard University Press, 2001.

Carrier, Toni. "Black Seminoles, Maroons and Freedom Seekers in Florida, Part 3: The Destruction of Angola." University of South Florida Africana Heritage Project, 2005. Http://www.africanaheritage.com/Black_Seminoles_Angola.asp.

Carter, Clarence Edwin, ed. *The Territorial Papers of the United States, Volumes 3 and 24: The Territory of Florida*. Washington, D.C.: Government Printing Office, 1959–62.

Chaplin, Joyce E. *An Anxious Pursuit: Agricultural Innovation and Modernity in the Lower South, 1730–1815*. Chapel Hill: University of North Carolina Press, 1993.

Chappell, Bruce. "A Report on the Documentation Relating to the History of the Diego Plains Region in Second Spanish Period Florida." Typescript, 1976. P. K. Yonge Library of Florida History, University of Florida, Gainesville.

Charles, Eunice A. *Precolonial Senegal: The Jolof Kingdom, 1800–1900*. African Studies Center, Boston University, 1977.

Charles, Joseph. "The Jay Treaty: The Origins of the American Party System." *William and Mary Quarterly*, 3rd ser., 12, no. 4 (October 1955): 581–630.

Chesnutt, David R., ed. *The Papers of Henry Laurens*. 16 vols. Columbia: University of South Carolina Press, 1968–2002.

Child, Lydia Maria. *Letters from New-York*. Ed. Bruce Mills. Athens: University of Georgia Press, 1998.

———. "Letters from New York.—No. 30." *National Anti-Slavery Standard*, July 7, 1842.

———. "Letter XXIII." *Letters from New York*. New York: Charles S. Francis, 1843.

Christie, Ian R. *Wars and Revolutions: Britain, 1760–1815*. Cambridge: Harvard University Press, 1982.

Christopher, Emma. *Slave Ship Sailors and Their Captive Cargoes, 1730–1807*. Cambridge: Cambridge University Press, 2006.

Coclanis, Peter A. *The Shadow of a Dream: Economic Life and Death in the South Carolina Low Country, 1670–1920*. New York: Oxford University Press, 1989.

Cohen, David W., and Jack P. Greene, eds. *Neither Slave Nor Free: The Freedman of African Descent in the Slave Societies of the New World*. Baltimore: Johns Hopkins University Press, 1972.

Coke, Daniel Parker, M.P. "Memorial of Zephaniah Kingsley." *The Royal Commission on the Losses and Services of American Loyalists, 1783–1785. Being the Notes of Mr. Daniel Parker Coke, M. P., One of the Commissioners During that Period*. London: Oxford University Press, 1915.

Coker, Kathy Roe. "The Punishment of Civil War Loyalists." Ph.D. diss., University of South Carolina, 1987.

Coker, P. C., III. *Charleston's Maritime Heritage, 1670–1865, an Illustrated history*. Charleston, S.C.: CokerCraft Press, 1991.

Condon, Ann Gorman. "The Loyalist Community in New Brunswick." In *Loyalists and Community in North America*, ed. Robert M. Calhoon, Timothy M. Barnes, and George A. Rawlyk, 161–74. Westport, Conn.: Greenwood Press, 1994.

Corbitt, D. C. "The Return of Spanish Rule to the St. Marys and the St. Johns." *Florida Historical Quarterly* 20, no. 1 (July 1941): 47–68.

Corse, Carita Doggett. *The Key to the Golden Islands*. Chapel Hill: University of North Carolina Press, 1931.

Coulter, Merton. *Thomas Spalding of Sapelo*. Baton Rouge: Louisiana University Press, 1940.

Covington, James W. "The Negro Fort." *Gulf Coast Historical Review* 5 (1990): 78–91.

———. *The Seminoles of Florida.* Gainesville: University Press of Florida, 1993.

Cratan, Michael. *Empire, Enslavement, and Freedom in the Caribbean.* Princeton, N.J.: Markus Weiner, 1997.

Crow, Jeffrey D. "Slave Rebelliousness and Social Conflict in North Carolina, 1775 to 1802." *William and Mary Quarterly*, 3rd ser., 37 (January 1980): 79–102.

Curtin, Philip D. *Economic Change in Precolonial Africa: Senegambia in the Era of the Slave Trade.* Madison: University of Wisconsin Press, 1975.

Cusick, James. "Across the Border: Commodity Flow and Merchants in Spanish St. Augustine." *Florida Historical Quarterly* 69, no. 3 (January 1991): 277–99.

———, comp. "East Florida Papers Oaths of Allegiance, 1793–1804." Vol. 2. Unpublished typescript. P. K. Yonge Library of Florida History, University of Florida, Gainesville.

———. *The Other War of 1812: The Patriot War and the American Invasion of Spanish East Florida.* Gainesville: University Press of Florida, 2003.

da Costa, Emilia Viotti. *Crowns of Glory, Tears of Blood: The Demerara Slave Rebellion of 1823.* New York: Oxford University Press, 1994.

Danish National Archives. "A Brief History of the Danish West Indies, 1666–1917." http://www.virgin-islands-history.dk/eng/vi_hist.asp.

Darcy, Cornelius P. *The Encouragement of the Fine Arts in Lancashire, 1760–1860.* Manchester, England: Manchester University Press, 1976.

Davis, Thomas Frederick. *MacGregor's Invasion of Florida, 1817; together with an account of his successors Irwin, Hubbard and Aury on Amelia Island, East Florida.* Deland: Florida Historical Society, 1928.

Davis, William G. "The Florida Legislative Council, 1822–1838." Master's thesis, Florida State University, 1970.

DeConde, Alexander. *The Quasi-War: The Politics and Diplomacy of the Undeclared War with France, 1797–1801.* New York: Scribner, 1966.

Degler, Carl. *Neither White Nor Black; Slavery and Race Relations in Brazil and the United States.* New York: MacMillan, 1971.

Derks, Scott, ed. "Composite Commodity Price Index." In *The Value of a Dollar: Prices and Incomes in the United States, 1860–1989,* ed. Scott Derks, 2. Detroit: A. Manly, 1994.

de Vries, Jan. "The Dutch Atlantic Economies." In *The Atlantic Economy during the Seventeenth and Eighteenth Centuries: Organization, Operation, Practice, and Personnel,* ed. Peter A. Coclanis, 2–29. Columbia: University of South Carolina Press, 2005.

Dillon, Merton L. *Benjamin Lundy and the Struggle for Negro Freedom.* Urbana: University of Illinois, 1966.

Dillwyn, William. "Diary of William Dillwyn during a Visit to Charleston in 1772." *South Carolina Historical and Genealogical Magazine* 36, no. 1 (January 1935): 1–6; no. 2 (April 1935): 29–35; no. 3 (July 1935): 73–78; no. 4 (October 1935): 107–10.

Diop, Brahim. "Traite Négrière, desertions rurales et occupation du sol dansl'arrière-pays de Gorée dans le traite Atlantique: Myths et Réalités." Ed. Djibril Samb, Initiations at etudes Africaines. Dakar: IFAN, 1997.

———. "Les villages désertés du Sénégal: Contribution à l'histoire de l'habit et de l'occupation du sol." *Archeoafrica*, Hambourg, 1997, 35–47.

Diouf, Mamadou. *Le Kajoor au XIXe siècle: Pouvoir ceddo et conquete colonial*. Paris: Karthala, 1990.

Dixon, Chris. *African Americans and Haiti's Emigration and Black Nationalism in the Nineteenth Century*. Westport, Conn.: Greenwood Press, 2000.

Dobson, David. *Directory of Scots in the Carolinas, 1680–1830*. Baltimore: Genealogical Publishing Company, 1986.

Dodge, Julia B. "An Island by the Sea." *Scribner's Magazine*, September 1877, 652–61.

Doggett, John. *Supplement to Doggett's New-York City Directory, July 19, 1845*. New York: John Doggett, Jr., 1845.

Donnan, Elizabeth. "The Slave Trade into South Carolina before the Revolution." *American Historical Review* 33, no. 4 (July 1928): 804–28.

Dookhan, Isaac. *A History of the Virgin Islands of the United States*. Charlotte Amalie, St. Thomas: Caribbean Universities Press, 1974.

Drescher, Seymour. "The Long Goodbye: Dutch Capitalism and Anti-Slavery in Comparative Perspective." *American Historical Review* 99, no. 1 (February 1994): 46–69.

Dresser, Madge. *Slavery Obscured: The Social History of the Slave Trade in an English Provincial Port*. London: Continuum Books, 2001.

Dubois, Laurent. *Avengers of the New World: The Story of the Haitian Revolution*. Cambridge: Harvard University Press, 2004.

———. *A Colony of Citizens: Revolution and Slave Emancipation in the French Caribbean, 1787–1804*. Chapel Hill: University of North Carolina Press, 2005.

———. *Haiti. The Aftershocks of History*. New York: Metropolitan Books, Henry Holt and Co., 2012.

———. "'The Price of Liberty': Victor Hugues and the Administration of Freedom in Guadeloupe, 1794–1798." *William and Mary Quarterly*, 3rd ser., 56 (1999): 363–92.

Dubois, Laurent, and John D. Garrigus. *Slave Revolution in the Caribbean, 1789–1804: A Brief History with Documents*. Boston: Bedford/St. Martins, 2006.

Duffy, Michael. *Soldiers, Sugar, and Seapower: The British Expeditions to the West Indies and the War against Revolutionary France*. Oxford, U.K.: Clarendon Press, 1987.

DuPlessis, Robert S. "Cloth and the Emergence of the Atlantic Economy." In *The Emergence of the Atlantic Economy*, ed. Peter A. Coclanis, 72–94. Columbia: University of South Carolina Press, 2005.

Earl, Peter. *The Making of the English Middle Class: Business, Society and Family Life in London, 1660–1730*. Berkeley: University of California Press, 1989.

Earle, Jonathan H. *Jacksonian Antislavery and the Politics of Free Soil, 1824–1854*. Chapel Hill: University of North Carolina Press, 2004.

Edgar, Walter. *South Carolina: A History*. Columbia: University of South Carolina Press, 1998.

Ekman, Ernst. "Sweden, the Slave Trade and Slavery." *Revue français d'histoire d'outre-mer*, nos. 226–27 (1975): 221–31.

Ellis, Joseph J. *Passionate Sage: The Character and Legacy of John Adams.* New York: Norton, 1993, 2001.

Ellsworth, Linda, and Lucius Ellsworth. *Pensacola: The Deep Water City.* Tulsa: Continental Heritage Press, 1982.

Eltis, David. "A Brief Overview of the Trans-Atlantic Slave Trade: The Middle Passage," Voyages: The Trans-Atlantic Slave Trade Database. Http://slavevoyages.org/tast/assessment/essays-intro-01.faces.

———. "The Volume and Structure of the Transatlantic Slave Trade: A Reassessment." *William and Mary Quarterly* 58, no. 1 (January 2001): 17–46.

———. "'Voyages: The Trans-Atlantic Slave Trade Database': Voyage 25457, Gustavia (1806)."

Eltis, David, and David Richardson. "A New Assessment of the Transatlantic Slave Trade." In *Voyages: The Trans-Atlantic Slave Trade Database,* at www.slavevoyages.org.

———. "The 'Numbers Game' and Routes to Slavery." *Slavery and Abolition: A Journal of Slave and Post-Slave Studies* 18, no. 1 (April 1997): 1–15.

———, eds. "Routes to Slavery: Direction, Ethnicity and Mortality in the Transatlantic Slave Trade." *Slavery and Abolition* 18, no. 1 (April 1997): 72–97, 98–121, and 122–45.

———. "West Africa and the Transatlantic Slave Trade: New Evidence of Long-Run Trends." *Slavery and Abolition: A Journal of Slave and Post-Slave Studies* 18, no. 1 (April 1997): 16–35.

Ernest, Joseph Albert. "The Currency Act Repeal Movement: A Study of Imperial Politics and Revolutionary Crisis, 1764–1767." *William and Mary Quarterly,* 3rd ser., 25, no. 2 (April 1968): 177–211.

Estes, Todd. *The Jay Treaty Debate: Public Opinion and the Evolution of Early American Political Culture.* Amherst: University of Massachusetts Press, 2006.

Fanning, Sarah Connors. "Haiti and the U.S.: African American Emigration and the Recognition Debate." Ph.D. diss., University of Texas at Austin. 2008.

Feldbaek, Ole. "The Danish Trading Companies of the Seventeenth and Eighteenth Centuries." *Scandinavian Economic History Review* 34, no. 3 (1986): 204–18.

Ferguson, T. Reed. *The John Couper Family at Cannon's Point.* Macon, Ga.: Mercer University Press, 1994.

Fewster, Joseph M. "The Jay Treaty and British Ship Seizures: The Martinique Cases." *William and Mary Quarterly,* 3rd ser., 45, no. 3 (July 1988): 426–52.

Fick, Caroline E. "The French Revolution in Saint Domingue: A Triumph or a Failure?" In *A Turbulent Time: The French Revolution and the Greater Caribbean,* ed. David Barry Gaspar and David Patrick Geggus, 51–77. Bloomington: Indiana University Press, 1997.

Fields, Barbara Jeanne. *Slavery and Freedom on the Middle Ground: Maryland during the Nineteenth Century.* New Haven: Yale University Press, 1985.

Fleszar, Mark J. "The Atlantic Mind: Zephaniah Kingsley, Slavery and the Politics of Race in the Atlantic World." Unpublished M.A. thesis, Georgia State University, 2009.

Follett, Richard. *The Sugar Masters: Planters and Slaves in Louisiana's Cane World, 1820–1860.* Baton Rouge: Louisiana State University Press, 2005.

Foner, Laura. "The Free People of Color in Louisiana and St. Domingue: A Comparative Portrait of Two Three-Caste Societies." *Journal of Social History* 3 (1970): 406–30.

Fraser, Walter J., Jr. *Charleston! Charleston! The History of a Southern City.* Columbia: University of South Carolina Press, 1989.

———. *Patriots, Pistols and Petticoats: "Poor Sinful Charles Town" during the American Revolution.* Columbia: University of South Carolina Press, Second Edition, 1993.

Fraser, Sir Walter. *The Annandale Family Book of the Johnstones.* 2 vols. Edinburgh, Scotland, 1894.

Fretwell, Jacqueline K. *Kingsley Beatty Gibbs and His Journal of 1840–1843.* St. Augustine: St. Augustine Historical Society, 1984.

Fyfe, Christopher. *A History of Sierra Leone.* London: Oxford University Press, 1962.

Gamble, David P. *The Wolof of Senegambia: together with notes on the Lebu and the Serer.* London: International African Institute, 1967.

Gannon, Michael V. *The Cross in the Sand: The Early Catholic Church in Florida, 1513–1870.* Gainesville: University Presses of Florida, 1982.

Garrigus, John D. *Before Haiti: Race and Citizenship in French Saint-Domingue.* New York: Palgrave Macmillan, 2006.

———. "Blue and Brown: Contraband Indigo at the Rise of a Free Colored Planter Class in French Saint-Domingue." *The Americas* 50, no. 2 (October 1993). 233–63.

Garvin, Russell. "The Free Negro in Florida before the Civil War." *Florida Historical Quarterly* 46 (July 1967): 9–17.

Geggus, David Patrick. "Jamaica and the Saint Domingue Slave Revolt, 1791–1793." http://abolition/nypl.org/content/images/480ff2e556288/jamaica_/st_domingue_revolt.pdf: 219–233.

———. *Slavery, War, and Revolution: The British Occupation of Saint Domingue, 1793–1798.* London: Oxford University Press, 1982.

———. "Slavery, War, and Revolution in the Greater Caribbean, 1789–1815." In *A Turbulent Time: The French Revolution and the Greater Caribbean,* ed. David Barry Gaspar and David Patrick Geggus, 1–50. Bloomington: Indiana University Press, 1997.

Genovese, Eugene D. *Roll, Jordan, Roll; The World the Slaves Made.* New York: Vintage Books, 1976.

Godbold, E. Stanly, Jr., and Robert H. Woody. *Christopher Gadsden and the American Revolution.* Knoxville: University of Tennessee Press, 1983.

Green-Pedersen, Svend E. "Colonial Trade under the Danish Flag: A Case Study of the Danish Slave Trade to Cuba 1790–1807." *Scandinavian Journal of History* 5 (1980): 93–119.

———. "The Economic Considerations behind the Danish Abolition of the Negro Slave Trade." In *The Uncommon Market: Essays in the Economic History of the Atlantic Slave Trade*, ed. Henry A. Gemery and Jan S. Hogendorn, 399–418. New York: Academic Press, Harcourt Brace Jovanovitch, 1979.

———. "The History of the Danish Negro Slave Trade: An Interim Survey Relating in Particular to Its Volume, Structure, Profitability and Abolition." *Revue Française d'Historie d'Outre Mer* 62 (1975): 196–220.

———. "The Scope and Structure of the Danish Negro Slave Trade." *Scandinavian Economic History Review* 19, no. 2 (1971): 149–97.

Griffin, Patricia C., ed. *The Odyssey of an African Slave, by Sitiki.* Gainesville: University Press of Florida, 2009.

Gritzner, Janet. "Tabby in the Colonial Southeast: The Culture History of an American Building Material." Ph.D. diss., Louisiana State University, 1978.

Guèye, Mbaye. L'Esclavage au Sénégal du XVIIe au XIXe siècle, these de IIIe cycle, Nantes, France, 1969.

Gutteridge, G. H. *The American Correspondence of a Bristol Merchant, 1766–1776.* Berkeley: University of California Press, 1934.

Hagy, James W., comp. *City Directories for Charleston, South Carolina.* Baltimore: Clearfield Company, 1995.

———, comp. *City Directories for Charleston, South Carolina for the Years 1803, 1806, 1807, 1809, 1813.* Baltimore: Clearfield Company, 1996.

Harper, Francis, ed. *Travels of William Bartram; Naturalist's Edition.* Athens: University of Georgia Press, 1998.

Harries, Patrick. "Slavery, Social Incorporation and Surplus Extraction: The Nature of Free and Unfree Labour in South-East Africa." *Journal of African History* 22, no. 3 (1981): 309–30.

Harris, Marvin. *Patterns of Race in the Americas.* New York: Norton, 1964.

Harris, P. M. G. *The History of Human Population.* Vol. 2, *Migration, Urbanization, and Structural Change.* Westport, Conn.: Praeger, 2003.

Heckard, Jennifer. "The Crossroads of Empire: The 1817 Liberation and Occupation of Amelia Island, East Florida." Unpublished Ph.D. diss., University of Connecticut, 2006.

Henshaw, William Wade, and Thomas Worth Marshall. *Encyclopedia of American Quaker Genealogy.* Vol. 2. Ann Arbor: Edward Brothers, 1940.

Hickey, Donald. *The War of 1812: A Forgotten Conflict.* Urbana: University of Illinois Press, 1990.

Highfield, Arnold R. "The Danish Atlantic and West Indian Slave Trade." In *The Danish West Indian Slave Trade: Virgin Islands Perspectives*, ed. George F. Tyson and Arnold

R. Highfield, 11–32. Christiansted, St. Croix: Virgin Islands Humanities Council, 1994.

Hill, Louise B. "George J. F. Clarke, 1774–1836." *Florida Historical Quarterly* 21, no. 3 (January 1943): 197–235.

Hoffman, Paul E. *Florida's Frontiers*. Bloomington: Indiana University Press, 2002.

Holcomb, Brent H., comp. *South Carolina Naturalizations, 1783–1850*. Baltimore: Clearfield Company, 1985.

Holmbert, Tom. "The Acts, Orders in Council, & c. of Great Britain [on Trade], 1793–1812." Research Subjects: Government & Politics, The Napoleon Series, 2003. Http://www.napoleon-series.org/research/government/british/decrees/ c_britdecrees1.html#source.

Holmes, Mrs. Basil. "Haunts of the London Quakers." In *The Antiquary: A Magazine Devoted to the Study of the Past*, ed. Edward Walford, John Charles Cox, and George Lattimer Apperson, vol. 35 (January–December 1899). London: Elliot Stock, 1899.

Holmes, Theodore C. *Loyalists to Canada: The 1783 Settlement of Quakers and others at Passamaquoddy*. Camden, Maine: Picton Press, 1992.

Holsoe, Svend E. "The Origin, Transport, Introduction and Distribution of Africans on St. Croix: An Overview." In *The Danish West Indian Slave Trade: Virgin Islands Perspectives*, ed. George F. Tyson and Arnold R. Highfield, 33–46. Christiansted, St. Croix: Virgin Islands Humanities Council, 1994.

———. "Slave Carrying Vessels between the Danish West Indies and Gorée and/or Cape Verde." Unpublished typescript, Department of Anthropology, University of Delaware, Wilmington, 1994.

Hooper, Kevin S. *The Early History of Clay County: A Wilderness That Could Be Tamed*. Charleston, S.C.: The History Press, 2006.

Hostettler, Eve. "Local History in Lincolnshire." *History Workshop*, no. 2 (Autumn 1976): 140–46.

Howe, Mark A. DeWolfe, ed. "Journal of Josiah Quincy, Junior, 1773." *Proceedings of the Massachusetts Historical Society* 49 (June 1916): 424–81.

Hudson, Winthrop S. "A Suppressed Chapter in Quaker History." *Journal of Religion* 24, no. 2 (April 1944): 108–18.

Hunt, Alfred N. *Haiti's Influence on Antebellum America: Slumbering Volcano in the Caribbean*. Baton Rouge: Louisiana State University Press, 1988.

Jackson, Jesse J. "The Negro and the Law in Florida, 1821–1921." Unpublished M.A. thesis, Florida State University, 1960.

Jackson, Melvin H. *Privateers in Charleston, 1793–1796: An Account of a French Palatinate in South Carolina*. Washington, D.C.: Smithsonian Institution Press, 1969.

Jervey, Hayward, collector. "Items from a South Carolina Almanac." *South Carolina Historical and Genealogical Magazine* 32, no. 1 (January 1931): 73–80.

Johnson, Michael P. "Runaway Slaves and the Slave Communities in South Carolina, 1799 to 1830." *William and Mary Quarterly*, 3rd ser., 38 (1981): 418–41.

Johnson, Sherry. "Climate, Community, and Commerce among Florida, Cuba, and the Atlantic World." *Florida Historical Quarterly* 80, no. 4 (Spring 2002): 455–81.

Johnson, Walter. *Soul by Soul: Life inside the Antebellum Slave Market.* Cambridge: Harvard University Press, 1999.

Johnston, Alexander, Jr. *General Account of the Family of Johnston of that Ilk, formerly of Caskieben.* Edinburgh, Scotland, 1832.

Johnston, T. B., and James A. Robertson. *Historical Geography of the Clans of Scotland.* 3rd ed. 1899.

Johnstone, C. L. *History of the Johnstones, 1171–1909.* Edinburgh, Scotland, 1909, supplement, Glasgow, 1925.

Jordan, Winthrop D. *The White Man's Burden: Historical Origins of Racism in the United States.* New York: Oxford University Press, 1974.

Joslin, Isaac. *West Florida Controversy, 1798–1813.* Baltimore: Johns Hopkins University Press, 1918.

Keith, Alice B. "Relaxations in British Restrictions on American Trade with the British West Indies, 1783–1802." *Journal of Modern History* 20, no. 1 (March 1948): 1–18.

Kingsley, Z[ephaniah]. *A Treatise on the Patriarchal, or Co-operative System of Society, As it Exists in some Governments, and Colonies in America, and in the United States, Under the Name of Slavery, With its Necessity and Advantages. By an Inhabitant of Florida.* Freeport, N.Y.: Books for Libraries Press, 1828, 1829, 1833, 1834; reprinted 1970.

Kingsley, Zephaniah, Jr. "Process of Manufacturing and Clarifying Sugar from weak or immature Juice, and of obtaining Sugar from Molasses." *Southern Agriculturalist and Register of Rural Affairs; Adapted to the Southern Section of the United States* 3, no. 2 (October 1830): 513–17.

Kiple, Kenneth F., and Brian T. Higgins. "Mortality Caused by Dehydration during the Middle Passage." In *The Atlantic Slave Trade: Effects on Economies, Societies, and Peoples in Africa, the Americas, and Europe,* ed. Joseph E. Inikori and Stanley L. Engerman, 321–38. Durham, N.C.: Duke University Press, 1992.

Klein, Herbert S. *The Atlantic Slave Trade.* Cambridge, U.K.: Cambridge University Press, 1999.

———. *Slavery in the Americas: A Comparative Study of Cuba and Virginia.* Chicago: University of Chicago Press, 1967.

———, comp. "Slave Trade to Havana, Cuba, 1790–1820." Computer file. Madison: University of Wisconsin Data and Program Library Service, 1978.

Klein, Martin A. "Servitude among the Wolof and Sereer of Senegambia." In *Slavery in Africa: Historical and Anthropological Perspectives,* ed. Igor Kopytoff and Suzanne Miers, 336–66. Madison: University of Wisconsin Press, 1977.

Knetsch, Joe. *Florida's Seminole Wars, 1817–1858.* Charleston, S.C.: Arcadia Publishing, 2003.

Knight, Franklin. *Slave Society in Cuba during the Nineteenth Century.* Madison: University of Wisconsin Press, 1970.

Koger, Larry. *Black Slaveowners: Free Black Slave Masters in South Carolina, 1790–1860.* Columbia: University of South Carolina Press, 1985.

Kulikoff, Allan. "Uprooted Peoples: Black Migrants in the Age of the American Revolution, 1790–1820." In *Slavery and Freedom in the Age of the American Revolution*, ed. Ira Berlin and Ronald Hoffman, 147–54. Charlottesville: University of Virginia Press, 1983.

Lambert, Robert Stansbury. *South Carolina Loyalists in the American Revolution.* Columbia: University of South Carolina Press, 1987.

Landers, Jane G. *Atlantic Creoles in the Age of Revolutions.* Cambridge: Harvard University Press, 2010.

———. *Black Society in Spanish Florida.* Urbana: University of Illinois Press, 1999.

———, ed. *Colonial Plantations and Economy in Florida.* Gainesville: University Press of Florida, 2000.

———. "Francisco Xavier Sánchez, Floridano Planter and Merchant." In Landers, *Colonial Plantations and Economy in Florida*, 83–97.

———. "Gracia Real de Santa Teresa de Mose: A Free Black Town in Spanish Colonial Florida." *American Historical Review* 95, no. 1 (1990): 9–30.

———. "Rebellion and Royalism in Spanish Florida: The French Revolution on Spain's Northern Colonial Frontier." In Gaspar and Geggus, *A Turbulent Time*, 156–77.

———. "Slave Resistance on the Southeastern Frontier: Fugitives, Maroons, and Banditti in the Age of Revolutions." *El Escribano: The Journal of St. Augustine Historical Society* 32 (1995): 12–49.

Lavoie, Yolande, Caroline Fick, and Francine M. Mayer. "A Particular Study of Slavery in the Caribbean Island of Saint Bartelemy: 1648–1846." *Caribbean Studies* 28, no. 2 (1995): 369–403.

Lawrence, Joseph Wilson. *The Judges of New Brunswick and Their Times.* Ed. and annotated by Alfred A. Stockton. Saint John, New Brunswick: J. & A. McMillan, 1883.

L'Engle, Madeleine. *The Summer of the Great-Grandmother.* New York: Farrar, Straus and Giroux, 1974.

Leyti, Oumar Ndiaye. "Le Joloff et ses Burbas." BIFAN, Series B, 31 (1969): 966–1008.

Lisenby, Julie Ann. "The Free Negro in Antebellum Florida." Unpublished master's thesis, Florida State University, 1967.

Littlefield, Daniel C. *Rice and Slavery: Ethnicity and the Slave Trade in Colonial South Carolina.* Baton Rouge: Louisiana State University Press, 1981.

Lloyd, Richard, Lieutenant Colonel. Original Correspondence to the Secretary of State, Colonial Office, National Archives, Kew, England.

Lloyd's List, Register of Ships. Entry no. 4186, January 22, 1805, Liverpool. London: Gregg International Publishers, Limited, 1969.

Lovejoy, Paul E. *Transformations in Slavery: A History of Slavery in Africa.* 2nd ed. New York: Cambridge University Press, 2000.

Lovejoy, Paul E., and David Richardson, "'This Horrid Hole': Royal Authority, Commerce and Credit at Bonny, 1690–1840." *Journal of African History* 45, no. 3 (2004): 363–92.

Lowe, Richard G. "American Seizure of Amelia Island." *Florida Historical Quarterly* 45, no. 1 (July 1966): 18–30.

Machado, Pedro. "A Forgotten Corner of the Indian Ocean: Gujarati Merchants, Portuguese India and the Mozambique Slave-Trade, c. 1730–1830." *Slavery and Abolition* 24, no. 2 (August 2003): 17–33.

———. "Without Scales and Balances: Gujarati Merchants in Mozambique, c.1680s–1800." *Portuguese Studies Review* 9, nos. 1–2 (2001): 254–88.

Mackenzie-Grieve, Averill. *The Last Years of the English Slave Trade: Liverpool, 1750–1807.* London: Frank Cass and Co., reprint of a 1941 first edition.

MacNutt, W. Stewart. "The Founders and Their Times." Special Collections, University of New Brunswick Library, no date.

———. *New Brunswick, A History: 1784–1867.* Toronto: Macmillan of Canada, 1967.

Mahon, John K. *History of the Second Seminole War, 1835–1842.* Rev. ed. Gainesville: University Press of Florida, 1991.

Mahon, John K., and Brent R. Weisman. "Florida's Seminole and Miccosukee Peoples." In *The New History of Florida*, ed. Michael Gannon, 183–206. Gainesville: University Press of Florida, 1996.

Marotti, Frank, Jr. *The Cana Sanctuary: History, Diplomacy, and Black Catholic Marriage in Antebellum St. Augustine, Florida.* Tuscaloosa: University of Alabama Press, 2012.

———. *Heaven's Soldiers: Free People of Color and the Spanish Legacy in Antebellum Florida.* Tuscaloosa: University of Alabama Press, 2013.

———. "Negotiating Freedom in St. Johns County, Florida, 1812–1862." Unpublished Ph.D. diss., University of Hawaii, August 2003.

Martin, Sidney W. *Florida during the Territorial Days.* Athens: University of Georgia Press, 1944.

Maxwell, Charles, Lieutenant Colonel. "Answers to Questions Proposed to Lt. Colonel Maxwell, Lieutenant Governor of Senegal and Gorée by His Majesty's Commissioner for Investigating the Forts and Settlements in Africa," January 1, 1811. Original Correspondence of the Secretarty of State, Series 267, vol. 29, Colonial Office, National Archives, Kew, England.

May, Philip S. "Zephaniah Kingsley, Nonconformist." *Florida Historical Quarterly* 23, no. 3 (January 1945): 145–59.

Mayer, Henry. *All on Fire: William Lloyd Garrison and the Abolition of Slavery.* New York: Norton, 1998.

McAlister, Lyle. "Pensacola during the Second Spanish Period." *Florida Historical Quarterly* 37, no. 3 (January 1959): 281–327.

McDiarmid, Kate. "Whistler's Mother: Her Life, Letters, and Journal." Unpublished biography. Special Collections, Glasgow University Library, Glasgow, Scotland.

McDonough, Daniel J. *Christopher Gadsden and Henry Laurens: The Parallel Lives of Two Americans.* Selingrove, Pa.: Susquehanna University Press, 2000.

McGowen, George Smith, Jr. *The British Occupation of Charleston, 1780–1782.* Columbia: University of South Carolina Press, 1972.

McIntosh, John Houstoun. "Communication." *National Intelligencer,* July 2, 1823, Washington, D.C.

McMillin, James A. *Final Victims: Foreign Slave Trade to North America, 1783–1810.* Columbia: University of South Carolina Press, 2004.

McQueen, John. *The letters of Don Juan McQueen to his family: written from Spanish East Florida, 1791–1807.* With a biographical sketch of notes by Walter Charlton Hartridge. Columbia, S.C.: Colonial Dames of America, by Bostick and Thornley, 1943.

Merrens, H. Roy, ed. "A View of Coastal South Carolina in 1778: The Journal of Ebenezer Hazard." *South Carolina Historical Magazine* 73 (October 1972): 177–93.

Miller, Janice Borton. "The Struggle for Free Trade in East Florida and the Cédula of 1793." *Florida Historical Quarterly* 55, no. 1 (July 1976): 48–59.

Miller, Joseph C. *Way of Death: Merchant Capitalism and the Angolan Slave Trade, 1730–1830.* Madison: University of Wisconsin Press, 1988.

Minchinton, Walter E. "Bristol—Metropolis of the West in the Eighteenth Century." *Transactions of the Royal Historical Society,* 5th ser., 4 (1954): 69–89.

———. "The Political Activities of Bristol Merchants with Respect to the Southern Colonies." *Virginia Magazine of History and Biography* 79, no. 2 (April 1971): 167–89.

———. "The Stamp Act Crises: Bristol and Virginia." *Virginia Magazine of History and Biography* 73, no. 2 (April 1965): 145–55.

Mintz, Sidney W. "From Plantations to Peasantries in the Caribbean." In *Caribbean Contours,* ed. Mintz and Sally Price, 127–53. Baltimore: Johns Hopkins University Press, 1985.

———. "Slavery and the Rise of Peasantries." In *Roots and Branches: Current Directions in Slave Studies,* ed. Michael Craton, 213–42. Oxford, England: Pergamon Press, 1979.

Monteil, Vincent. "Le Dyolof et Al-Bouri Ndiaye." Dakar, Senegal: BIFAN 28, no. 3–4 (1966): 595–620.

Moore, Christopher. *The Loyalists: Revolution, Exile, Settlement.* Toronto: Macmillan of Canada, 1984.

Morgan, Kenneth. "Bristol and the Atlantic Trade in the Eighteenth Century." *English Historical Review* 107, no. 424 (July 1992): 626–50.

———. "Liverpool's Dominance in the British Slave Trade, 1740–1807." In *Liverpool and Transatlantic Slavery,* ed. David Richardson, Suzanne Schwarz, and Anthony Tibbles, 14–42. Liverpool: Liverpool University Press, 2000.

———. "Shipping Patterns and the Atlantic Trade of Bristol, 1740–1770." *William and Mary Quarterly,* 3rd ser., 46, no. 3 (July 1989): 506–38.

———. "Slave Sales in Colonial Charleston." *English Historical Review* 113, no. 453 (September 1998): 905–27.

Morgan, Philip D. "Black Society in the Lowcountry, 1760–1810." In *Slavery and Free-*

dom in the Age of Revolution, ed. Ira Berlin and Ronald Hoffman, 82–142. Charlottesville: University of Virginia Press, 1983.

———. "Cultural Implications of the Atlantic Slave Trade: African Regional Origins, American Destinations and New World Developments." *Slavery and Abolition: A Journal of Slave and Post-Slave Studies* 18, no. 1 (1997): 122–45.

———. "Labor and the Shaping of Slave Life in the Americas." In Berlin and Morgan, *Cultivation and Culture*, 1–45.

———. *Slave Counterpoint: Black Culture in the Eighteenth-Century Chesapeake and Low Country*. Chapel Hill: University of North Carolina Press, 1998.

———. "Task and Gang Systems: The Organization of Labor on New World Plantations." In *Work and Labor in Early America*, ed. Stephen Innes, 189–220. Chapel Hill: University of North Carolina Press, 1998.

Morris, Allen, and Amelia Rea Maguire. "Beginnings of Popular Government in Florida." *Florida Historical Quarterly* 57, no. 1 (July 1978): 19–38.

Morriss, Roger. *Cockburn and the British Navy in Transition: Admiral Sir George Cockburn, 1772–1753*. Columbia: University of South Carolina Press, 1997.

Moser, Harold D., Harriet Chappell Owsley, David R. Hoth, Sharon Macpherson, John H. Reinbold, and Sam B. Smith, eds. *The Papers of Andrew Jackson*. Vol. 5, *1821–1824*. Knoxville: University of Tennessee Press, 1996.

Mouser, Bruce L. *American Colony on the Rio Pongo: The War of 1812, Continuing Slave Trade, and Plans for a Settlement of African Americans, 1810–1830*. Trenton, N.J.: Africa World Press, 2013.

———. "Baltimore's African Experiment, 1822–1827." *Journal of Negro History* 80, no. 3 (Summer 1995): 113–30.

———. "Landlords-Strangers: A Process of Accommodation and Assimilation." *International Journal of African Historical Studies* 8, no. 3 (1975): 425–40.

———. "Trade and Politics in the Nunez and Pongo Rivers, 1790–1865." Unpublished Ph.D. diss., Indiana University, 1972.

———. "Trade, Coasters, and Conflict in the Rio Pongo from 1790 to 1808." *Journal of African History* 14, no. 1 (January 1973): 45–64.

"Mr. Robinson's Tour," no. 15, *The American Agriculturalist and Farmer's Cabinet* 9 (March 1850): 93–95. New York: C.M. Saxton, 1850.

Mullin, Gerald W. *Flight and Rebellion: Slave Resistance in Eighteenth-Century Virginia*. New York: Oxford University Press, 1972.

Mullin, Michael. *Africa in America: Slave Acculturation and Resistance in the American South and the British Caribbean, 1736–1831*. Urbana: University of Illinois Press, 1992.

Mulroy, Kevin. *Freedom on the Border: The Seminole Maroons in Florida, the Indian Territory, Coahuila, and Texas*. Lubbock: Texas Tech University Press, 1993.

Nash, R. C. "The Organization of Trade and Finance in the Atlantic Economy: Britain and South Carolina, 1670–1775." In *Money, Trade, and Power*, ed. Jack P. Greene, Rosemary Brana-Shute, and Randy J. Sparks, 74–107. Columbia: University of South Carolina Press, 2001.

Newitt, Malyn. *A History of Mozambique*. Bloomington: Indiana University Press, 1995.

Newton, John. *Thoughts on the African Slave Trade*. London: J. Buckland and J. Johnson, 1788.

Nicholls, C. S. *The Swahili Coast: Politics, Diplomacy and Trade on the East African Littoral, 1798–1856*. New York: Africana Publishing Corporation, 1971.

Nicholson, John. *Bygone Lincolnshire*. Ed. William Andrews. London: Simpkin, Marshall Hamilton, Kent and Company, 1891.

Nissen, Johan Peter. *Reminiscences of a 46 Years' Residence in the Island of St. Thomas, in the West Indies*. Nazareth, Pa.: Senseman & Co., 1838.

Nørregard, Georg. *Danish Settlements in West Africa, 1658–1850*, Boston: Boston University Press, 1966.

Notes of an Invalid, no. 9, "The Rich Mr. K. with His Black Consort and Offspring." *Christian Register and Boston Observer*, September 30, 1837.

Olsbert, R. Nicholas. "Ship Registers in the South Carolina Archives, 1734–1780." *South Carolina Historical Magazine* 74, no. 4 (1973): 189–279.

Owsley, Frank, Jr., and Gene A. Smith. *Filibusters and Expansionists: Jeffersonian Manifest Destiny, 1800–1821*. Tuscaloosa: University of Alabama Press, 1997.

Paisley, Clifton. *The Red Hills of Florida, 1528–1865*. Tuscaloosa: University of Alabama Press, 1989.

Palmer, Gregory. *Biographical Sketches of Loyalists of the American Revolution*. Westport, Conn.: Meckler Publishing, 1984.

Palmer, Michael. *Stoddert's War: Naval Operations during the Quasi-War with France, 1798–1801*. Columbia: University of South Carolina Press, 1987.

Pamphile, Leon D. "Emigration of Black Americans to Haiti, 1821–1863." *The Crisis* 90 (1983): 43–44.

———. *Haitians and African Americans: A Heritage of Tragedy and Hope*. Gainesville: University Press of Florida, 2001.

Paquette, Robert L. *Sugar Is Made with Blood: The Conspiracy of La Escalera and the Conflict between Empires over Slavery in Cuba*. Middletown, Conn.: Wesleyan University Press, 1988.

Parker, Susan. "Men without God or King: Rural Settlers of East Florida, 1784–1790." *Florida Historical Quarterly* 69, no. 2 (October 1990): 135–55.

———. "Success through Diversification: Francis Philip Fatio's New Switzerland Plantation." In Landers, *Colonial Plantations and Economy in Florida*, 69–82.

Patrick, Rembert Wallace. *Aristocrat in Uniform: General Duncan L. Clinch*. Gainesville: University of Florida Press, 1963.

———. *Florida Fiasco: Rampant Rebels on the Florida-Georgia Border, 1810–1815*. Athens: University of Georgia Press, 1951.

Perotin-Dumon, Ann. "Cabotage, Contraband, and Corsairs: The Port Cities of Guadeloupe and Their Inhabitants, 1650–1800." In *Atlantic Port Cities: Economy, Culture, and Society in the Atlantic World, 1650–1850*, ed. Peggy K. Liss and Franklin W. Knight, 58–86. Knoxville: University of Tennessee Press, 1991.

Pons, Frank Moya. *The Dominican Republic: A National History*. New Rochelle, N.Y.: Hispaniola Books, 1994.

Popkin, Jeremy D. *Facing Racial Revolution: Eyewitness Accounts of the Haitian Insurrection*. Chicago: University of Chicago Press, 2007.

———. *You Are All Free: The Haitian Revolution and the Abolition of Slavery*. New York: Cambridge University Press, 2010.

Porter, Kenneth W. *The Black Seminoles: History of a Freedom-Seeking People*. Rev. and ed. Alcione M. Amos and Thomas P. Senter. Gainesville: University Press of Florida, 1996.

Poston, Jonathan H. *The Buildings of Charleston: A Guide to the City's Architecture*. Columbia: University of South Carolina Press, 1997.

"Prejudice against Color." *Working Man's Advocate* (New York), October 1, 1831.

Puig Ortiz, Jose Augusto. *Emigracion de Libertos NorteAmericanos a Puerto Plata en la Primera Mitad del Siglo XIX*. Dominican Republic: La Iglesia Metodista Wesleyana, 1978.

Rainey, George P. *Cases Argued and Adjudged in the Supreme Court of Florida, During the years 1882–1883*. Vol. 19. Tallahassee, Florida, 1883.

Rediker, Marcus. *The Slave Ship: A Human History*. New York: Penguin Books, 2007.

Rice, C. Duncan. "The Anti-Slavery Mission of George Thompson to the United States, 1834–1835." *Journal of American Studies* 2, no. 1 (April 1968): 13–31.

Richardson, David. "Shipboard Revolts, African Authority, and the Atlantic Slave Trade." *William and Mary Quarterly*, 3rd ser., 58, no. 1 (January 2001): 69–92.

———. "Slavery and Bristol's 'Golden Age.'" *Slavery and Abolition* 26, no. 1 (April 2005): 35–54.

Richardson, David, Suzanne Schwarz, and Anthony Tibbles, eds. *Liverpool and Transatlantic Slavery*. Liverpool: Liverpool University Press, 2007.

Rigby, S. H. "'Sore Decay' and 'Fair Dwellings': Boston and Urban Decline in the Later Middle Ages." *Midlands History* 10, no. 1 (1985): 47–61.

Riley, Sandra. *Homeward Bound: A History of the Bahama Islands to 1850, with a Definitive Study of Abaco in the American Loyalist Period*. Miami: Riley Hall, 1983.

Rivers, Larry Eugene. *Slavery in Florida: Territorial Days to Emancipation*. Gainesville: University Press of Florida, 2000.

Robinson, David. "The Islamic Revolution of Futa Toro." *International Journal of African Historical Studies* 8, no. 2 (1975): 185–221.

Rogers, George C. *Charleston in the Age of the Pinckneys*. Norman: University of Oklahoma Press, 1969.

———. "The Charleston Tea Party: The Significance of December 3, 1773." *South Carolina Historical Magazine* 75 (July 1974): 153–68.

Rohrer, Katherine E. "David B. Mitchell (1766–1837)." In *New Georgia Encyclopedia*, http://www.georgia encyclopedia.org/nge.

Rollins, Mrs. John. "Fort George Island." Unpublished memoir, 1904. Kingsley Plantation Vertical File, Department of College Archives and Special Collections, Olin Library, Rollins College, Winter Park, Florida.

Salmon, Thomas. "The Present state of Zanguebar." In *Modern History of the Present State of All Nations. Describing their respective situations, persons, and buildings....* 3rd ed., vol. 3. London: T. Longman and T. Shewell, 1746.

Schafer, Daniel L. *Anna Madgigine Jai Kingsley: African Princess, Florida Slave, Plantation Slaveowner.* Gainesville: University Press of Florida, 2003.

———. "'A Class of People Neither Freemen Nor Slaves': From Spanish to American Race Relations in Florida, 1821–1861." *Journal of Social History* 26, no. 3 (Spring 1993): 587–609.

———. "Family Ties That Bind: Anglo-African Slave Traders in Africa and Florida, John Fraser and His Descendants." *Slavery and Abolition* 20, no. 3 (December 1999): 1–21. Reprinted in Heuman, Gad, and James Walvin. *The Slavery Reader.* London: Routledge, 2003, 778–95.

———. "Freedom was as Close as the River: African Americans and the Civil War in Florida." In *The African American Heritage of Florida*, ed. David R. Colburn and Jane L. Landers, 157–84. Gainesville: University Press of Florida, 1995.

———. *Governor James Grant's Villa: A British East Florida Indigo Plantation.* St. Augustine: The Augustine Historical Society, 2000.

———. "'A Swamp of an Investment'?: Richard Oswald's British East Florida's Plantation Experiment." In Landers, *Colonial Plantations and Economy in Florida*, 11–38.

———. *Thunder on the River: The Civil War in Northeast Florida.* Gainesville: University Press of Florida, 2009.

———. *William Bartram and the Ghost Plantations of British East Florida.* Gainesville: University Press of Florida, 2010.

———. "'Yellow silk ferret tied round their wrists': African Americans in British East Florida, 1763–1784." In Colburn and Landers, *The African American Heritage of Florida*, 71–103.

Schene, Michael G. "Robert and John Grattan Gamble: Middle Florida Entrepreneurs." *Florida Historical Quarterly* 54, no. 1 (July 1975): 61–87.

———. "Sugar along the Manatee: Major Robert Gamble, Jr. and the Development of Gamble Plantation." *Tequesta: The Journal of the Historical Society of Southern Florida* 41 (1981): 69–81.

Scott, Julius S. "Crisscrossing Empires: Ships, Sailors, and Resistance in the Lesser Antilles in the Eighteenth Century." In *The Lesser Antilles in the Age of European Expansion*, ed. Robert L. Paquette and Stanley L. Engerman, 128–43. Gainesville: University Press of Florida, 1996.

———. "'Negroes in Foreign Bottoms': Sailors, Slaves, and Communication." In *Origins of the Black Atlantic: Rewriting Histories*, ed. Laurent Dubois and Julius S. Scott, 69–98. New York: Routledge, 2009.

Searcy, Martha Condray. *The Georgia-Florida Contest in the American Revolution, 1776–1778.* Tuscaloosa: University of Alabama Press, 1985.

Searing, James F. *West African Slavery and Atlantic Commerce: The Senegal River Valley, 1700–1860.* Cambridge: Cambridge University Press, 1993.

Sellers, Leila. *Charleston Business on the Eve of the American Revolution.* Chapel Hill: University of North Carolina Press, 1934.

Sheriff, Abdul. *Slaves, Spices, and Ivory in Zanzibar.* London: James Currey, 1987.

Sherman, Gordon E. "Orders in Council and the Laws of the Sea." *American Journal of International Law* 16, no. 3 (July 1922): 400–419.

Sidbury, James. "Saint Domingue in Virginia: Ideology, Local Meaning, and Resistance to Slavery, 1790–1800." *Journal of Southern History* 63, no. 3 (August 1997): 531–52.

Siebert, Wilbur. "The Early Sugar Industry in Florida." *Florida Historical Quarterly* 35, no. 4 (April 1957): 312–19.

Sitterson, Carlyle. "Ante-Bellum Sugar Culture in the South Atlantic States." *Journal of Southern History* 3, no. 2 (May 1937): 175–87.

———. "Financing and Marketing the Sugar Crop of the Old South." *Journal of Southern History* 10, no. 2 (May 1944): 188–99.

Smallwood, Stephanie E. *Saltwater Slavery: A Middle Passage from Africa to American Diaspora.* Cambridge: Harvard University Press, 2007.

Smelser, Marshall. "The Passage of the Naval Act of 1794." *Military Affairs* 22, no. 1 (Spring 1958): 1–12.

Smith, Julia Floyd. *Slavery and Plantation Growth in Antebellum Florida, 1821–1860.* Gainesville: University of Florida Press, 1973.

Smith, Raymond T. *British Guiana.* London: Oxford University Press, 1962.

———. *The Matrifocal Family: Power, Pluralism, and Politics.* New York: Routledge, 1996.

Soliene de González, Nancy L. "The Consanguineal Household and Matrifocality." *American Anthropologist* 67, no. 6 (1965): 1541–49.

Sosin, Jack M. *Agents and Merchants: British Colonial Policy and the Origins of the American Revolution, 1763–1765.* Lincoln: University of Nebraska Press, 1965.

Steel, D. J. *Sources for Nonconformist Genealogy and Family History.* Vol. 2. London: Phillimore, published for the Society of Genealogists, 1973.

Stephens, Jean B. "Zephaniah Kingsley and the Recaptured Africans." *El Escribano: The Journal of the St. Augustine Historical Society* 15 (1978): 71–75.

Stevens, Michael E. "'To get as many slaves as you can': An 1807 Slaving Voyage." *South Carolina Historical Magazine* 87, no. 3 (July 1986): 187–92.

Stowell, Daniel W., ed. *Balancing Evils Judiciously: The Proslavery Writings of Zephaniah Kingsley.* Gainesville: University Press of Florida, 2000.

———. *Timucuan Ecological and Historic Preserve: Historic Resource Study.* Atlanta: National Park Service, Southeast Field Area, 1996.

Sullivan, Buddy. "Ecology as History in the Sapelo Island National Estuarine Research Reserve." *Occasional Papers of the Sapelo Island NERR.* Vol. 1, 2008. 1–22.

Swanson, Gail. *Slave Ship Guerrero*. West Conshohocken, Pa.: Infinity Publishing, 2005.

Tannenbaum, Frank. *Slave and Citizen: The Negro in the Americas*. New York: Knopf, 1947.

Thomas, Hugh. *The Slave Trade: The Story of the Atlantic Slave Trade, 1440–1870*. New York: Simon & Schuster, 1979.

Thompson, Leslie A. *Manual or Digest of the Statute Law of the State of Florida, Including Law of the United States Relative to the Government of Florida*. Boston: C. C. Little and J. Brown, 1847.

Thompson, Pishey. *The History and Antiquities of Boston*. London: Longman and Company, 1856.

Thornton, John. *Africa and Africans in the Making of the Atlantic World, 1400–1680*. New York: Cambridge University Press, 1992.

Tourziari, Georgia, ed. "The Correspondence of Anna McNeill Whistler." In *The Correspondence of Anna McNeill Whistler, 1855–1880*, ed. Margaret F. MacDonald, Patricia de Montfort, and Nigel Thorp. University of Glasgow, Scotland. Http://www.whistler.arts.gla.ac.uk/correspondence.

Trollope, Anthony. *The West Indies and the Spanish Main*. London: Chapman and Hall, 1859.

Troxler, Carole Watterson. "The Migration of Carolina and Georgia Loyalists to Nova Scotia and New Brunswick." Ph.D. diss., University of North Carolina, Chapel Hill, 1974.

United States. Works Progress Administration. Historical Records Survey. *Spanish Land Grants in Florida*. Tallahassee: State Library Board, 1942. Florida State Archives, Tallahassee.

Vaugondy, Robert. *Atlas Portatif Universel*. Paris: Robert de Vaugondy, 1748.

Vlach, John Michael. "Not Mansions . . . But Good Enough: Slave Quarters as Bi-Cultural Expression." In *Black and White Cultural Interaction in the Antebellum South*, ed. Ted Owenby, 89–124. Jackson: University of Mississippi Press, 1993.

Wadstrom, Carl B. *Observations on the Slave Trade and Some Part of the Coast of Guinea during a Voyage Made in 1787 and 1788*. Vol. 1. London: J. Philips, 1789.

Watt, Margaret Gibbs. "The Gibbs Family of Long Ago and Near at Hand, 1337–1967." Jacksonville: Privately printed, 1967.

Wayne, Lucy B. *Sweet Cane: The Architecture of the Sugar Works of East Florida*. Tuscaloosa: University of Alabama Press, 2010.

Webb, James L. A. *Desert Frontier: Ecological and Economic Change Along the Western Sahel, 1600–1850*. Madison: University of Wisconsin Press, 1995.

Webber, Mabel L., comp. "Extracts from the Journal of Mrs. Ann Manigault, 1754–1781." *South Carolina Historical and Genealogical Magazine* 21, no. 1 (January 1921): 10–23.

———, comp. "Marriage and Death Notices from the City Gazette." *South Carolina Historical Magazine* 25, no. 1 (January 1924): 43; and 26, no. 2 (April 1925): 133.

———. "Records of the Quakers in Charleston." *South Carolina Historical Magazine* 28 (January–April 1927): 22–43, 94–107, and 176–97.

———, comp. "William Hort's Journal." *South Carolina Historical and Genealogical Magazine* 24, no. 2 (July 1923): 40–47.

Weber, David J. *The Spanish Frontier in North America.* New Haven: Yale University Press, 1992.

Whistler, James McNeill. "The Correspondence of James McNeill Whistler: The On-line Edition," University of Glasgow, 2004–2007. www.whistler.arts.gla.ac.uk/correspondence/.

Wildes, Tara. "The McIntosh Family of Camden and McIntosh Counties, Georgia, and Alachua and Duval Counties, Florida." Typescript, April 17, 1998. Department of History, University of North Florida.

Williams, Greg H. *The French Assault on American Shipping, 1793–1813: A History and Comprehensive Report of Merchant Marine Losses.* Jefferson, N.C.: Mcfarland, 2009.

Williams, John Lee. *The Territory of Florida or Sketches of the Topography, Civil and Natural History, of the Country, the Climate, and the Indian Tribes, From the First Discovery to the Present Time, with a Map, Views, &c.* A Facsimile Reproduction of the 1827 Edition with an Introduction by Herbert J. Doherty, Jr. Gainesville: University of Florida Press, 1962.

Wilson, Gertrude Rollins. "Notes Concerning the Old Plantation on Fort George Island, 1868–1869." Transcribed by Emily Palmer, March 13, 2009. Timucuan Ecological and Historic Preserve, Florida, National Park Service, Jacksonville, Florida. www.nps.gov/timu/historyculture/timu_fla_notes_plantation.htm.

Wood, Wayne W. *Jacksonville's Architectural Heritage: Landmarks for the Future.* Jacksonville: University of North Florida Press, 1989.

Woodson, Carter G., ed. *Free Negro Owners of Slaves in the United States: Together with Absentee Ownership of Slaves in the United States in 1830.* Washington, D.C.: Association for the Study of Negro Life and History, 1924.

Wright, Esther Clark. *The Loyalists of New Brunswick.* Yarmouth, Nova Scotia: Sentinel Printing Ltd., 1955 (5th printing, 1985).

Wright, James Leitch, Jr. "A Note on the First Seminole War as Seen by the Indians, Negroes and Their British Advisors." *Journal of Southern History* 34, no. 4 (November 1968): 565–75.

Wu, Kathleen Gibbs Johnson. "Manumission of Anna: Another Interpretation." *El Escribano: The St. Augustine Journal of History* 46 (2009): 51–68.

Wyllys, Rufus Kay, "The East Florida Revolution of 1812–1814." *Hispanic Historical Review* 9, no. 4 (November 1929): 415–45.

Index

Bay of Fundy, 27–28

Bedon's Alley, Charleston, 7, 14, 19

Behrendt, Stephen, 75

Bennett Taylor and Company, 23, 25, 72

Berlin, Ira, 173

Bethune, Farquhar, 114, 233

Biassou, Jorge, 49, 104

Big Hammock, 147

Black Legend, 114

Black Seminoles, 145, 206

Bolster, W. Jeffrey, 99

Bonafi, slave carpenter, 81, 198, 237, 295n26, 296n34; and sale of family, 239–40, 245, 249, 251

Bonaparte, Napoléon, 48

Bouteille, Jean, 35

Bowden, John M., 96, 106

Bowers, David, 62–63, 77

Bowles, William Augustus, 103

Boyer, Jean-Pierre, 210, 214, 218, 222

Bozales, 73, 89, 94, 98. *See also* New Negro

Brandywine (ship), 58

Brenian, Mr., 26

Brewton, Miles, 16

Bristol, England, 7–10, 23–25

British seizure of U.S. ships, 38–42

Bronson, Isaac H., 225, 227

Brown, John F., 179–80, 184

Brown, Robert, 179

Brugal, Pablo Juan, 220

Buena Vista Plantation, 156, 188, 201–3, 254

Buena Vista Point. *See* Orange Grove Plantation

Burritt, Samuel L., 225

Buurba Jolof, 89, 91–93

Cabaret (also Cabarete), 160, 215, 217–20, 222–24, 229, 233

Cabaret Creek, 219

Calhoun, John C., 149

Callen, Patrick, 64–65

Camara, Sidi, 164, 284n10

Cameron, Gail, 74

Campbell, Archibald, 20

Campbell, William, 17, 20

Camp New Hope, 126–27, 293n30

Cape Fear, North Carolina, 32

Cape of Good Hope, 78, 84

Cape Verde, West Africa, 72, 78, 90–91, 267n9

Cap Haitien, 213

Carey, Obid, 228

Carleton, Thomas, 28–30

Carpenter Bill, 81, 198; wife and children of, 237–40, 249, 251

Castillo de San Marcos, 126

Cayor, 89–90, 93, 274n12, 275nn17,19

Cedar Point, 128

Ceddo, 89–91, 93, 274n12

Chaires, Benjamin, 205

Charleston: and British troop withdrawal and Loyalist exile, 22–23; and city markets, 14–15; and extremes of wealth and poverty, 14, 17; and Charles Johnston, 7, 11, 37; Kingsley family and, 7, 11–12, 14–15, 19, 25–26; and Kingsley Jr.'s slaving voyage to East Africa, 74, 84–86; and Kingsley Sr. as fervent Loyalist, 18–20; and Kingsley Sr.'s mercantile businesses and residences, 7, 12, 19, 23–25, 28; and military occupations, 17–23; as port of call for Kingsley Jr., 34–36, 44–45, 53, 84–87, 207, 209; and post-revolution political societies, 39; and revolutionary tension and violence, 13, 17–20, 21–23, 38; and slavery, 15–17, 71, 84; and Society of Friends, 12; and threat of epidemic diseases, 11

Charlotte, slave of Mary Hobkirk, 184

Charlotte Amalie: and Kingsley's loyalty oath, 53; and Kingsley in transit trade, 57–58, 65–67, 61–65, 71–73, 87, 94–95, 97; as natural harbor, 54; as trade center and transshipment port, 54

Charlton, Mary Kingsley (sister), 7, 12, 18, 30

Chesterfield (farm), 233. *See also* Kingsley, Anna

Chidgigane, Sophy, 106, 113, 189–90, 197; children of, 202–3, 220, 289n15

Child, Lydia Maria, 95, 150, 208, 218, 222–23, 229–30

Chipman, Ward, 29

Gibbs, George, III: financial troubles of, 66; as partner of Kingsley, 59, 66, 78, 84, 89; and trust deed, 198

Gibbs, Kingsley B.: and bequests from Kingsley, 226; Fort George Island and, 165, 219, 224–27, 231; as Kingsley's attorney, 204, 223–27; and labor routine, 173–76; slave property and, 204

Gibbs, Zephaniah C., 195–98, 198

Gillespie, David, 14

Gilman, Howard, 172

Gonaïves, Haiti, 213–14

Goodbys Creek, 198–99, 126, 156

Graham, John, 7, 16, 262n2

Grant, James, 167

Gray, Vincent, 60, 62

Great Hall of Exchange, 14

Greene, Nathanael, 22

Greenfield Plantation, 117–18

Green-Pedersen, Svend E., 57

Grey, Charles, 41

Guadeloupe, 43–44

Gulf of Maine, 32

Gullah Jack, 80–81

Gustavia (ship), 74–78, 80–82, 84–86, 88, 112, 271n15, 273n4

Habanera (ship), 131

Haiti, 46, 104, 153–54, 183–84, 209

Hambly, William, 146

Hamilton, James, 58

Hamilton Plantation, 60

Hammond River, 26, 30, 263n19

Hanahan, Abraham, 72; Sophy Chidgigane and, 113, 190, 197; emancipation of, 106; and emigration to Haiti, 220, 292n20; militia raids and, 100–103; as plantation manager, 98, 277n18; Seminole raids and, 125

Hanahan, Flora. *See* Kingsley, Flora Hanahan

Harper, Henry, 225

Harris, Buckner, 128, 138

Harry, slave of Mary Hobkirk, 184

Havana, Cuba: and Fernandina, 153; and Kingsley Jr., 73, 87, 91, 93–96, 99, 108; as slave trade center, 59–68

Hawkins, Benjamin, 148

Head rights land grants, 26, 69, 121

Head tax, 179–80, 200

Heineken, Theodore J., 215

Henly, J. D., 154

Hernandez, Joseph, 146, 152, 155, 225, 227–28

Hickman, Joshua, 184

Higginbotham, Ralph, 223

Highfield, Arnold R., 57

Hill, Theophilus, 74–79, 81–82, 84, 86

Hobkirk, Mary, 184

Hoffman, Paul E., 115

Holdover planters, 183

Horse Landing, 97, 99

Horseshoe Bend, Battle of, 145, 149

Hugues, Victor, 43–45

Immutable (ship), 131

Indentured laborers, 188–90, 215, 217, 220, 223, 242

Industria (ship), 98

Ingenac, B., 214, 223

Inland Passage, 128, 135

Inventory of property: of Spicer Christopher, 116, 278n33; of George Kingsley, 254; of Zephaniah Kingsley Jr., 188–90, 230–37, 239

Irving, George, 117

Isaacs, Ralph, 122

Island of Liberty (Haiti), 210–11, 218, 224

Jackson, Andrew, 145, 149, 197, 206, 211

Jai, Anna. *See* Kingsley, Anna

James Murphy and Company, 72

Jamoa, Moca Province, Dominican Republic, 224

Jay, John, and Treaty, 43

Jean-François, 49

Jefferson, Thomas, embargo policy, 69

Jekyll Island, 61, 142

Jennings, John P., 58

Jeremie, Grand Anse, Saint-Domingue, 38, 46, 49, 51

224–25; and Charleston/Caribbean coffee trade, 38–46; childhood and education of, 8–14, 19–22; and destruction of Florida economy during Patriot War, 121–27, 130–34, 139–42, 144–45; as family patriarch, 191–98, 200–204; and fate of slaves, 234–40, 241–45; and imprisonment at Martinique, 41–44; and introduction to slavery, 15–17; "Kingsley's fleet," 134–35; last will and testament of, 226–27, 230–34; locations of plantations and businesses in Florida, 106, 108, 156, 159, 198, 283n1; and loyalty to Denmark, 52–53; and loyalty to Spain, 67, 69, 71, 73, 105; and loyalty to the United States, 34, 39; and New Brunswick and Nova Scotia, 25–28, 31–32; and patriarchal system of slavery, 154–63, 173–77, 186–90; as a plantation owner in Spanish East Florida, 69, 71, 105, 111–13; as ship captain and Caribbean trader, 29–32; and ships seized at sea, 35–36, 41–42, 45; slaves owned by, 111–14, 140–45, 168, 188–91, 195–98, 226, 234–37; as a slave trader, 53–61, 63–64; and temporary residence in the south of Saint-Domingue, 50; and three-caste vs. two-caste race and social structure, 178–85;

Kingsley, Zephaniah, Sr.: childhood and Quaker ancestry in Lancashire, 8; and emigration to Wilmington, North Carolina; and family in Charleston, 7–11, 19; at London and Bristol, 8–10; as Loyalist in revolutionary city, 12–13, 17–23, 25–26; as merchant and ship owner at St. John, New Brunswick, 28–31; and New Brunswick and Caribbean trade, 32; and New Brunswick land grants, 259n7, 262n7; as resident of Fredericton, New Brunswick, 264n24; and speculation concerning his death, 264n29; and University of New Brunswick, 29

Kingsley Brook, New Brunswick, 30
Kingsley Point, 131

Klein, Herbert S., 82

Lake George, 106, 111, 156, 187–88, 201
Lamotte, John, 229, 293n40
Landers, Jane G., 114
Laurel Grove Plantation, 71–74, 108–10, 156; Anna Kingsley at, 96–97; mercantile business at, 74, 99–100, 106; militia raids on, 101–3, 106; slaves and management of, 72–73, 98, 111–13, 161, 190, 197–98
Laurens, Henry, 14, 24
Lawson, William, 117
Lébron, Tony, 199
Leclerc, Charles Victor Emmanuel, 48
Lee, Charles, 18
Legislative council. *See* Florida Territorial Council
L'Engle, Madeleine, 199
L'Engle, Susan Philippa Fatio, 198–99
Leslie, Alexander, 22
Leslie, John, 116
Letter of marque and reprisal, 35. *See also* Privateers
Liberal manumission policies, 177, 180–81, 190, 209, 212, 240
Liberty Boys. *See* Sons of Liberty
Lincoln, Benjamin, 20–21
Little Jim (ship, alias *Laurel*), 72–73
Little San José Plantation, 156, 202
Liverpool, England, 64, 66, 71, 73–78, 115, 117
Llorente, Thomas, 129–34, 134–35, 137
Lloyd, Richard, 91
Long Island, 18
Lottery, Esther, 244–45
Lottery, Quash, 244
Louisa Plantation, 117
Louverture, Toussaint, 46, 49, 51–52, 104
Lovejoy, Paul, 64
Loyalists: in Charleston, 17–21, 23; as exiles in England and Canada, 25, 27–30, 32
Loyalty oath, Kingsley Jr.'s pledge to: Denmark, 53; Spain, 67, 69, 71, 73, 105; United States, 34, 39

Lukas, John, 172
Lundy, Benjamin, 211

"Ma-am Anna" house at Fort George Island, 159, 193–94, 201
MacGregor, Gregor, 152–55
Maclean, Andrew, 102
Madgigine (Madgiguéne), Anna. See Kingsley, Anna
Maitland, General Thomas, 51
Man, Spencer John, 74. See also Gustavia
Manatee River, 146–47, 150
Manigault, Mrs. Ann, 11
Manning, Lawrence, 127
Manumission, 174, 177–78; Kingsley and manumission, 180–81, 190, 209, 212, 240. See also Anti-manumission statute of 1829
Marotti, Frank, 114
Martinique, 36–37, 39, 165; and imprisonment of Kingsley, 41–42, 45, 241
Mathews, George, 122–24
Mattier, Luis, 195
Mayne, Father Edward, 194–96
Mayorasgo de Koka, 215, 294n6. See also Cabaret
McClure, John, 117
McDonald, James, 237
McGundo, Fatimah (daughter). See Kingsley, Fatimah McGundo (daughter)
McGundo, Munsilna, 88, 194–95, 201–3, 220
M'Choolay Moreema, 81
McIntosh, John H., 70, 105, 114–15, 122–23, 127, 135, 281n28
McIntosh, John H., Jr., 110, 169, 235, 250, 253
McIntosh, William, Lower Creek chief, 149–50
McNeill, Charles Johnston, 191; and inheritance, 226, 234; as overseer, 218, 231–32, 236–37; and Reddy Point, 242; and slaves of, 234–37, 244–45, 253, 255
McNeill, Daniel, 34
McNeill, Martha Kingsley (sister), 18, 30, 33, 34, 232; and challenge to Kingsley Jr.'s will, 231, 233; as grandmother of James Abbott McNeill Whistler, 258n2

McQueen, John, 115, 158
Memorial to Congress, 182
Miccosukee: as lake, 148; as villages, 148–49
Middle Passage, 85, 88, 94
Militias: American, 49; free black, 103, 106, 126, 130, 177; Georgia, 126; Jacksonville, 206; Spanish, 128, 151
Miller, Charles, 150
Mill's Ferry, 151
Mitchell, David Brydie, 124, 147–50, 154
Montarro, enslaved blacksmith, 109, 111, 125
Montserrat, 40
Moore, Christopher, 27
Moore, Ophelia, 244
Moreno, José Antonio, 130–34
Morgan, Philip D., 173
Mouser, Bruce L., 276n30
Mumford, Giles, 98–99
Murphy, Sarah. See Kingsley, Sarah Murphy
Murray, Romeo, 236, 249, 251, 254

Napoleon, George Gaston, 254–55, 295n26, 296n34
Naranjal de San Jose, 156, 201
Nash, R. C., 10
Nat Turner rebellion, 206
Navarro, Joaquin, 137
Ndiaye, Anta Majigeen. See Kingsley, Anna
Ndiaye, Mba Kompas, Buurba Jolof, 1762–1797, 92
Ndiaye, Njaajaan, founder of Empire of Jolof, 89
Negro Fort, Prospect Bluff, Apalachicola River, 145–49
Neutral flag, 39, 52, 55, 67
New Brunswick, 25–33, 148
New Hope Plantation, 197–98, 202, 293n29
Newitt, Malyn, 79
Newnan, Daniel, 126
New Negro, 16, 60–61, 63, 65, 112–13, 190. See also Bozales
New Switzerland Plantation, 126
Newton, John, 83–84
Nicholls, Edward, 145–47
Niger Delta, 64

DANIEL L. SCHAFER is Professor of History Emeritus and University Distinguished Professor, University of North Florida. The author of numerous journal articles on African American and Florida history, his recent publications include *Anna Madgigine Jai Kingsley: African Princess, Florida Slave, Plantation Slaveowner*; *Thunder on the River: The Civil War in Northeast Florida*; and *William Bartram and the Ghost Plantations of British East Florida*.

The University Press of Florida is the scholarly publishing agency for the State University System of Florida, comprising Florida A&M University, Florida Atlantic University, Florida Gulf Coast University, Florida International University, Florida State University, New College of Florida, University of Central Florida, University of Florida, University of North Florida, University of South Florida, and University of West Florida.

Printed in the USA
CPSIA information can be obtained
at www.ICGtesting.com
JSHW022147240924
70151JS00002B/9

9 780813 080789